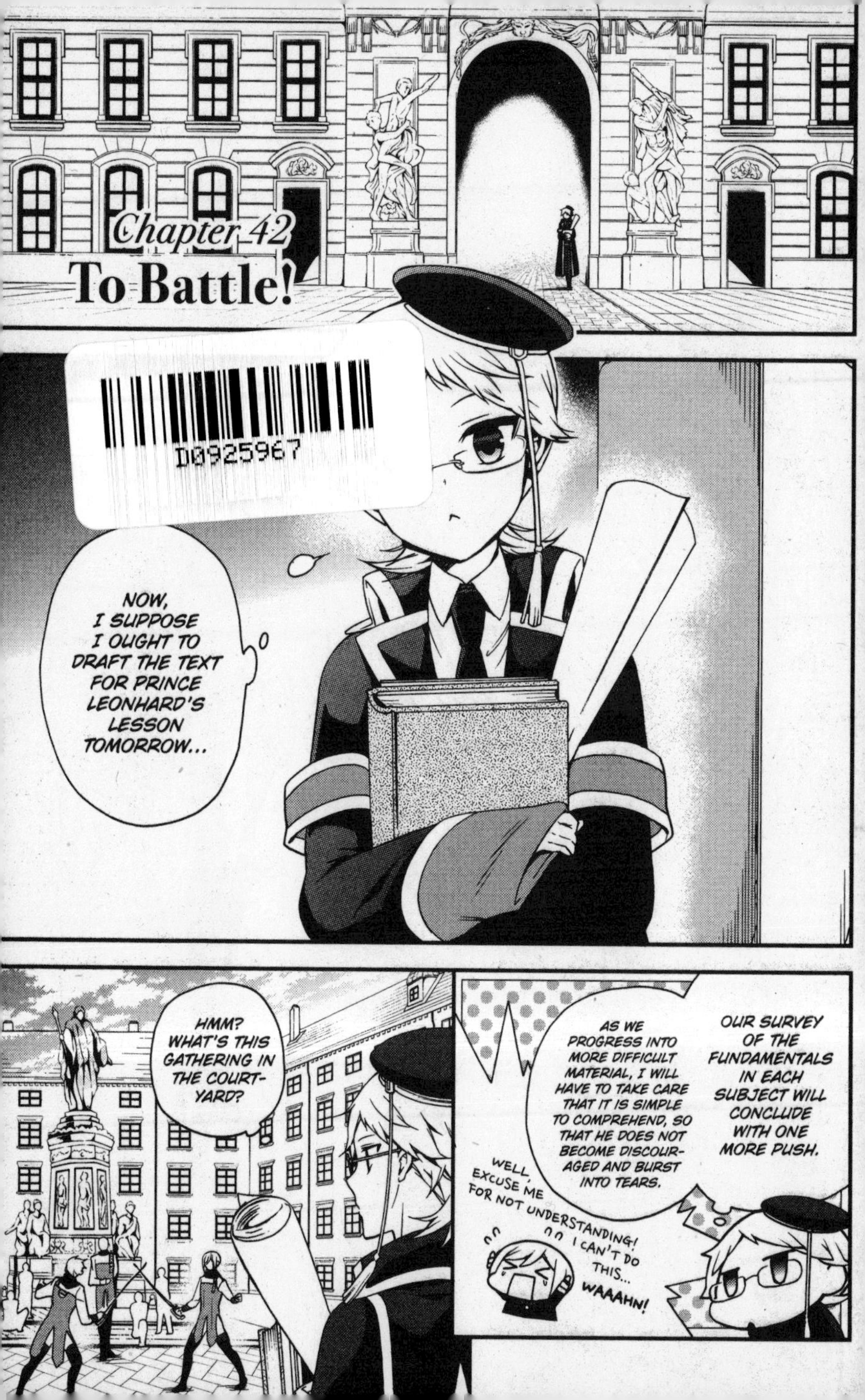
Chapter 42
To Battle!
NOW, I SUPPOSE I OUGHT TO DRAFT THE TEXT FOR PRINCE LEONHARD'S LESSON TOMORROW...
OUR SURVEY OF THE FUNDAMENTALS IN EACH SUBJECT WILL CONCLUDE WITH ONE MORE PUSH.
AS WE PROGRESS INTO MORE DIFFICULT MATERIAL, I WILL HAVE TO TAKE CARE THAT IT IS SIMPLE TO COMPREHEND, SO THAT HE DOES NOT BECOME DISCOURAGED AND BURST INTO TEARS.
WELL, EXCUSE ME FOR NOT UNDERSTANDING!
I CAN'T DO THIS...
WAAAHN!
HMM? WHAT'S THIS GATHERING IN THE COURTYARD?

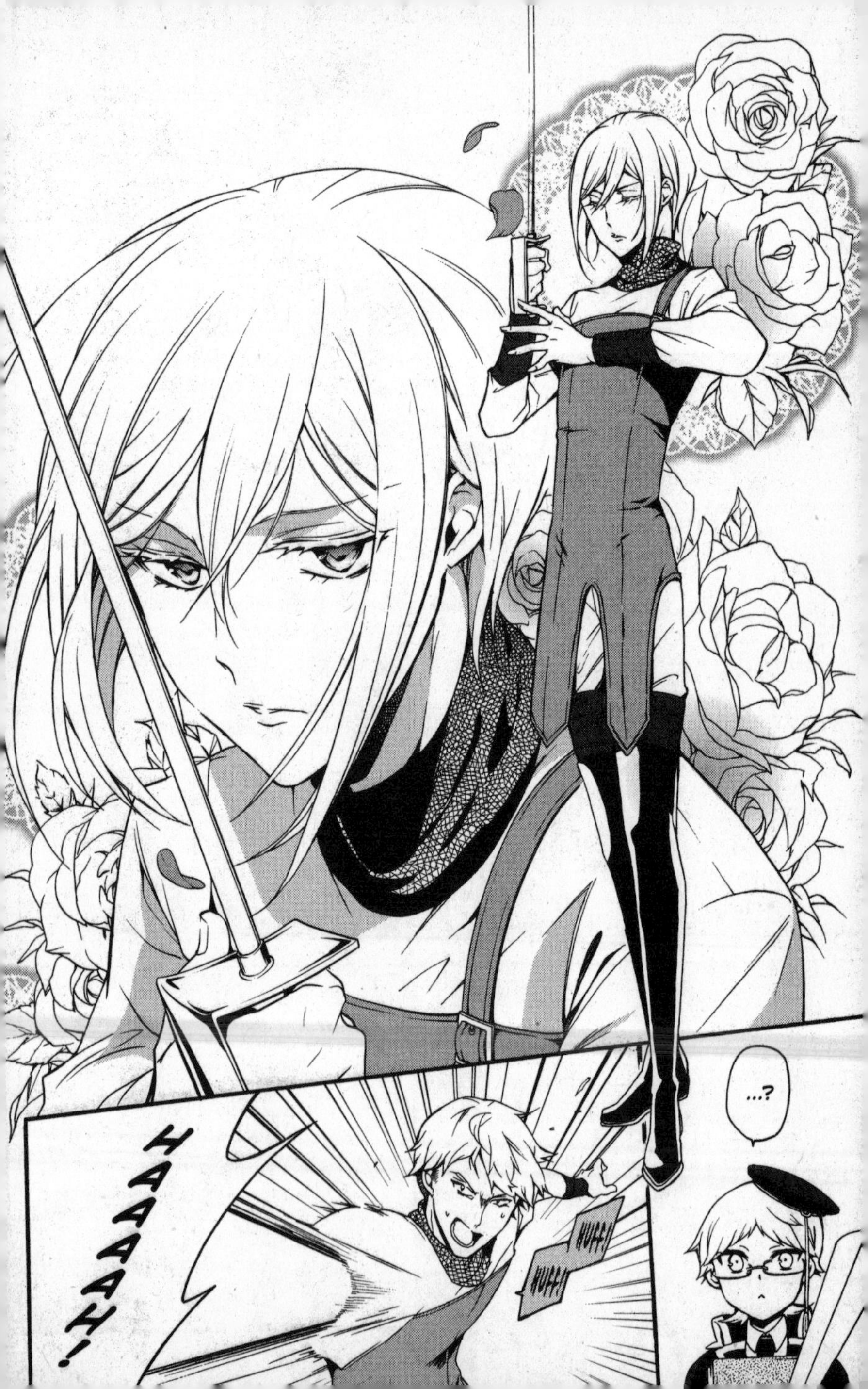
...?
HUFF!
HUFF!
HAAAAAH!

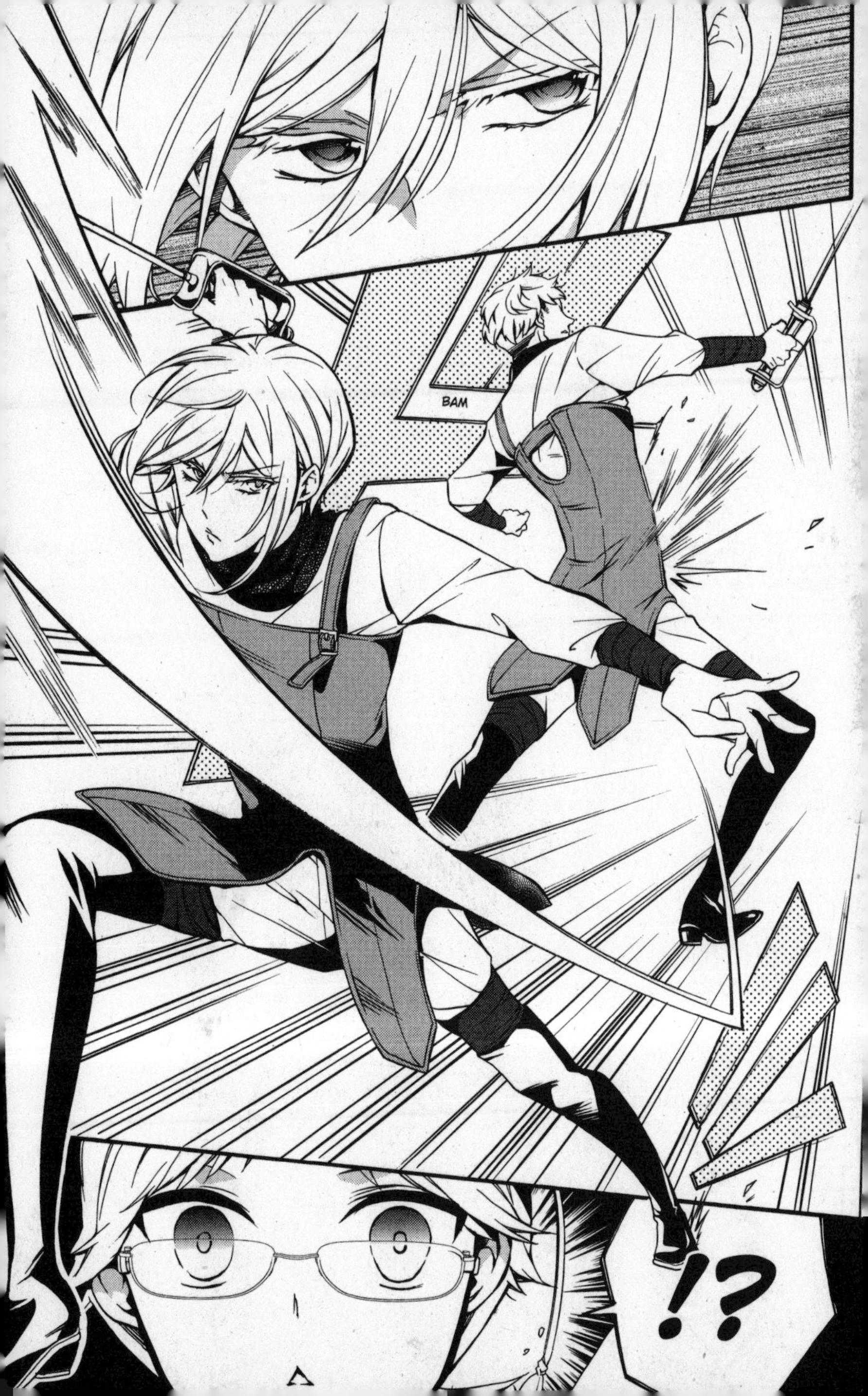
BAM
!?

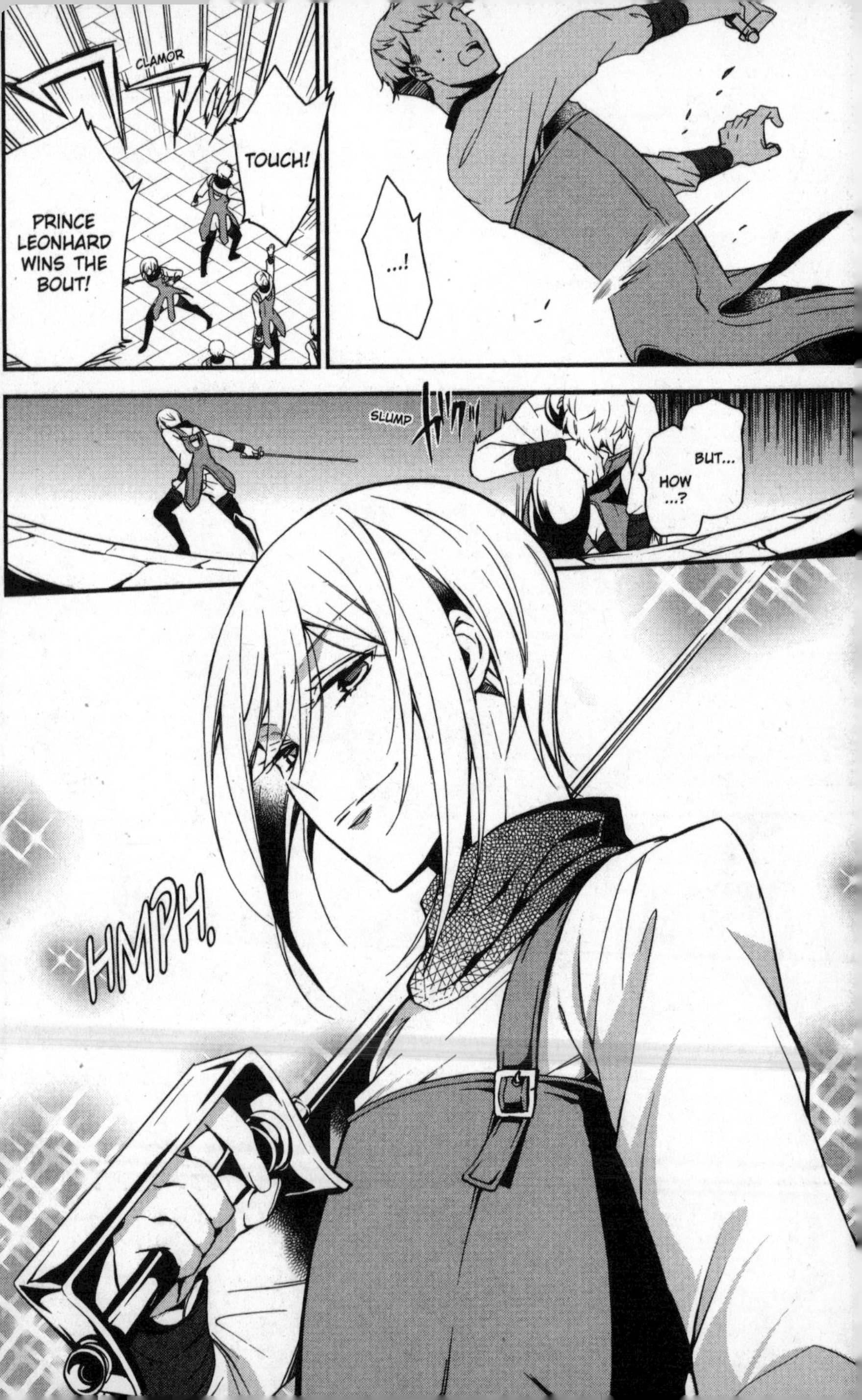

...!
CLAMOR
TOUCH!
PRINCE LEONHARD WINS THE BOUT!
SLUMP
BUT... HOW ...?
HMPH.

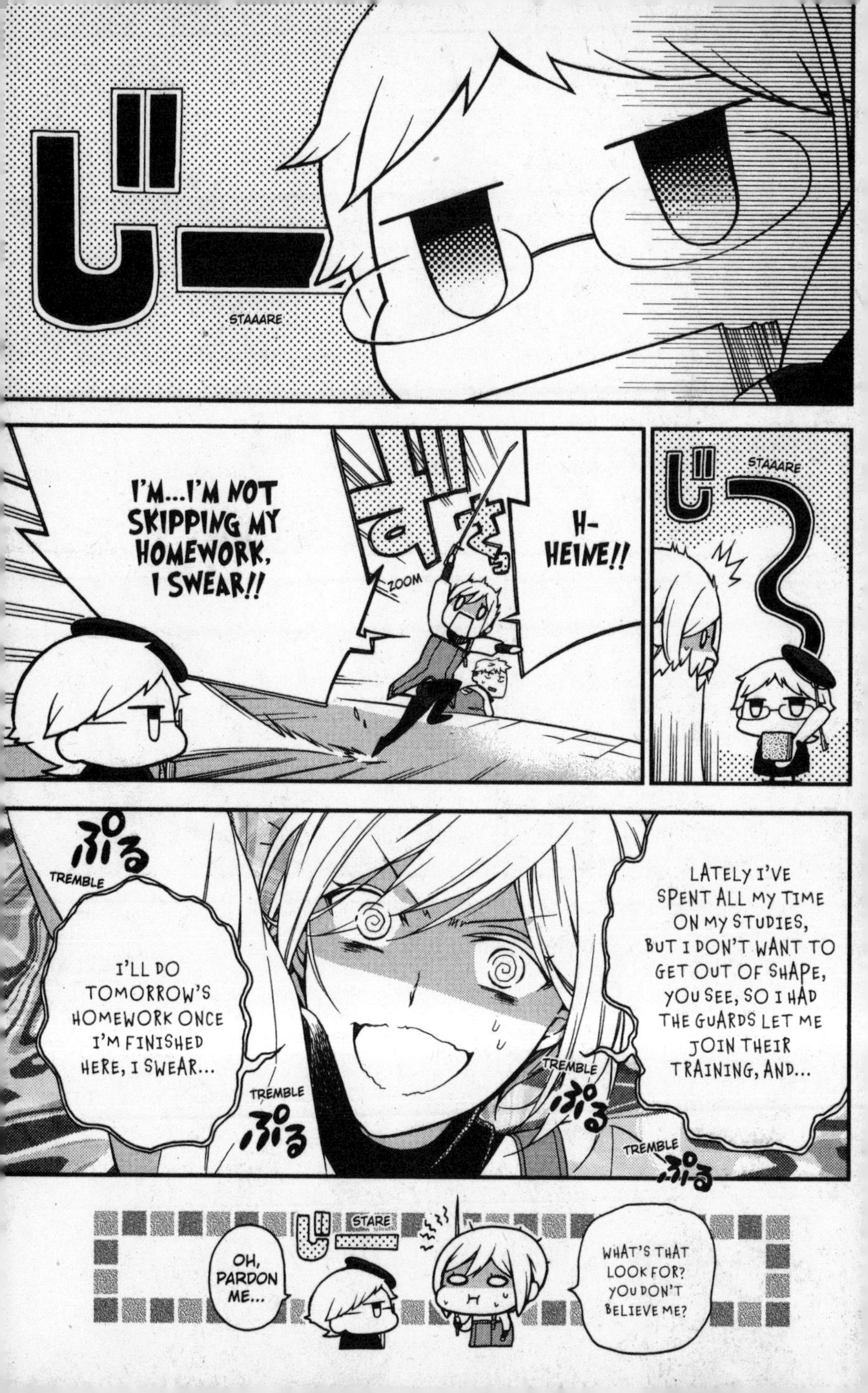
じーー
STAAARE
じっ
STAAARE
H-HEINE!!
ZOOM
I'M...I'M NOT SKIPPING MY HOMEWORK, I SWEAR!!
ぷる
TREMBLE
LATELY I'VE SPENT ALL MY TIME ON MY STUDIES, BUT I DON'T WANT TO GET OUT OF SHAPE, YOU SEE, SO I HAD THE GUARDS LET ME JOIN THEIR TRAINING, AND...
TREMBLE
ぷる
I'LL DO TOMORROW'S HOMEWORK ONCE I'M FINISHED HERE, I SWEAR...
TREMBLE
ぷる
TREMBLE
ぷる
WHAT'S THAT LOOK FOR? YOU DON'T BELIEVE ME?
じー
STARE
OH, PARDON ME...

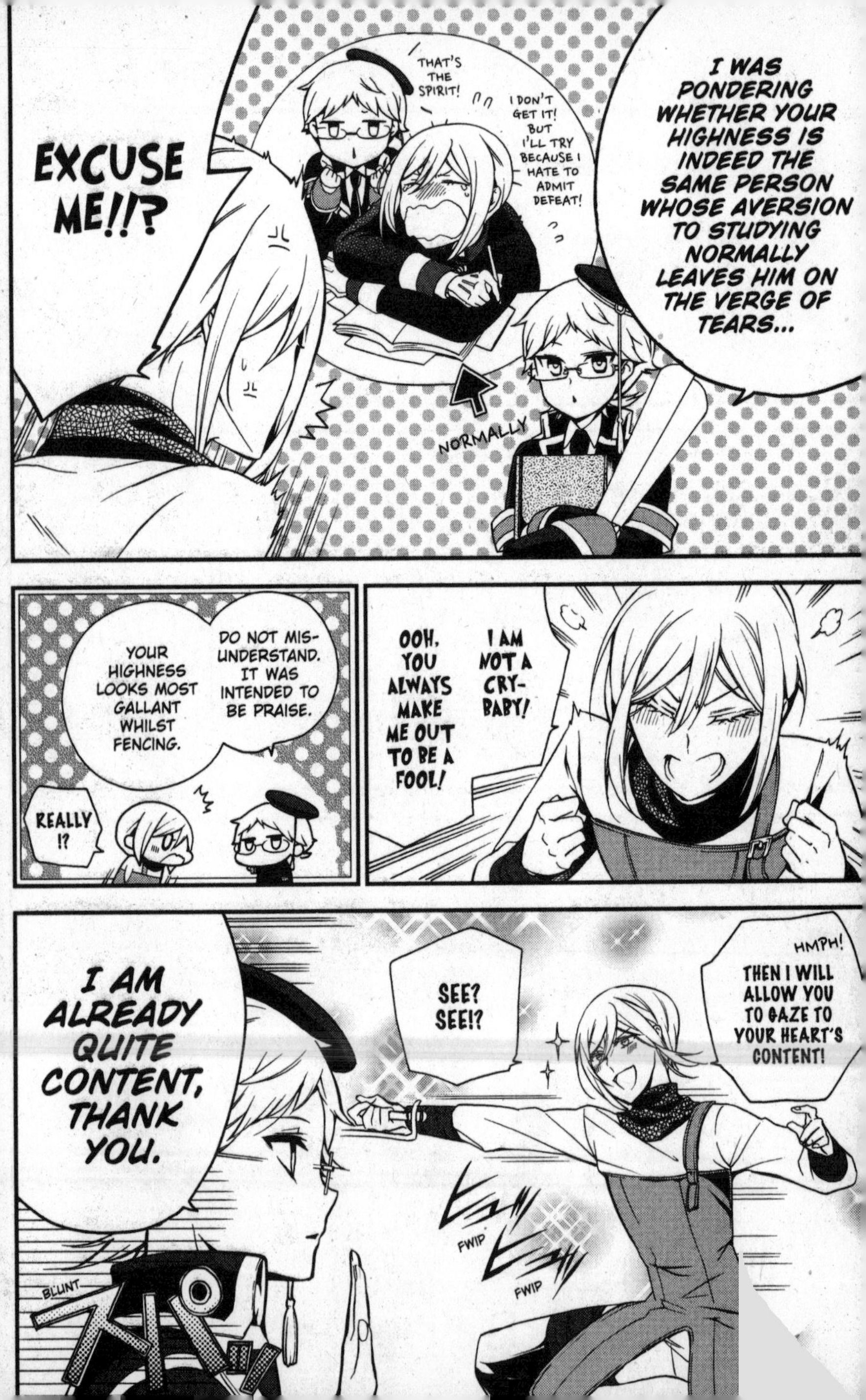
I WAS PONDERING WHETHER YOUR HIGHNESS IS INDEED THE SAME PERSON WHOSE AVERSION TO STUDYING NORMALLY LEAVES HIM ON THE VERGE OF TEARS...
I DON'T GET IT! BUT I'LL TRY BECAUSE I HATE TO ADMIT DEFEAT!
THAT'S THE SPIRIT!
NORMALLY
EXCUSE ME!!?
I AM NOT A CRY-BABY!
OOH, YOU ALWAYS MAKE ME OUT TO BE A FOOL!
DO NOT MIS-UNDERSTAND. IT WAS INTENDED TO BE PRAISE.
YOUR HIGHNESS LOOKS MOST GALLANT WHILST FENCING.
REALLY!?
HMPH! THEN I WILL ALLOW YOU TO GAZE TO YOUR HEART'S CONTENT!
SEE? SEE!?
I AM ALREADY QUITE CONTENT, THANK YOU.
FWIP
FWIP
BLUNT

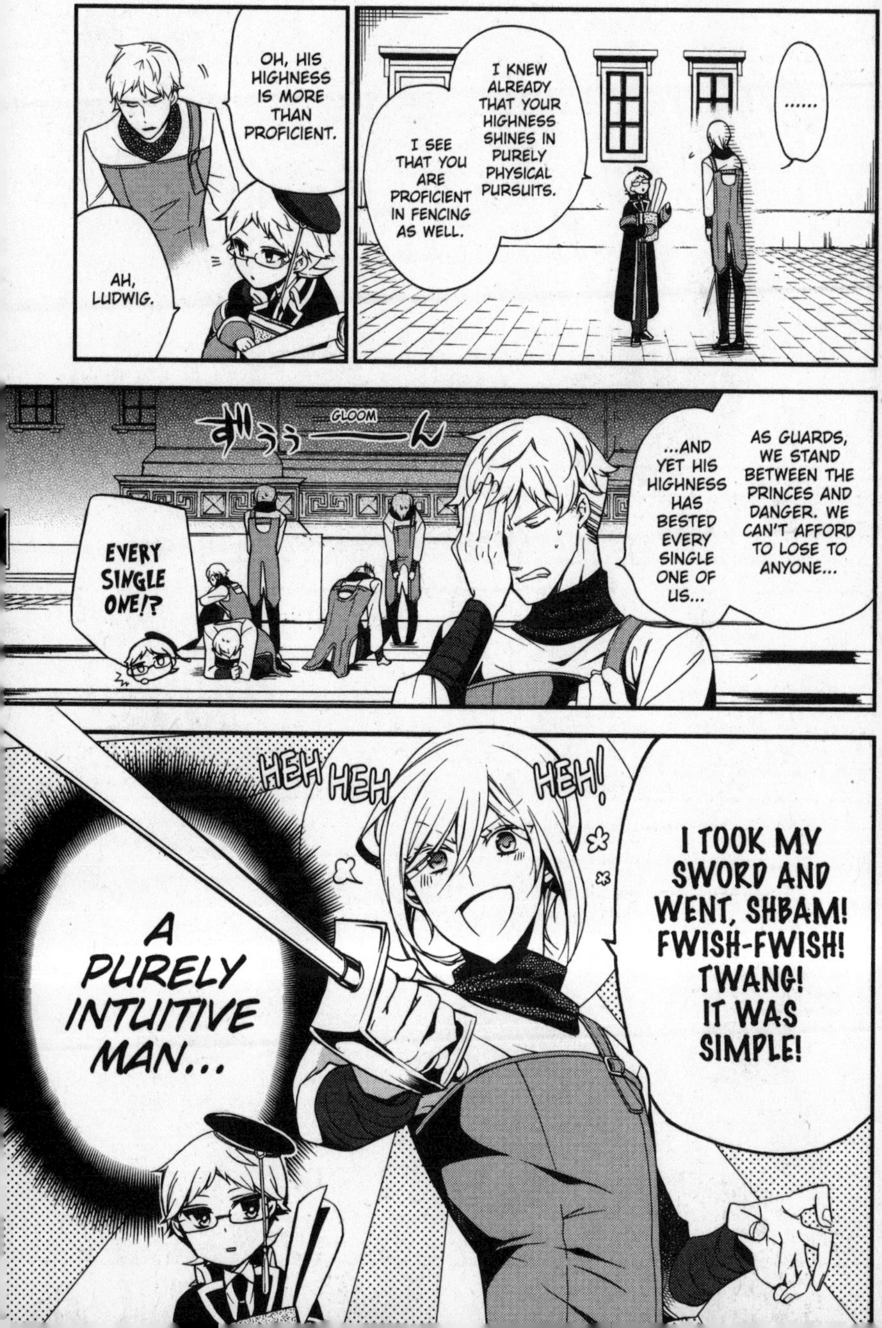
......
I KNEW ALREADY THAT YOUR HIGHNESS SHINES IN PURELY PHYSICAL PURSUITS.
I SEE THAT YOU ARE PROFICIENT IN FENCING AS WELL.
OH, HIS HIGHNESS IS MORE THAN PROFICIENT.
AH, LUDWIG.
AS GUARDS, WE STAND BETWEEN THE PRINCES AND DANGER. WE CAN'T AFFORD TO LOSE TO ANYONE...
...AND YET HIS HIGHNESS HAS BESTED EVERY SINGLE ONE OF US...
GLOOM
EVERY SINGLE ONE!?
I TOOK MY SWORD AND WENT, SHBAM! FWISH-FWISH! TWANG! IT WAS SIMPLE!
HEH HEH HEH!
A PURELY INTUITIVE MAN...

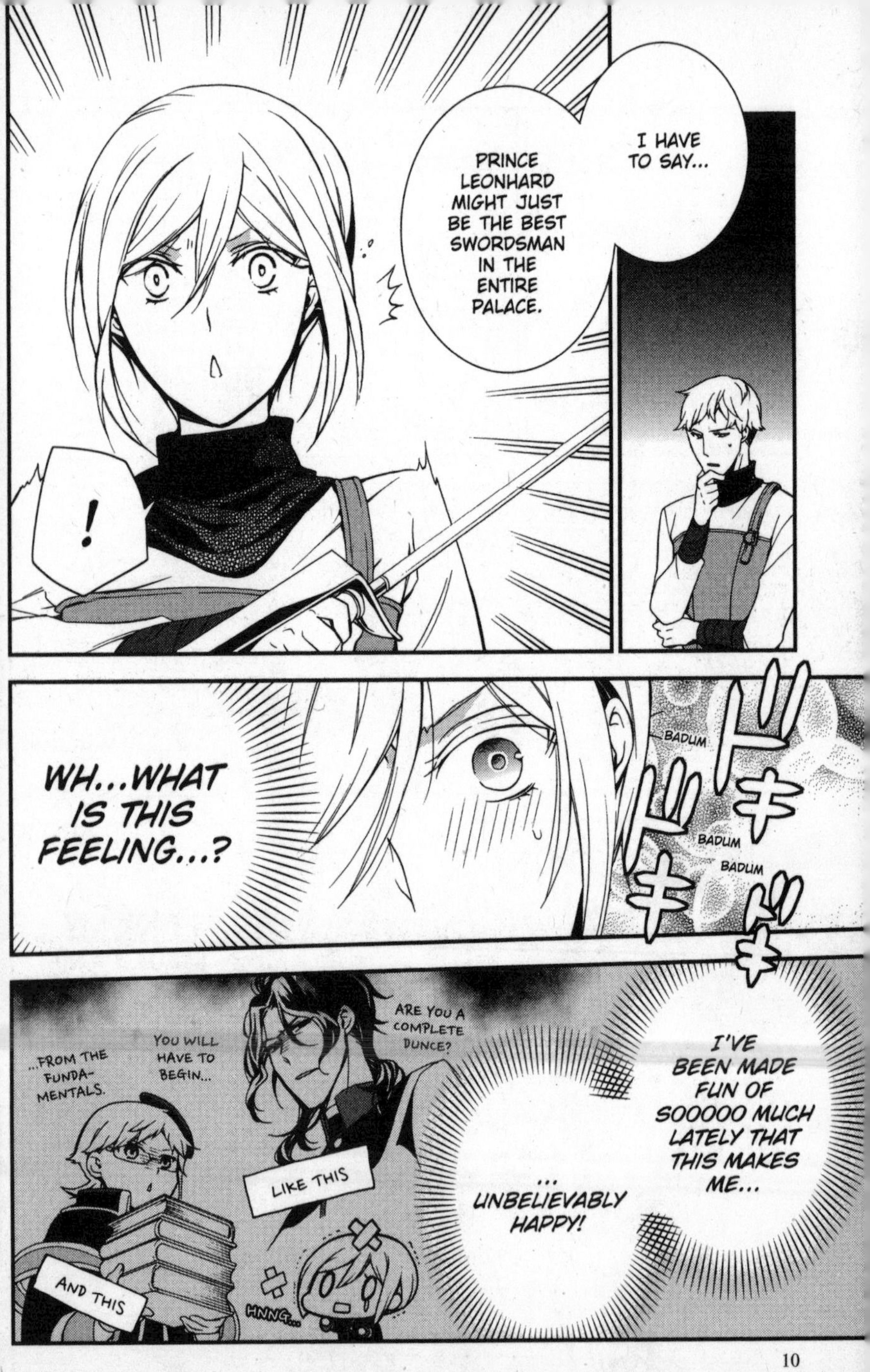
I HAVE TO SAY...
PRINCE LEONHARD MIGHT JUST BE THE BEST SWORDSMAN IN THE ENTIRE PALACE.
!
BADUM
BADUM
BADUM
WH...WHAT IS THIS FEELING...?
I'VE BEEN MADE FUN OF SOOOOO MUCH LATELY THAT THIS MAKES ME...
...UNBELIEVABLY HAPPY!
ARE YOU A COMPLETE DUNCE?
LIKE THIS
YOU WILL HAVE TO BEGIN...
...FROM THE FUNDA-MENTALS.
AND THIS
HNNG...

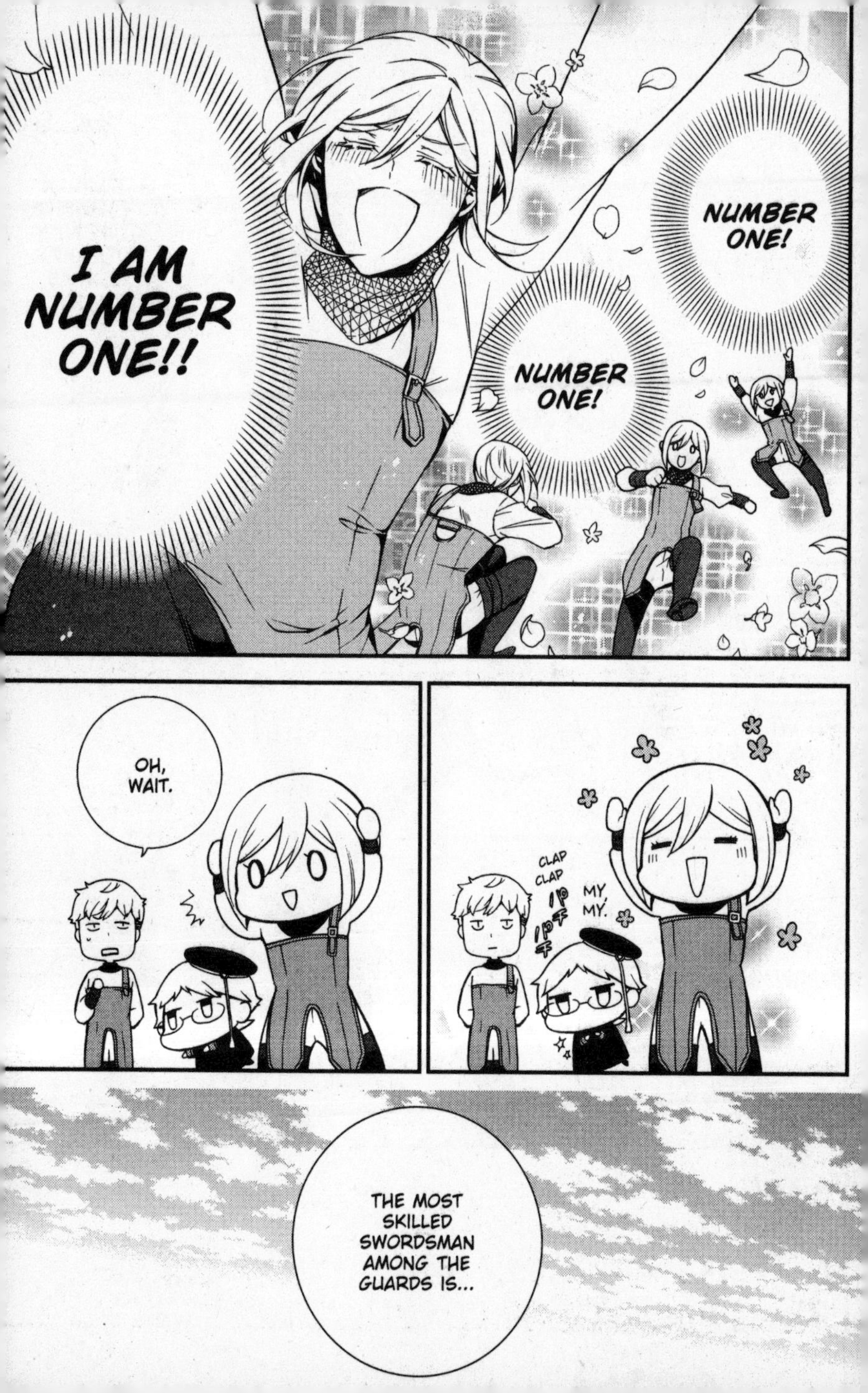
NUMBER ONE!
NUMBER ONE!
I AM NUMBER ONE!!
MY, MY.
CLAP CLAP
OH, WAIT.
THE MOST SKILLED SWORDSMAN AMONG THE GUARDS IS...

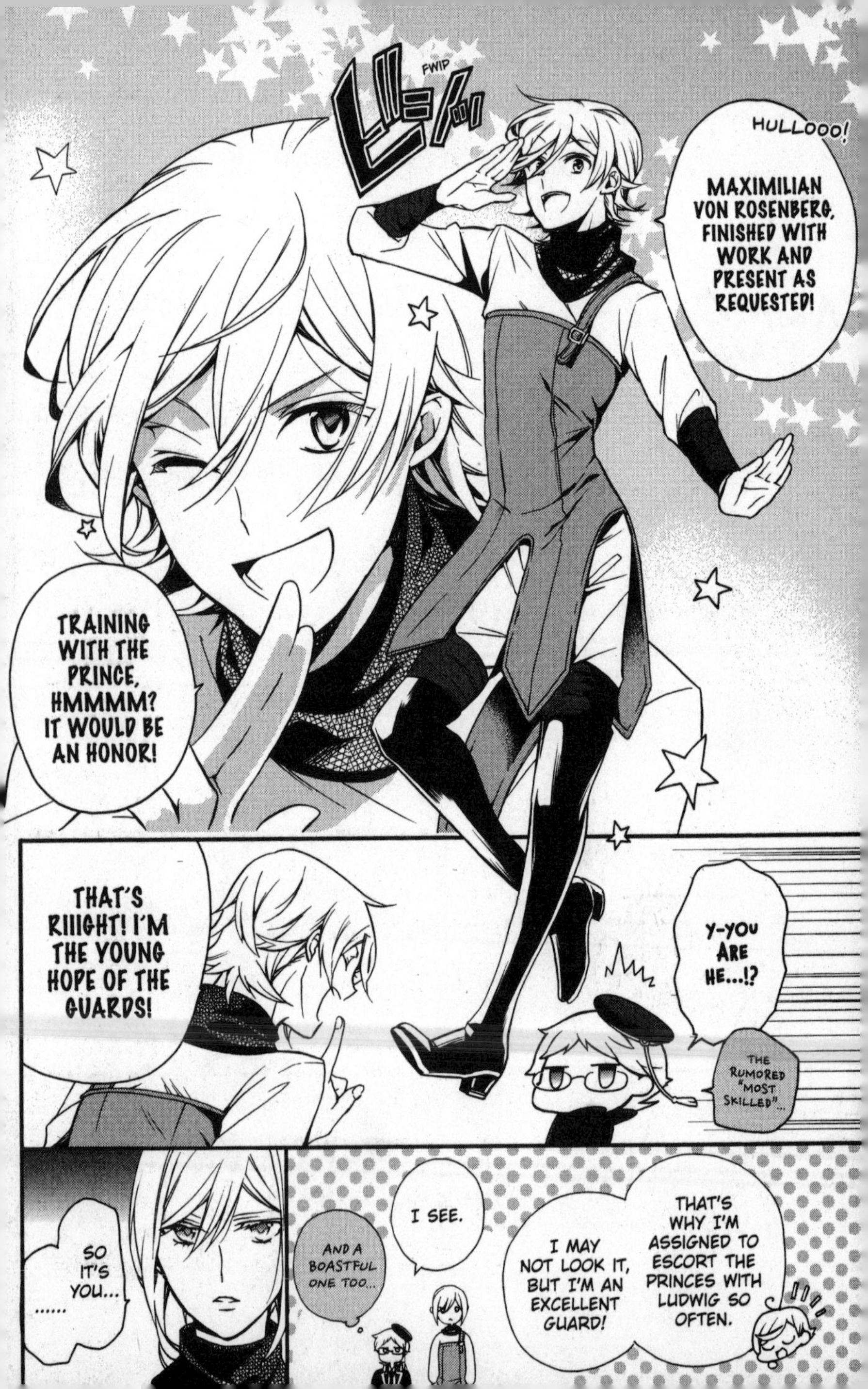
FWIP
HULLOOO!
MAXIMILIAN VON ROSENBERG, FINISHED WITH WORK AND PRESENT AS REQUESTED!
TRAINING WITH THE PRINCE, HMMMM? IT WOULD BE AN HONOR!
Y-YOU ARE HE...!?
THE RUMORED "MOST SKILLED"...
THAT'S RIIIGHT! I'M THE YOUNG HOPE OF THE GUARDS!
THAT'S WHY I'M ASSIGNED TO ESCORT THE PRINCES WITH LUDWIG SO OFTEN.
I MAY NOT LOOK IT, BUT I'M AN EXCELLENT GUARD!
I SEE.
AND A BOASTFUL ONE TOO...
SO IT'S YOU... ......

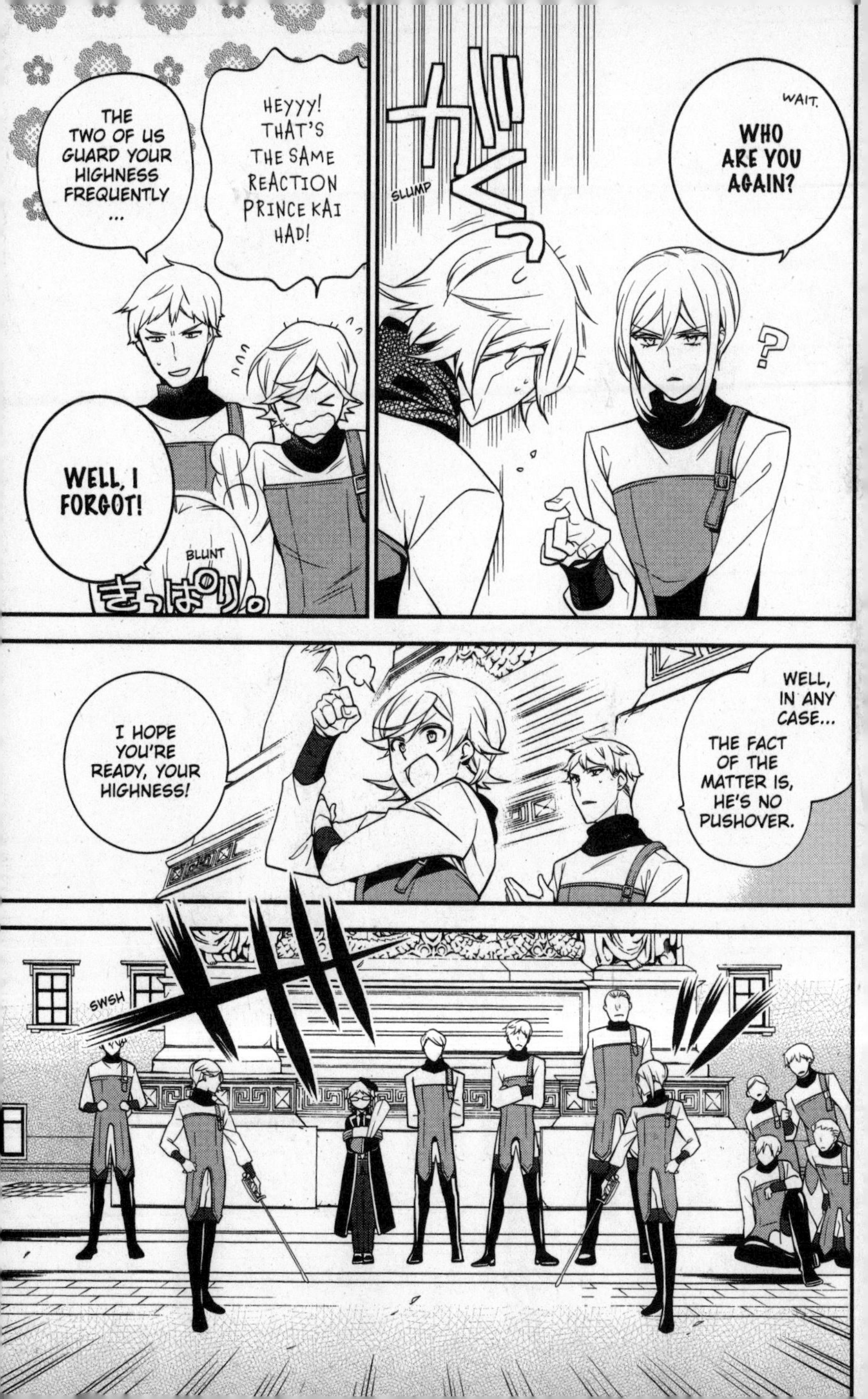
SLUMP
WAIT. WHO ARE YOU AGAIN?
HEYYY! THAT'S THE SAME REACTION PRINCE KAI HAD!
THE TWO OF US GUARD YOUR HIGHNESS FREQUENTLY ...
WELL, I FORGOT!
BLUNT
きっぱり。
WELL, IN ANY CASE... THE FACT OF THE MATTER IS, HE'S NO PUSHOVER.
I HOPE YOU'RE READY, YOUR HIGHNESS!
SWSH

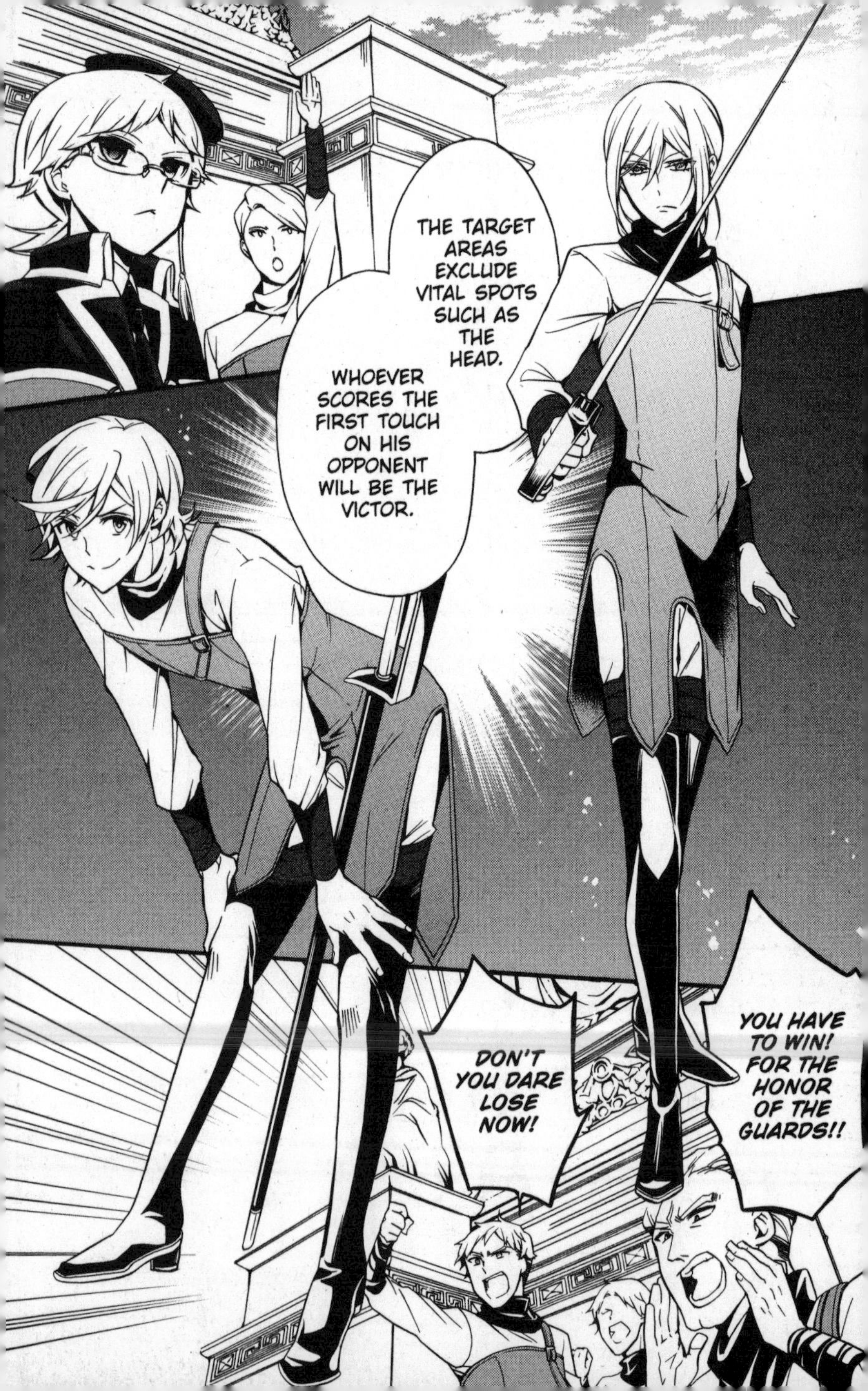
THE TARGET AREAS EXCLUDE VITAL SPOTS SUCH AS THE HEAD.
WHOEVER SCORES THE FIRST TOUCH ON HIS OPPONENT WILL BE THE VICTOR.
YOU HAVE TO WIN! FOR THE HONOR OF THE GUARDS!!
DON'T YOU DARE LOSE NOW!

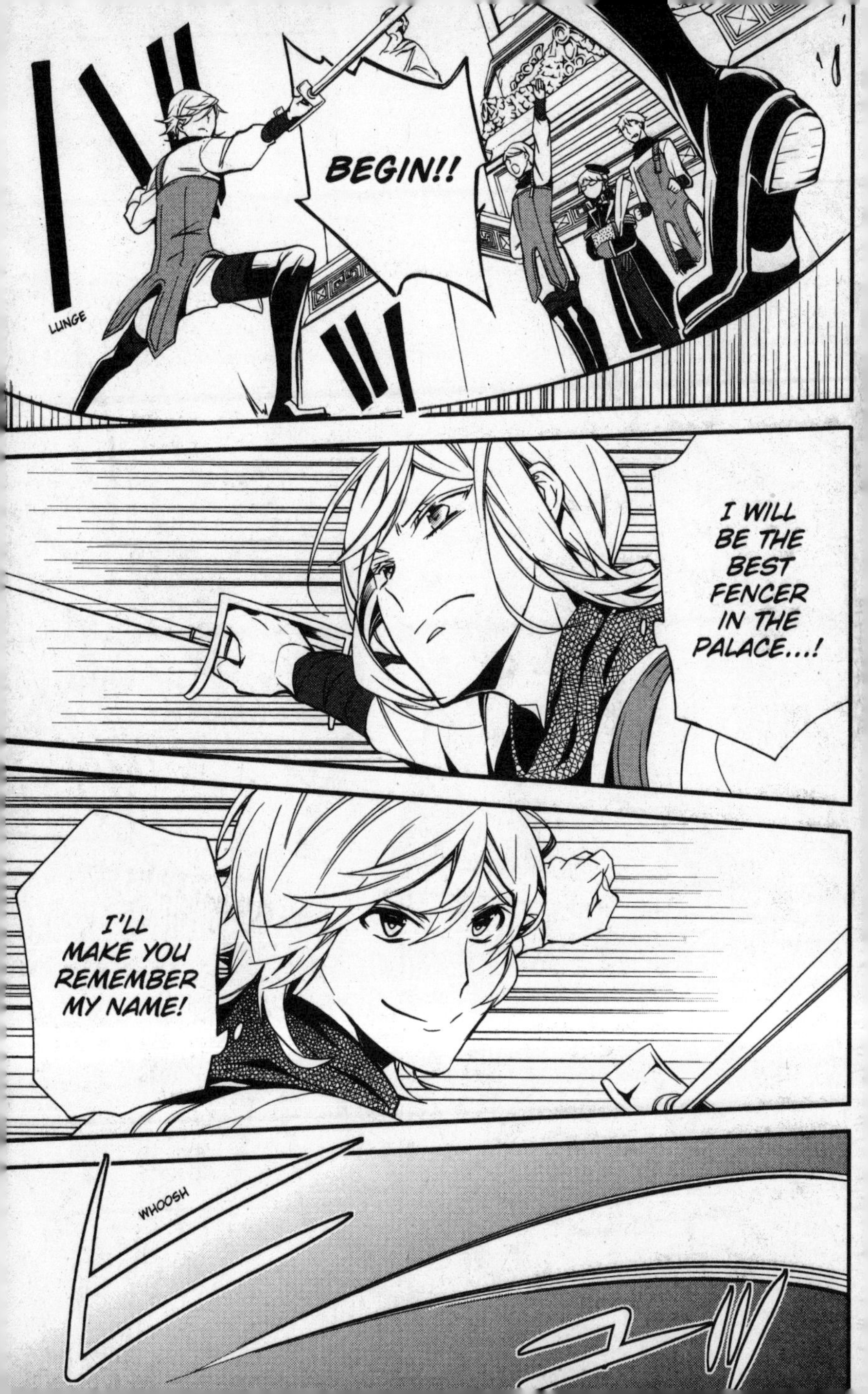
BEGIN!!
LUNGE
I WILL BE THE BEST FENCER IN THE PALACE...!
I'LL MAKE YOU REMEMBER MY NAME!
WHOOSH

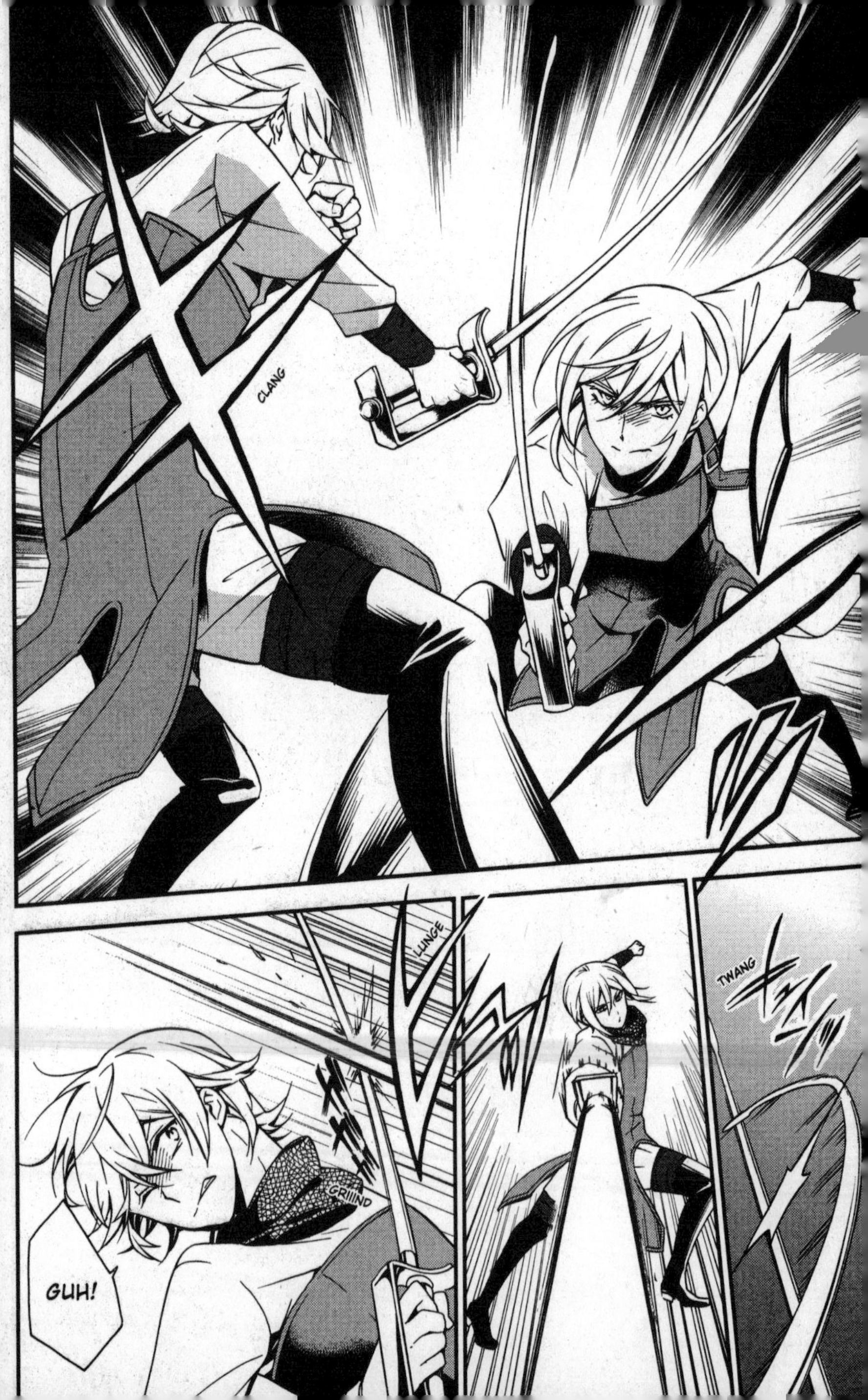
CLANG
TWANG
LUNGE
GRIIIND
GUH!

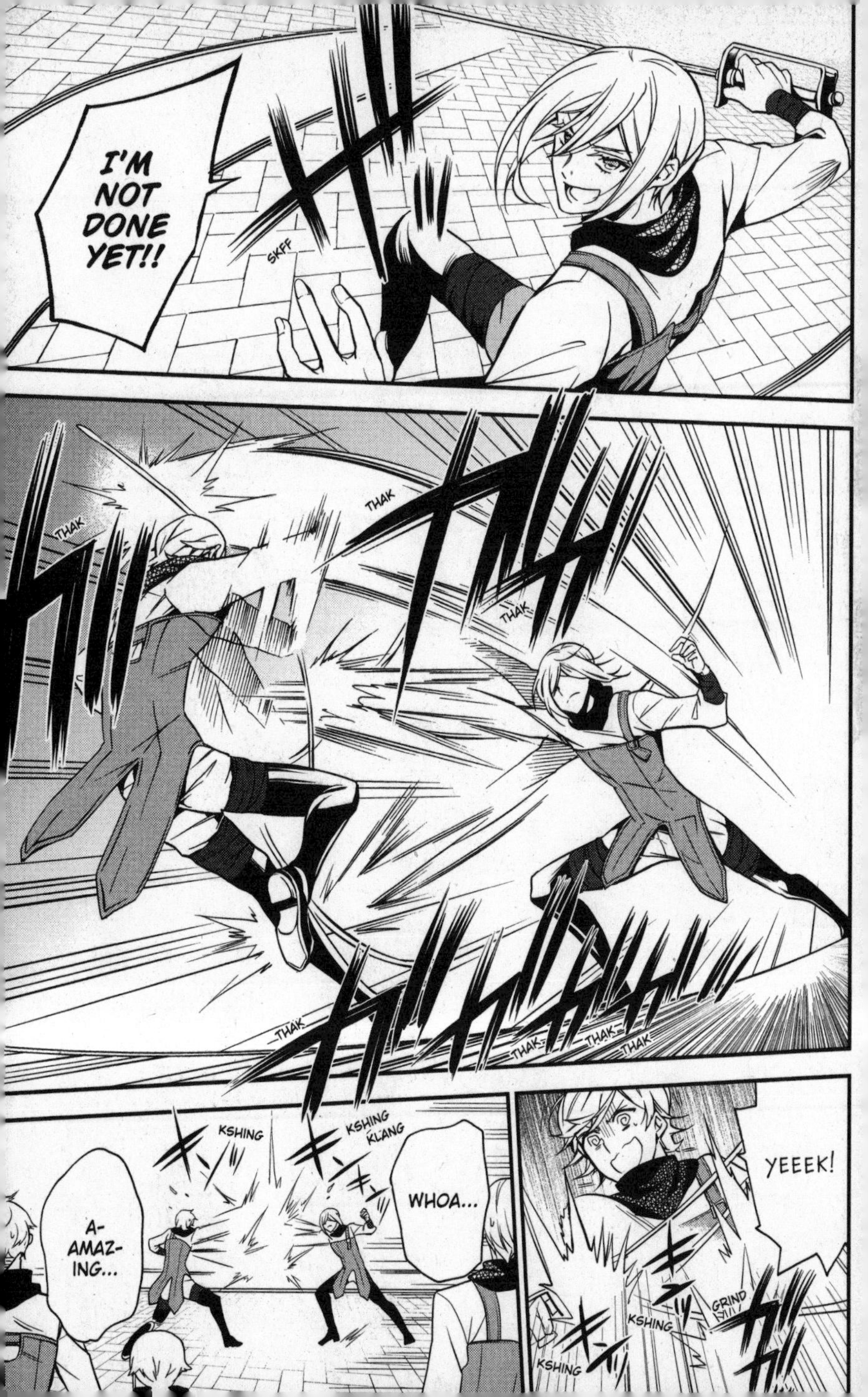
I'M NOT DONE YET!!
SKFF
THAK
THAK
THAK
THAK
THAK
THAK
THAK
YEEEK!
KSHING
KSHING
GRIND
KSHING
KLANG
KSHING
WHOA...
A-AMAZING...

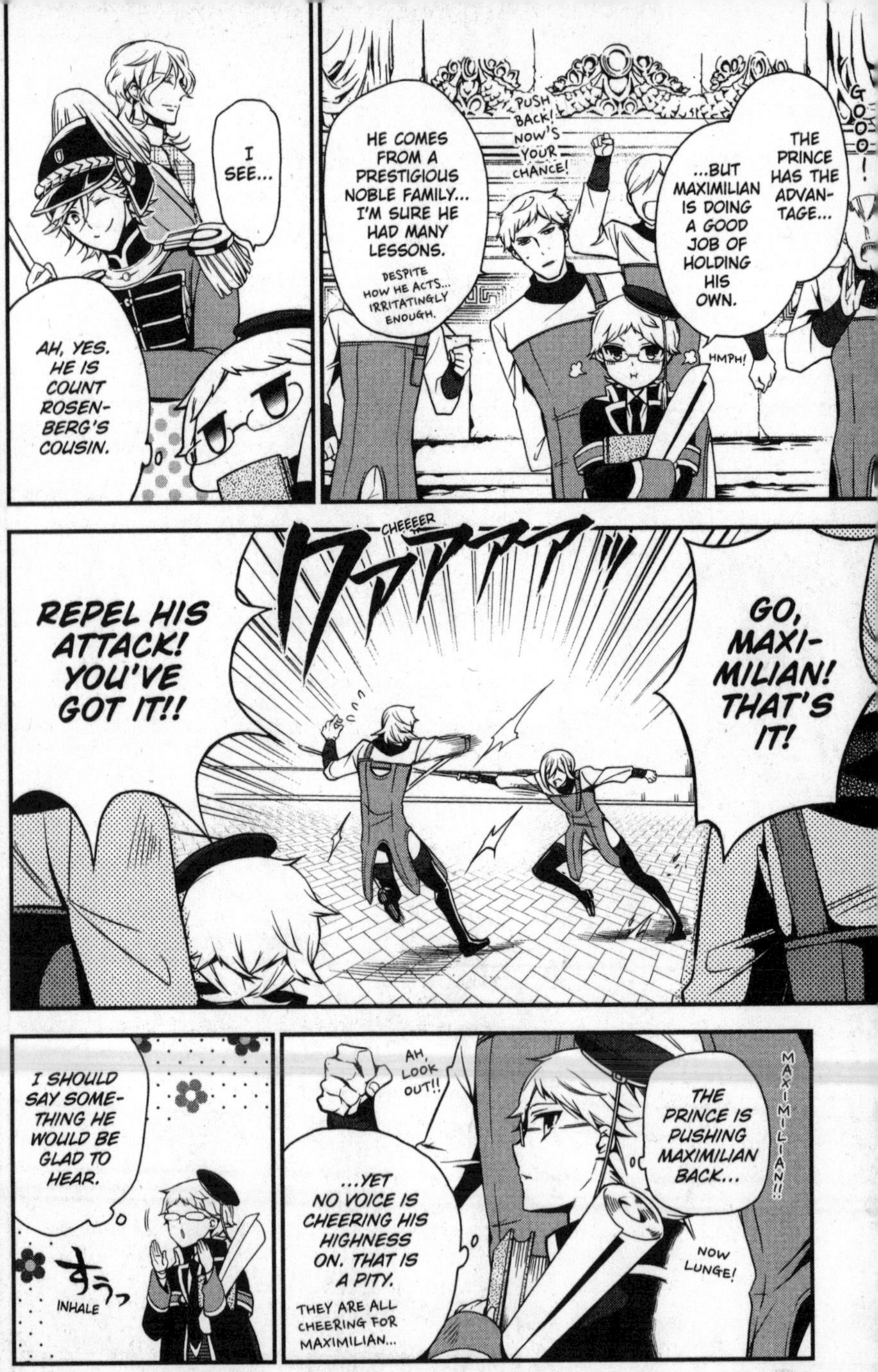
GOOOO!
THE PRINCE HAS THE ADVANTAGE...
...BUT MAXIMILIAN IS DOING A GOOD JOB OF HOLDING HIS OWN.
HMPH!
PUSH BACK! NOW'S YOUR CHANCE!
HE COMES FROM A PRESTIGIOUS NOBLE FAMILY... I'M SURE HE HAD MANY LESSONS.
DESPITE HOW HE ACTS... IRRITATINGLY ENOUGH.
I SEE...
AH, YES. HE IS COUNT ROSENBERG'S COUSIN.
GO, MAXIMILIAN! THAT'S IT!
CHEEEER
REPEL HIS ATTACK! YOU'VE GOT IT!!
MAXIMILIAN!!
THE PRINCE IS PUSHING MAXIMILIAN BACK...
AH, LOOK OUT!!
NOW LUNGE!
...YET NO VOICE IS CHEERING HIS HIGHNESS ON. THAT IS A PITY.
THEY ARE ALL CHEERING FOR MAXIMILIAN...
I SHOULD SAY SOMETHING HE WOULD BE GLAD TO HEAR.
INHALE

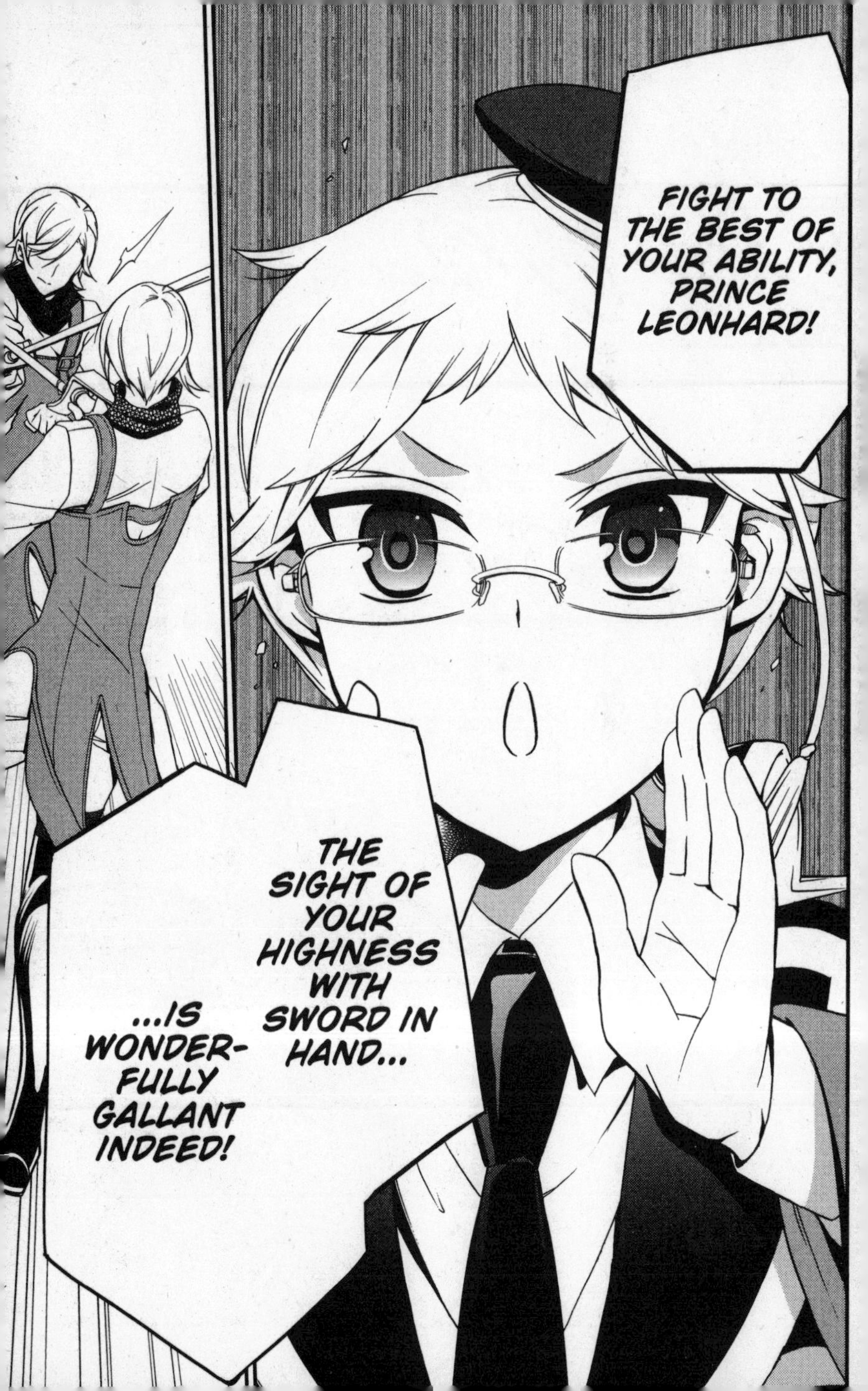
FIGHT TO THE BEST OF YOUR ABILITY, PRINCE LEONHARD!
THE SIGHT OF YOUR HIGHNESS WITH SWORD IN HAND...
...IS WONDER-FULLY GALLANT INDEED!

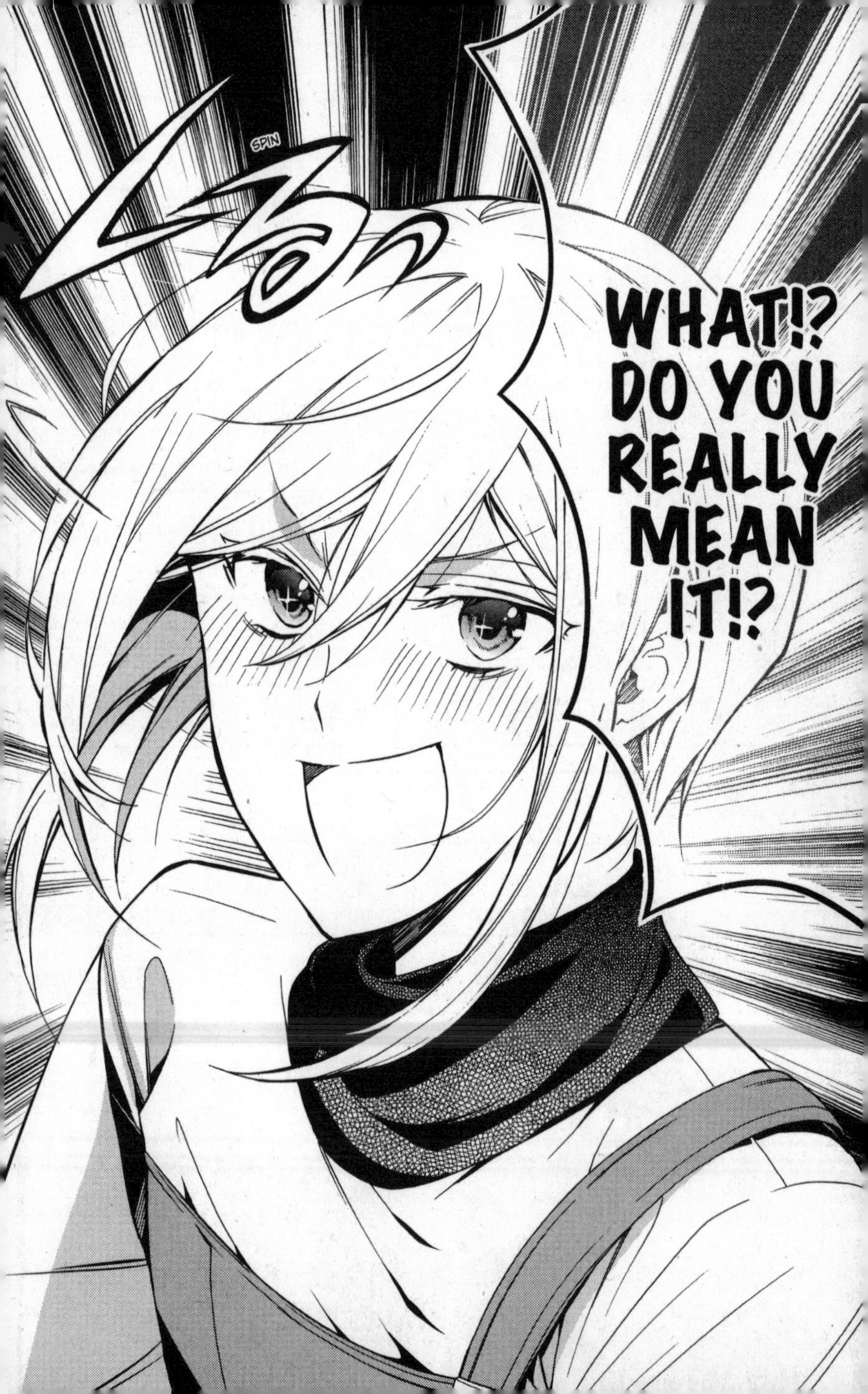
SPIN
WHAT!? DO YOU REALLY MEAN IT!?

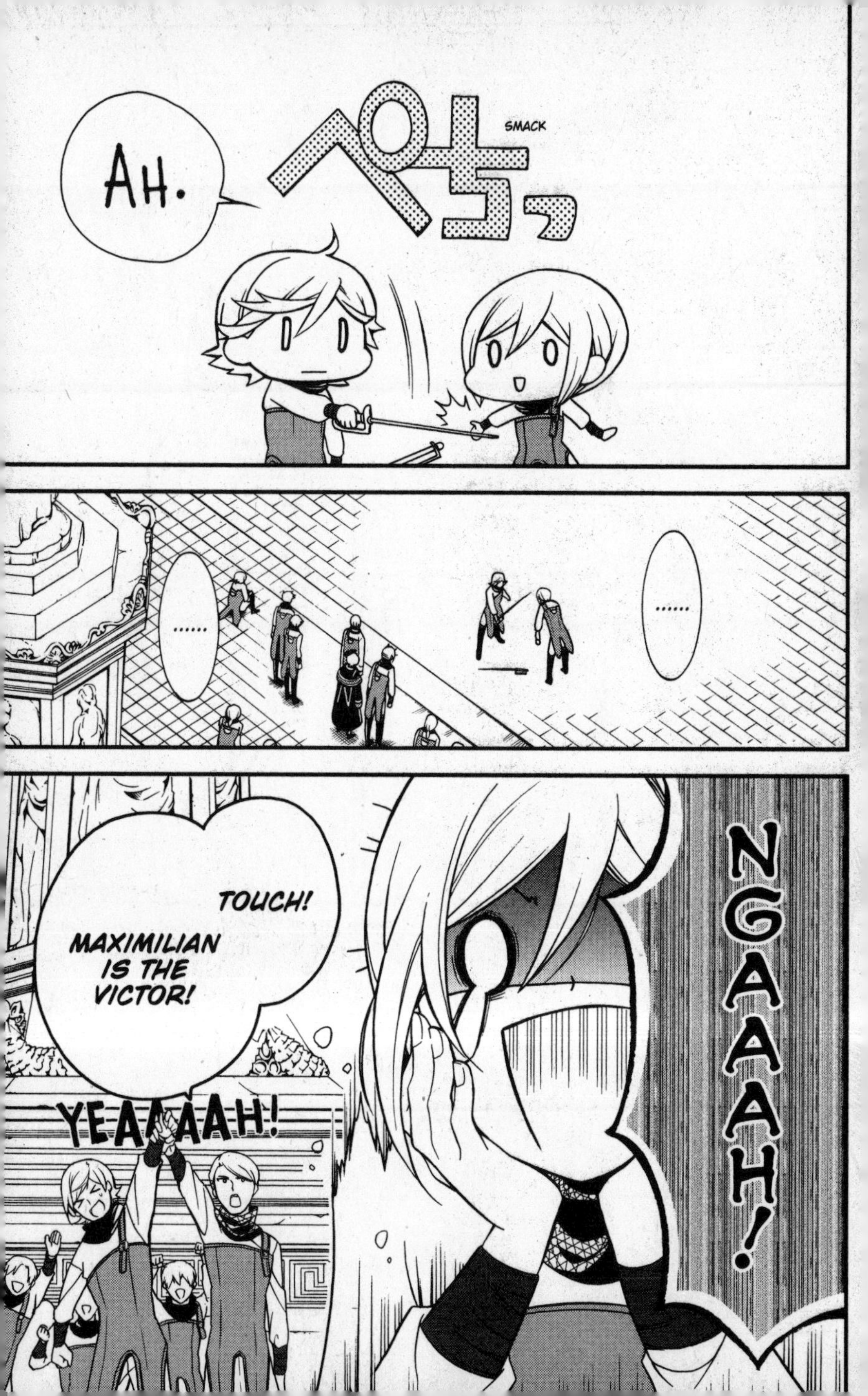
ペちっ
SMACK
AH.
......
......
NGAAAH!
TOUCH! MAXIMILIAN IS THE VICTOR!
YEAAAAH!

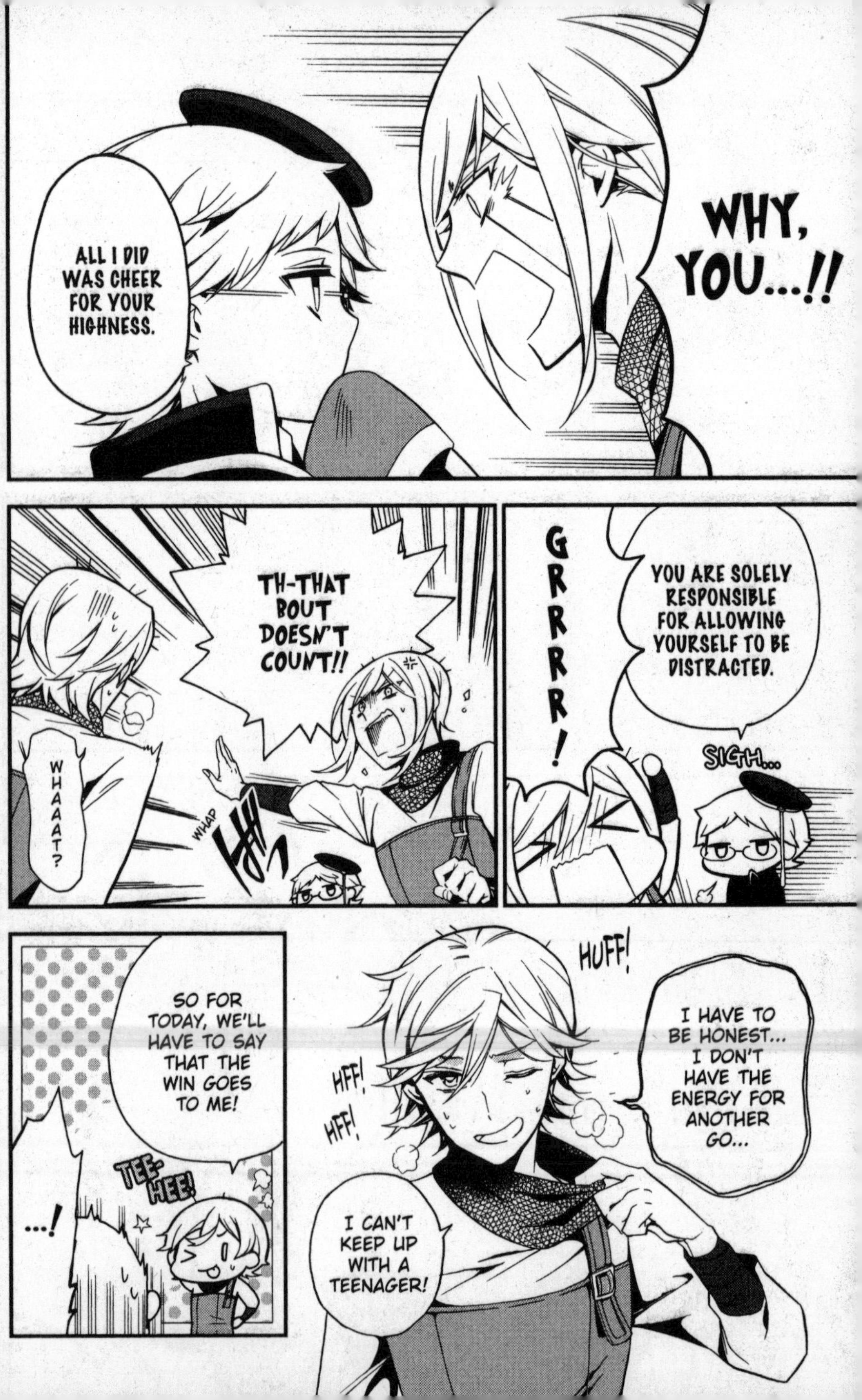
WHY, YOU...!!
ALL I DID WAS CHEER FOR YOUR HIGHNESS.
GRRRR!
YOU ARE SOLELY RESPONSIBLE FOR ALLOWING YOURSELF TO BE DISTRACTED.
SIGH...
TH-THAT BOUT DOESN'T COUNT!!
WHAAAAT?
WHAP
HUFF!
I HAVE TO BE HONEST... I DON'T HAVE THE ENERGY FOR ANOTHER GO...
HFF!
HFF!
I CAN'T KEEP UP WITH A TEENAGER!
SO FOR TODAY, WE'LL HAVE TO SAY THAT THE WIN GOES TO ME!
TEE-HEE!
...!

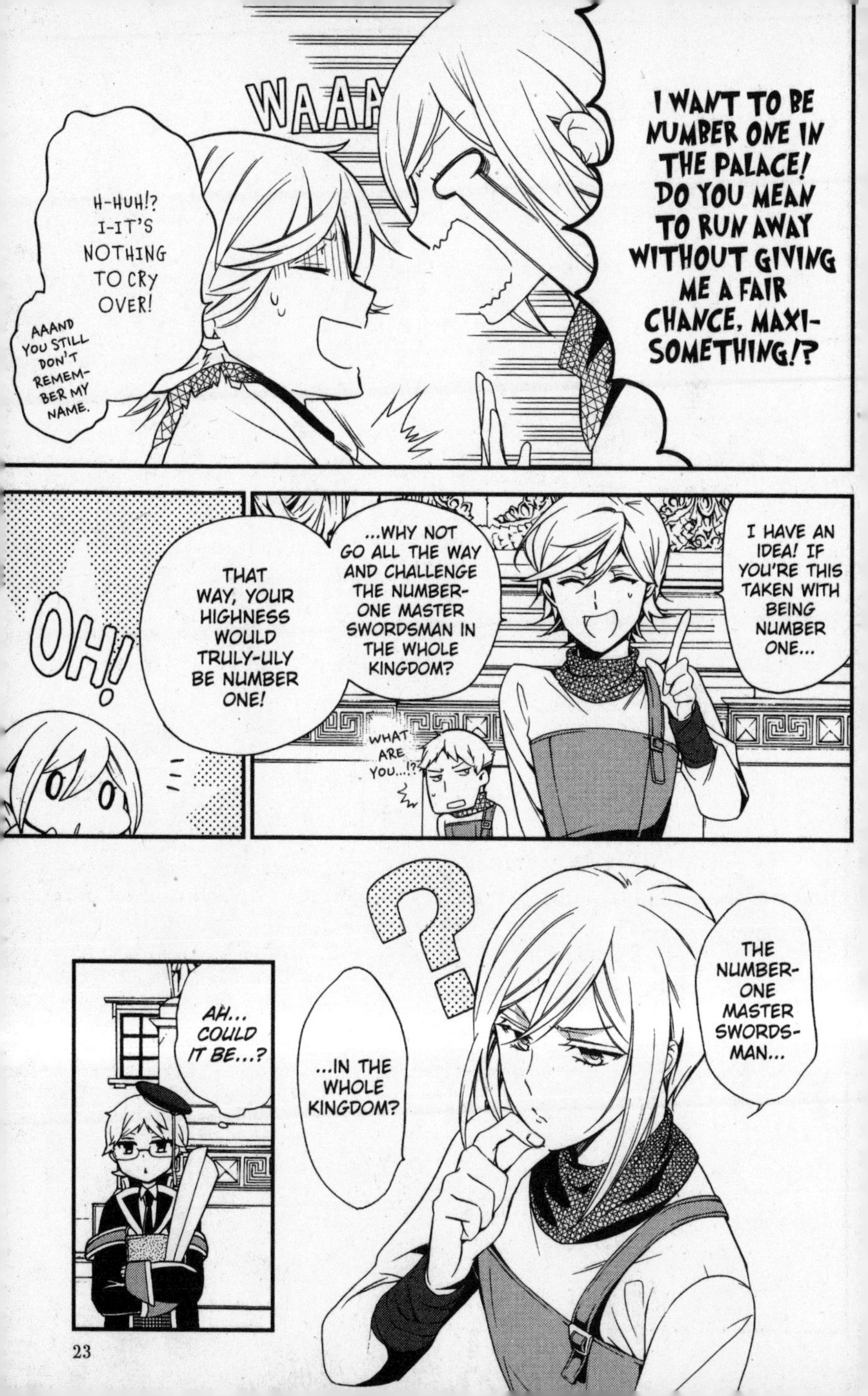
WAAA
I WANT TO BE NUMBER ONE IN THE PALACE! DO YOU MEAN TO RUN AWAY WITHOUT GIVING ME A FAIR CHANCE, MAXI-SOMETHING!?
H-HUH!? I-IT'S NOTHING TO CRY OVER!
AAAND YOU STILL DON'T REMEM-BER MY NAME.
I HAVE AN IDEA! IF YOU'RE THIS TAKEN WITH BEING NUMBER ONE...
...WHY NOT GO ALL THE WAY AND CHALLENGE THE NUMBER-ONE MASTER SWORDSMAN IN THE WHOLE KINGDOM?
WHAT ARE YOU...!?
THAT WAY, YOUR HIGHNESS WOULD TRULY-ULY BE NUMBER ONE!
OH!
THE NUMBER-ONE MASTER SWORDS-MAN...
...IN THE WHOLE KINGDOM?
AH... COULD IT BE...?

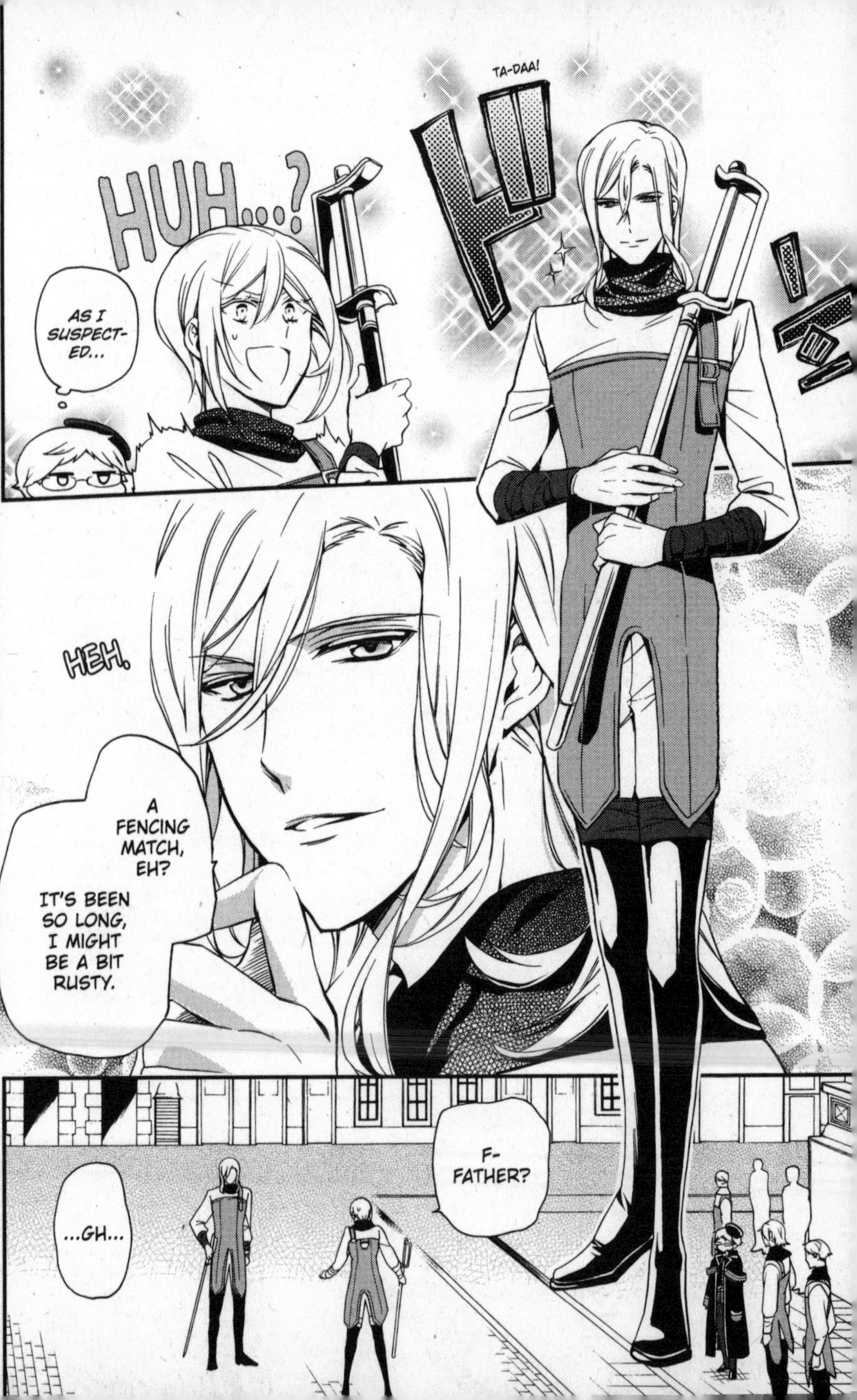
TA-DAA!
HUH...?
AS I SUSPECT-ED...
HEH.
A FENCING MATCH, EH?
IT'S BEEN SO LONG, I MIGHT BE A BIT RUSTY.
F-FATHER?
...GH...

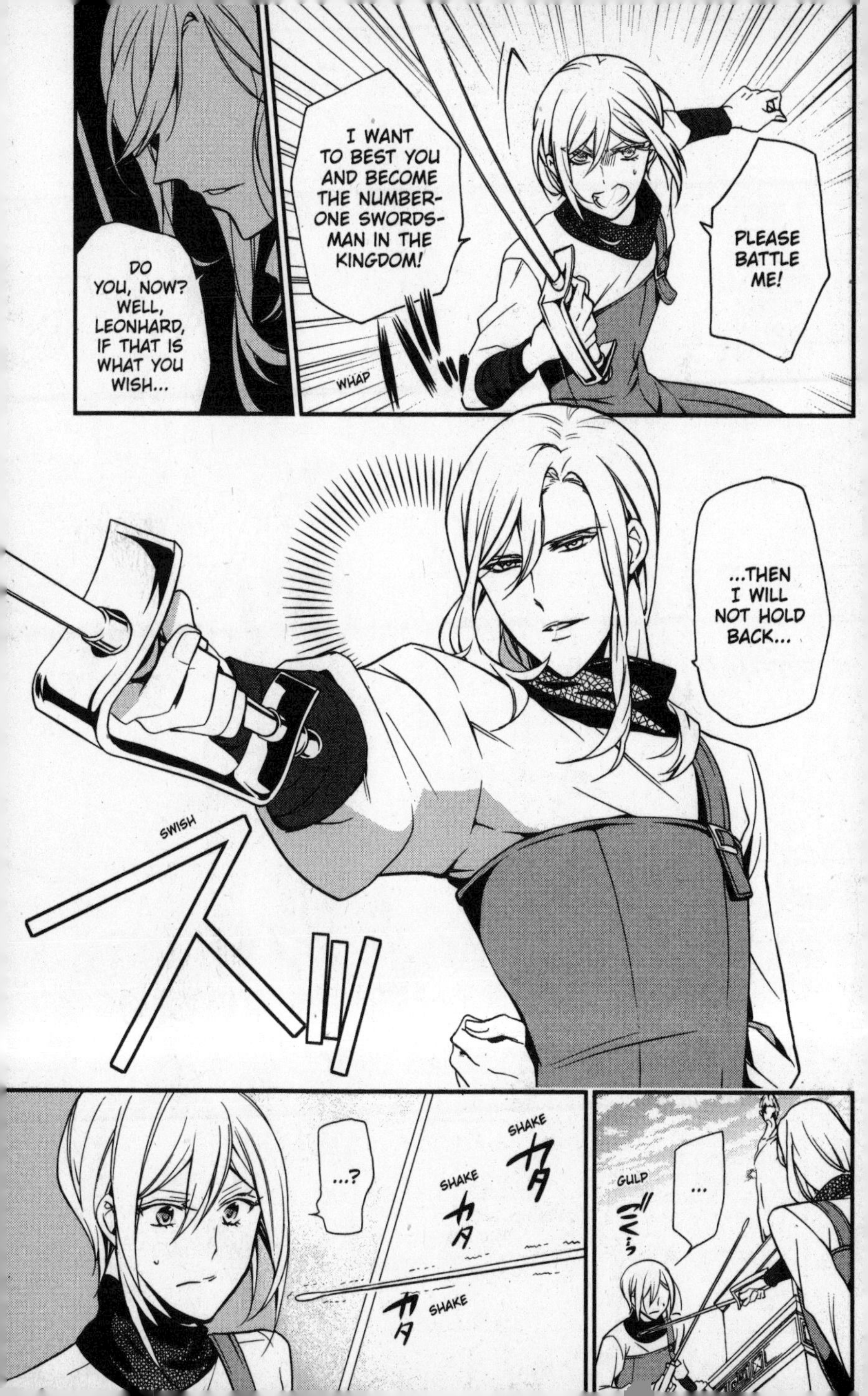
I WANT TO BEST YOU AND BECOME THE NUMBER-ONE SWORDSMAN IN THE KINGDOM!
PLEASE BATTLE ME!
WHAP
DO YOU, NOW? WELL, LEONHARD, IF THAT IS WHAT YOU WISH...
...THEN I WILL NOT HOLD BACK...
SWISH
GULP
...
SHAKE
SHAKE
SHAKE
...?

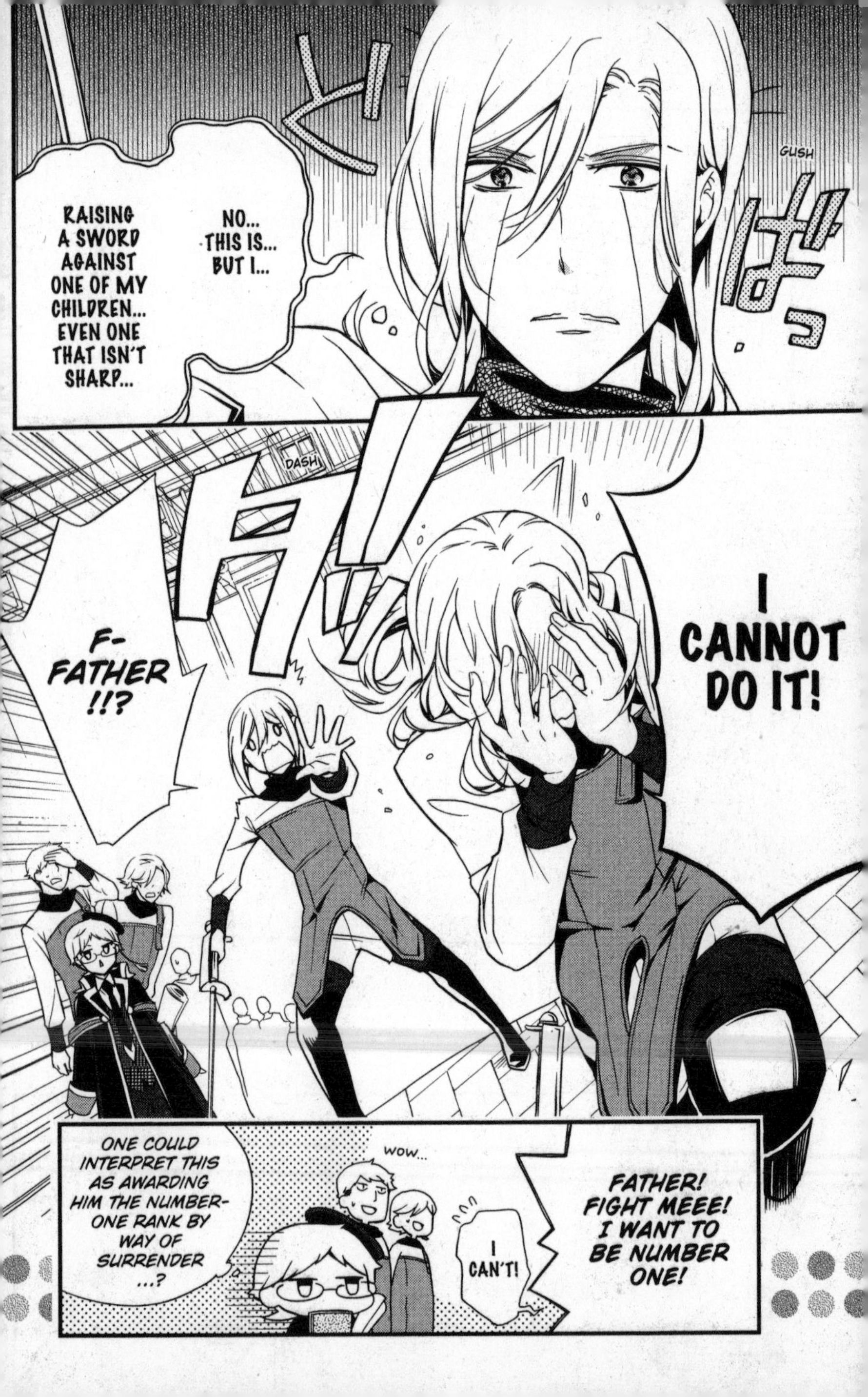
GUSH
NO... THIS IS... BUT I...
RAISING A SWORD AGAINST ONE OF MY CHILDREN... EVEN ONE THAT ISN'T SHARP...
DASH
I CANNOT DO IT!
F-FATHER!!?
FATHER! FIGHT MEEE! I WANT TO BE NUMBER ONE!
I CAN'T!
WOW...
ONE COULD INTERPRET THIS AS AWARDING HIM THE NUMBER-ONE RANK BY WAY OF SURRENDER ...?

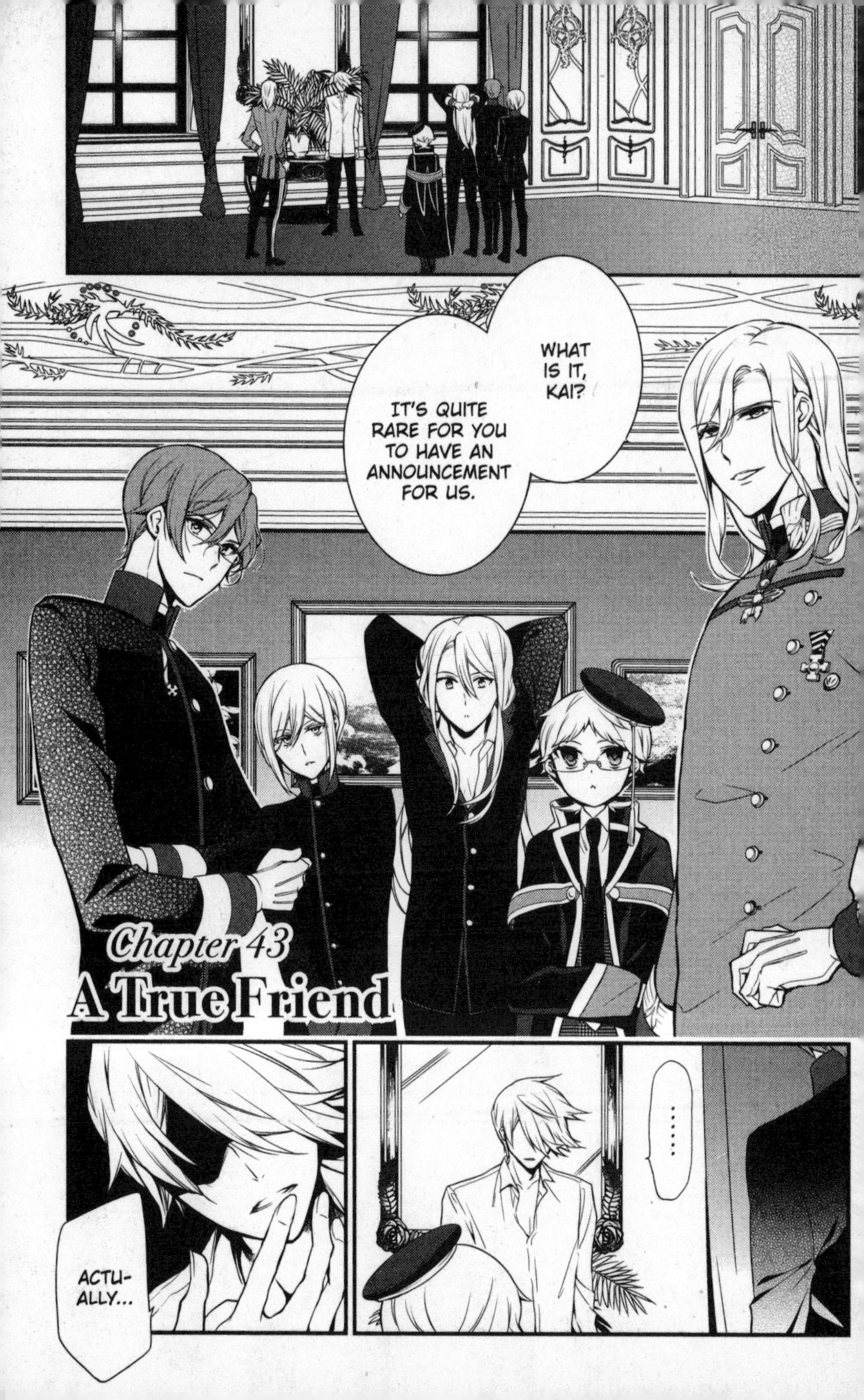
WHAT IS IT, KAI? IT'S QUITE RARE FOR YOU TO HAVE AN ANNOUNCEMENT FOR US.
Chapter 43
A True Friend
......
ACTU-ALLY...

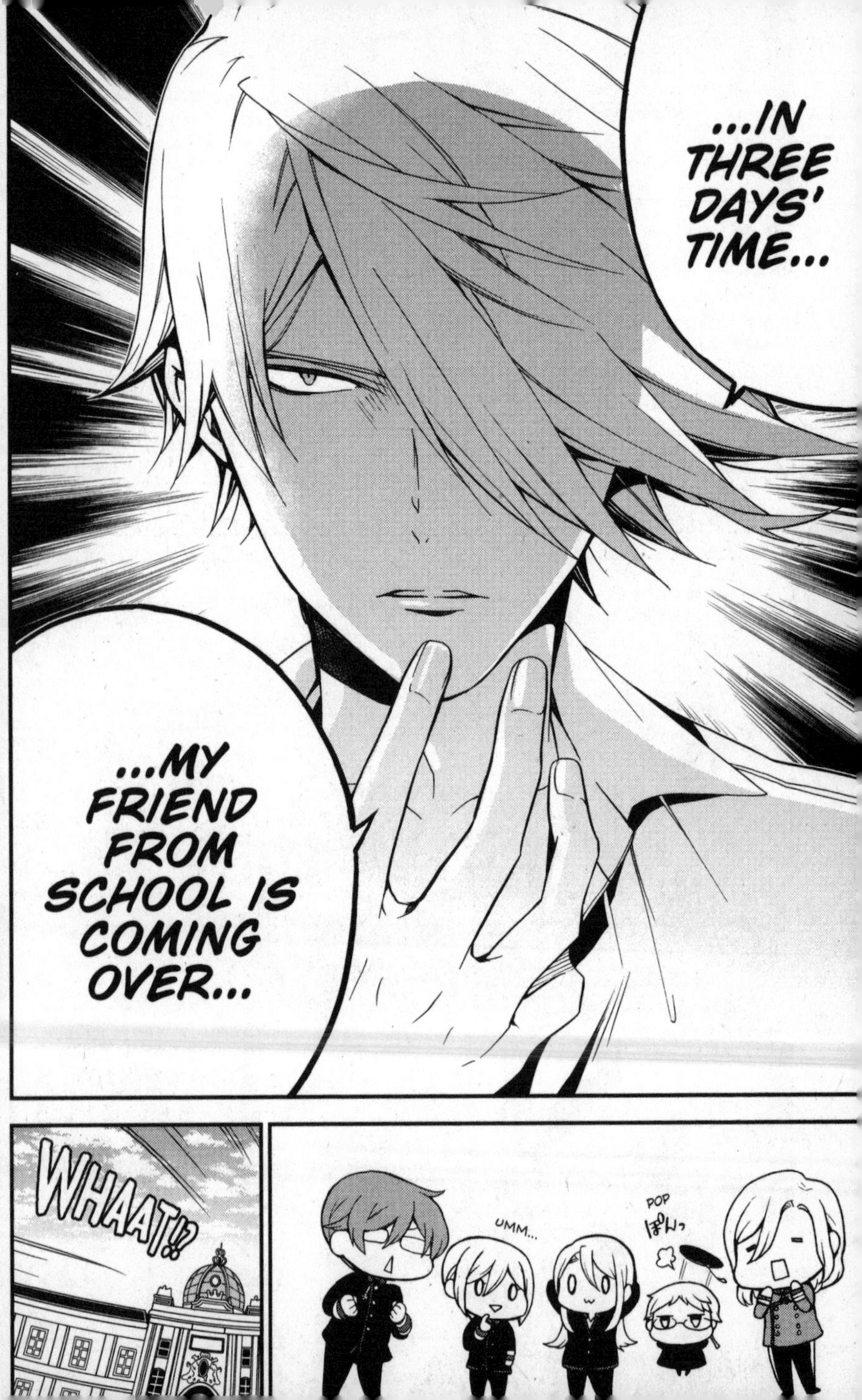
...IN THREE DAYS' TIME...
...MY FRIEND FROM SCHOOL IS COMING OVER...
UMM...
POP
ぽんっ
WHAAT!!?

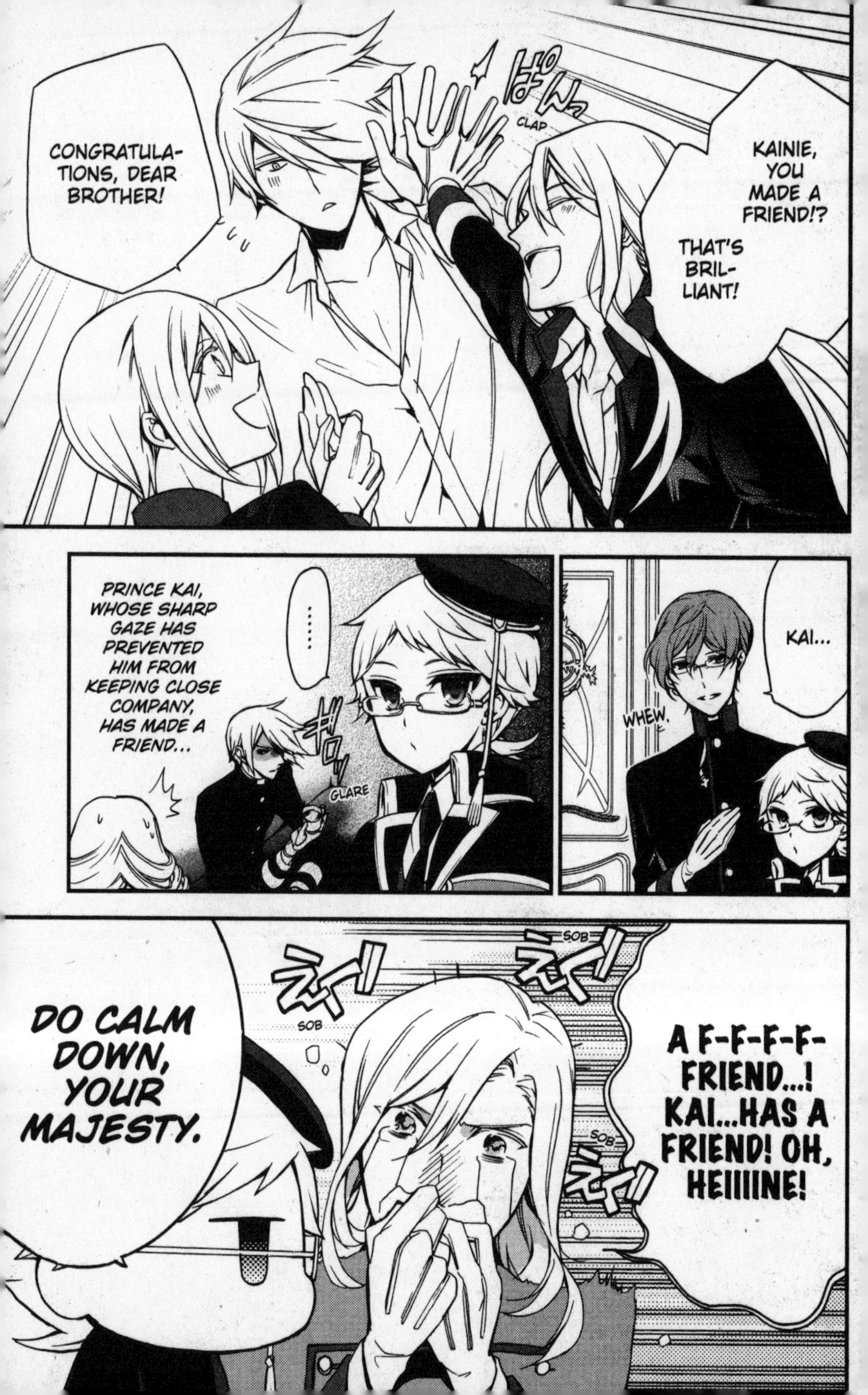
KAINIE, YOU MADE A FRIEND!?
THAT'S BRILLIANT!
ぱんっ
CLAP
CONGRATULATIONS, DEAR BROTHER!
KAI...
WHEW.
......
PRINCE KAI, WHOSE SHARP GAZE HAS PREVENTED HIM FROM KEEPING CLOSE COMPANY, HAS MADE A FRIEND...
GLARE
A F-F-F-F-FRIEND...! KAI...HAS A FRIEND! OH, HEIIIINE!
SOB
SOB
SOB
DO CALM DOWN, YOUR MAJESTY.

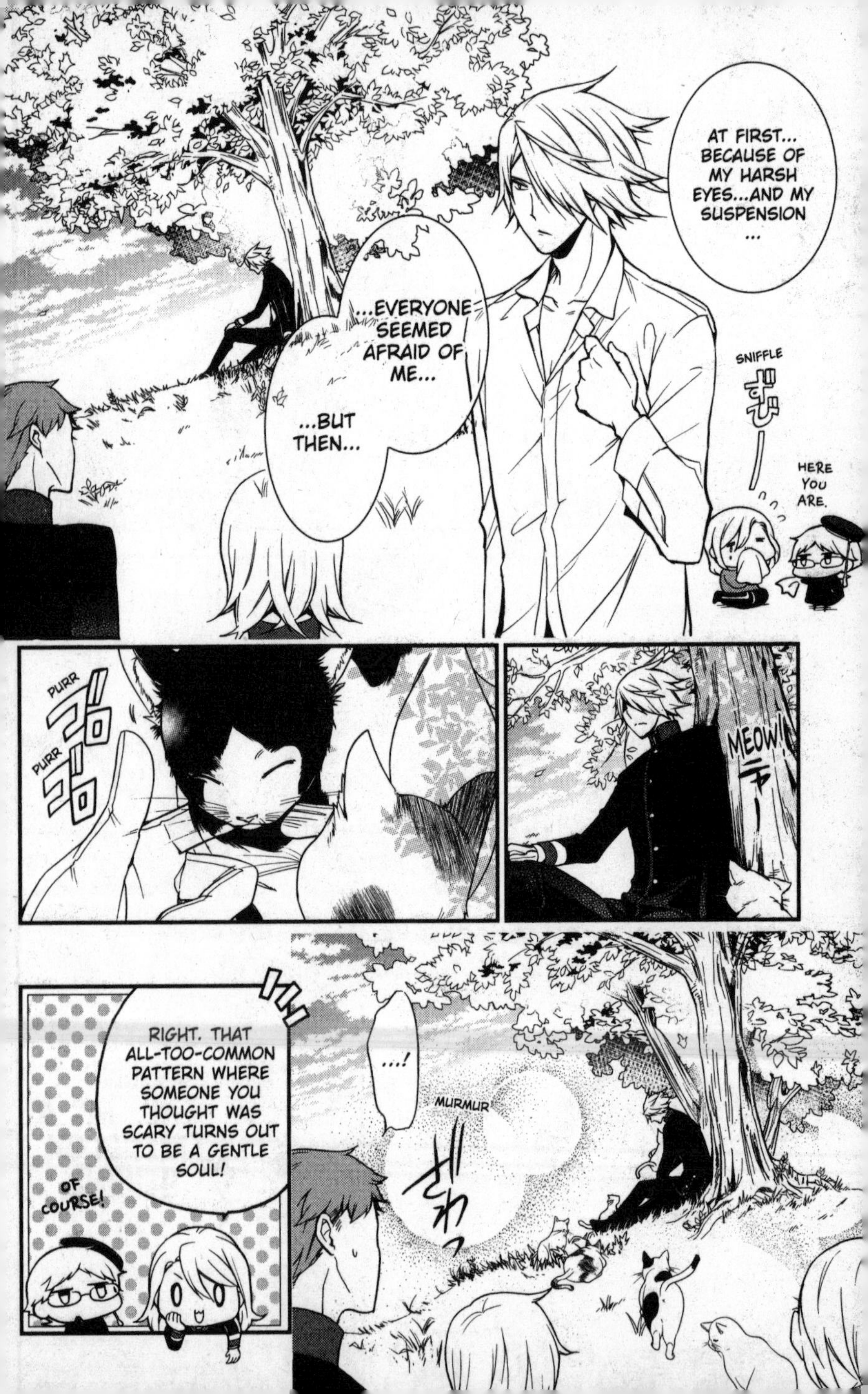
AT FIRST... BECAUSE OF MY HARSH EYES...AND MY SUSPENSION ...
...EVERYONE SEEMED AFRAID OF ME...
...BUT THEN...
SNIFFLE
ずびー
HERE YOU ARE.
MEOW!
ニャー
PURR
ゴロ
PURR
ゴロ
...!
MURMUR
ざわっ
RIGHT. THAT ALL-TOO-COMMON PATTERN WHERE SOMEONE YOU THOUGHT WAS SCARY TURNS OUT TO BE A GENTLE SOUL!
OF COURSE!

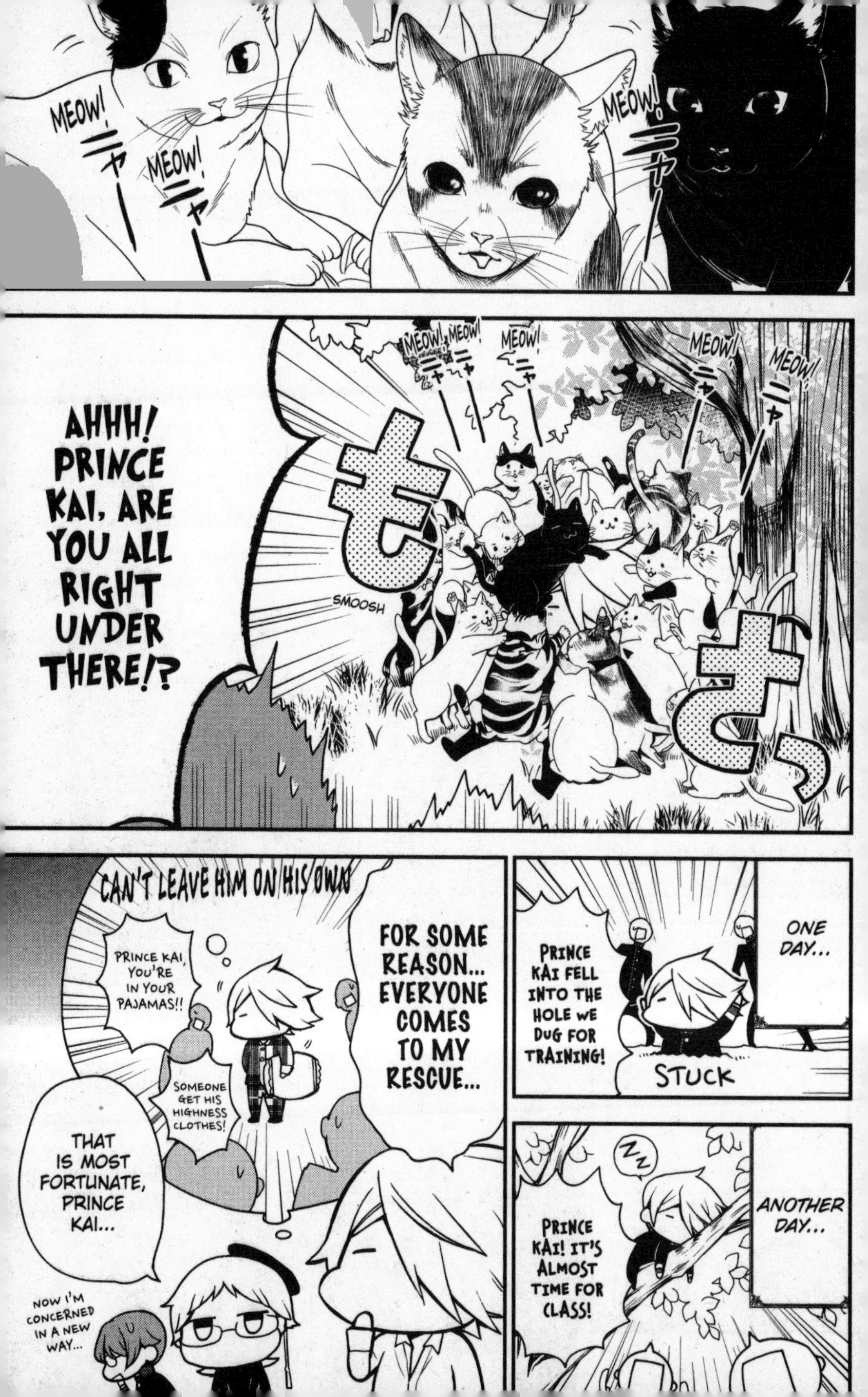
MEOW!
ニャー
MEOW!
ニャー
MEOW!
ニャー
MEOW!
ニャー
MEOW!
ニャー
MEOW!
ニャー
MEOW!
ニャー
MEOW!
ニャー
もさっ
SMOOSH
AHHH! PRINCE KAI, ARE YOU ALL RIGHT UNDER THERE!?
ONE DAY...
PRINCE KAI FELL INTO THE HOLE WE DUG FOR TRAINING!
STUCK
ANOTHER DAY...
PRINCE KAI! IT'S ALMOST TIME FOR CLASS!
CAN'T LEAVE HIM ON HIS OWN
FOR SOME REASON... EVERYONE COMES TO MY RESCUE...
PRINCE KAI, YOU'RE IN YOUR PAJAMAS!!
SOMEONE GET HIS HIGHNESS CLOTHES!
THAT IS MOST FORTUNATE, PRINCE KAI...
NOW I'M CONCERNED IN A NEW WAY...

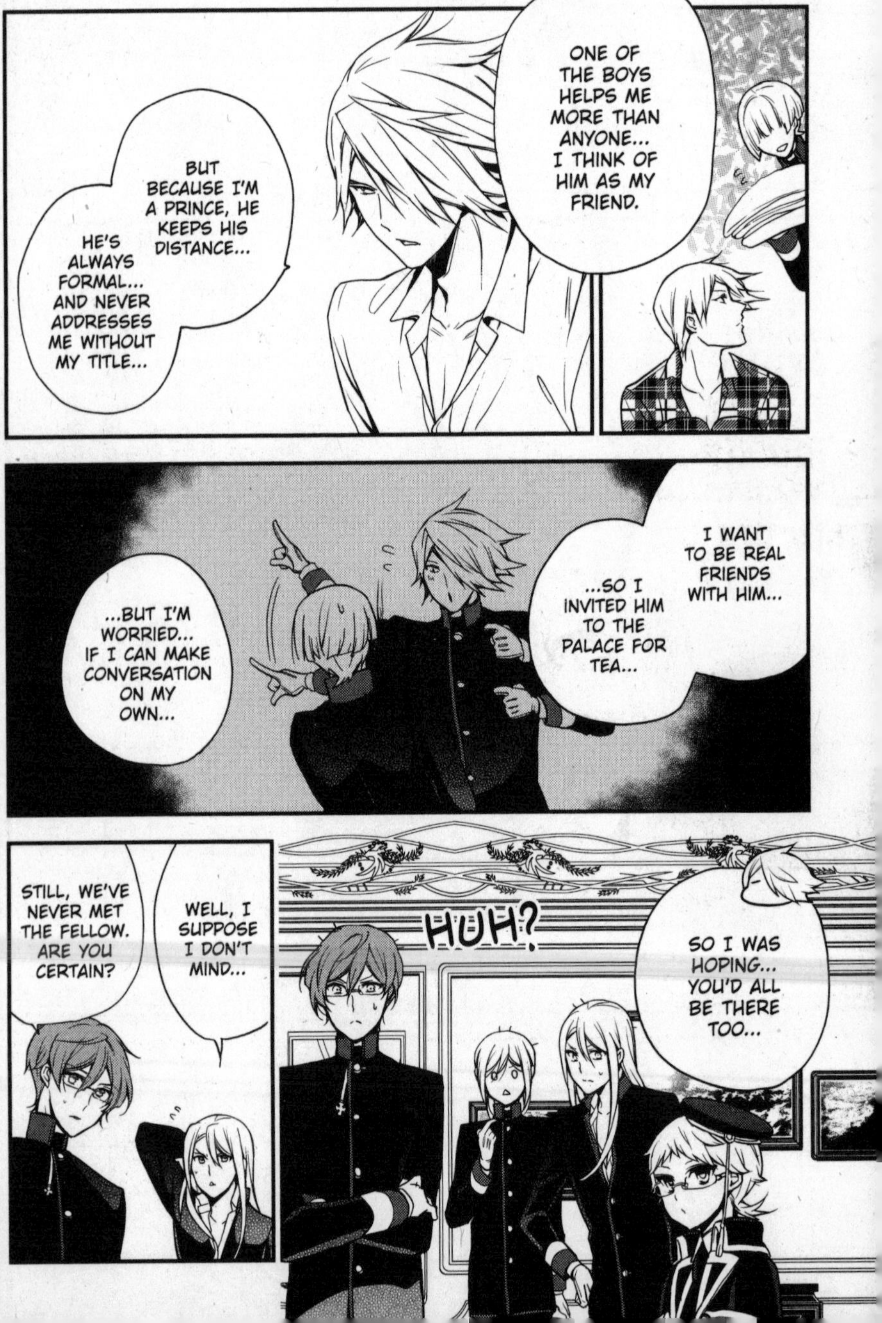
ONE OF THE BOYS HELPS ME MORE THAN ANYONE... I THINK OF HIM AS MY FRIEND.
BUT BECAUSE I'M A PRINCE, HE KEEPS HIS DISTANCE...
HE'S ALWAYS FORMAL... AND NEVER ADDRESSES ME WITHOUT MY TITLE...
I WANT TO BE REAL FRIENDS WITH HIM...
...SO I INVITED HIM TO THE PALACE FOR TEA...
...BUT I'M WORRIED... IF I CAN MAKE CONVERSATION ON MY OWN...
SO I WAS HOPING... YOU'D ALL BE THERE TOO...
HUH?
WELL, I SUPPOSE I DON'T MIND...
STILL, WE'VE NEVER MET THE FELLOW. ARE YOU CERTAIN?

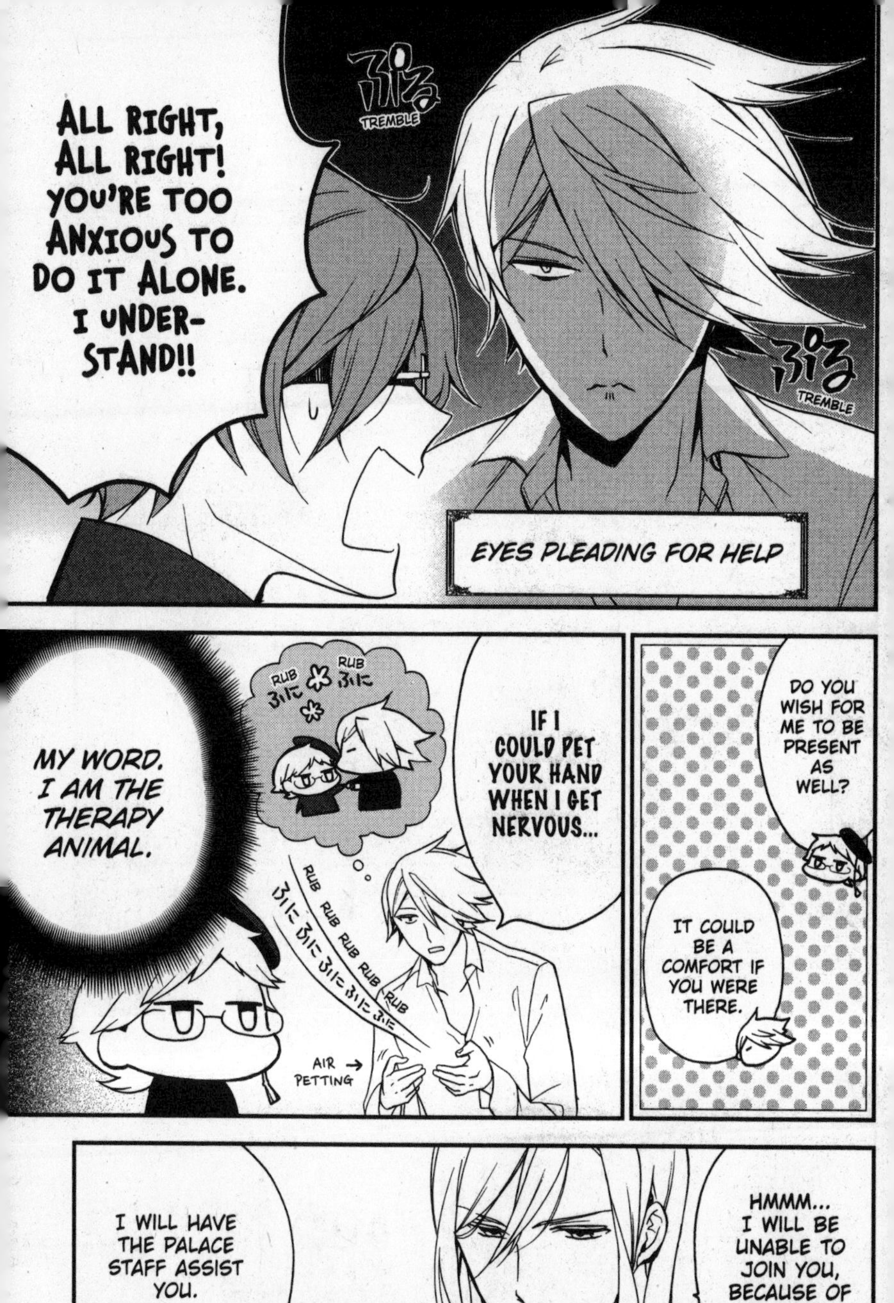
ぷる
TREMBLE
ぷる
TREMBLE
ALL RIGHT, ALL RIGHT! YOU'RE TOO ANXIOUS TO DO IT ALONE. I UNDER-STAND!!
EYES PLEADING FOR HELP
DO YOU WISH FOR ME TO BE PRESENT AS WELL?
IT COULD BE A COMFORT IF YOU WERE THERE.
IF I COULD PET YOUR HAND WHEN I GET NERVOUS...
RUB ふに RUB ふに
RUB RUB RUB RUB RUB ふに ふに ふに ふに ふに
AIR PETTING
MY WORD. I AM THE THERAPY ANIMAL.
HMMM... I WILL BE UNABLE TO JOIN YOU, BECAUSE OF MY WORK...
I WILL HAVE THE PALACE STAFF ASSIST YOU.

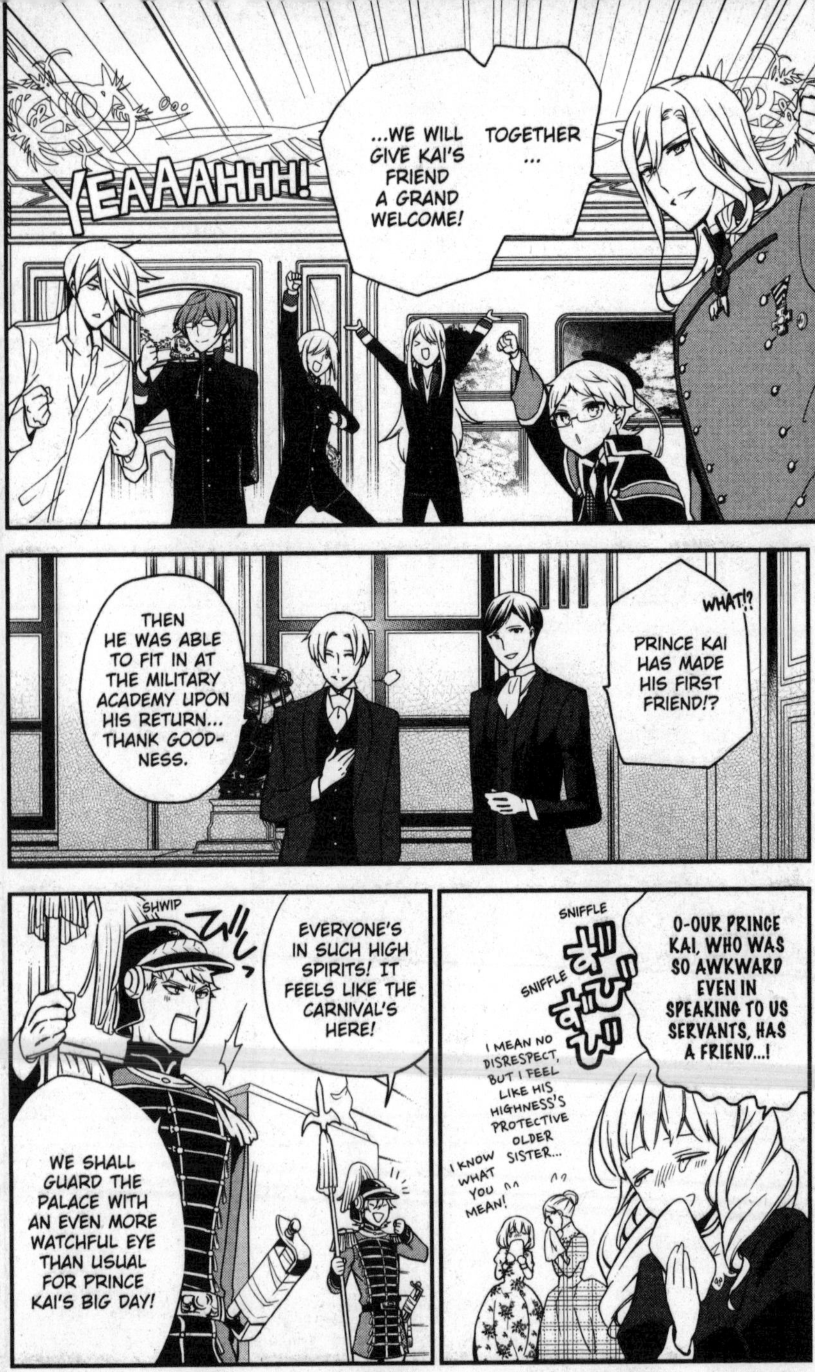
TOGETHER...
...WE WILL GIVE KAI'S FRIEND A GRAND WELCOME!
YEAAAHHH!
WHAT!?
PRINCE KAI HAS MADE HIS FIRST FRIEND!?
THEN HE WAS ABLE TO FIT IN AT THE MILITARY ACADEMY UPON HIS RETURN... THANK GOODNESS.
SNIFFLE
SNIFFLE
O-OUR PRINCE KAI, WHO WAS SO AWKWARD EVEN IN SPEAKING TO US SERVANTS, HAS A FRIEND...!
I MEAN NO DISRESPECT, BUT I FEEL LIKE HIS HIGHNESS'S PROTECTIVE OLDER SISTER...
I KNOW WHAT YOU MEAN!
EVERYONE'S IN SUCH HIGH SPIRITS! IT FEELS LIKE THE CARNIVAL'S HERE!
SHWIP
WE SHALL GUARD THE PALACE WITH AN EVEN MORE WATCHFUL EYE THAN USUAL FOR PRINCE KAI'S BIG DAY!

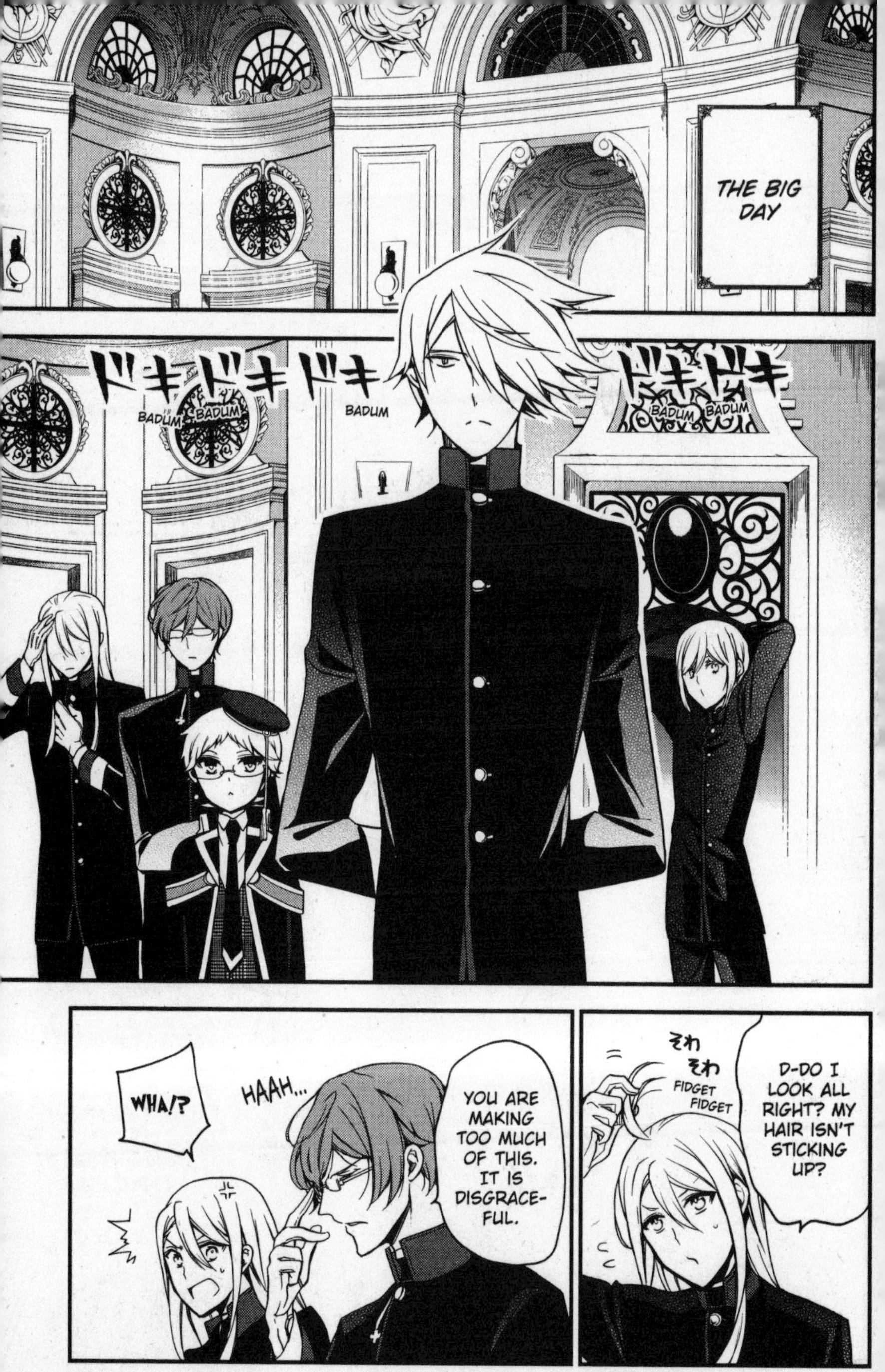
THE BIG DAY
ドキドキ
BADUM BADUM
ドキドキドキ
BADUM
BADUM BADUM
そわそわ
FIDGET FIDGET
D-DO I LOOK ALL RIGHT? MY HAIR ISN'T STICKING UP?
YOU ARE MAKING TOO MUCH OF THIS. IT IS DISGRACE-FUL.
HAAH...
WHA!?

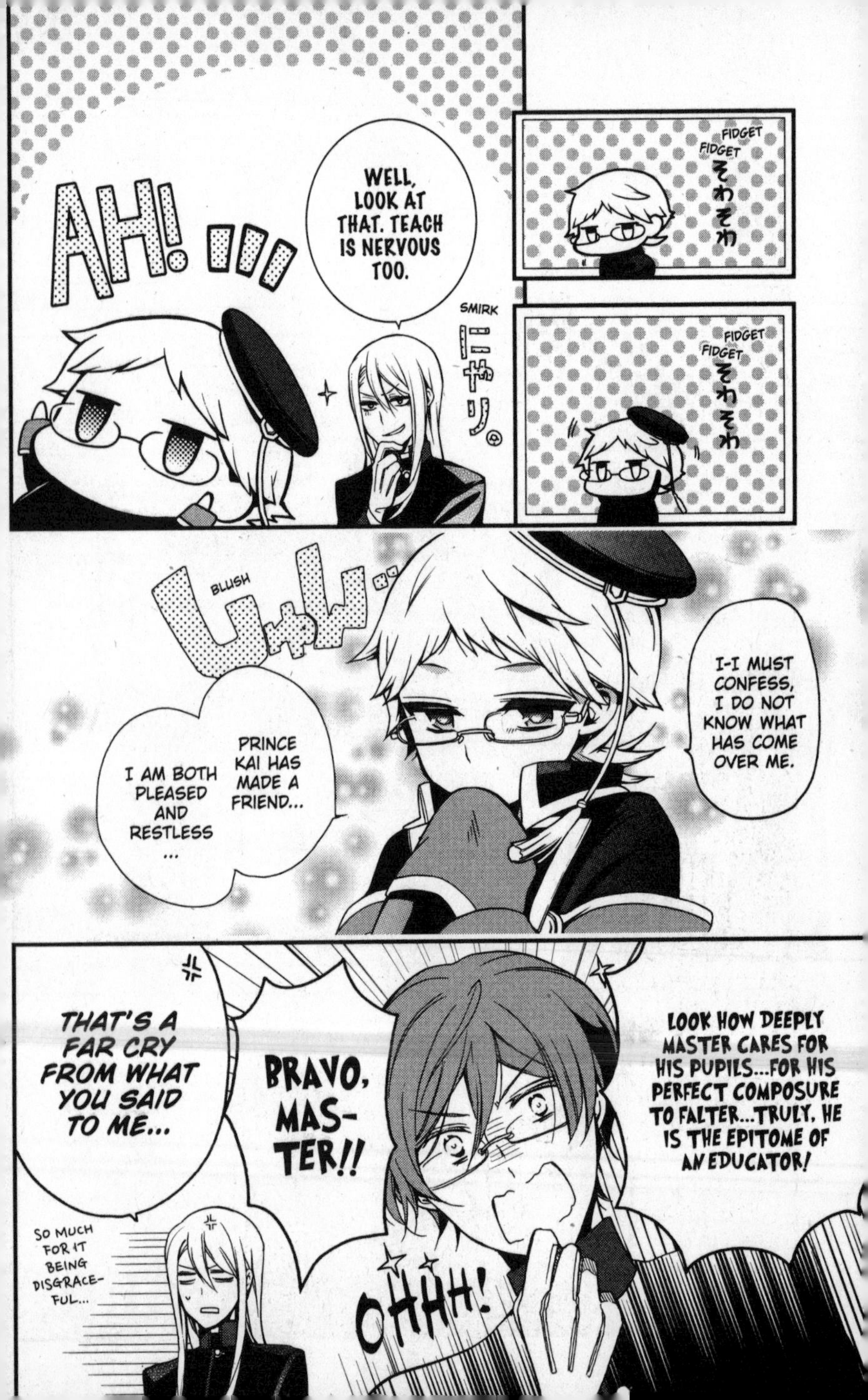
FIDGET
FIDGET
そわそわ
FIDGET
FIDGET
そわそわ
WELL, LOOK AT THAT. TEACH IS NERVOUS TOO.
SMIRK
にやり
AH!
BLUSH
I-I MUST CONFESS, I DO NOT KNOW WHAT HAS COME OVER ME.
PRINCE KAI HAS MADE A FRIEND...
I AM BOTH PLEASED AND RESTLESS ...
LOOK HOW DEEPLY MASTER CARES FOR HIS PUPILS...FOR HIS PERFECT COMPOSURE TO FALTER...TRULY, HE IS THE EPITOME OF AN EDUCATOR!
BRAVO, MAS-TER!!
OHHH!
THAT'S A FAR CRY FROM WHAT YOU SAID TO ME...
SO MUCH FOR IT BEING DISGRACE-FUL...

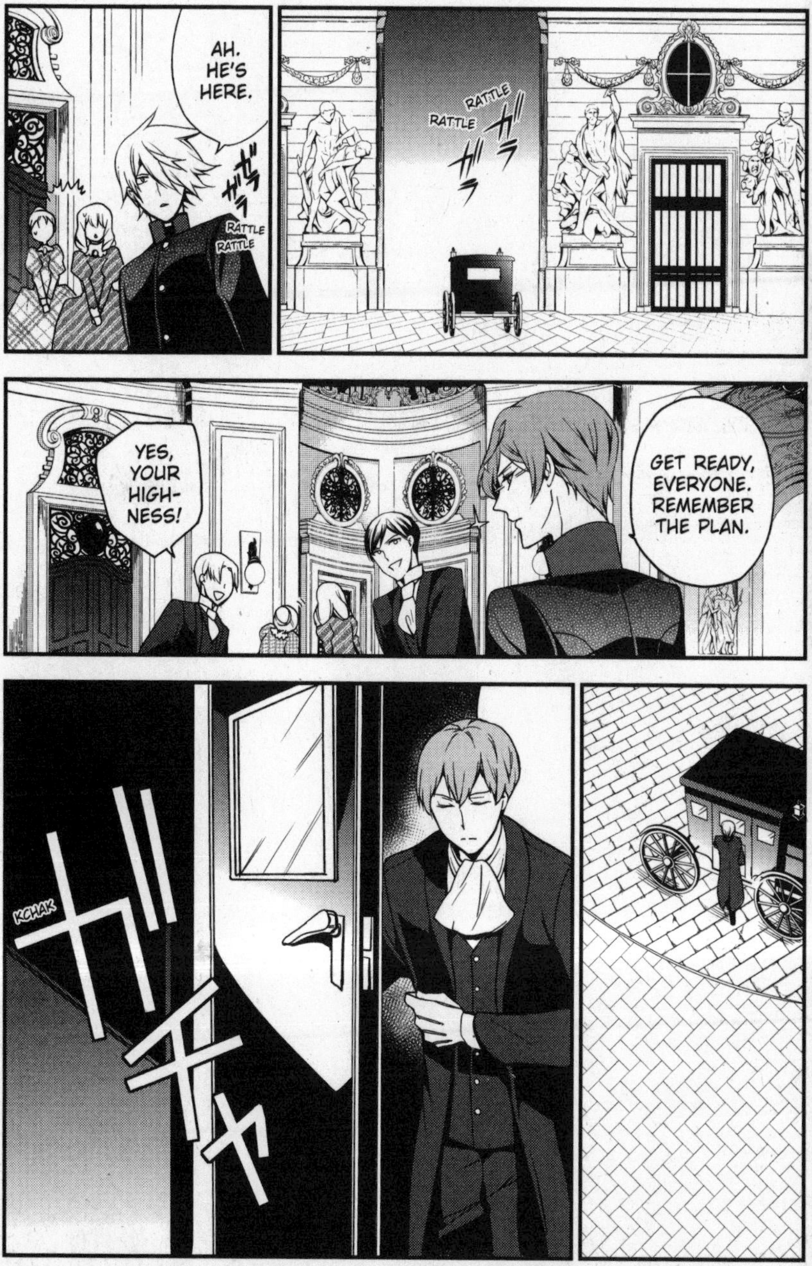
RATTLE
RATTLE
AH. HE'S HERE.
RATTLE
RATTLE
GET READY, EVERYONE. REMEMBER THE PLAN.
YES, YOUR HIGH-NESS!
KCHAK

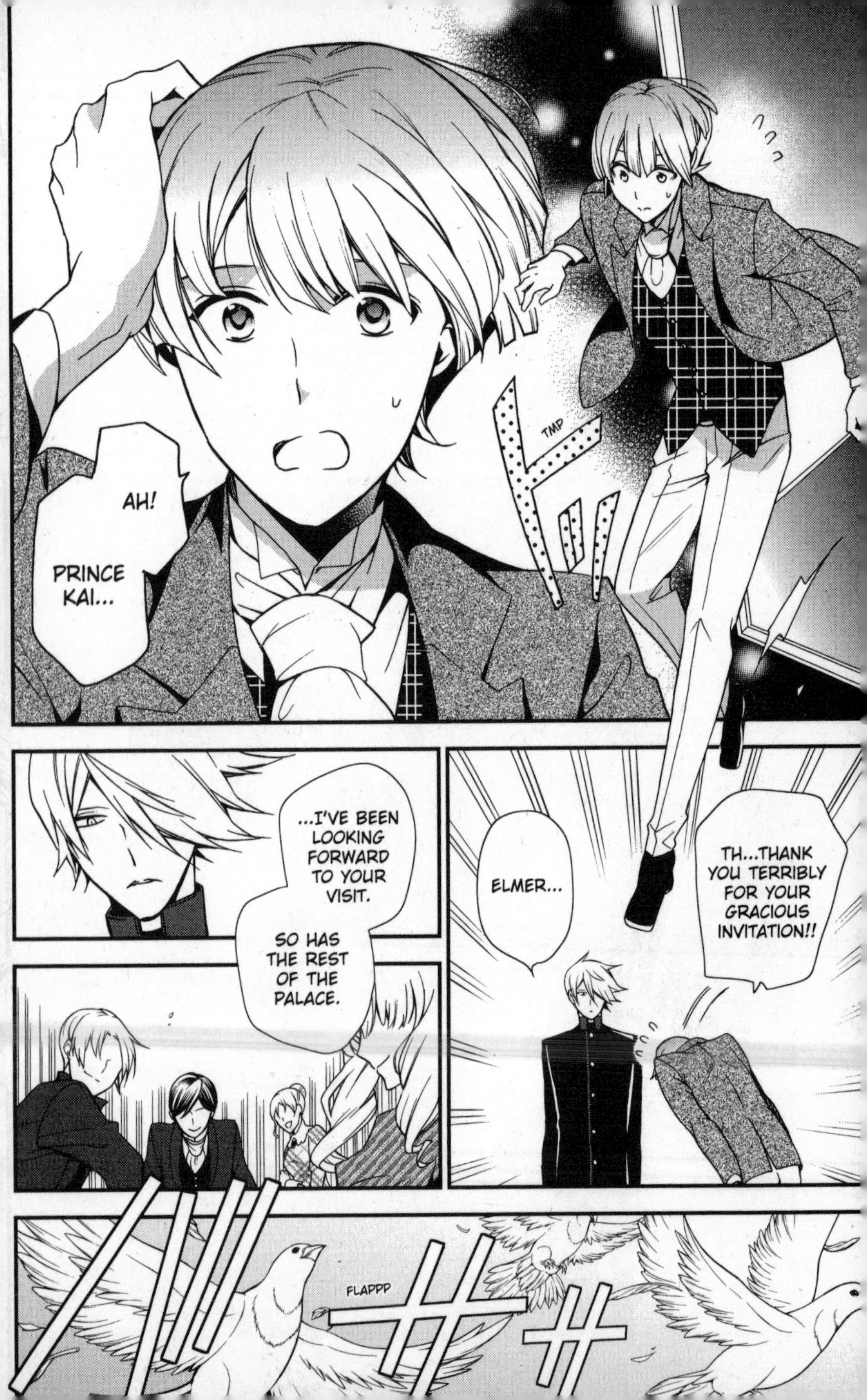
TMP
AH!
PRINCE KAI...
TH...THANK YOU TERRIBLY FOR YOUR GRACIOUS INVITATION!!
ELMER...
...I'VE BEEN LOOKING FORWARD TO YOUR VISIT.
SO HAS THE REST OF THE PALACE.
FLAPPP

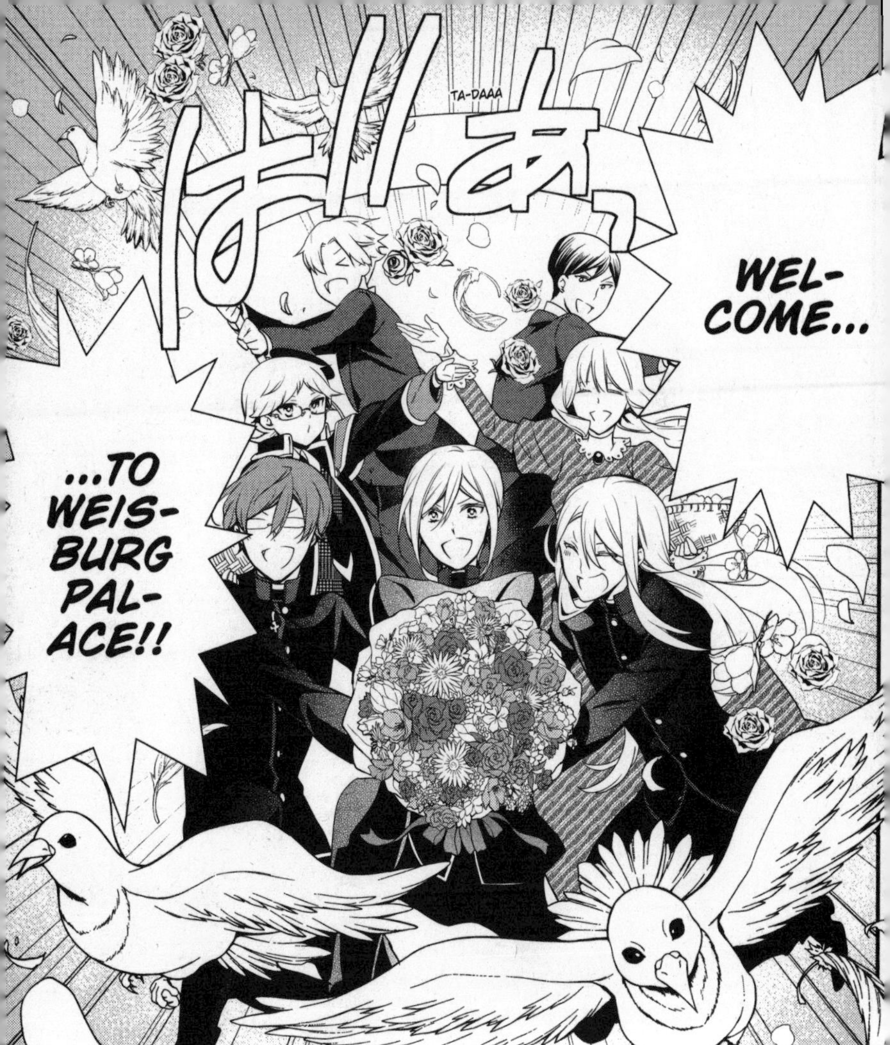
TA-DAAA
WEL-
COME...
...TO
WEIS-
BURG
PAL-
ACE!!
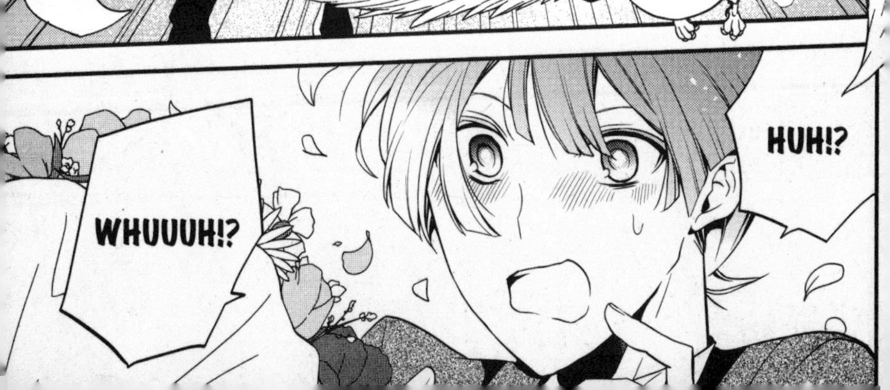
HUH!?
WHUUUH!?

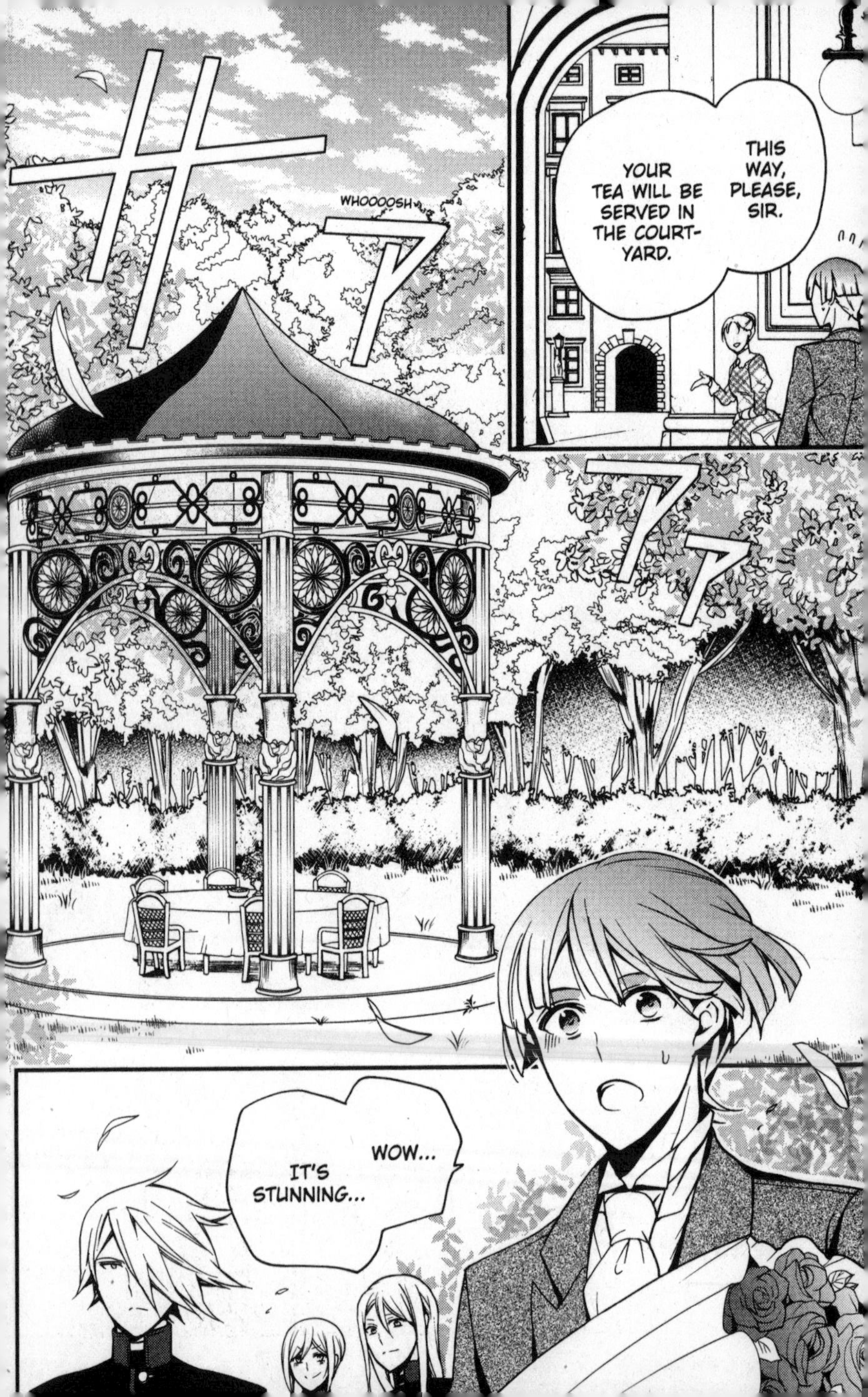
THIS WAY, PLEASE, SIR.
YOUR TEA WILL BE SERVED IN THE COURT-YARD.
WHOOOOSH
WOW...
IT'S STUNNING...

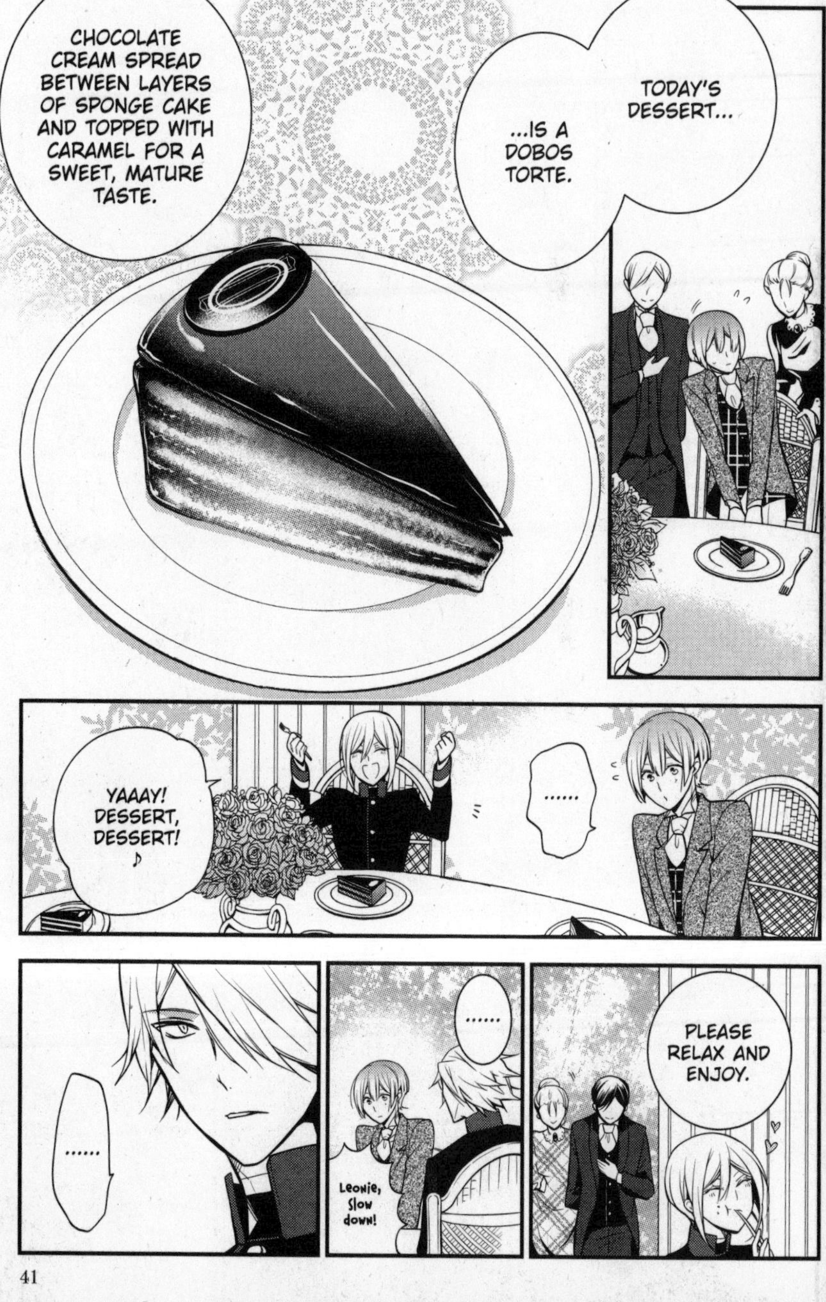
TODAY'S DESSERT...
...IS A DOBOS TORTE.
CHOCOLATE CREAM SPREAD BETWEEN LAYERS OF SPONGE CAKE AND TOPPED WITH CARAMEL FOR A SWEET, MATURE TASTE.
......
YAAAY! DESSERT, DESSERT! ♪
PLEASE RELAX AND ENJOY.
......
Leonie, Slow down!
......

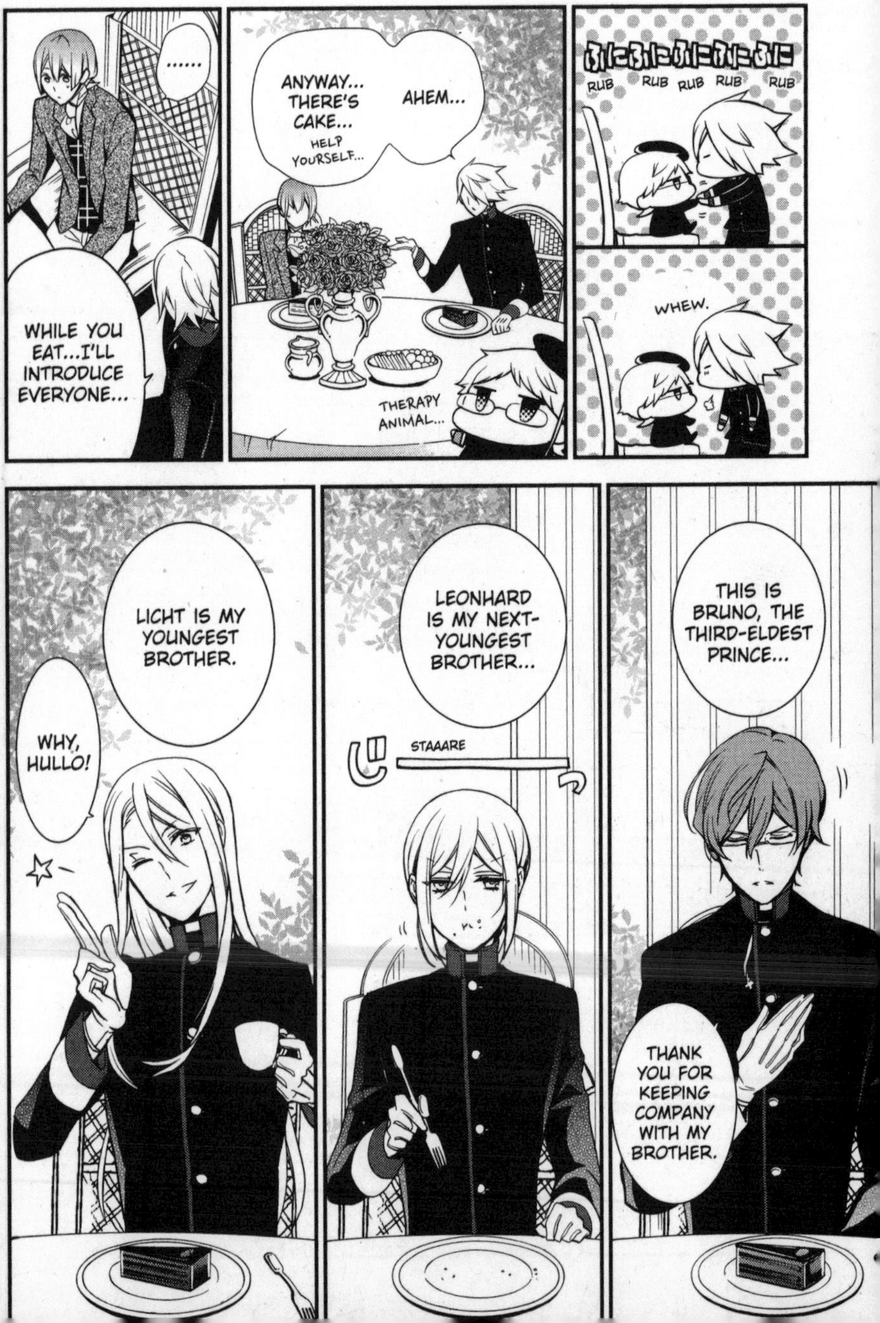

ふにふにふにふにふに
RUB RUB RUB RUB RUB
WHEW.
AHEM...
ANYWAY... THERE'S CAKE...
HELP YOURSELF...
THERAPY ANIMAL...
......
WHILE YOU EAT...I'LL INTRODUCE EVERYONE...
THIS IS BRUNO, THE THIRD-ELDEST PRINCE...
THANK YOU FOR KEEPING COMPANY WITH MY BROTHER.
LEONHARD IS MY NEXT-YOUNGEST BROTHER...
じー
STAAARE
LICHT IS MY YOUNGEST BROTHER.
WHY, HULLO!

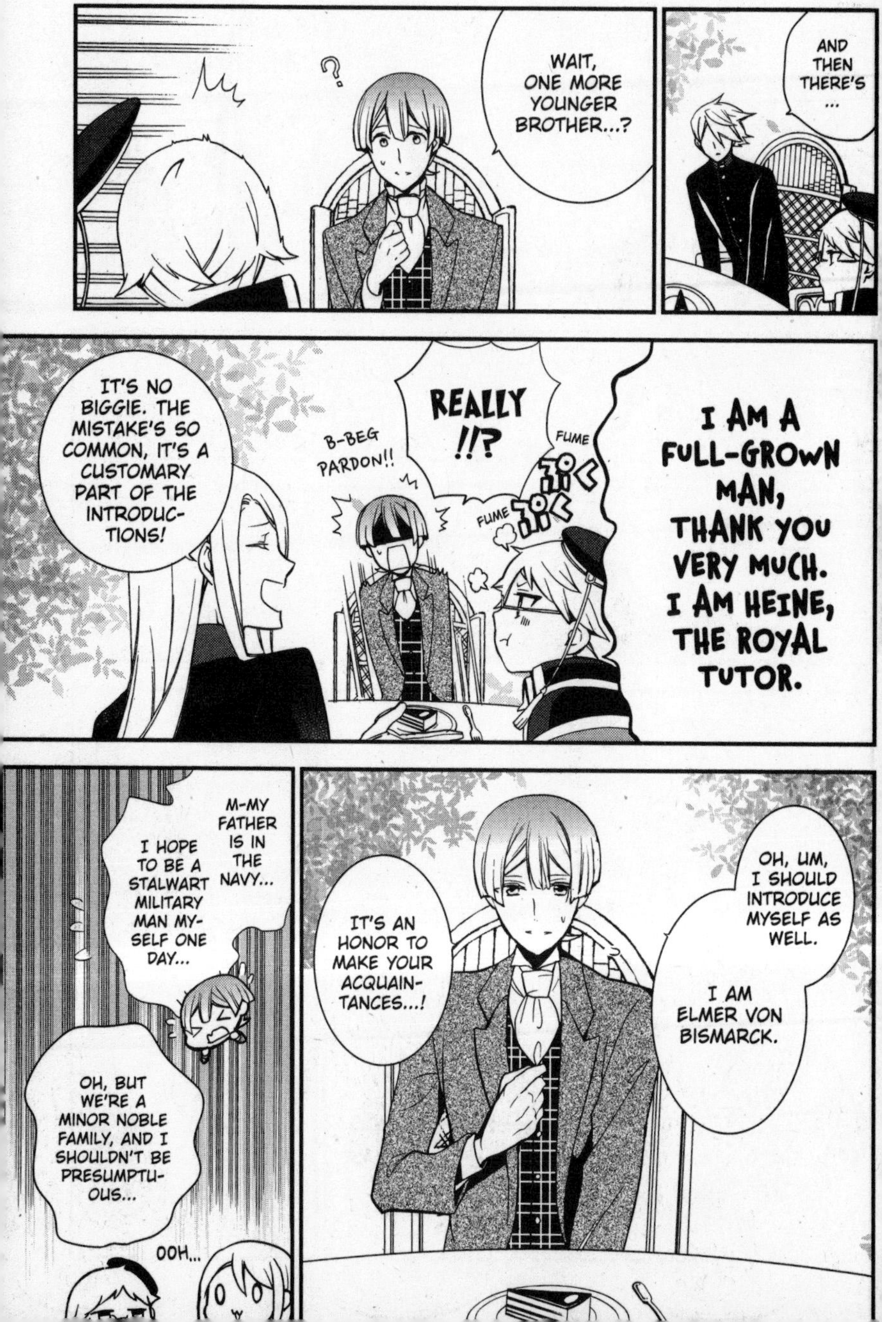
AND THEN THERE'S ...
WAIT, ONE MORE YOUNGER BROTHER...?
I AM A FULL-GROWN MAN, THANK YOU VERY MUCH. I AM HEINE, THE ROYAL TUTOR.
FUME
ぷく
FUME
ぷく
REALLY !!?
B-BEG PARDON!!
IT'S NO BIGGIE. THE MISTAKE'S SO COMMON, IT'S A CUSTOMARY PART OF THE INTRODUCTIONS!
OH, UM, I SHOULD INTRODUCE MYSELF AS WELL.
I AM ELMER VON BISMARCK.
IT'S AN HONOR TO MAKE YOUR ACQUAINTANCES...!
M-MY FATHER IS IN THE NAVY...
I HOPE TO BE A STALWART MILITARY MAN MYSELF ONE DAY...
OH, BUT WE'RE A MINOR NOBLE FAMILY, AND I SHOULDN'T BE PRESUMPTUOUS...
OOH...

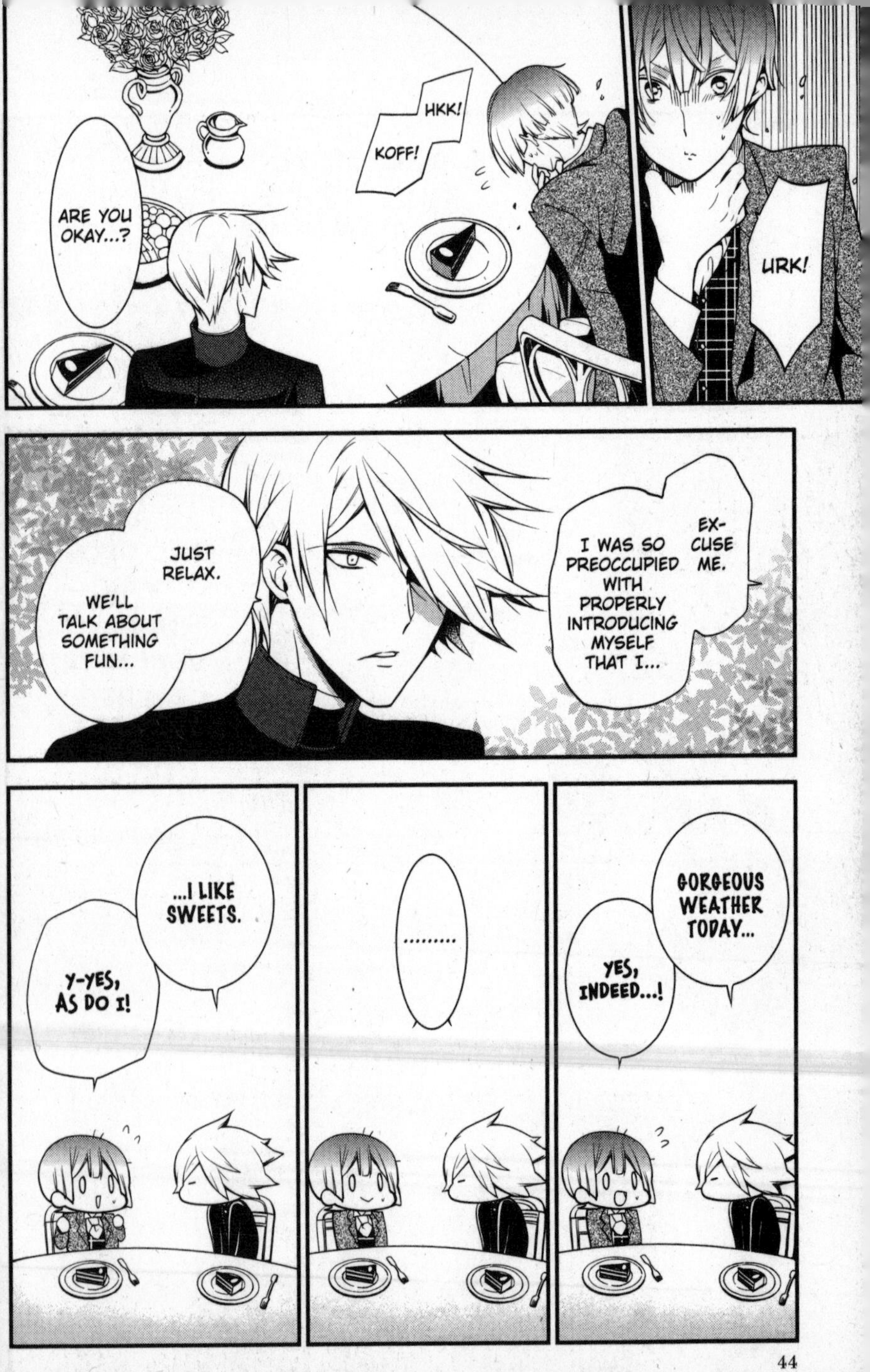
URK!
HKK!
KOFF!
ARE YOU OKAY...?
EX-CUSE ME.
I WAS SO PREOCCUPIED WITH PROPERLY INTRODUCING MYSELF THAT I...
JUST RELAX.
WE'LL TALK ABOUT SOMETHING FUN...
GORGEOUS WEATHER TODAY...
YES, INDEED...!
....
...I LIKE SWEETS.
Y-YES, AS DO I!

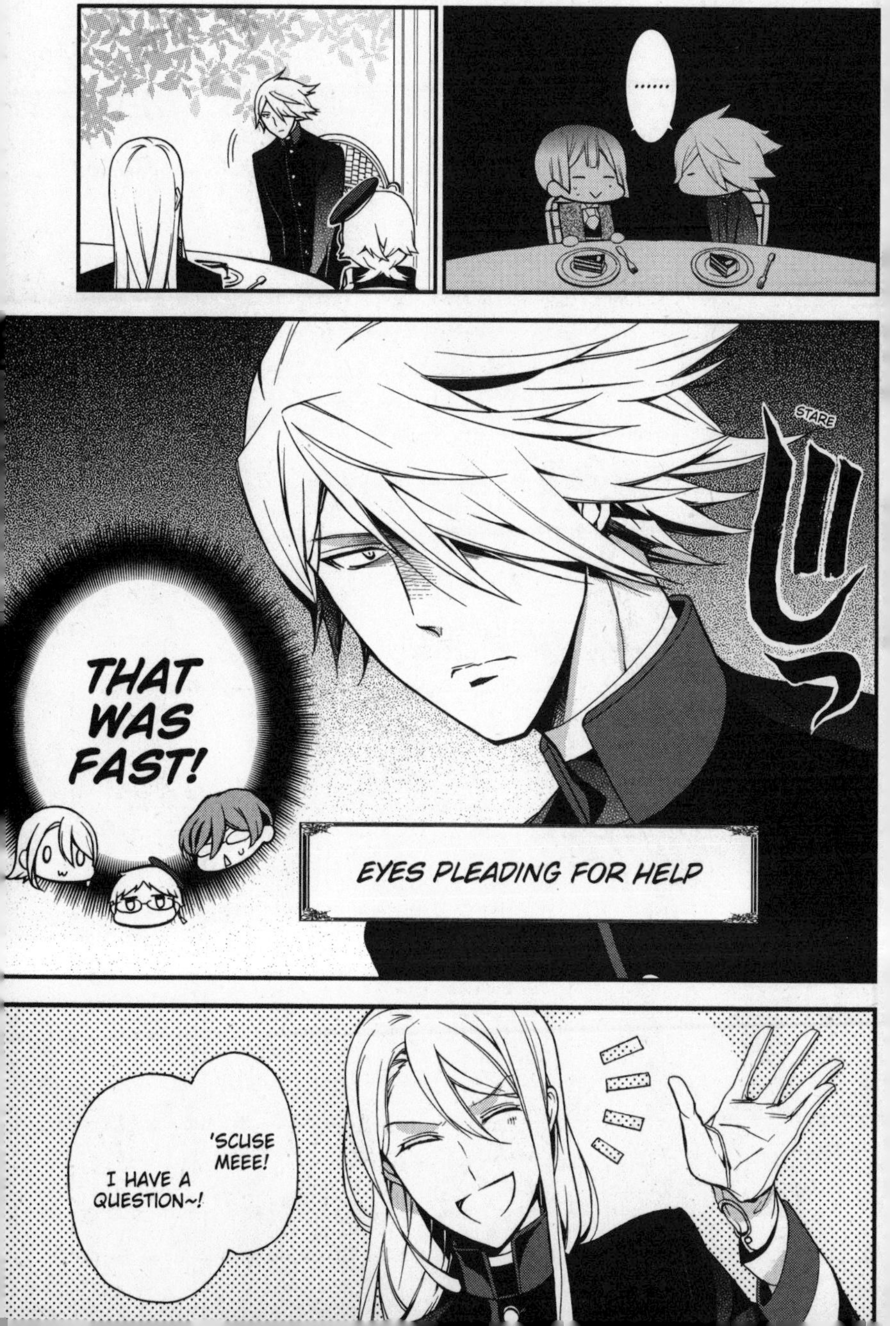
……
STARE
THAT WAS FAST!
EYES PLEADING FOR HELP
'SCUSE MEEE!
I HAVE A QUESTION~!

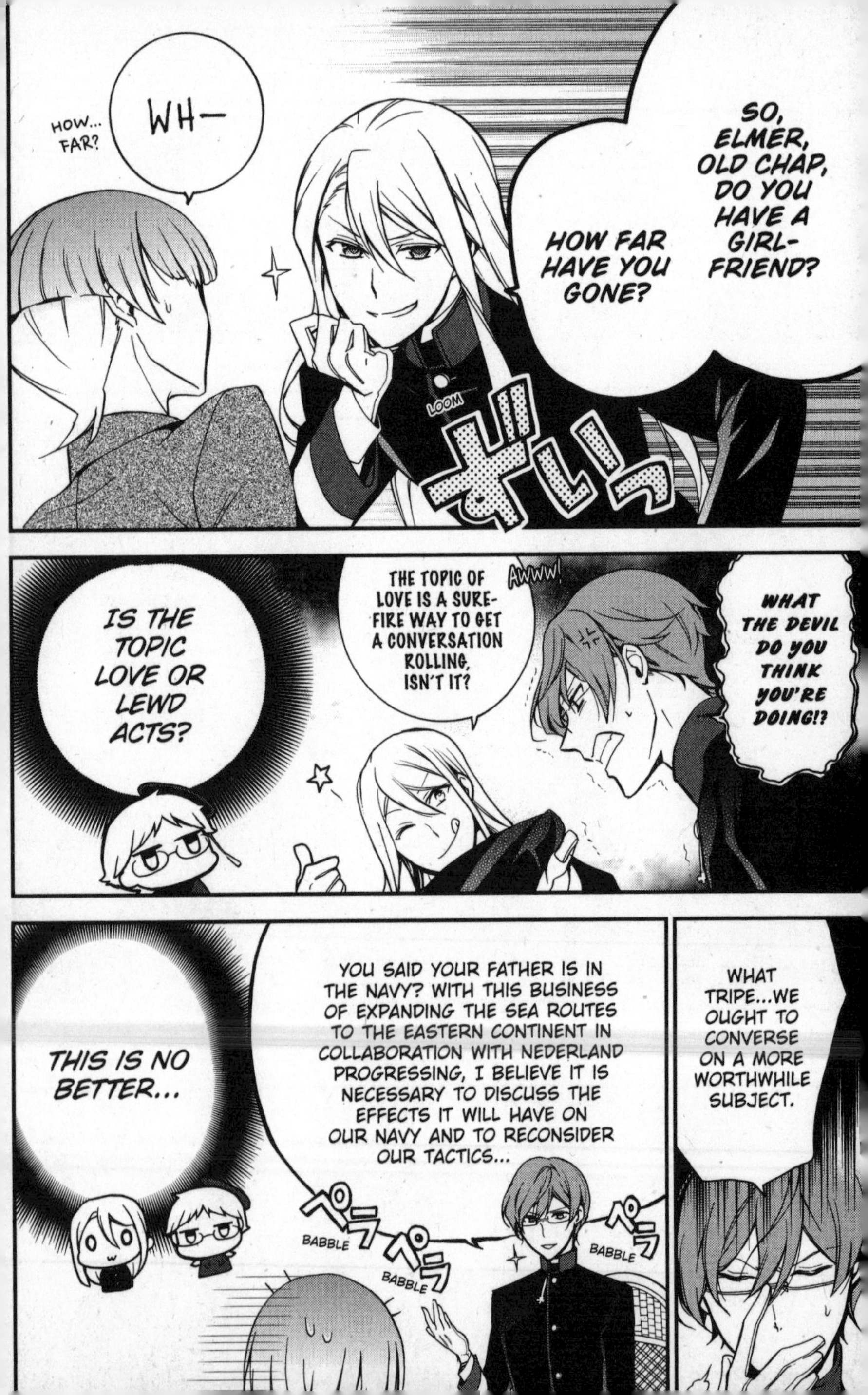
SO, ELMER, OLD CHAP, DO YOU HAVE A GIRL-FRIEND?
HOW FAR HAVE YOU GONE?
LOOM
WH—
HOW... FAR?
WHAT THE DEVIL DO YOU THINK YOU'RE DOING!?
AWWW!
THE TOPIC OF LOVE IS A SURE-FIRE WAY TO GET A CONVERSATION ROLLING, ISN'T IT?
IS THE TOPIC LOVE OR LEWD ACTS?
WHAT TRIPE...WE OUGHT TO CONVERSE ON A MORE WORTHWHILE SUBJECT.
YOU SAID YOUR FATHER IS IN THE NAVY? WITH THIS BUSINESS OF EXPANDING THE SEA ROUTES TO THE EASTERN CONTINENT IN COLLABORATION WITH NEDERLAND PROGRESSING, I BELIEVE IT IS NECESSARY TO DISCUSS THE EFFECTS IT WILL HAVE ON OUR NAVY AND TO RECONSIDER OUR TACTICS...
BABBLE
BABBLE
BABBLE
THIS IS NO BETTER...

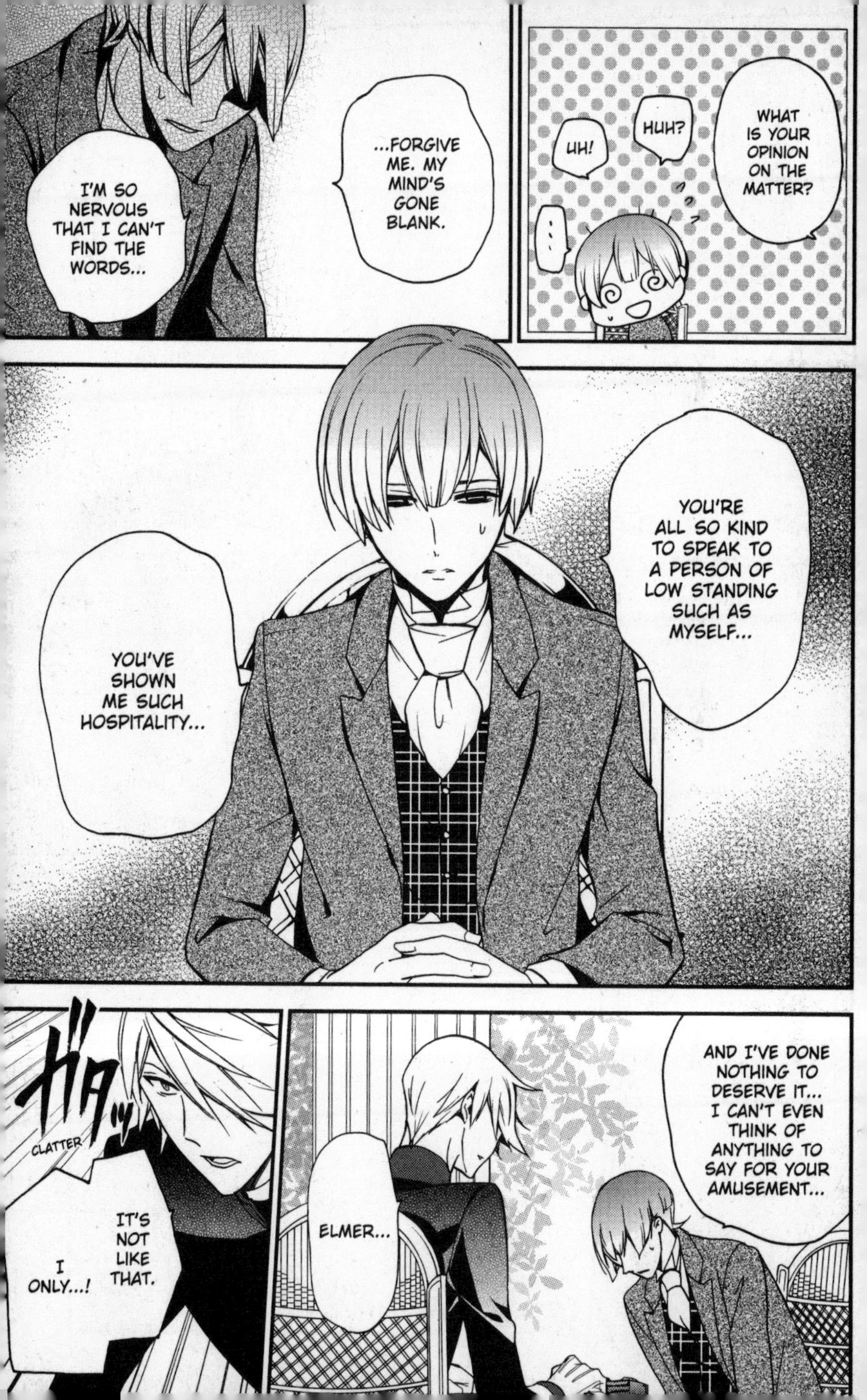
WHAT IS YOUR OPINION ON THE MATTER?
HUH?
UH!
...
...FORGIVE ME. MY MIND'S GONE BLANK.
I'M SO NERVOUS THAT I CAN'T FIND THE WORDS...
YOU'RE ALL SO KIND TO SPEAK TO A PERSON OF LOW STANDING SUCH AS MYSELF...
YOU'VE SHOWN ME SUCH HOSPITALITY...
AND I'VE DONE NOTHING TO DESERVE IT... I CAN'T EVEN THINK OF ANYTHING TO SAY FOR YOUR AMUSEMENT...
ELMER...
ガタッ
CLATTER
IT'S NOT LIKE THAT.
I ONLY...!

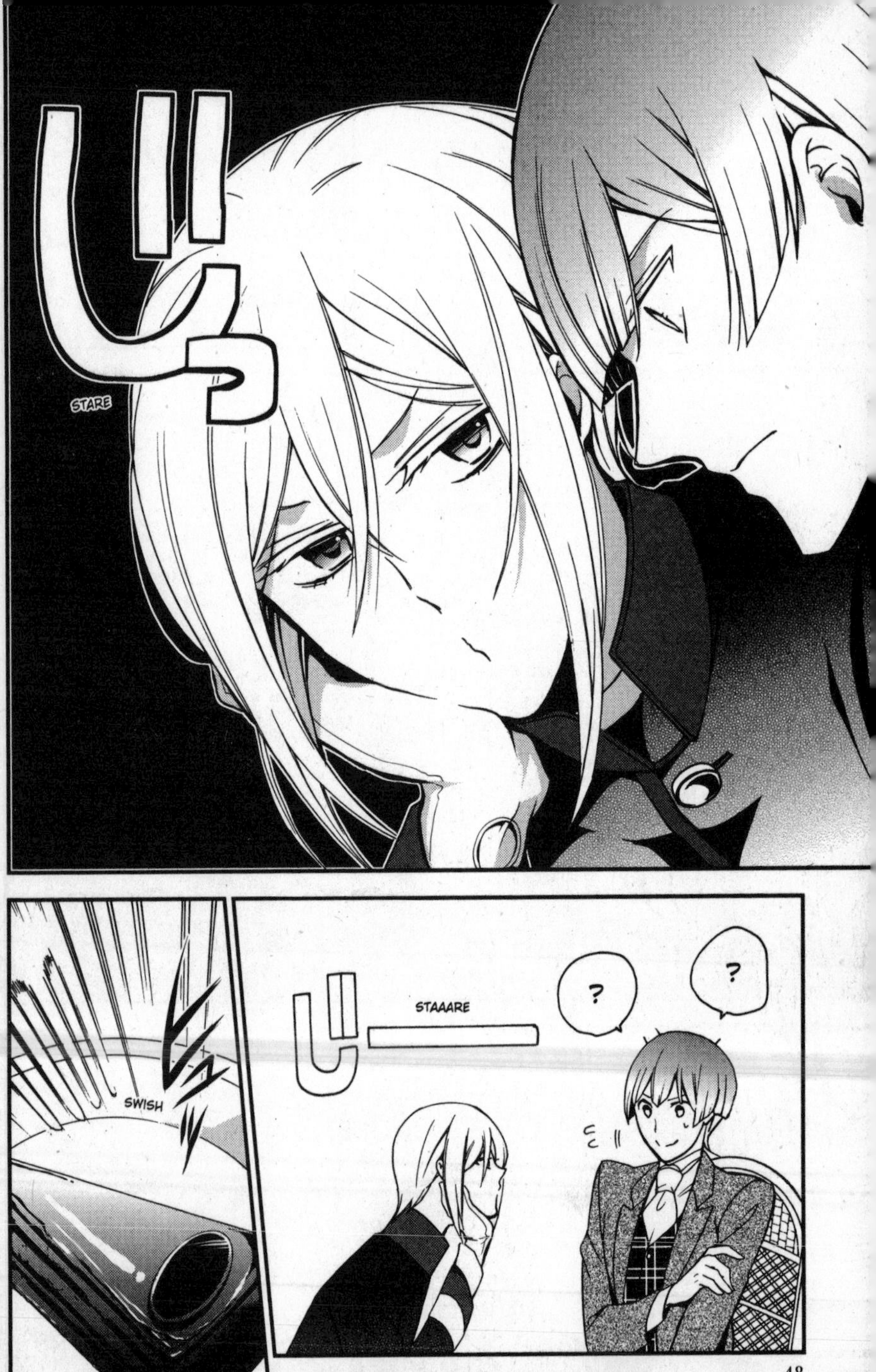
じーっ
STARE
じー
STAAARE
?
?
SWISH

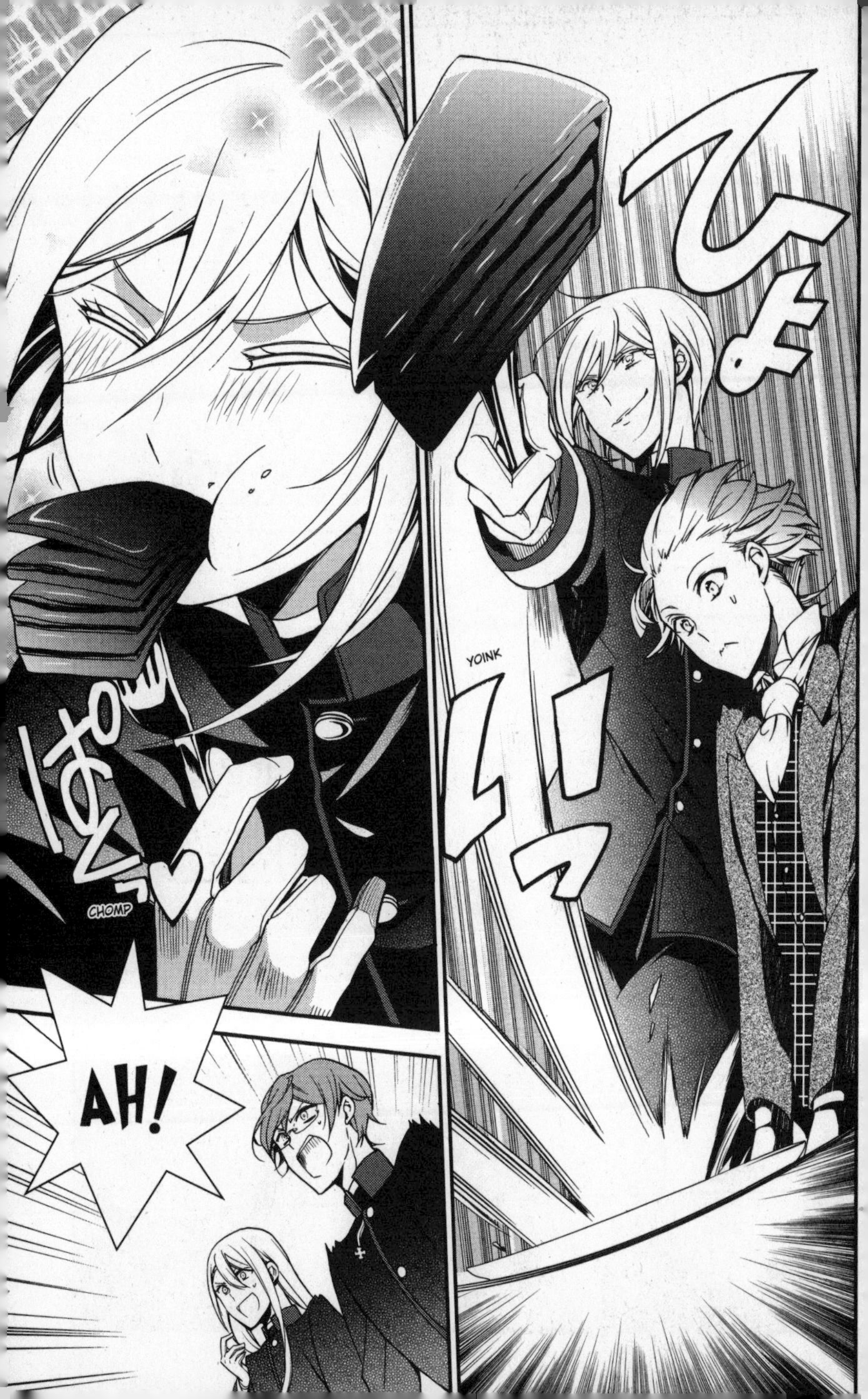
ひょい
YOINK
はむ
CHOMP
AH!

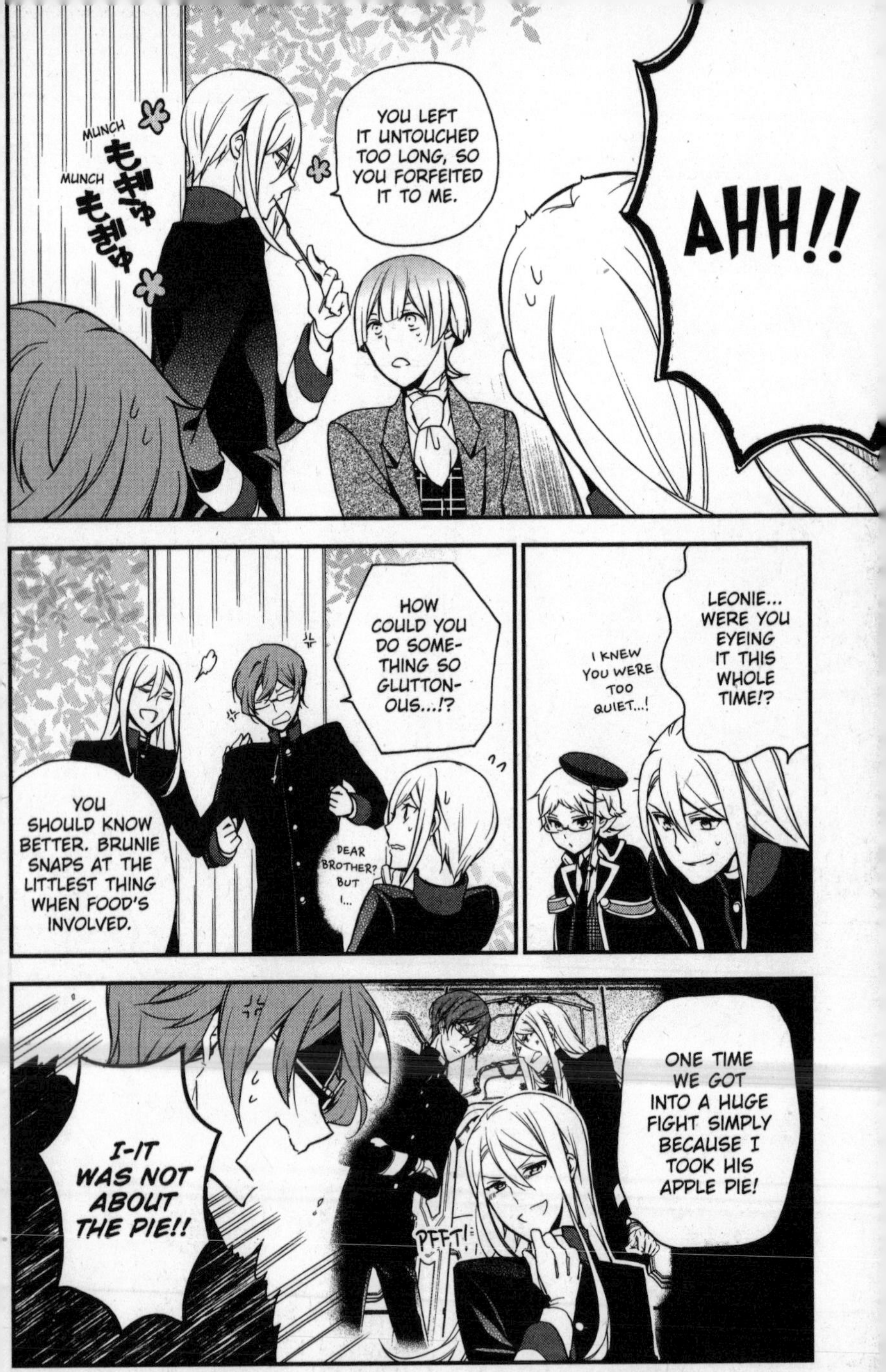
AHH!!
YOU LEFT IT UNTOUCHED TOO LONG, SO YOU FORFEITED IT TO ME.
MUNCH もぎゅ
MUNCH もぎゅ
LEONIE... WERE YOU EYEING IT THIS WHOLE TIME!?
I KNEW YOU WERE TOO QUIET...!
HOW COULD YOU DO SOMETHING SO GLUTTONOUS...!?
DEAR BROTHER? BUT I...
YOU SHOULD KNOW BETTER. BRUNIE SNAPS AT THE LITTLEST THING WHEN FOOD'S INVOLVED.
ONE TIME WE GOT INTO A HUGE FIGHT SIMPLY BECAUSE I TOOK HIS APPLE PIE!
PFFT!
I-IT WAS NOT ABOUT THE PIE!!

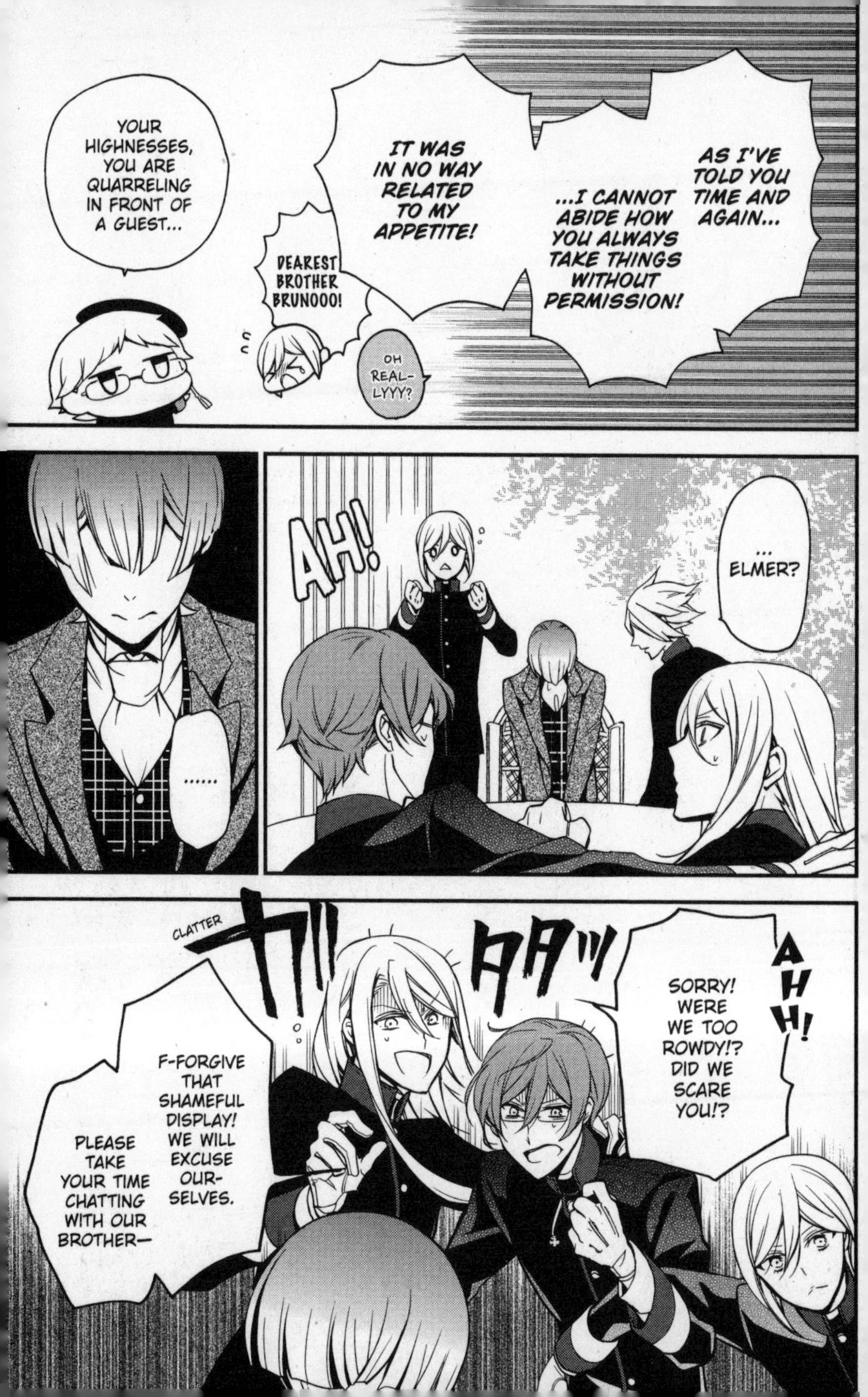
AS I'VE TOLD YOU TIME AND AGAIN...
...I CANNOT ABIDE HOW YOU ALWAYS TAKE THINGS WITHOUT PERMISSION!
IT WAS IN NO WAY RELATED TO MY APPETITE!
OH REAL-LYYY?
DEAREST BROTHER BRUNOOO!
YOUR HIGHNESSES, YOU ARE QUARRELING IN FRONT OF A GUEST...
...ELMER?
AH!
......
AHH!
SORRY! WERE WE TOO ROWDY!? DID WE SCARE YOU!?
タタッ
ガ
CLATTER
F-FORGIVE THAT SHAMEFUL DISPLAY! WE WILL EXCUSE OUR-SELVES.
PLEASE TAKE YOUR TIME CHATTING WITH OUR BROTHER—

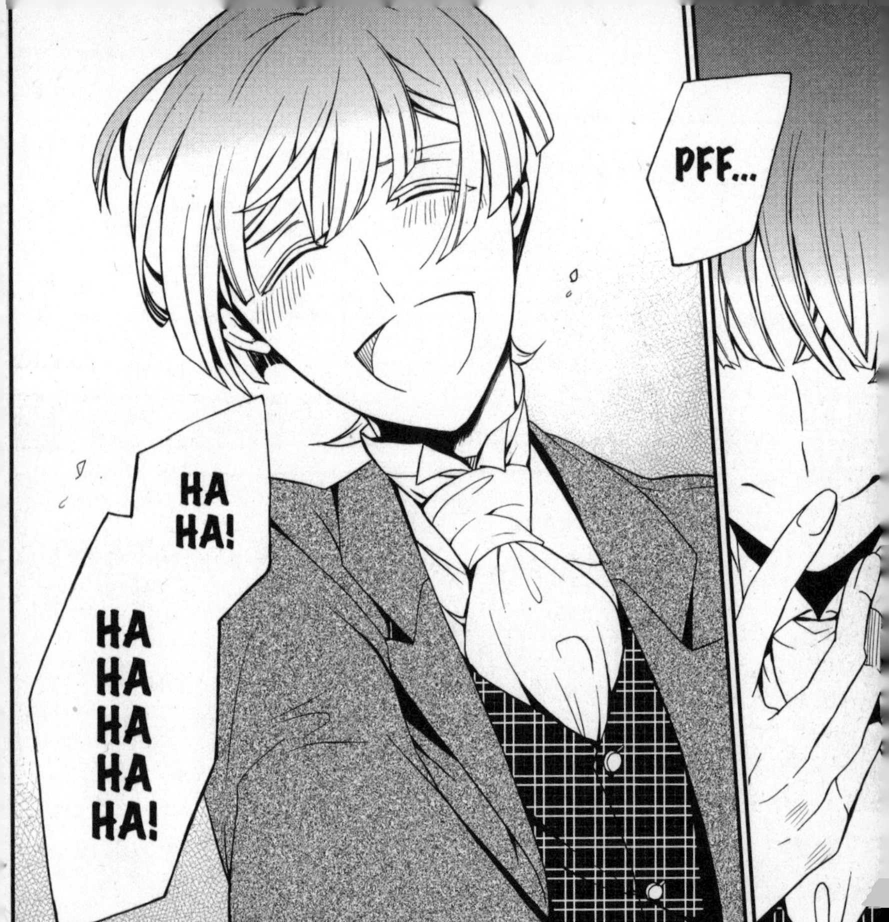
PFF...
HA HA!
HA HA HA HA HA!
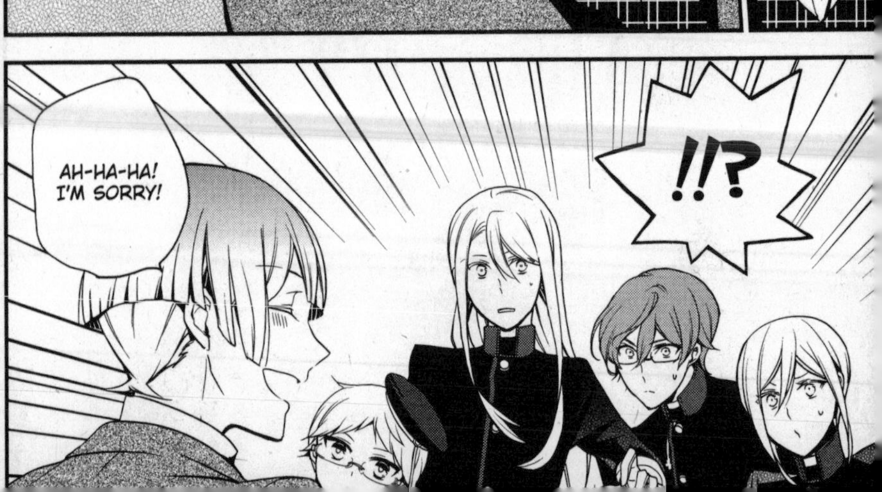
!!?
AH-HA-HA! I'M SORRY!

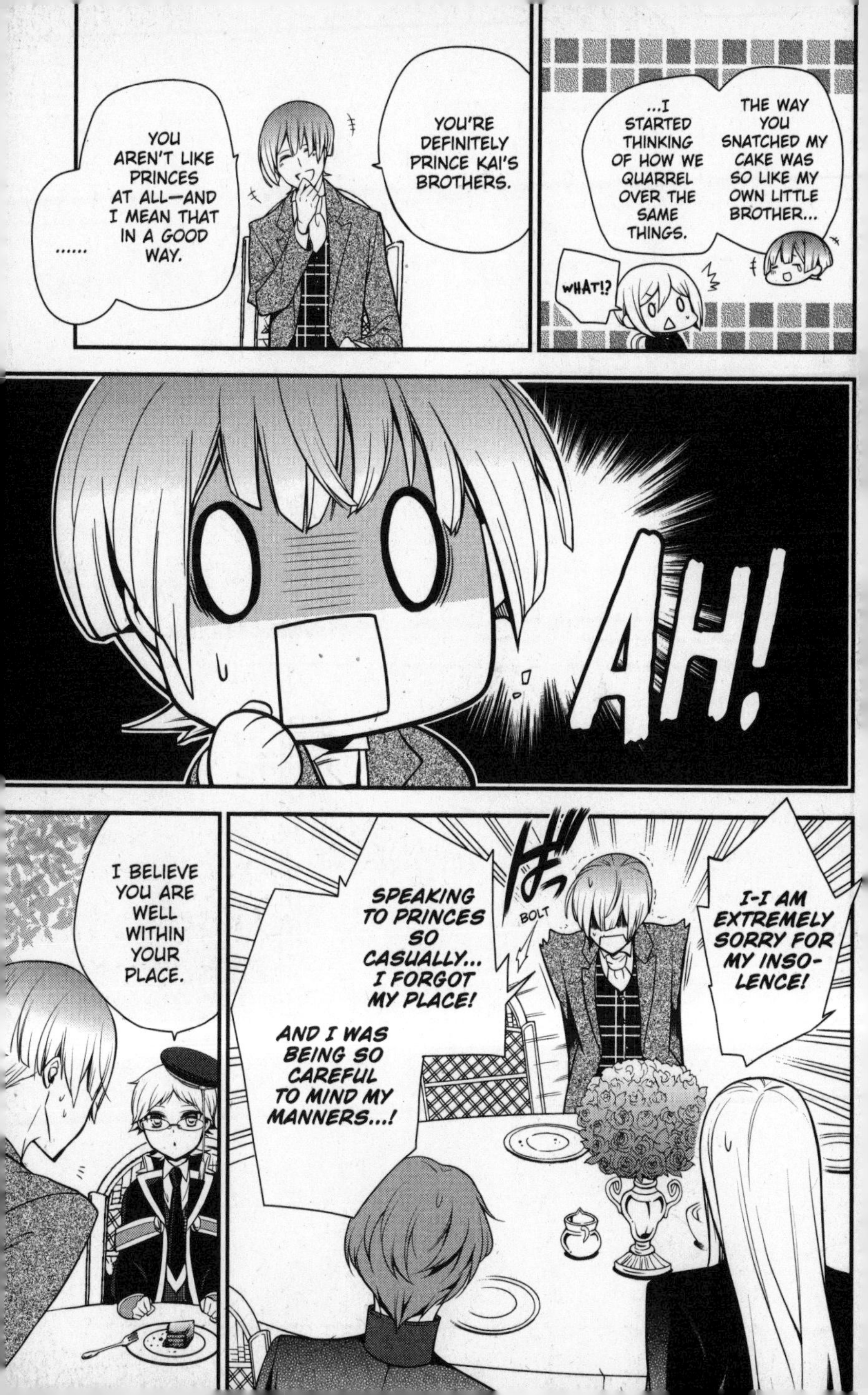
THE WAY YOU SNATCHED MY CAKE WAS SO LIKE MY OWN LITTLE BROTHER...
...I STARTED THINKING OF HOW WE QUARREL OVER THE SAME THINGS.
WHAT!?
YOU'RE DEFINITELY PRINCE KAI'S BROTHERS.
YOU AREN'T LIKE PRINCES AT ALL—AND I MEAN THAT IN A GOOD WAY.
......
AH!
I-I AM EXTREMELY SORRY FOR MY INSO-LENCE!
ばっ
BOLT
SPEAKING TO PRINCES SO CASUALLY... I FORGOT MY PLACE!
AND I WAS BEING SO CAREFUL TO MIND MY MANNERS...!
I BELIEVE YOU ARE WELL WITHIN YOUR PLACE.

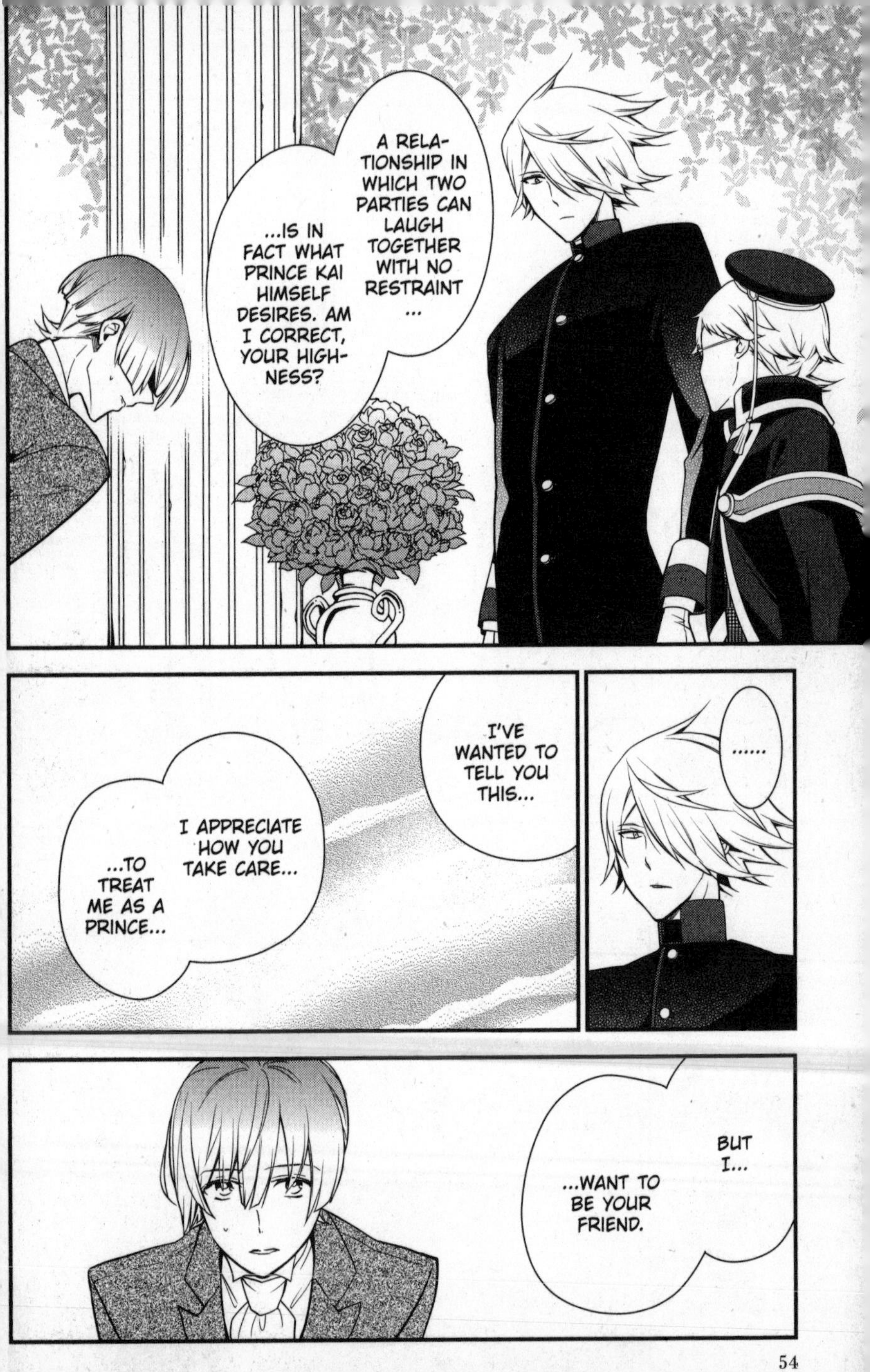
A RELATIONSHIP IN WHICH TWO PARTIES CAN LAUGH TOGETHER WITH NO RESTRAINT...
...IS IN FACT WHAT PRINCE KAI HIMSELF DESIRES. AM I CORRECT, YOUR HIGHNESS?
......
I'VE WANTED TO TELL YOU THIS...
I APPRECIATE HOW YOU TAKE CARE...
...TO TREAT ME AS A PRINCE...
BUT I...
...WANT TO BE YOUR FRIEND.

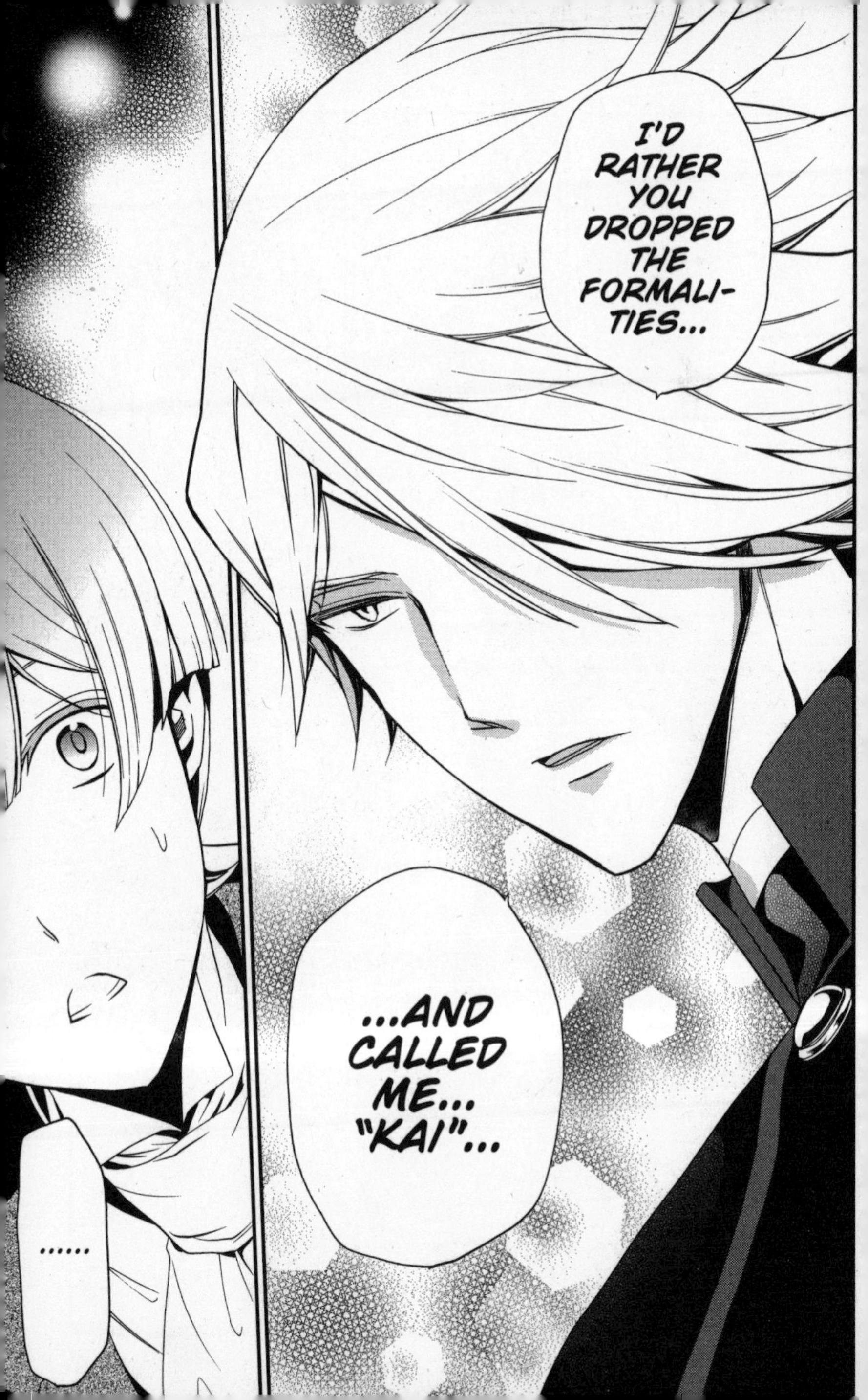
I'D RATHER YOU DROPPED THE FORMALI-TIES...
...AND CALLED ME... "KAI"...
......

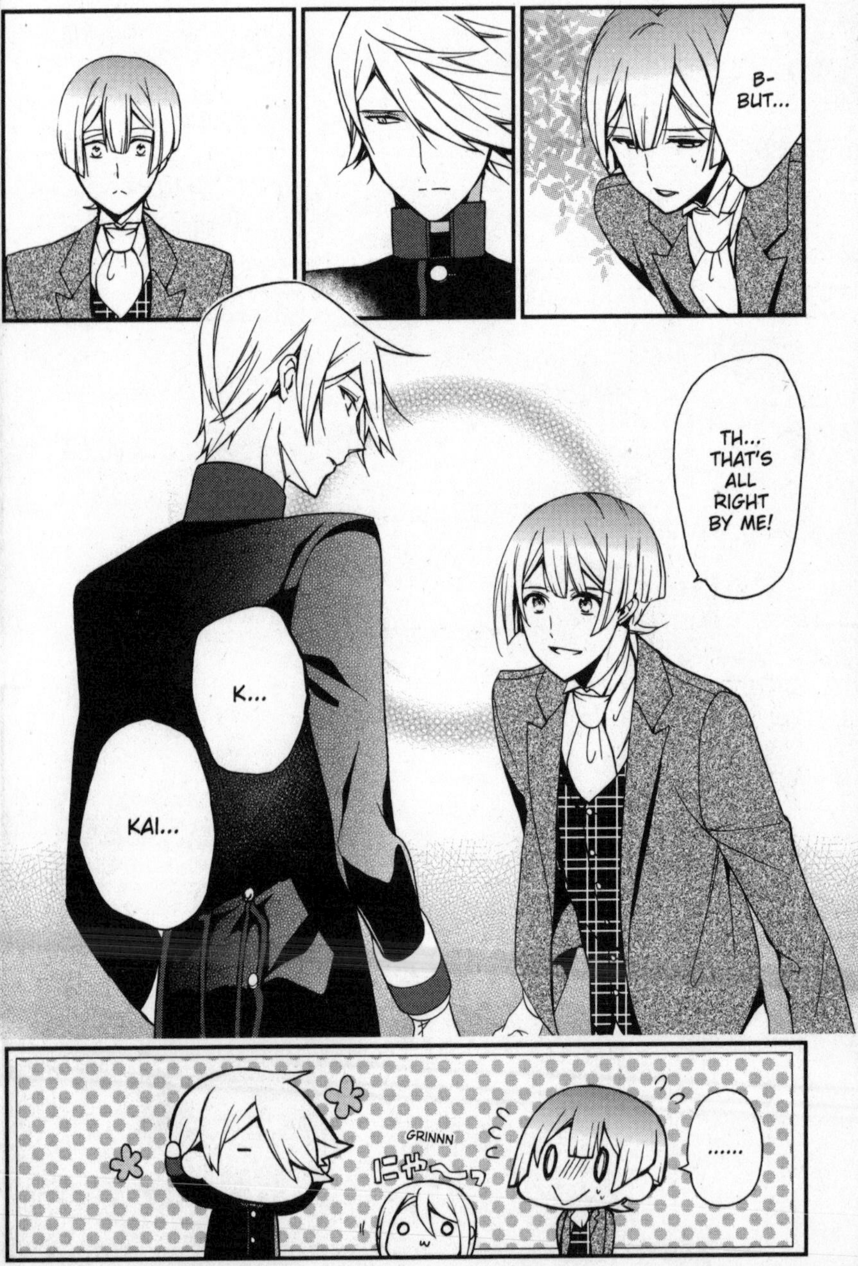
B-BUT...
TH... THAT'S ALL RIGHT BY ME!
K...
KAI...
......
GRINNN
にゃ〜っ

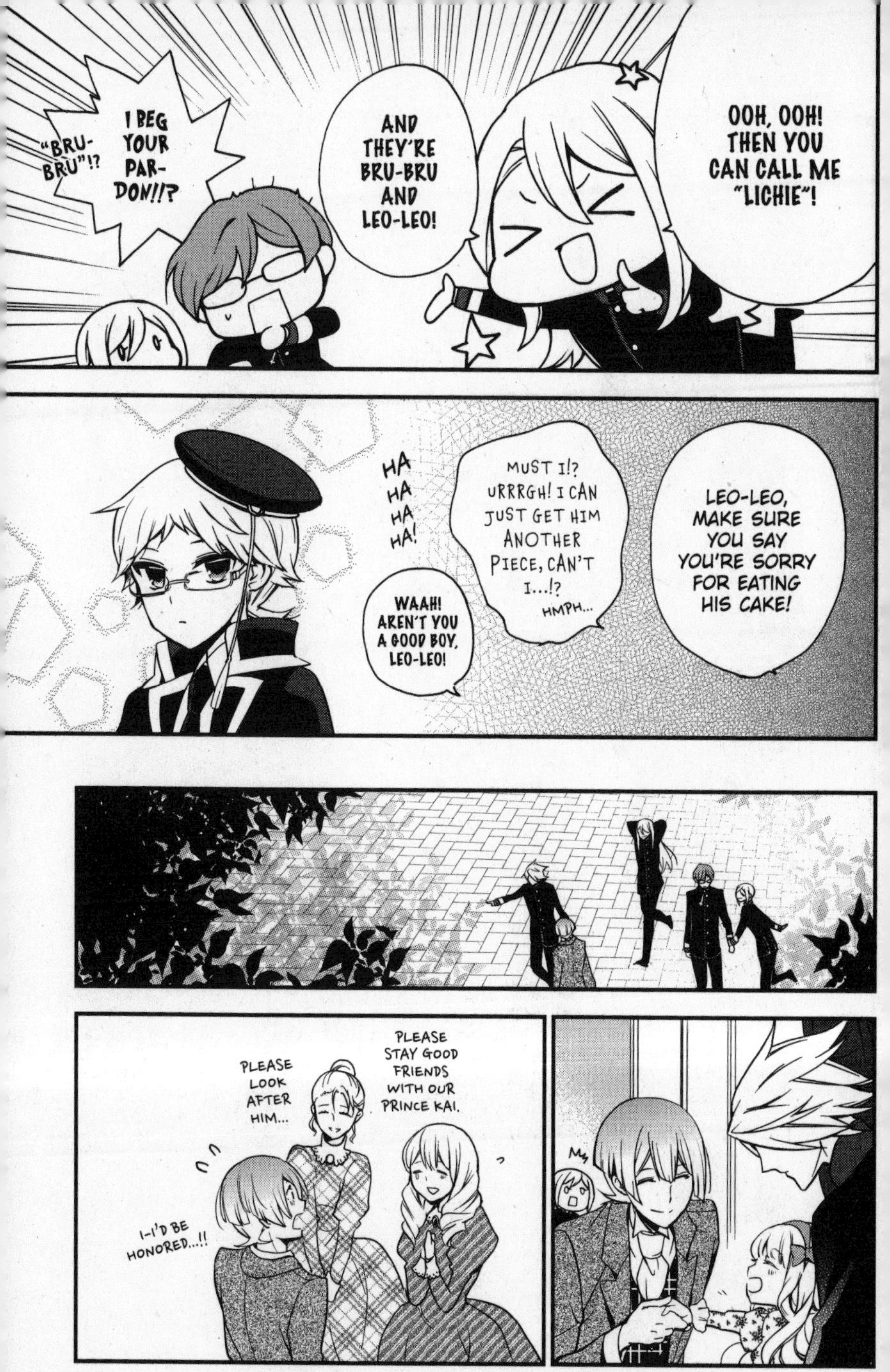
OOH, OOH! THEN YOU CAN CALL ME "LICHIE"!
AND THEY'RE BRU-BRU AND LEO-LEO!
I BEG YOUR PAR-DON!!?
"BRU-BRU"!?
LEO-LEO, MAKE SURE YOU SAY YOU'RE SORRY FOR EATING HIS CAKE!
MUST I!? URRRGH! I CAN JUST GET HIM ANOTHER PIECE, CAN'T I...!?
HMPH...
HA HA HA HA!
WAAH! AREN'T YOU A GOOD BOY, LEO-LEO!
PLEASE STAY GOOD FRIENDS WITH OUR PRINCE KAI.
PLEASE LOOK AFTER HIM...
I-I'D BE HONORED...!!

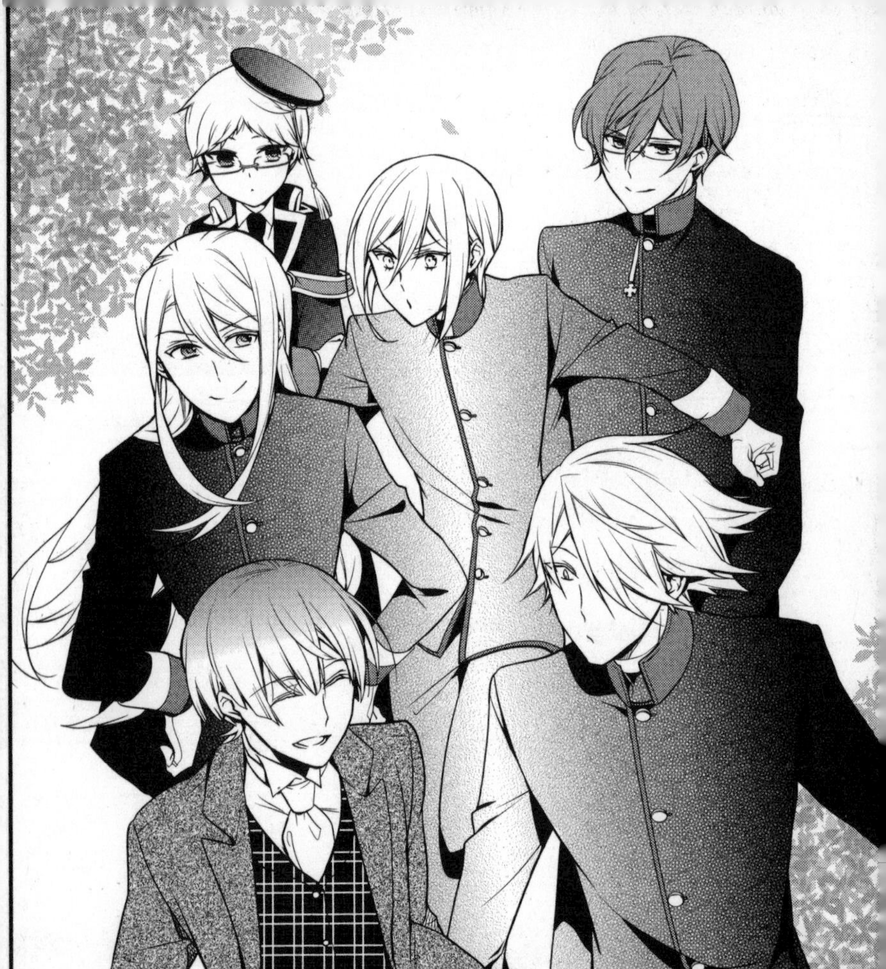
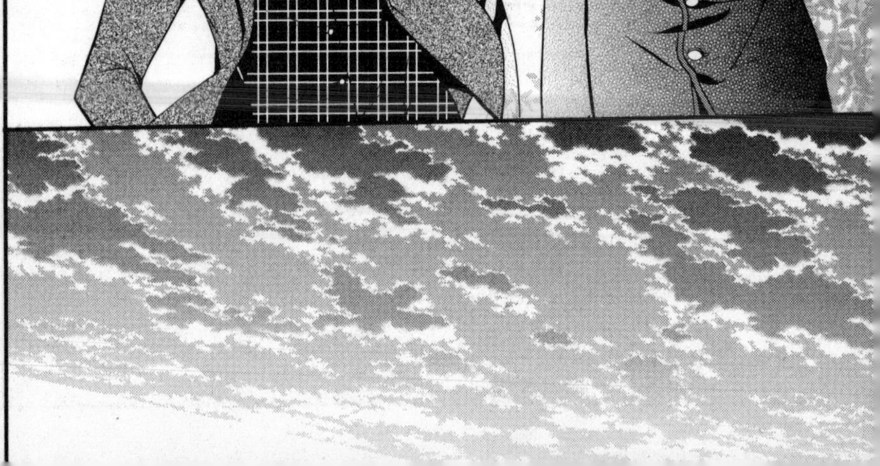

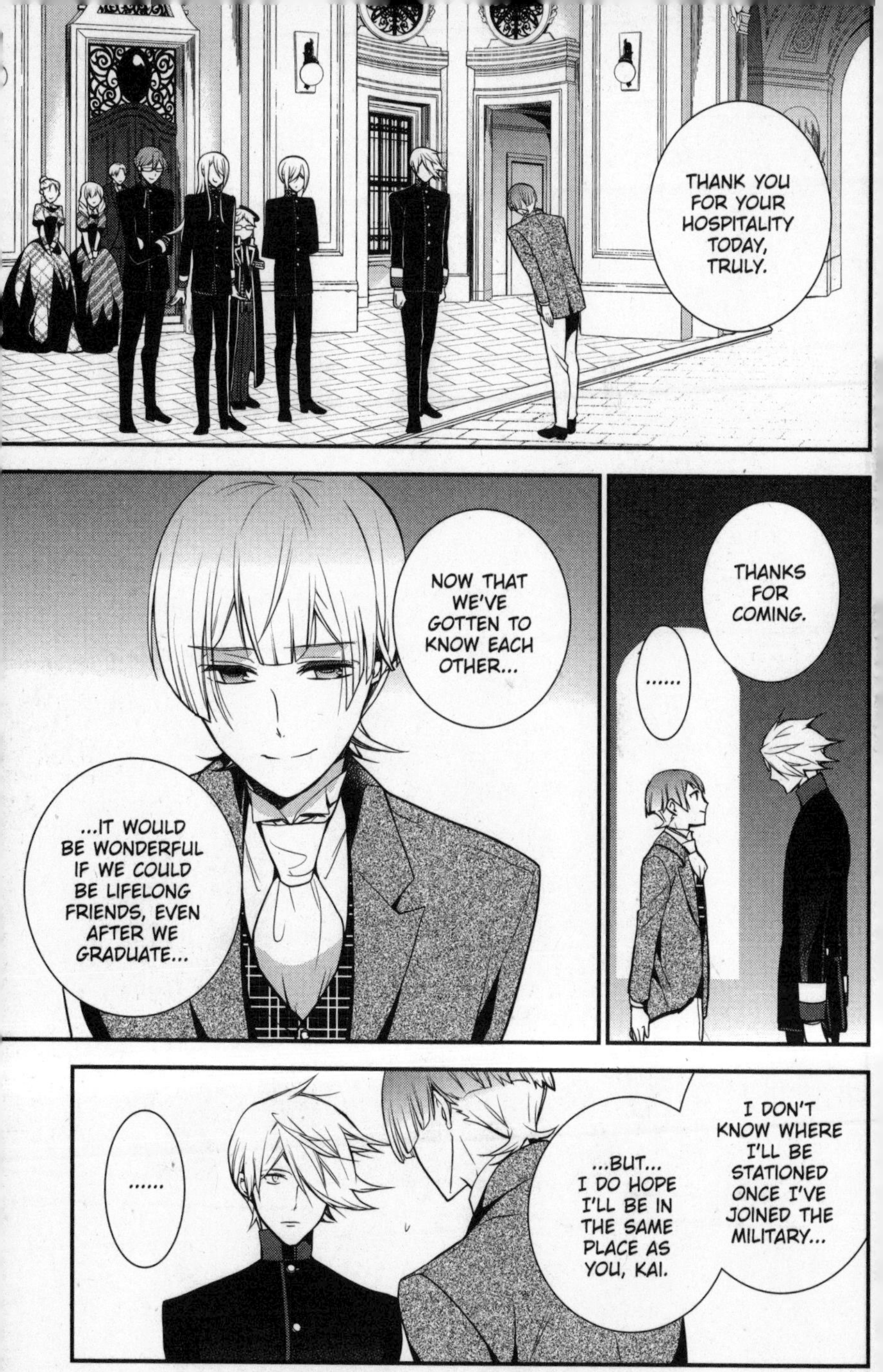
THANK YOU FOR YOUR HOSPITALITY TODAY, TRULY.
THANKS FOR COMING.
......
NOW THAT WE'VE GOTTEN TO KNOW EACH OTHER...
...IT WOULD BE WONDERFUL IF WE COULD BE LIFELONG FRIENDS, EVEN AFTER WE GRADUATE...
I DON'T KNOW WHERE I'LL BE STATIONED ONCE I'VE JOINED THE MILITARY...
...BUT... I DO HOPE I'LL BE IN THE SAME PLACE AS YOU, KAI.
......

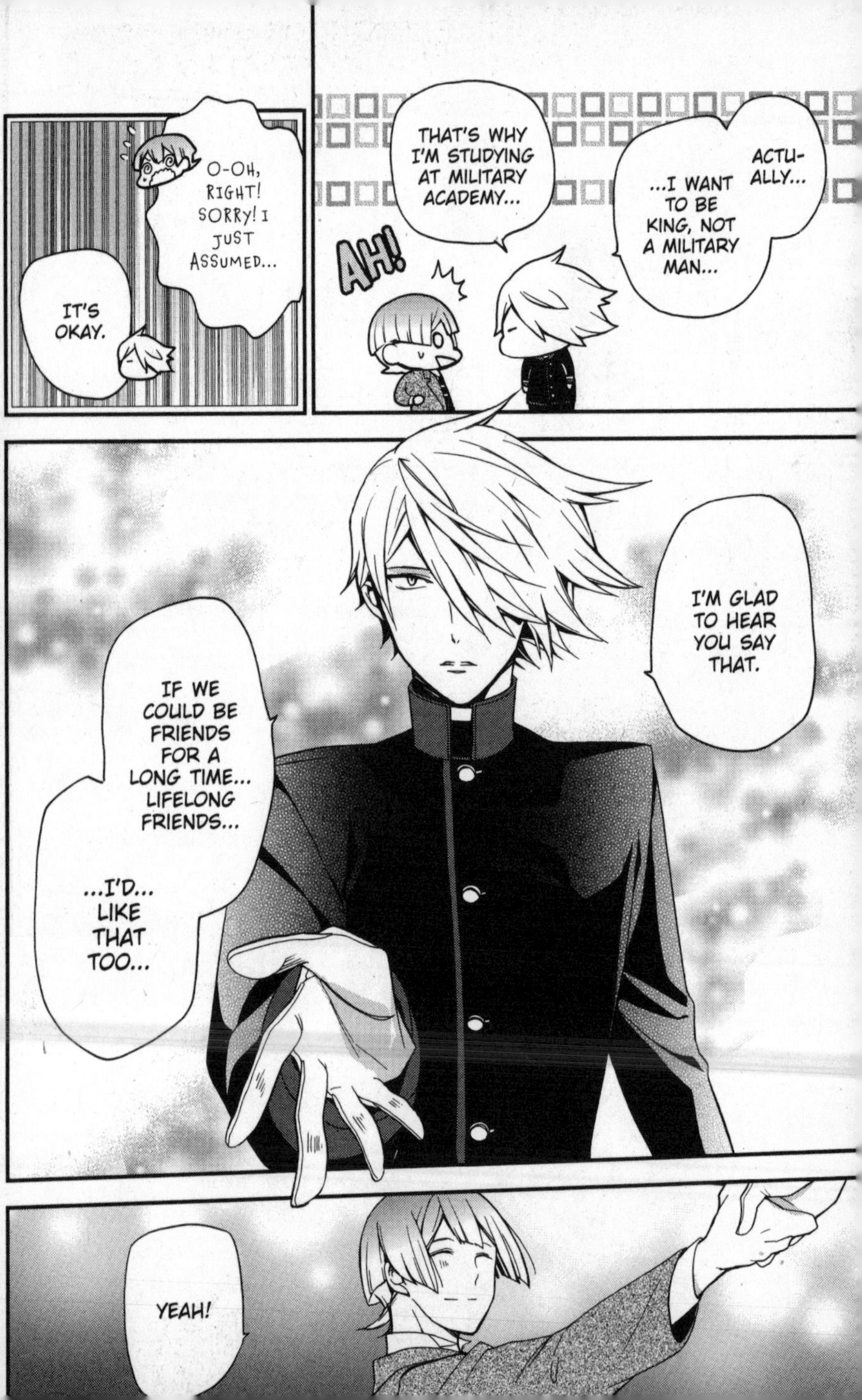
ACTU-ALLY...
...I WANT TO BE KING, NOT A MILITARY MAN...
THAT'S WHY I'M STUDYING AT MILITARY ACADEMY...
AH!
O-OH, RIGHT! SORRY! I JUST ASSUMED...
IT'S OKAY.
I'M GLAD TO HEAR YOU SAY THAT.
IF WE COULD BE FRIENDS FOR A LONG TIME... LIFELONG FRIENDS...
...I'D... LIKE THAT TOO...
YEAH!

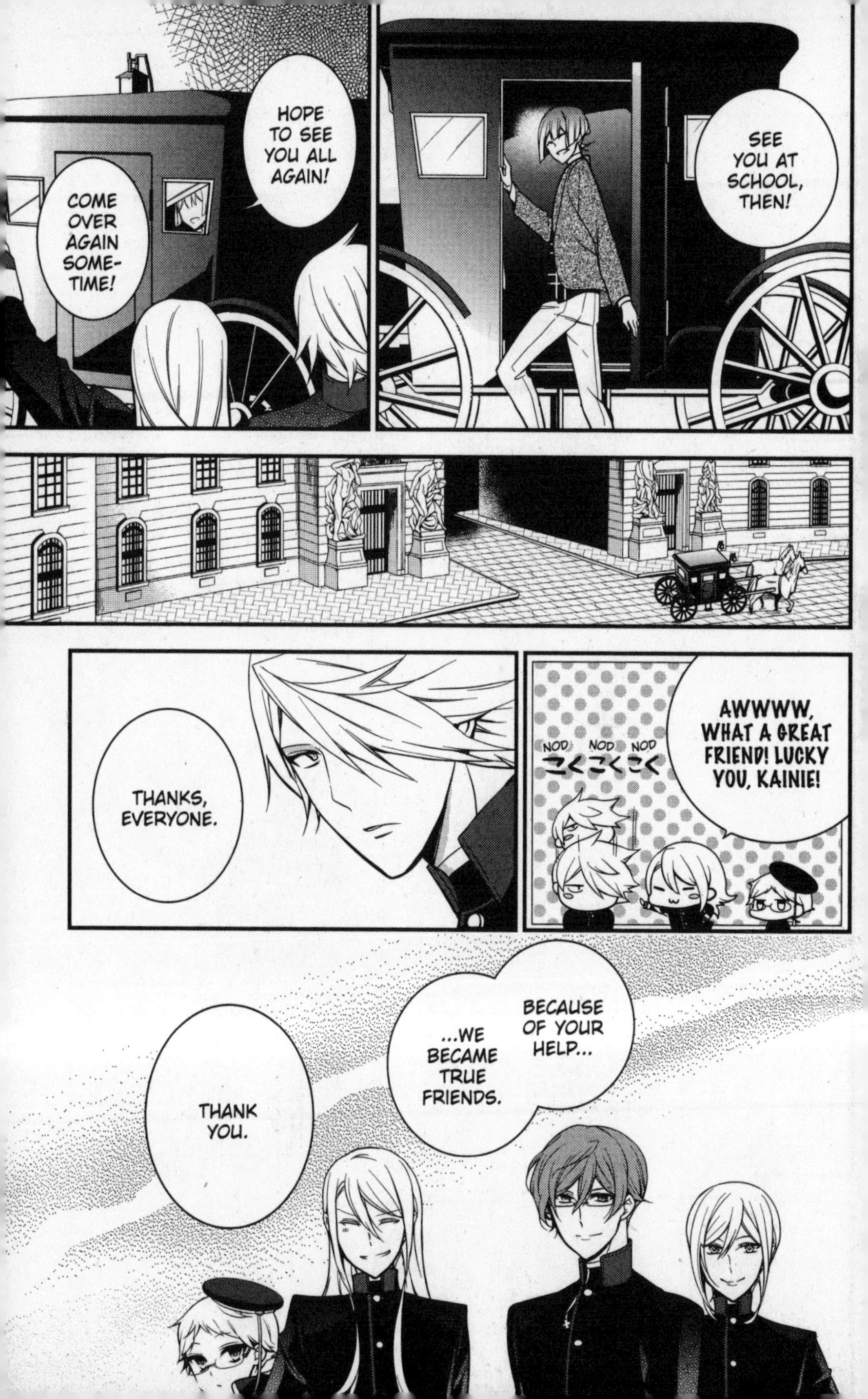
SEE YOU AT SCHOOL, THEN!
HOPE TO SEE YOU ALL AGAIN!
COME OVER AGAIN SOME-TIME!
AWWWW, WHAT A GREAT FRIEND! LUCKY YOU, KAINIE!
NOD NOD NOD
こくこくこく
THANKS, EVERYONE.
BECAUSE OF YOUR HELP...
...WE BECAME TRUE FRIENDS.
THANK YOU.

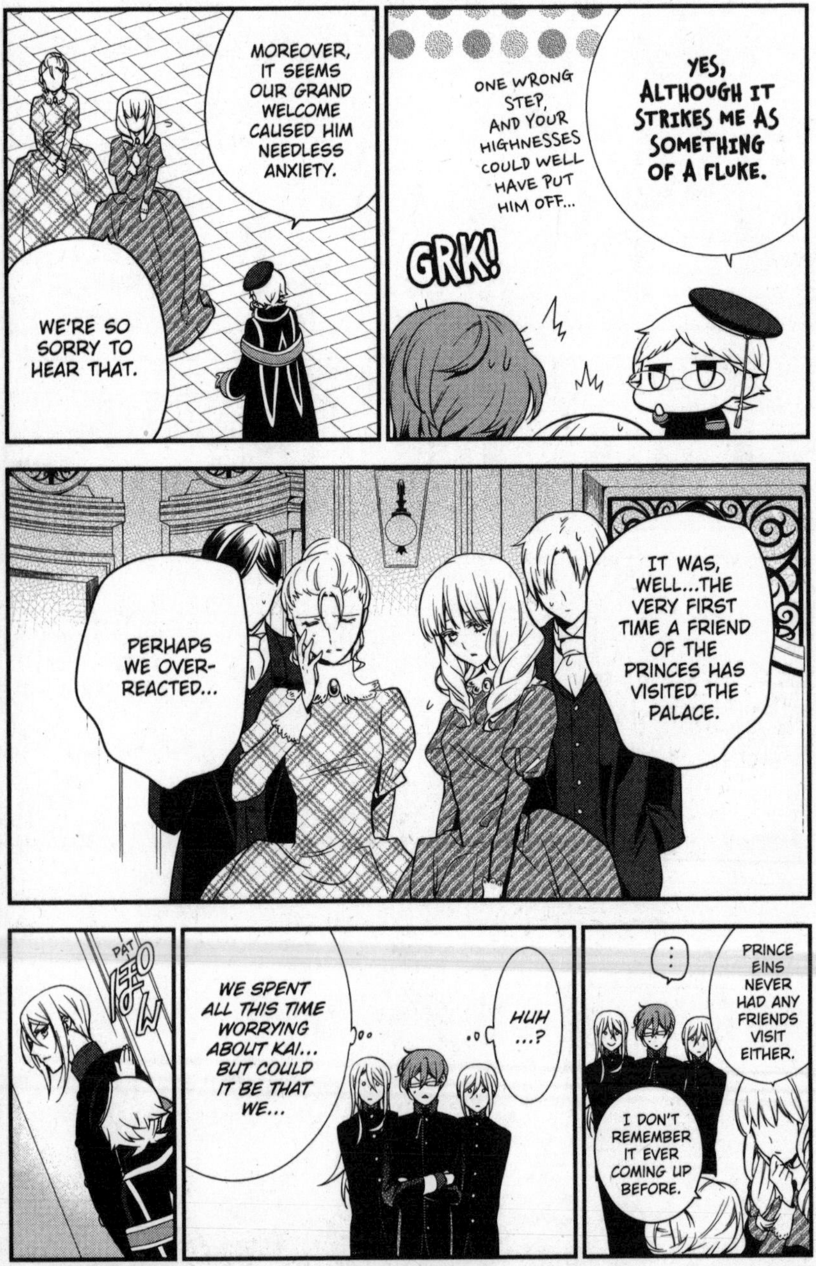
YES, ALTHOUGH IT STRIKES ME AS SOMETHING OF A FLUKE.
ONE WRONG STEP, AND YOUR HIGHNESSES COULD WELL HAVE PUT HIM OFF...
GRK!
MOREOVER, IT SEEMS OUR GRAND WELCOME CAUSED HIM NEEDLESS ANXIETY.
WE'RE SO SORRY TO HEAR THAT.
IT WAS, WELL...THE VERY FIRST TIME A FRIEND OF THE PRINCES HAS VISITED THE PALACE.
PERHAPS WE OVER-REACTED...
PRINCE EINS NEVER HAD ANY FRIENDS VISIT EITHER.
...
I DON'T REMEMBER IT EVER COMING UP BEFORE.
HUH ...?
WE SPENT ALL THIS TIME WORRYING ABOUT KAI... BUT COULD IT BE THAT WE...
PAT

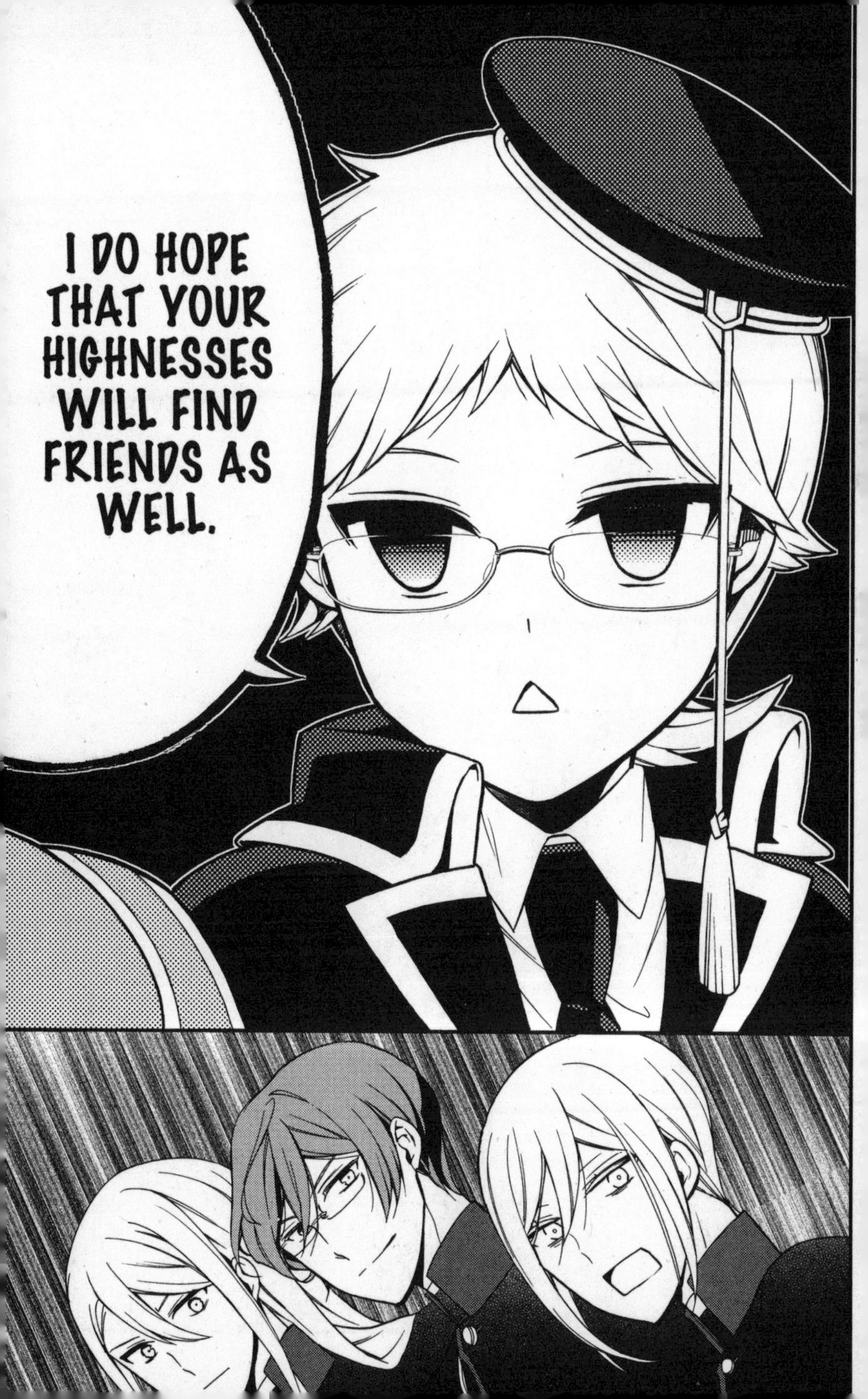
I DO HOPE THAT YOUR HIGHNESSES WILL FIND FRIENDS AS WELL.

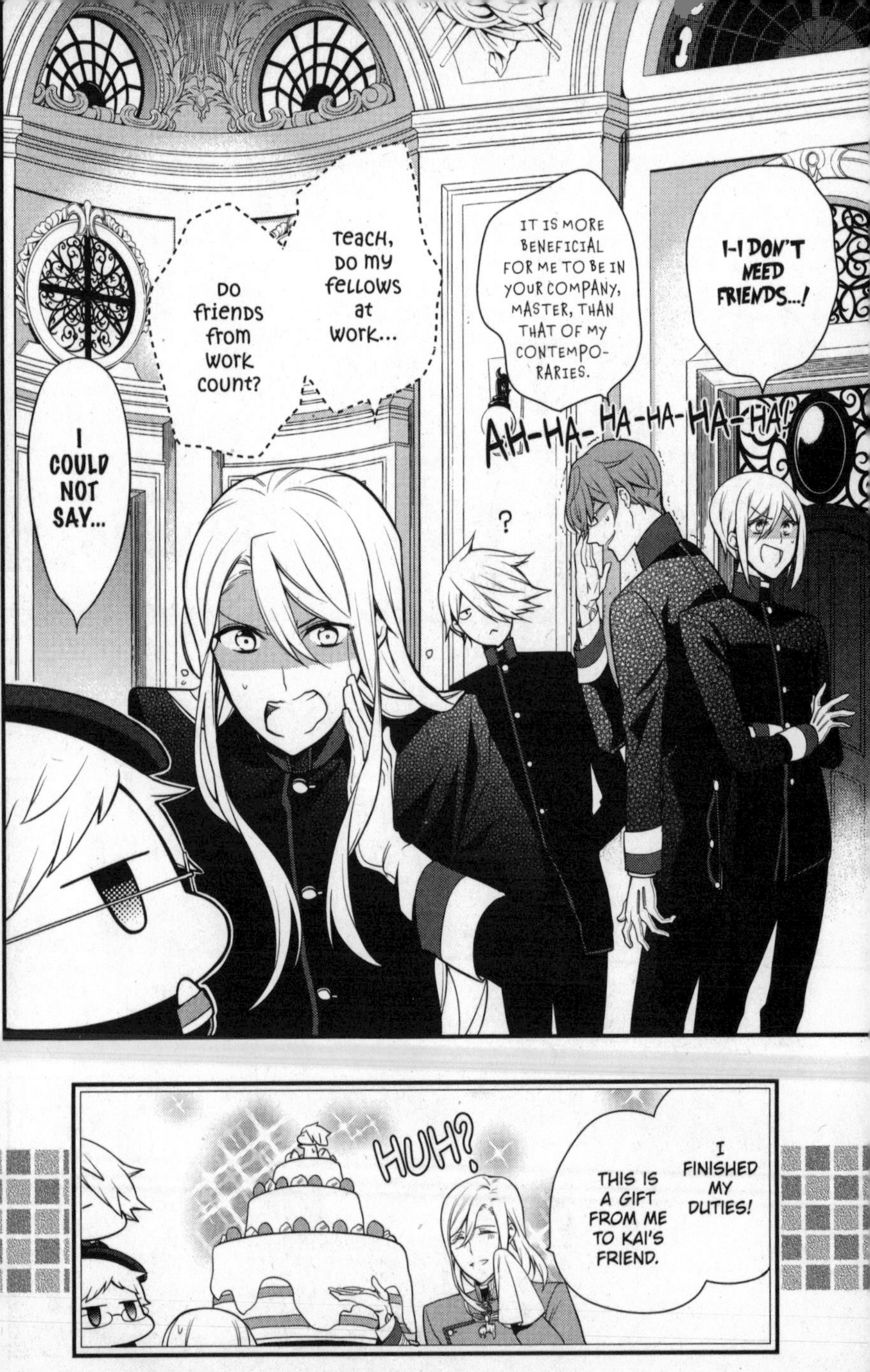
I-I DON'T NEED FRIENDS...!
IT IS MORE BENEFICIAL FOR ME TO BE IN YOUR COMPANY, MASTER, THAN THAT OF MY CONTEMPO-RARIES.
AH-HA-HA-HA-HA-HA!
TEACH, DO MY FELLOWS AT WORK...
DO FRIENDS FROM WORK COUNT?
?
I COULD NOT SAY...
I FINISHED MY DUTIES!
THIS IS A GIFT FROM ME TO KAI'S FRIEND.
HUH?

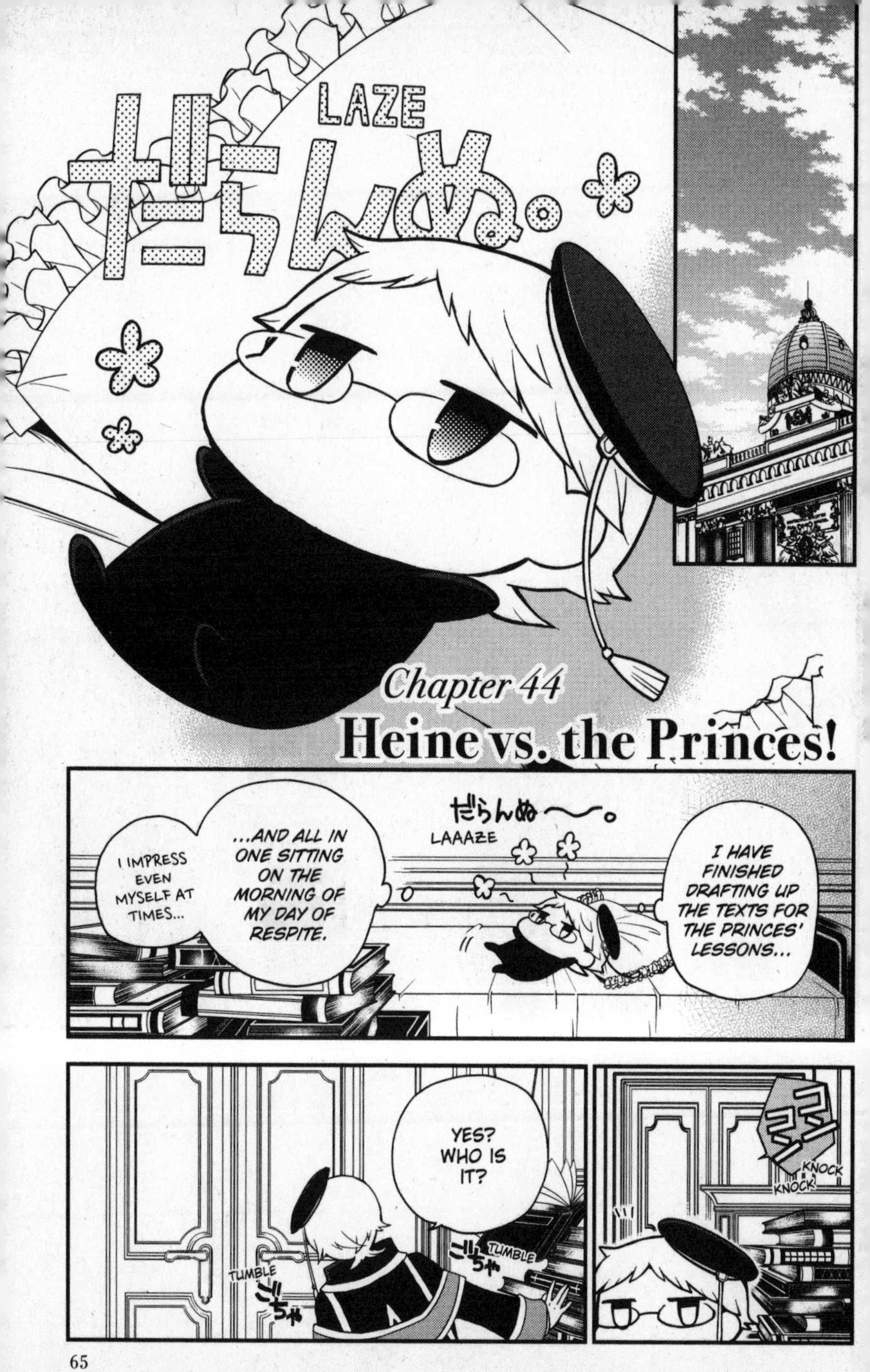

だらんぬ。
LAZE
Chapter 44
Heine vs. the Princes!
I HAVE FINISHED DRAFTING UP THE TEXTS FOR THE PRINCES' LESSONS...
だらんぬ〜〜。
LAAAZE
...AND ALL IN ONE SITTING ON THE MORNING OF MY DAY OF RESPITE.
I IMPRESS EVEN MYSELF AT TIMES...
コンコン
KNOCK KNOCK
YES? WHO IS IT?
ごちゃ
TUMBLE
ごちゃ
TUMBLE

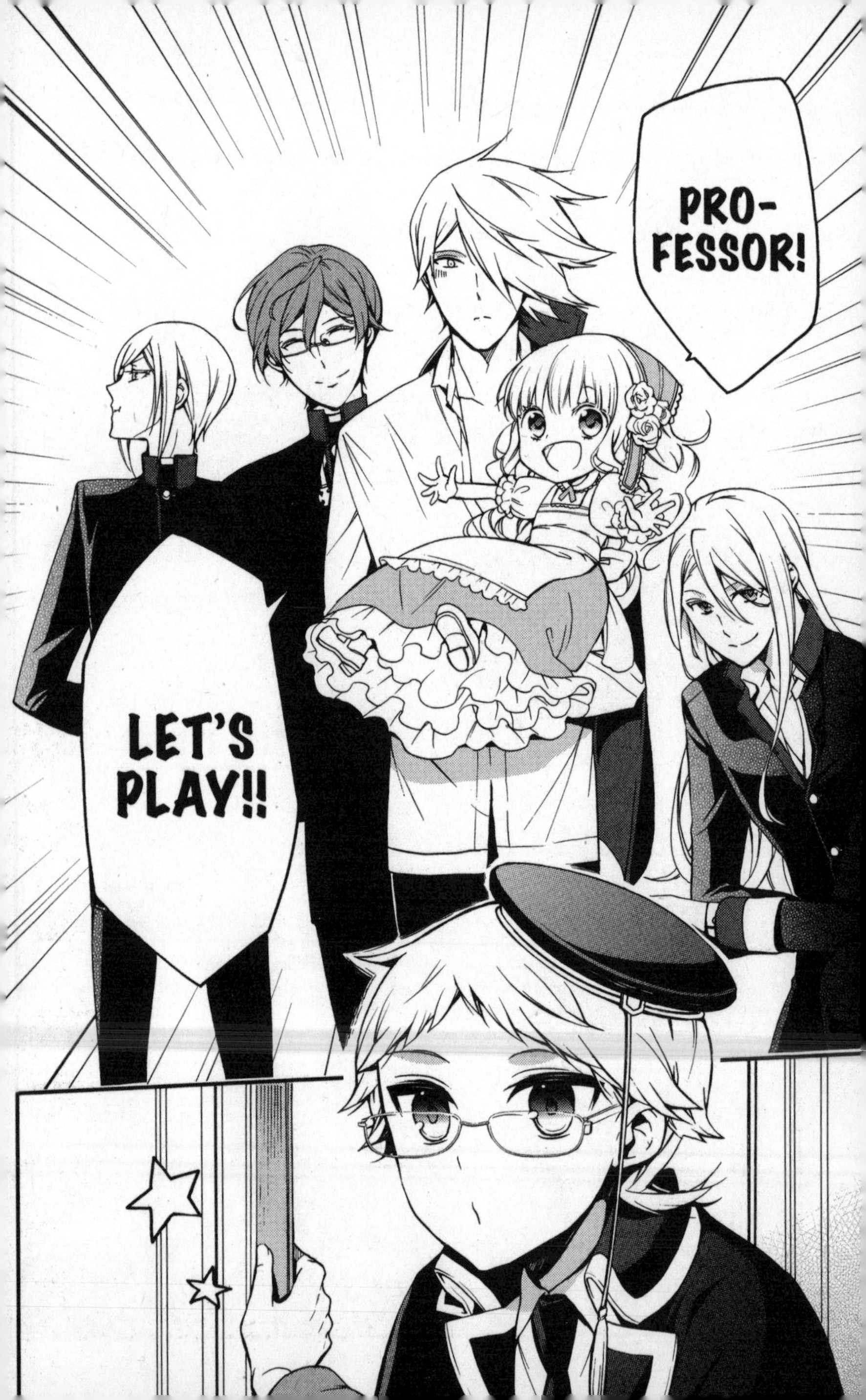
PRO-FESSOR!
LET'S PLAY!!

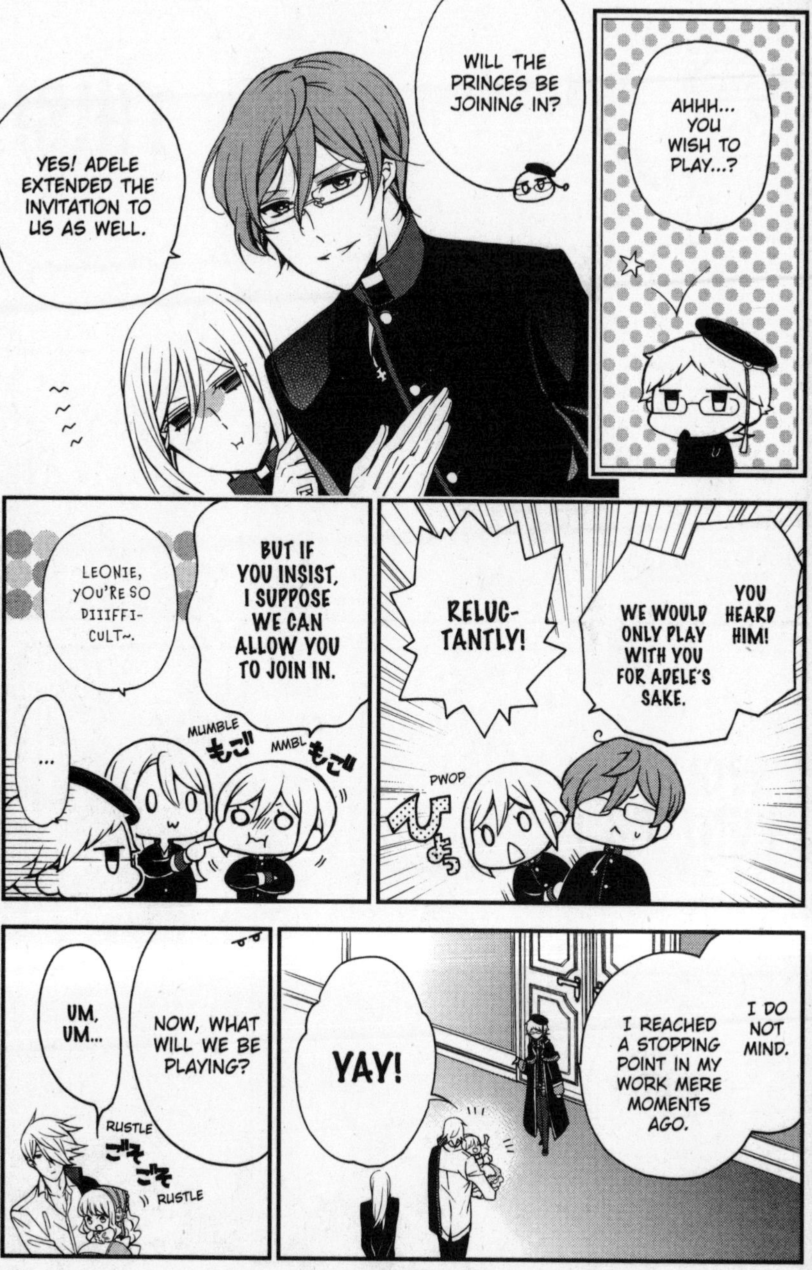
AHHH... YOU WISH TO PLAY...?
WILL THE PRINCES BE JOINING IN?
YES! ADELE EXTENDED THE INVITATION TO US AS WELL.
YOU HEARD HIM!
WE WOULD ONLY PLAY WITH YOU FOR ADELE'S SAKE.
RELUC-TANTLY!
PWOP
BUT IF YOU INSIST, I SUPPOSE WE CAN ALLOW YOU TO JOIN IN.
LEONIE, YOU'RE SO DIIIFFI-CULT~.
MMBL もご
MUMBLE もご
...
I DO NOT MIND.
I REACHED A STOPPING POINT IN MY WORK MERE MOMENTS AGO.
YAY!
NOW, WHAT WILL WE BE PLAYING?
UM, UM...
RUSTLE ごそ
ごそ RUSTLE

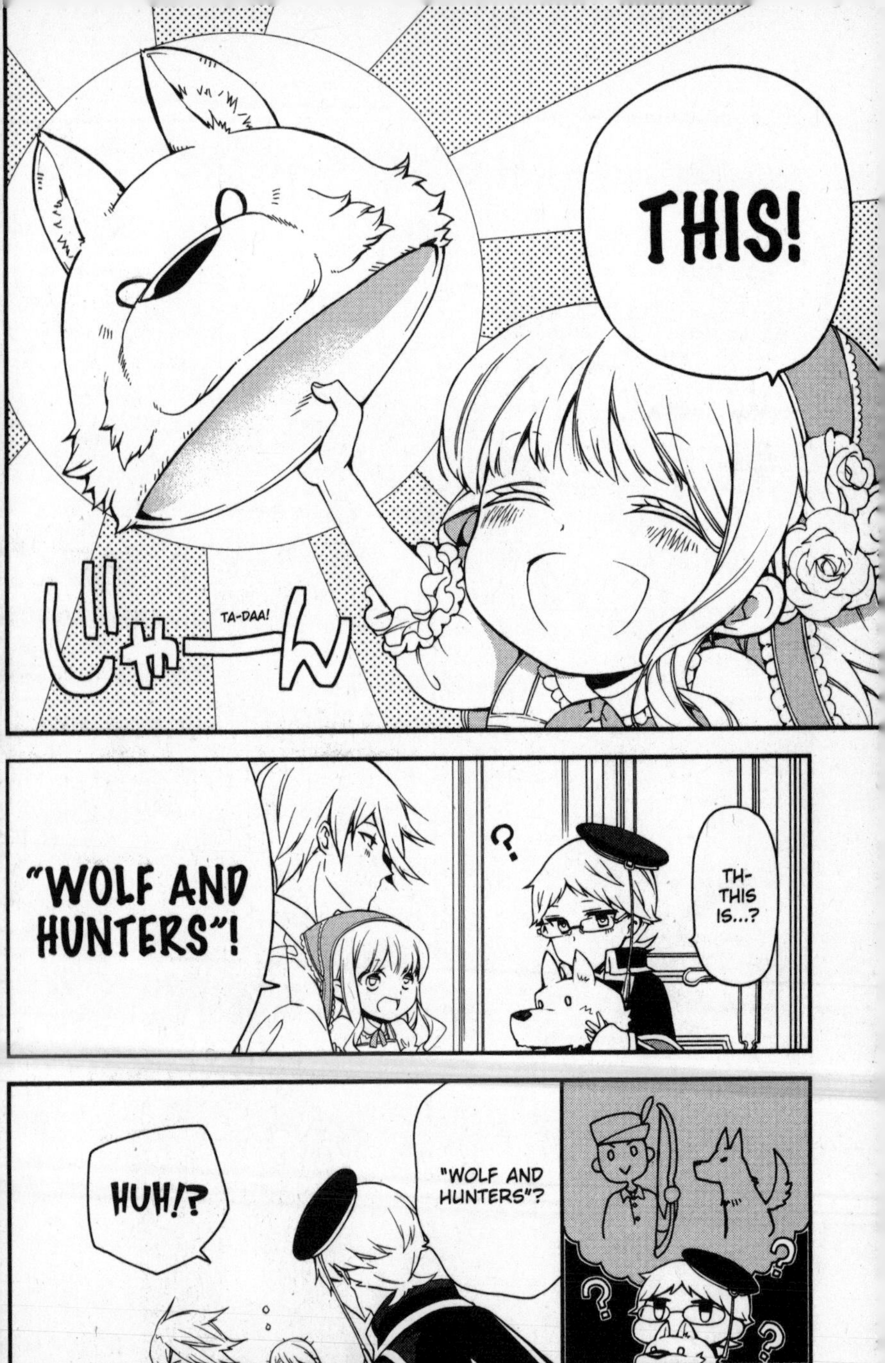
THIS!
じゃーん
TA-DAA!
TH-THIS IS...?
"WOLF AND HUNTERS"!
"WOLF AND HUNTERS"?
HUH!?

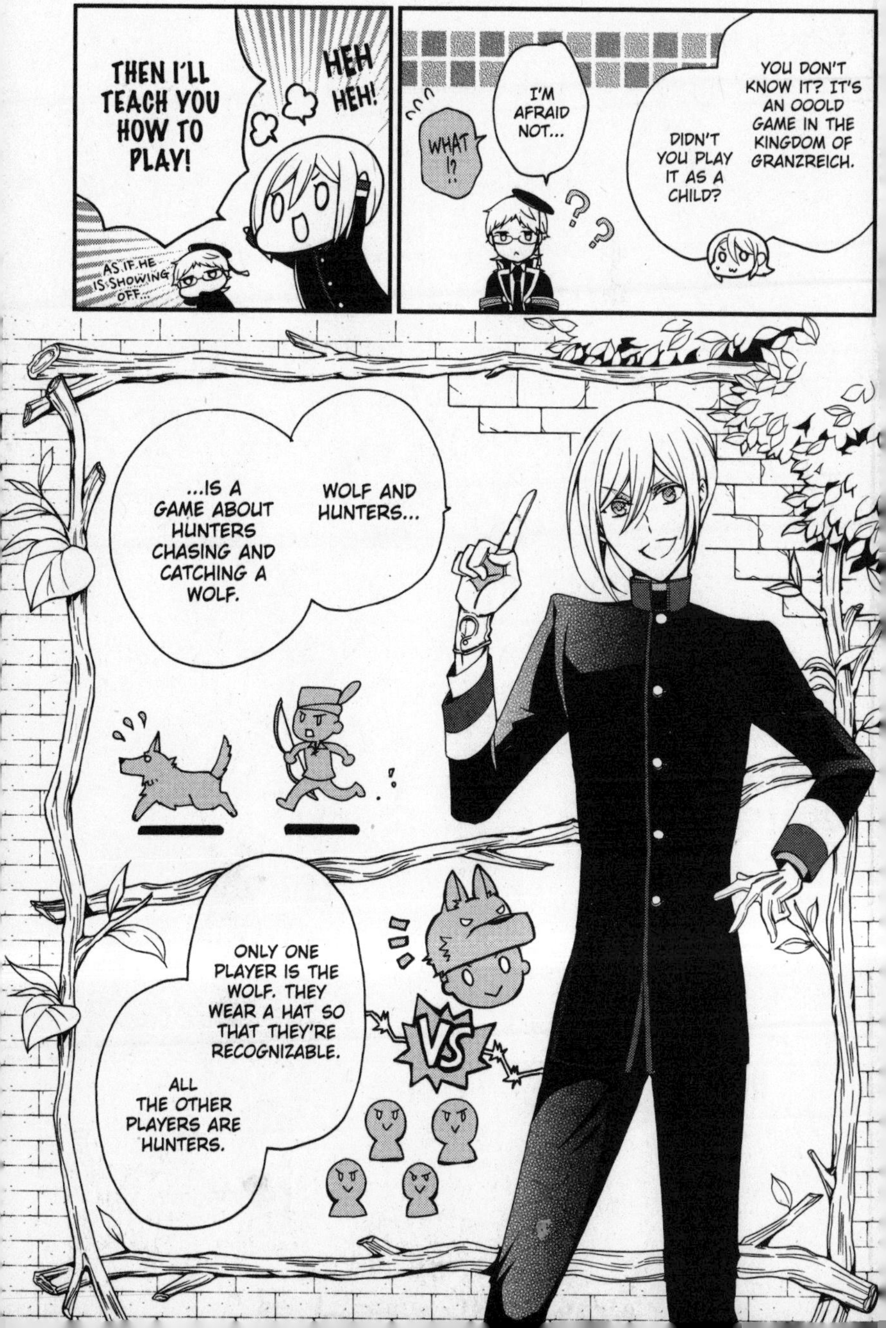
YOU DON'T KNOW IT? IT'S AN OOOLD GAME IN THE KINGDOM OF GRANZREICH.
DIDN'T YOU PLAY IT AS A CHILD?
I'M AFRAID NOT...
WHAT !?
HEH HEH!
THEN I'LL TEACH YOU HOW TO PLAY!
AS IF HE IS SHOWING OFF...
WOLF AND HUNTERS...
...IS A GAME ABOUT HUNTERS CHASING AND CATCHING A WOLF.
ONLY ONE PLAYER IS THE WOLF. THEY WEAR A HAT SO THAT THEY'RE RECOGNIZABLE.
ALL THE OTHER PLAYERS ARE HUNTERS.
VS

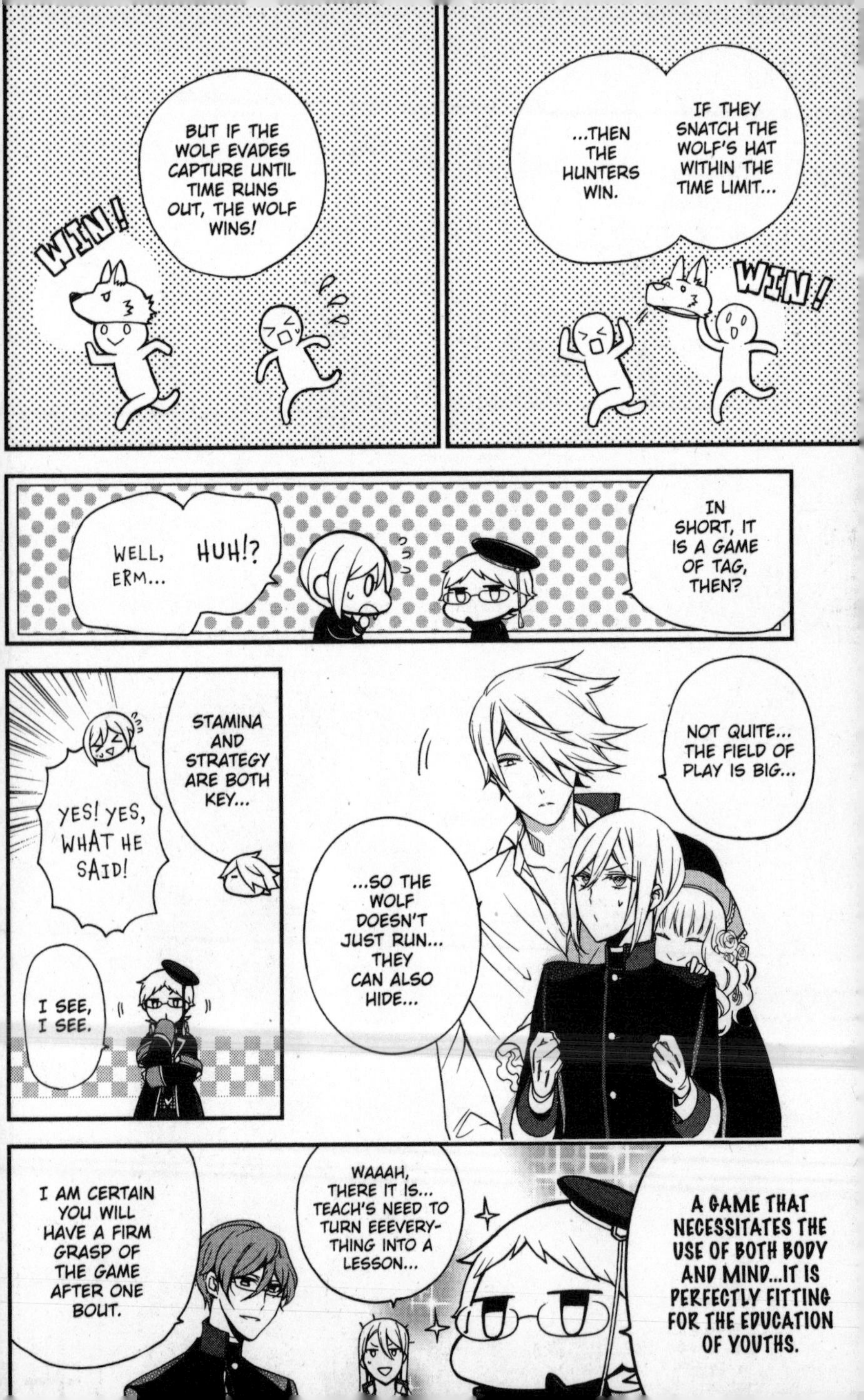

IF THEY SNATCH THE WOLF'S HAT WITHIN THE TIME LIMIT...
...THEN THE HUNTERS WIN.
WIN!
BUT IF THE WOLF EVADES CAPTURE UNTIL TIME RUNS OUT, THE WOLF WINS!
WIN!
IN SHORT, IT IS A GAME OF TAG, THEN?
HUH!?
WELL, ERM...
NOT QUITE... THE FIELD OF PLAY IS BIG...
...SO THE WOLF DOESN'T JUST RUN... THEY CAN ALSO HIDE...
STAMINA AND STRATEGY ARE BOTH KEY...
YES! YES, WHAT HE SAID!
I SEE, I SEE.
A GAME THAT NECESSITATES THE USE OF BOTH BODY AND MIND...IT IS PERFECTLY FITTING FOR THE EDUCATION OF YOUTHS.
WAAAH, THERE IT IS... TEACH'S NEED TO TURN EEEVERY-THING INTO A LESSON...
I AM CERTAIN YOU WILL HAVE A FIRM GRASP OF THE GAME AFTER ONE BOUT.

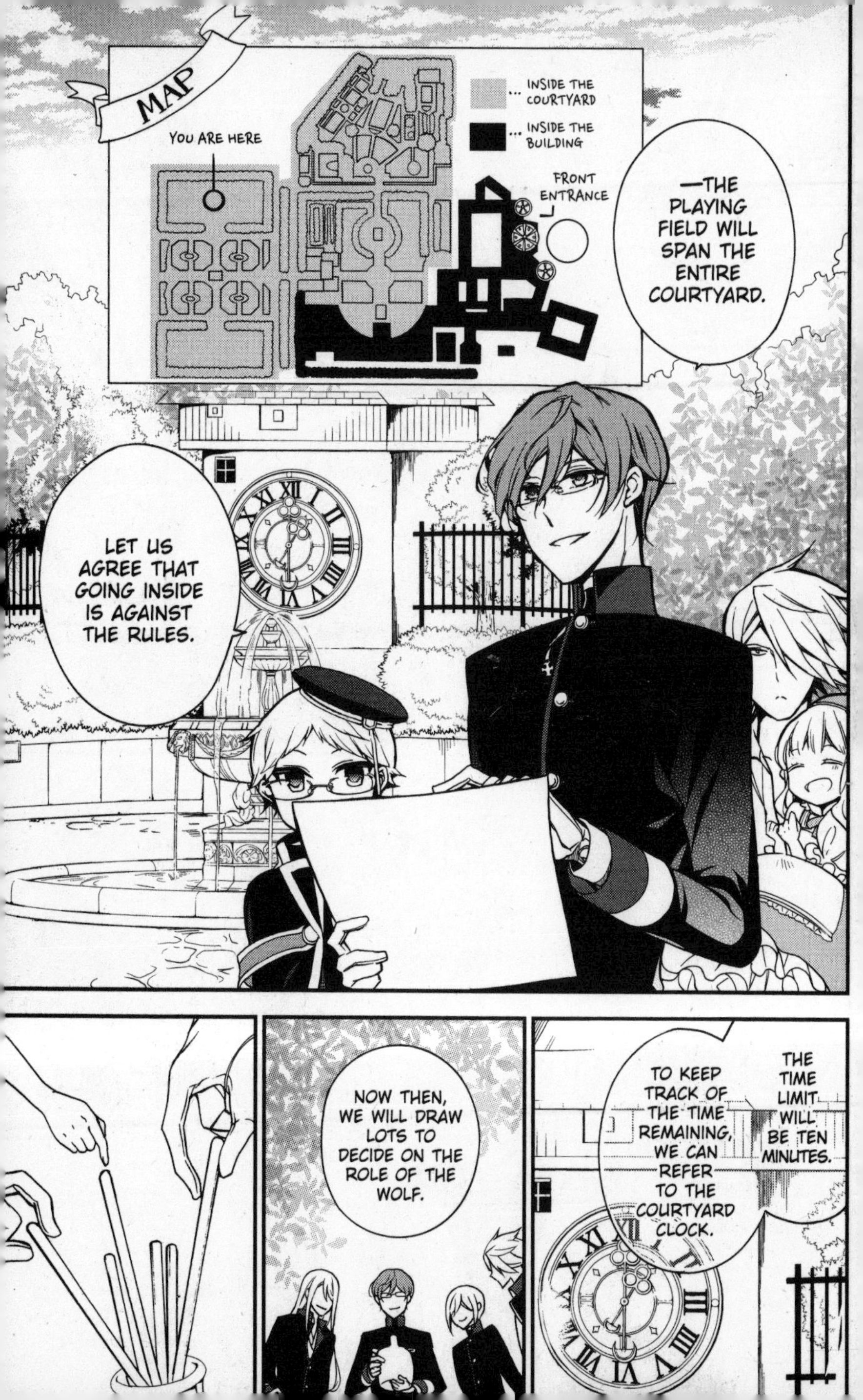
MAP
... INSIDE THE COURTYARD
... INSIDE THE BUILDING
YOU ARE HERE
FRONT ENTRANCE
—THE PLAYING FIELD WILL SPAN THE ENTIRE COURTYARD.
LET US AGREE THAT GOING INSIDE IS AGAINST THE RULES.
THE TIME LIMIT WILL BE TEN MINUTES.
TO KEEP TRACK OF THE TIME REMAINING, WE CAN REFER TO THE COURTYARD CLOCK.
NOW THEN, WE WILL DRAW LOTS TO DECIDE ON THE ROLE OF THE WOLF.

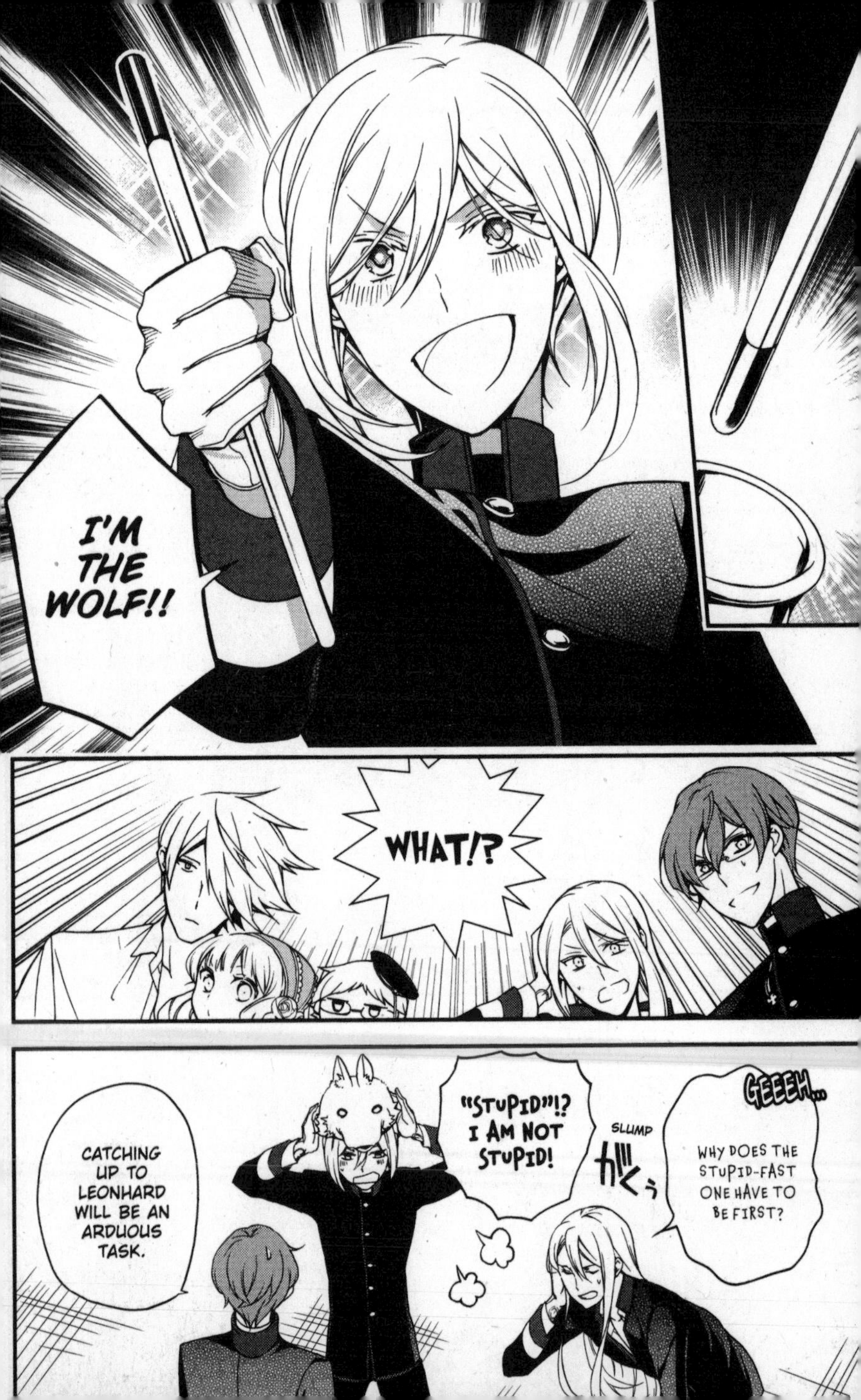
I'M THE WOLF!!
WHAT!?
GEEEH...
WHY DOES THE STUPID-FAST ONE HAVE TO BE FIRST?
SLUMP
"STUPID"!? I AM NOT STUPID!
CATCHING UP TO LEONHARD WILL BE AN ARDUOUS TASK.

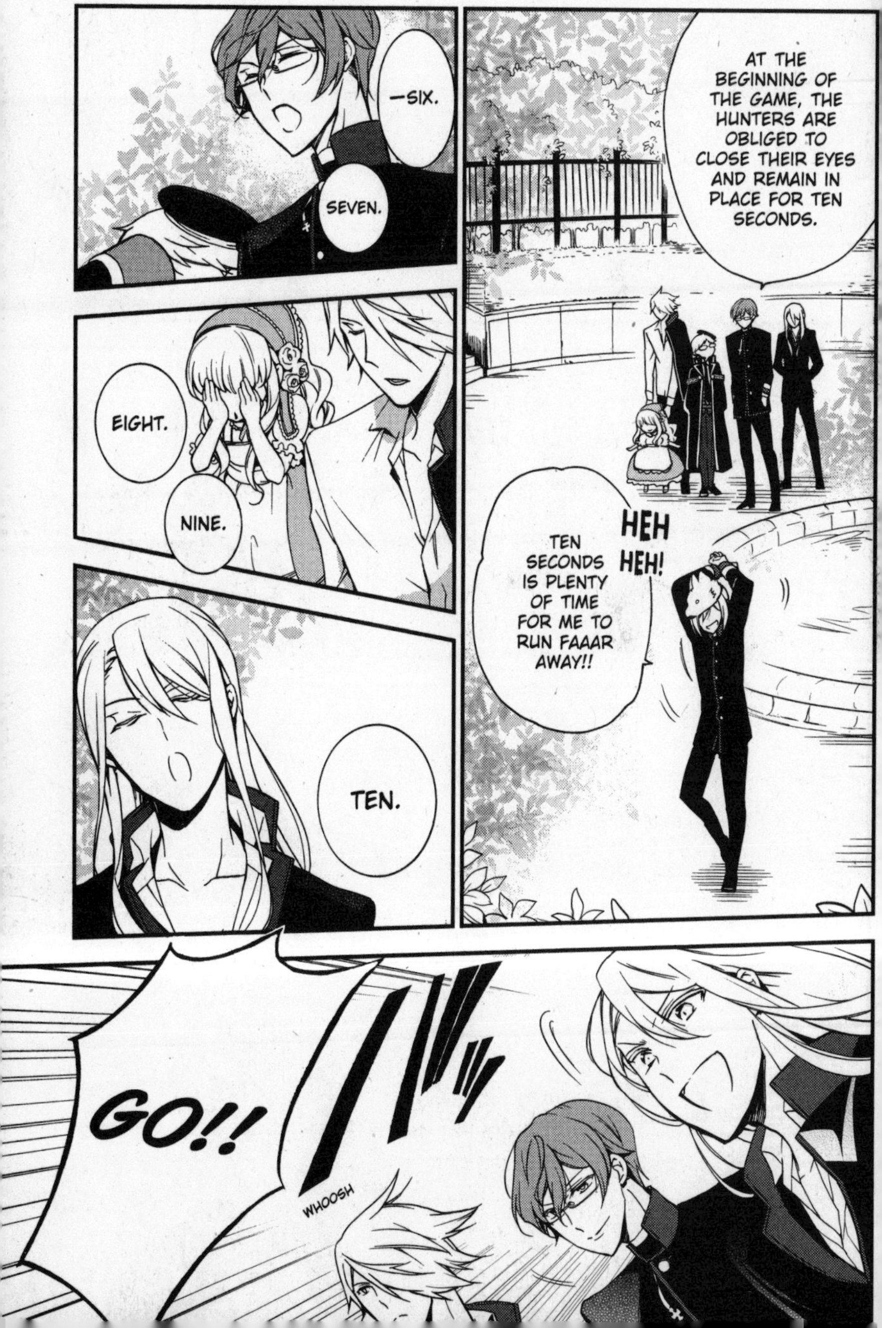
AT THE BEGINNING OF THE GAME, THE HUNTERS ARE OBLIGED TO CLOSE THEIR EYES AND REMAIN IN PLACE FOR TEN SECONDS.
HEH HEH!
TEN SECONDS IS PLENTY OF TIME FOR ME TO RUN FAAAR AWAY!!
—SIX.
SEVEN.
EIGHT.
NINE.
TEN.
GO!!
WHOOSH

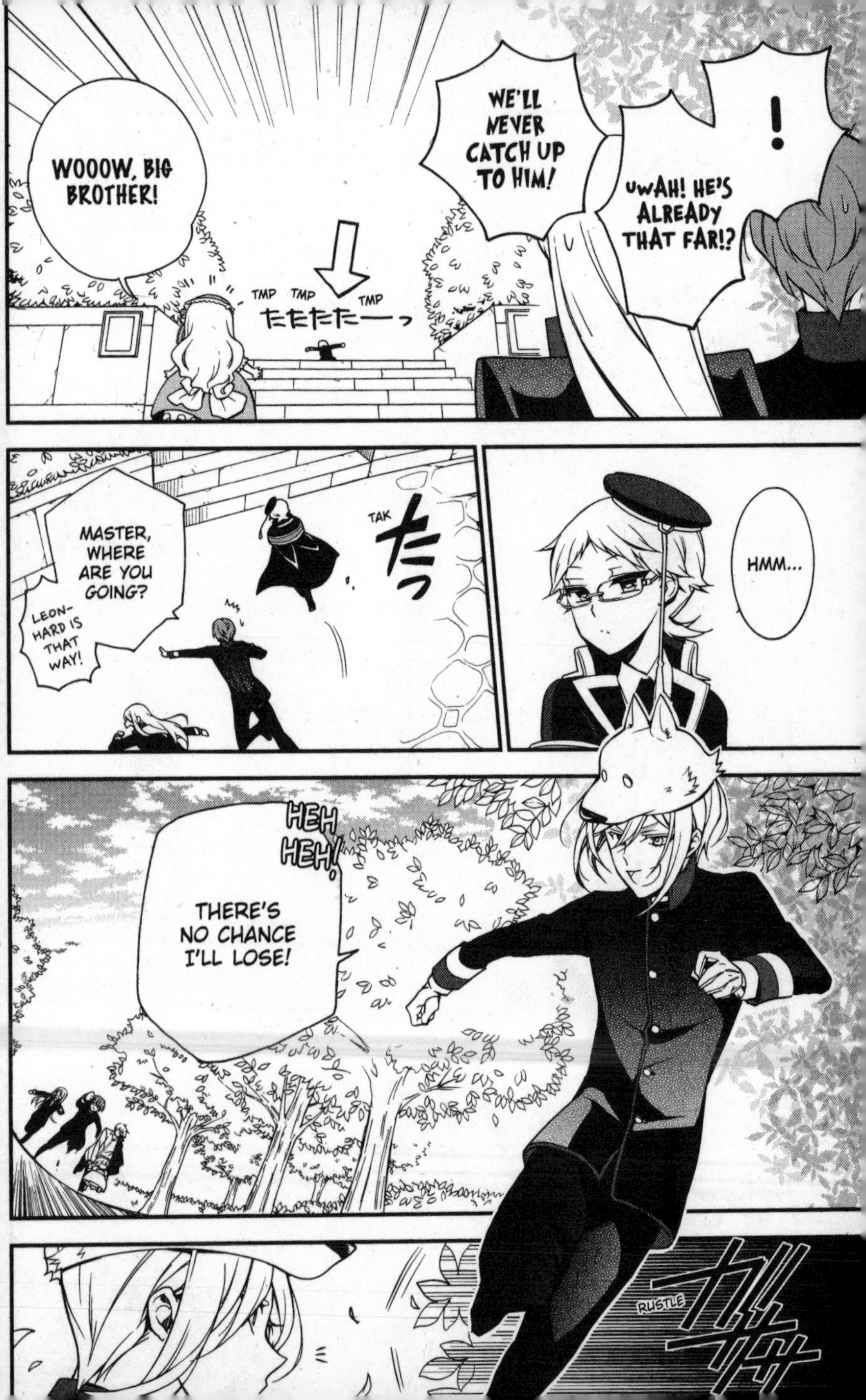
!
UWAH! HE'S ALREADY THAT FAR!?
WE'LL NEVER CATCH UP TO HIM!
TMP TMP TMP
たたたたーっ
WOOOW, BIG BROTHER!
HMM...
TAK
たっ
MASTER, WHERE ARE YOU GOING?
LEONHARD IS THAT WAY!
HEH HEH!
THERE'S NO CHANCE I'LL LOSE!
RUSTLE

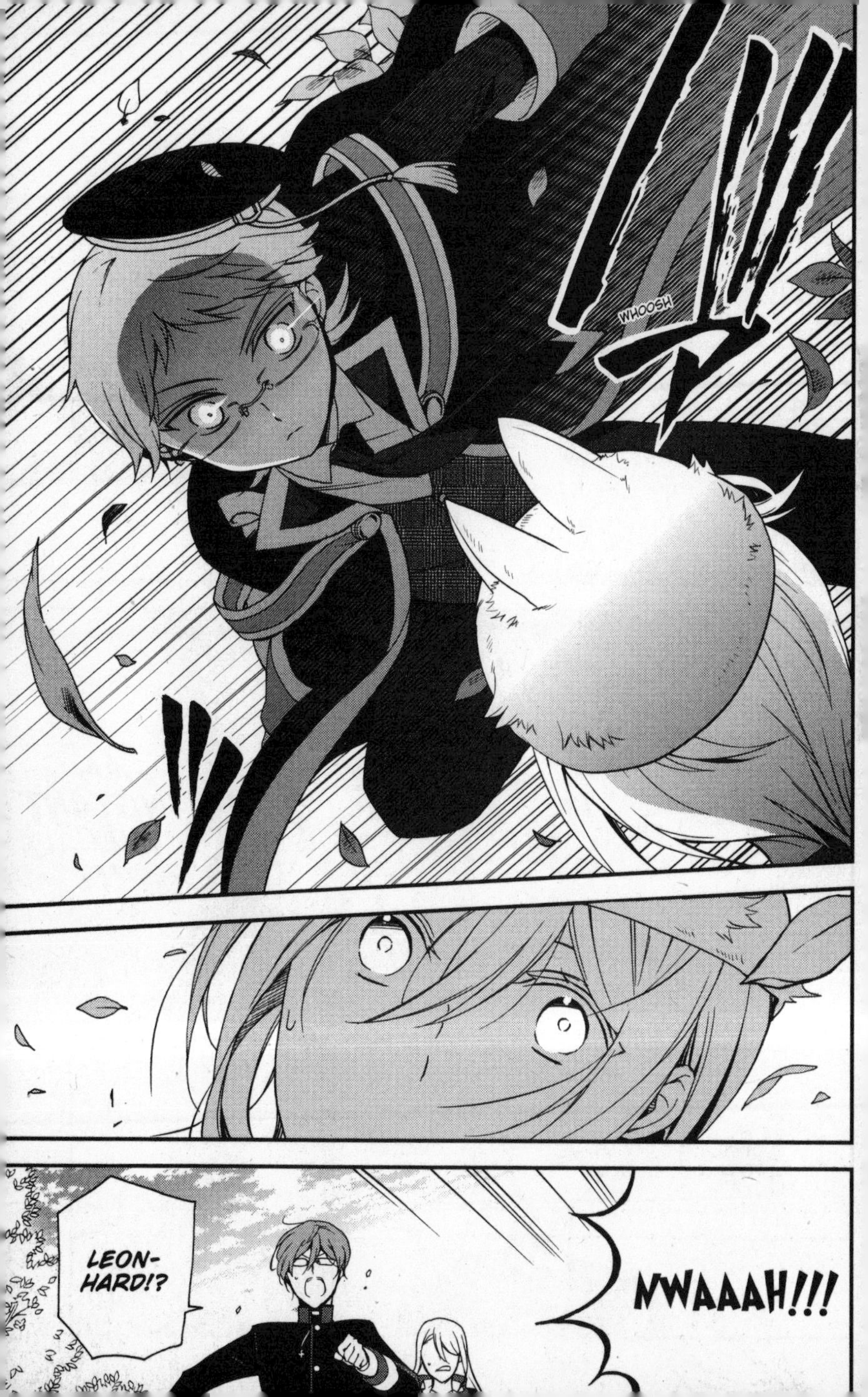
WHOOSH
NWAAAH!!!
LEON-HARD!?

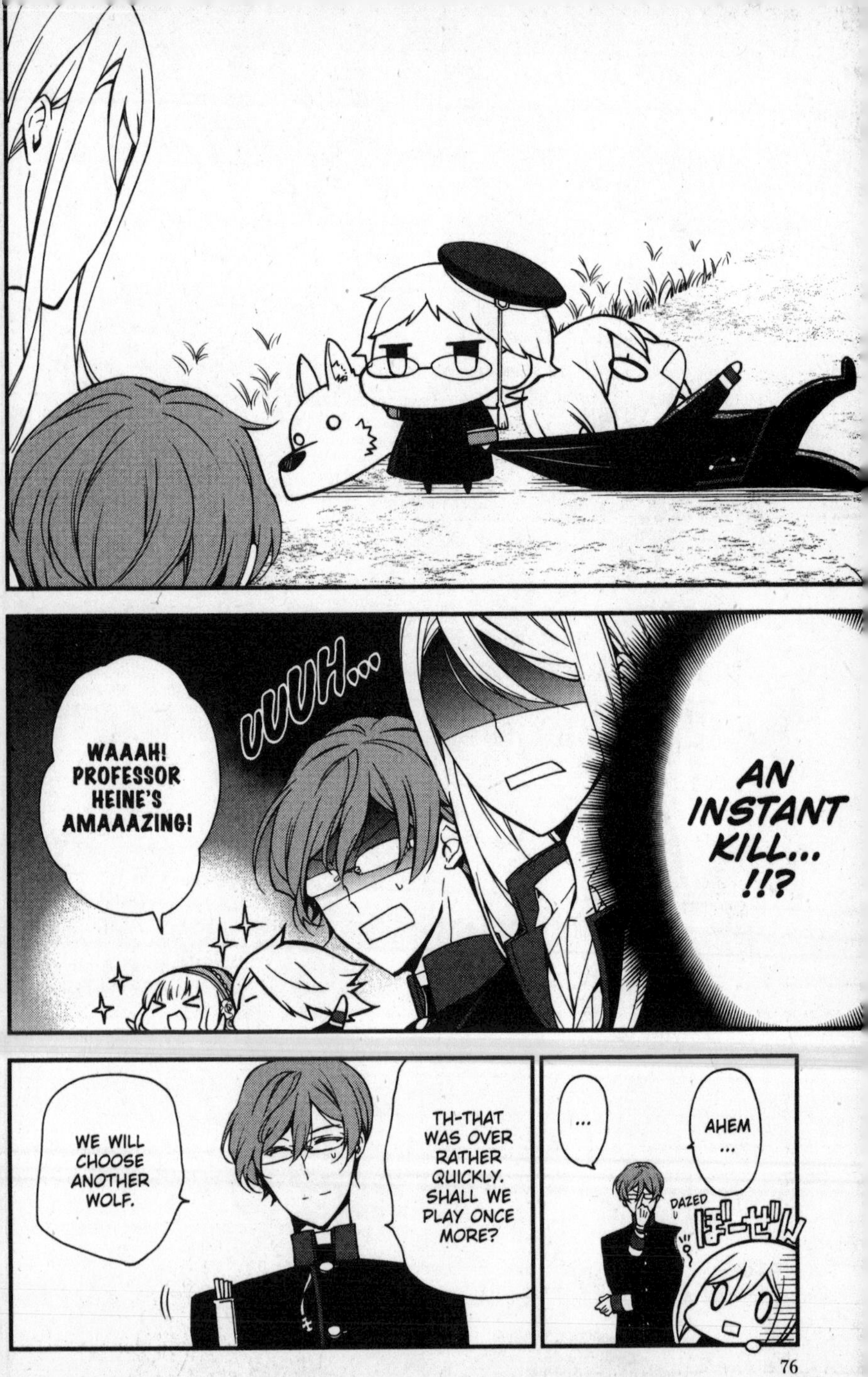

AN INSTANT KILL... !!?
UUUH...
WAAAH! PROFESSOR HEINE'S AMAAAZING!
AHEM ...
...
DAZED
ぼーぜん
TH-THAT WAS OVER RATHER QUICKLY. SHALL WE PLAY ONCE MORE?
WE WILL CHOOSE ANOTHER WOLF.

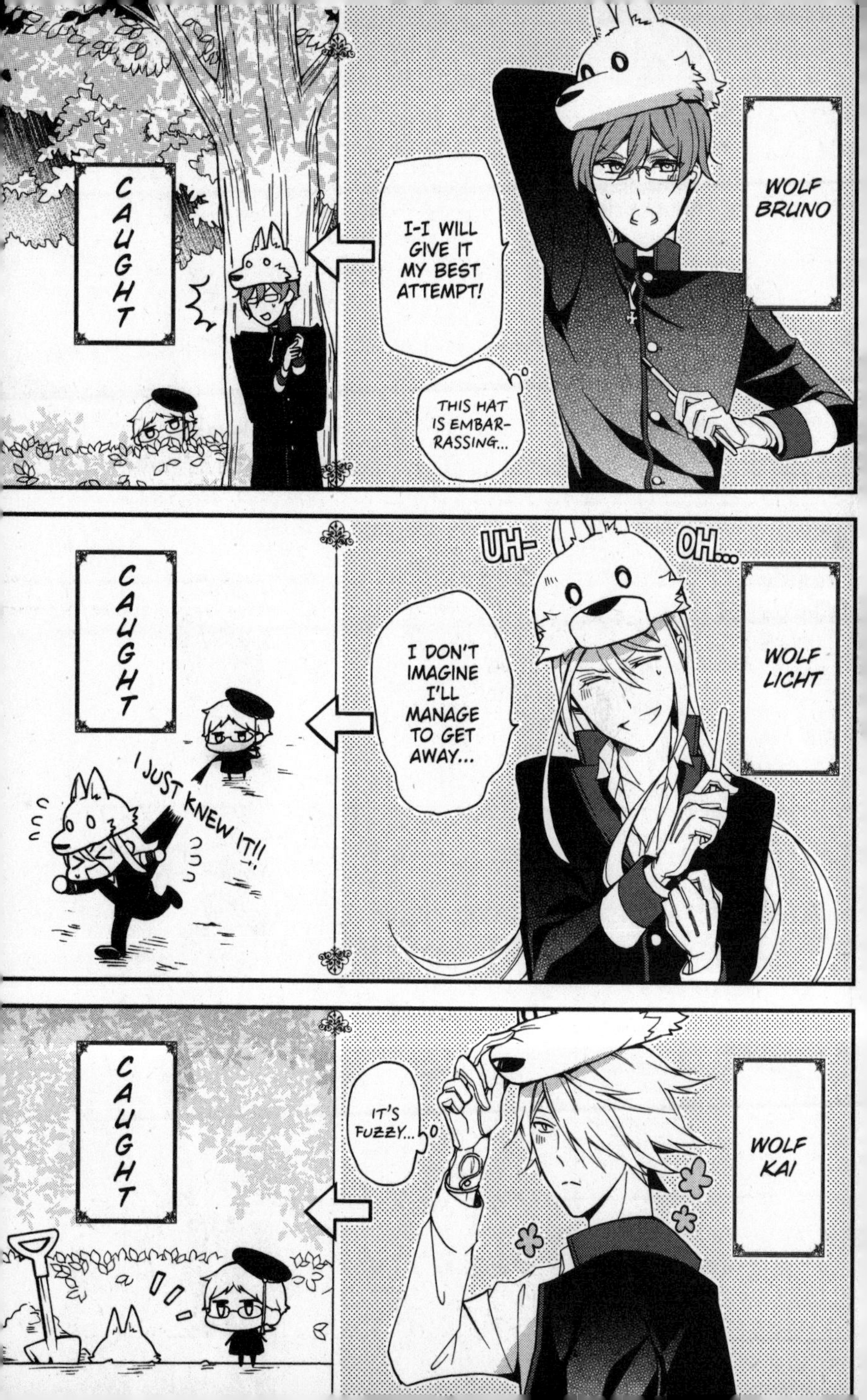
WOLF BRUNO
I-I WILL GIVE IT MY BEST ATTEMPT!
THIS HAT IS EMBARRASSING...
CAUGHT
UH-OH...
WOLF LICHT
I DON'T IMAGINE I'LL MANAGE TO GET AWAY...
CAUGHT
I JUST KNEW IT!!
WOLF KAI
IT'S FUZZY...
CAUGHT

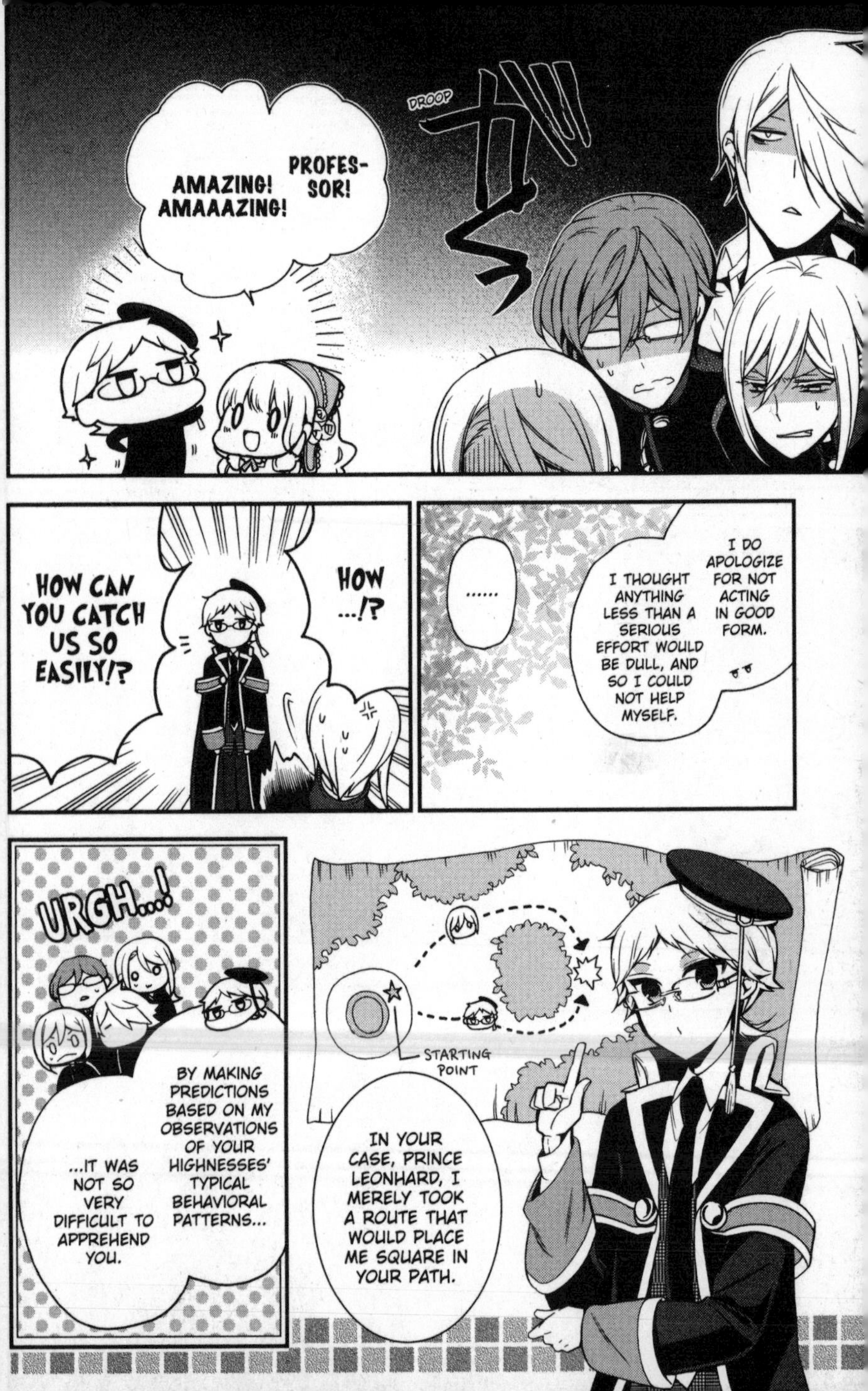
DROOP
PROFES-SOR! AMAZING! AMAAAZING!
I DO APOLOGIZE FOR NOT ACTING IN GOOD FORM.
I THOUGHT ANYTHING LESS THAN A SERIOUS EFFORT WOULD BE DULL, AND SO I COULD NOT HELP MYSELF.
......
HOW ...!?
HOW CAN YOU CATCH US SO EASILY!?
STARTING POINT
IN YOUR CASE, PRINCE LEONHARD, I MERELY TOOK A ROUTE THAT WOULD PLACE ME SQUARE IN YOUR PATH.
URGH...!
BY MAKING PREDICTIONS BASED ON MY OBSERVATIONS OF YOUR HIGHNESSES' TYPICAL BEHAVIORAL PATTERNS...
...IT WAS NOT SO VERY DIFFICULT TO APPREHEND YOU.

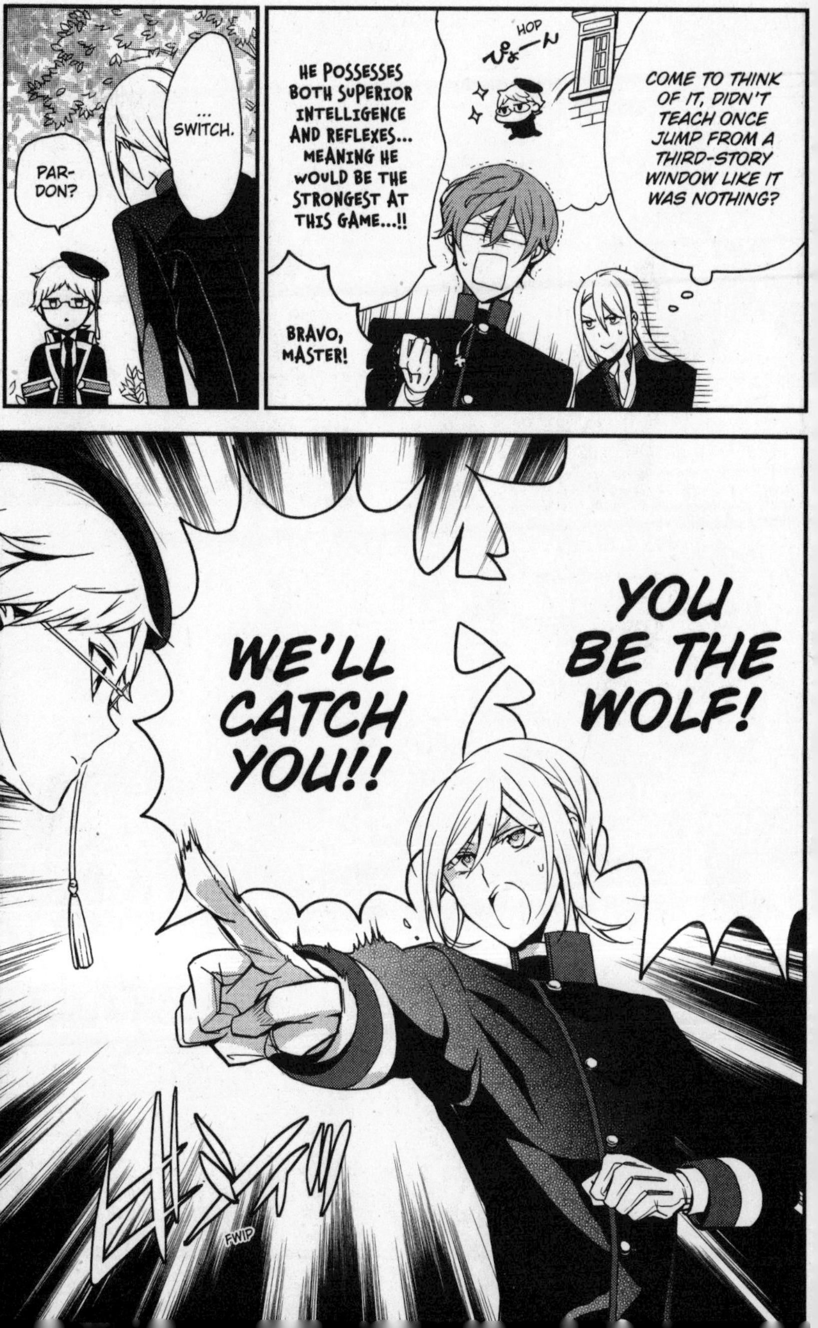
COME TO THINK OF IT, DIDN'T TEACH ONCE JUMP FROM A THIRD-STORY WINDOW LIKE IT WAS NOTHING?
HOP
HE POSSESSES BOTH SUPERIOR INTELLIGENCE AND REFLEXES... MEANING HE WOULD BE THE STRONGEST AT THIS GAME...!!
BRAVO, MASTER!
... SWITCH.
PAR-DON?
YOU BE THE WOLF!
WE'LL CATCH YOU!!
FWIP

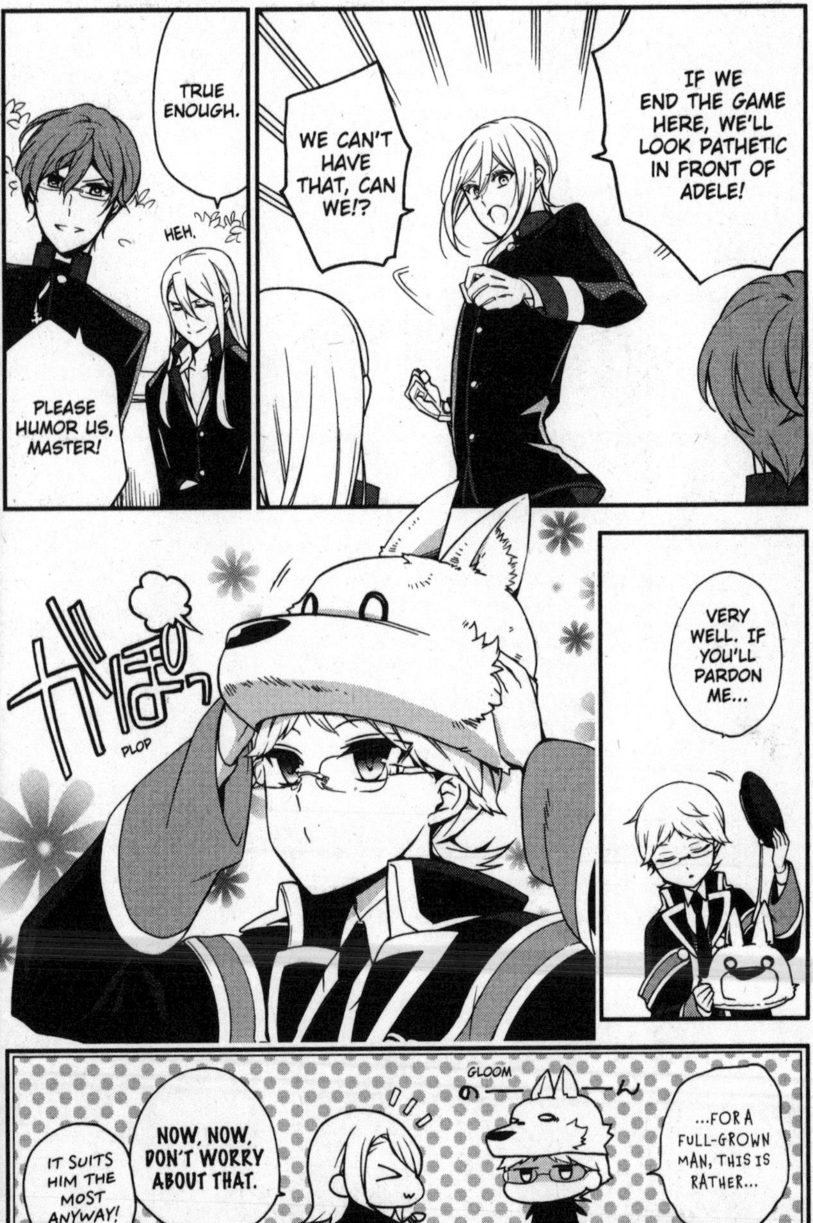
IF WE END THE GAME HERE, WE'LL LOOK PATHETIC IN FRONT OF ADELE!
WE CAN'T HAVE THAT, CAN WE!?
TRUE ENOUGH.
HEH.
PLEASE HUMOR US, MASTER!
VERY WELL. IF YOU'LL PARDON ME...
ガぽっ
PLOP
...FOR A FULL-GROWN MAN, THIS IS RATHER...
GLOOM
の———ん
NOW, NOW, DON'T WORRY ABOUT THAT.
IT SUITS HIM THE MOST ANYWAY!

WHOOSH

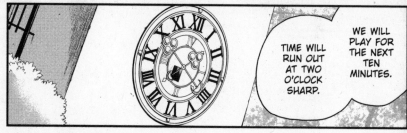

WE WILL PLAY FOR THE NEXT TEN MINUTES.

TIME WILL RUN OUT AT TWO O'CLOCK SHARP.

ONE.

TWO.

THREE.

FOUR.

—FIVE.

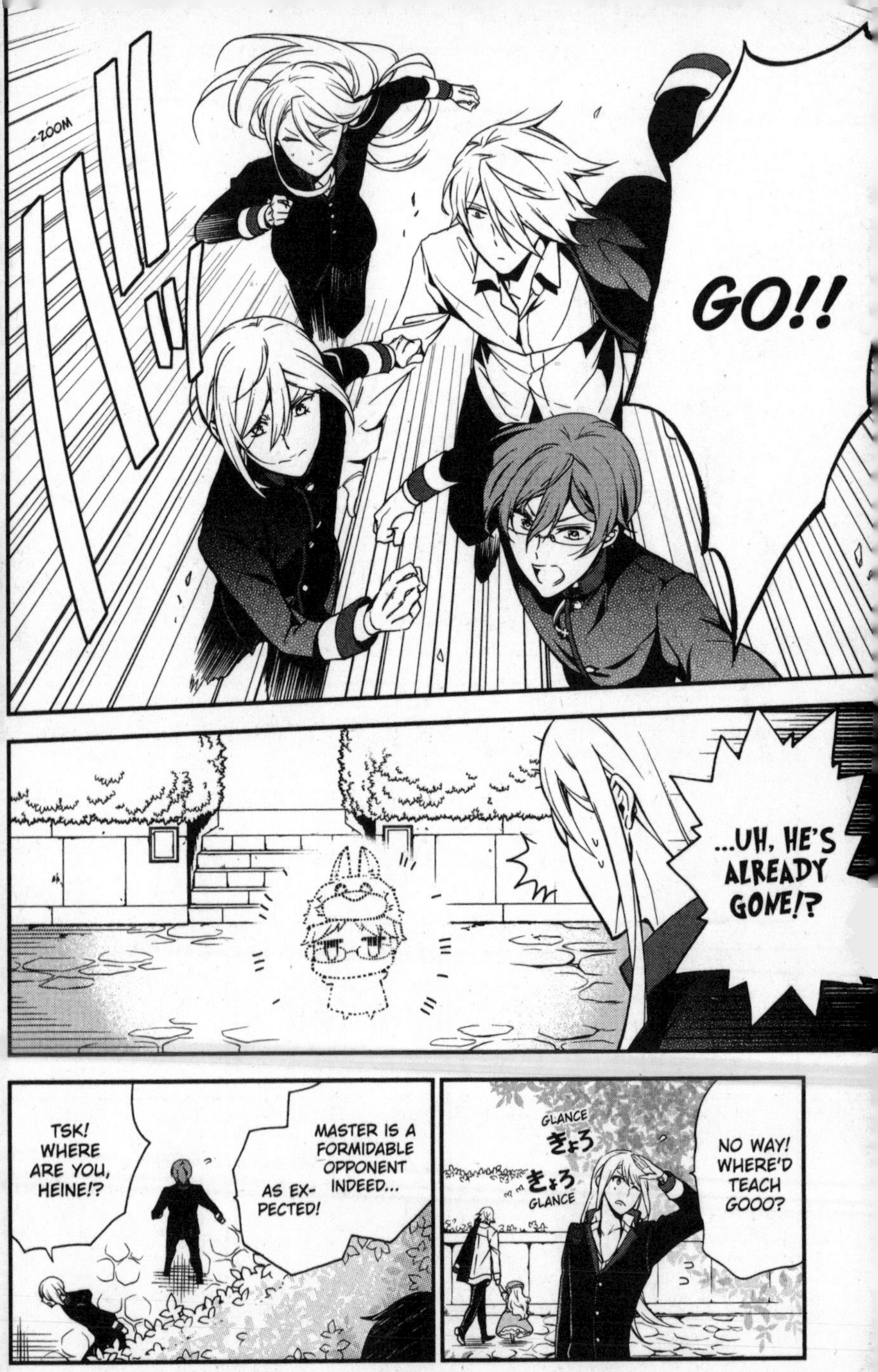
GO!!
ZOOM
...UH, HE'S ALREADY GONE!?
NO WAY! WHERE'D TEACH GOOO?
GLANCE
きょろ
きょろ
GLANCE
MASTER IS A FORMIDABLE OPPONENT INDEED...
AS EX-PECTED!
TSK! WHERE ARE YOU, HEINE!?

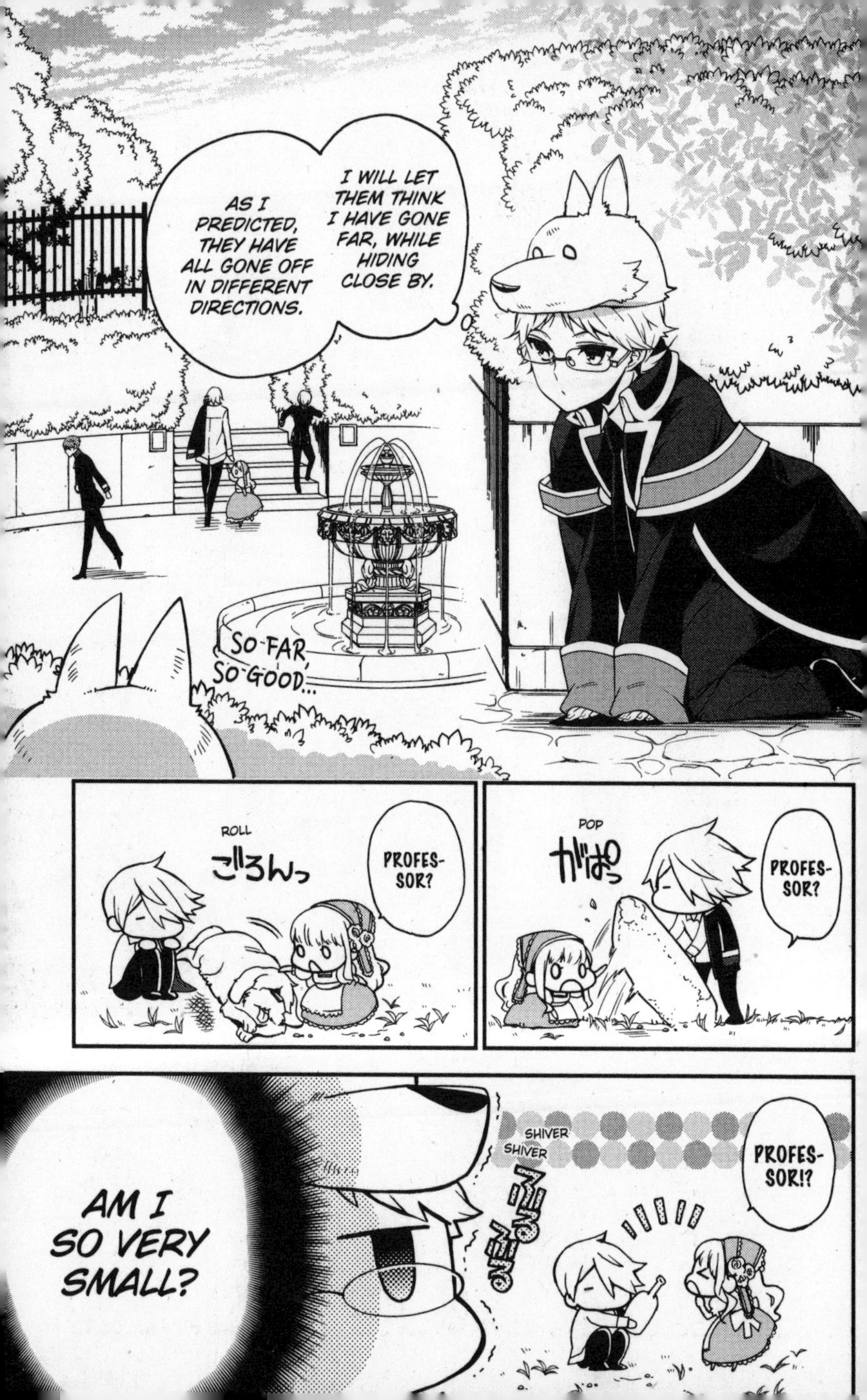
AS I PREDICTED, THEY HAVE ALL GONE OFF IN DIFFERENT DIRECTIONS.
I WILL LET THEM THINK I HAVE GONE FAR, WHILE HIDING CLOSE BY.
SO FAR, SO GOOD...
POP
がぱっ
PROFESSOR?
ROLL
ごろんっ
PROFESSOR?
PROFESSOR!?
SHIVER SHIVER
AM I SO VERY SMALL?

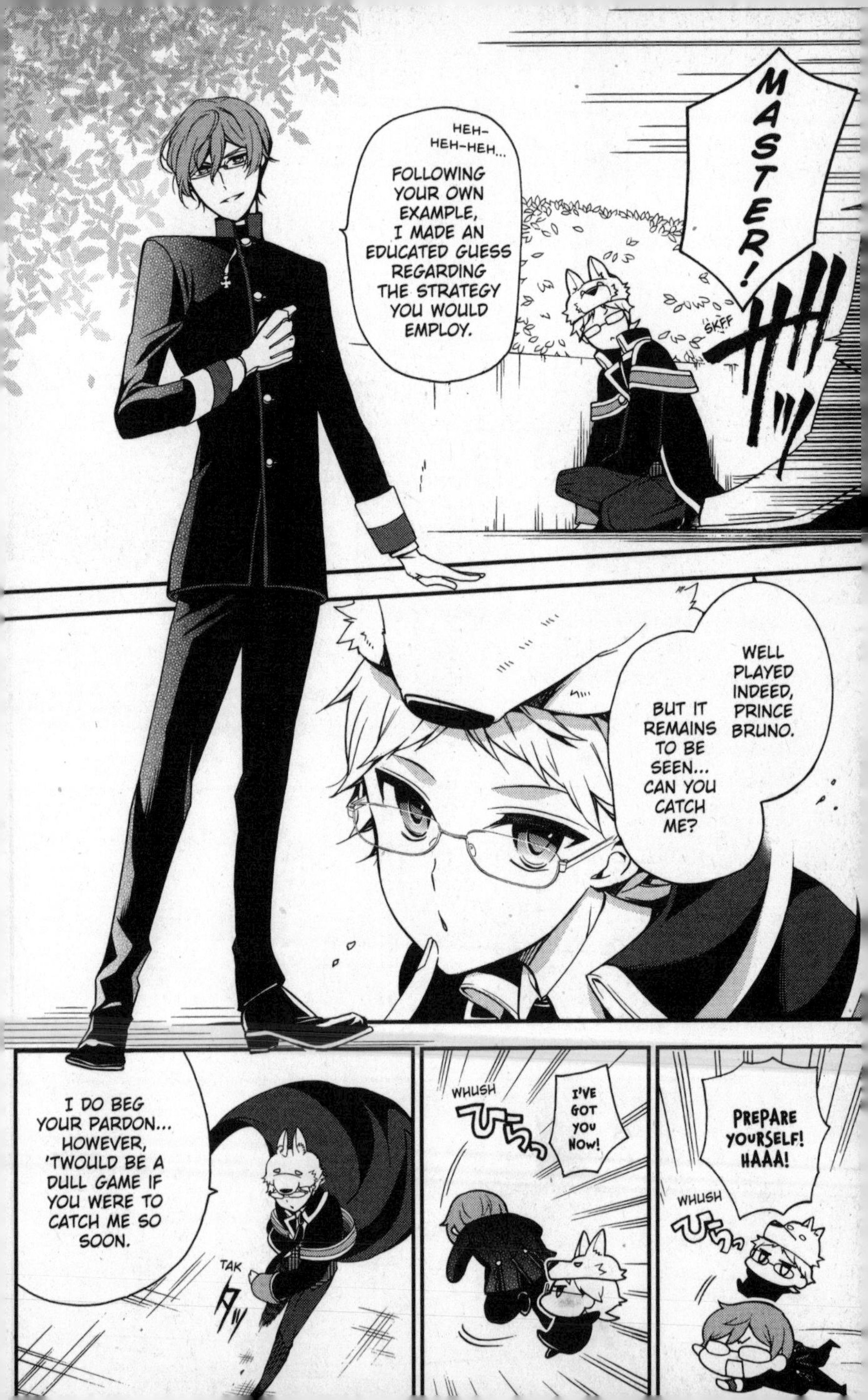
MASTER!
SKFF
HEH-HEH-HEH...
FOLLOWING YOUR OWN EXAMPLE, I MADE AN EDUCATED GUESS REGARDING THE STRATEGY YOU WOULD EMPLOY.
WELL PLAYED INDEED, PRINCE BRUNO.
BUT IT REMAINS TO BE SEEN... CAN YOU CATCH ME?
PREPARE YOURSELF! HAAA!
WHUSH
I'VE GOT YOU NOW!
WHUSH
I DO BEG YOUR PARDON... HOWEVER, 'TWOULD BE A DULL GAME IF YOU WERE TO CATCH ME SO SOON.
TAK

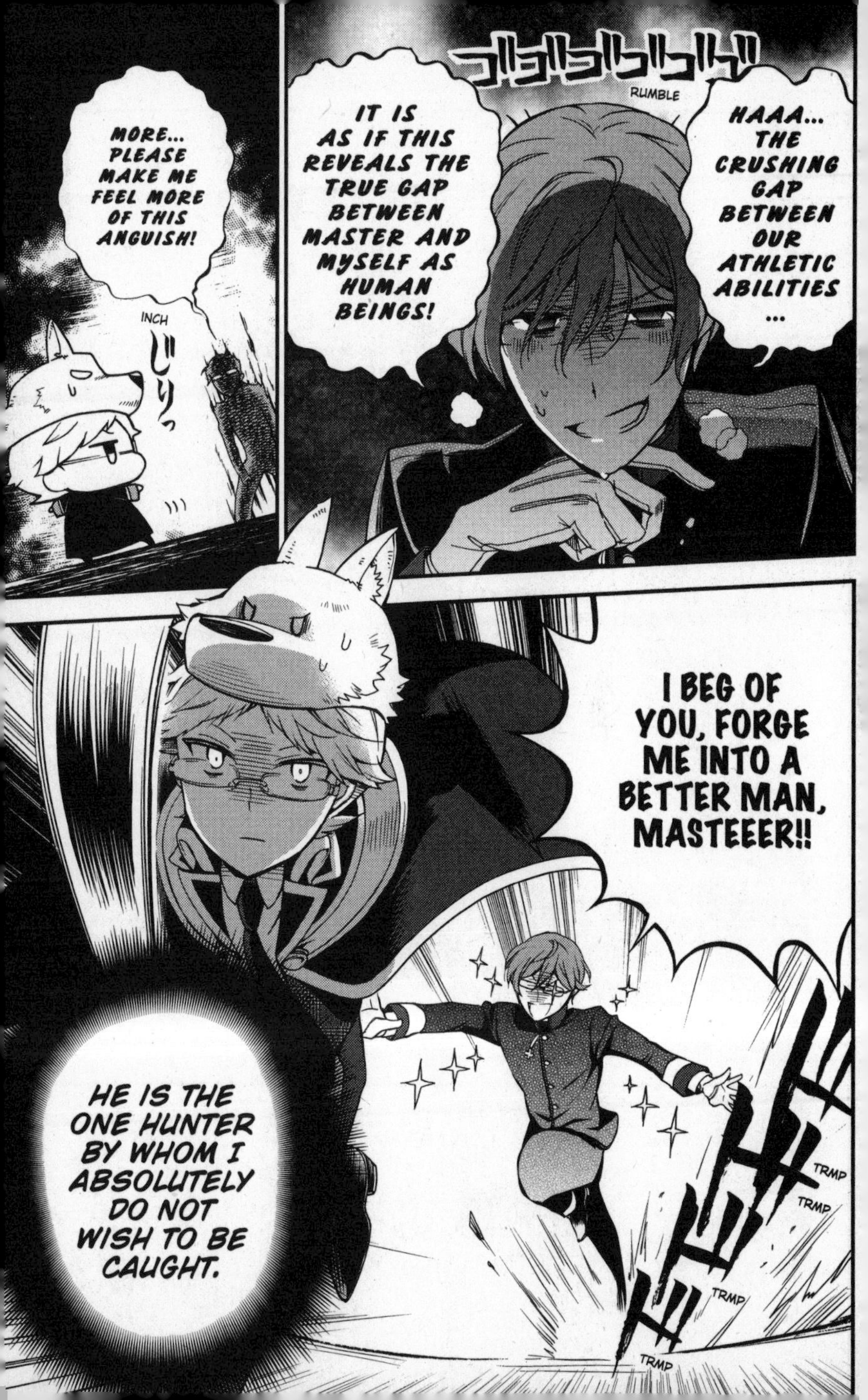
RUMBLE
HAAA... THE CRUSHING GAP BETWEEN OUR ATHLETIC ABILITIES...
IT IS AS IF THIS REVEALS THE TRUE GAP BETWEEN MASTER AND MYSELF AS HUMAN BEINGS!
MORE... PLEASE MAKE ME FEEL MORE OF THIS ANGUISH!
INCH
じりっ
I BEG OF YOU, FORGE ME INTO A BETTER MAN, MASTEEER!!
HE IS THE ONE HUNTER BY WHOM I ABSOLUTELY DO NOT WISH TO BE CAUGHT.
TRMP
TRMP
TRMP
TRMP

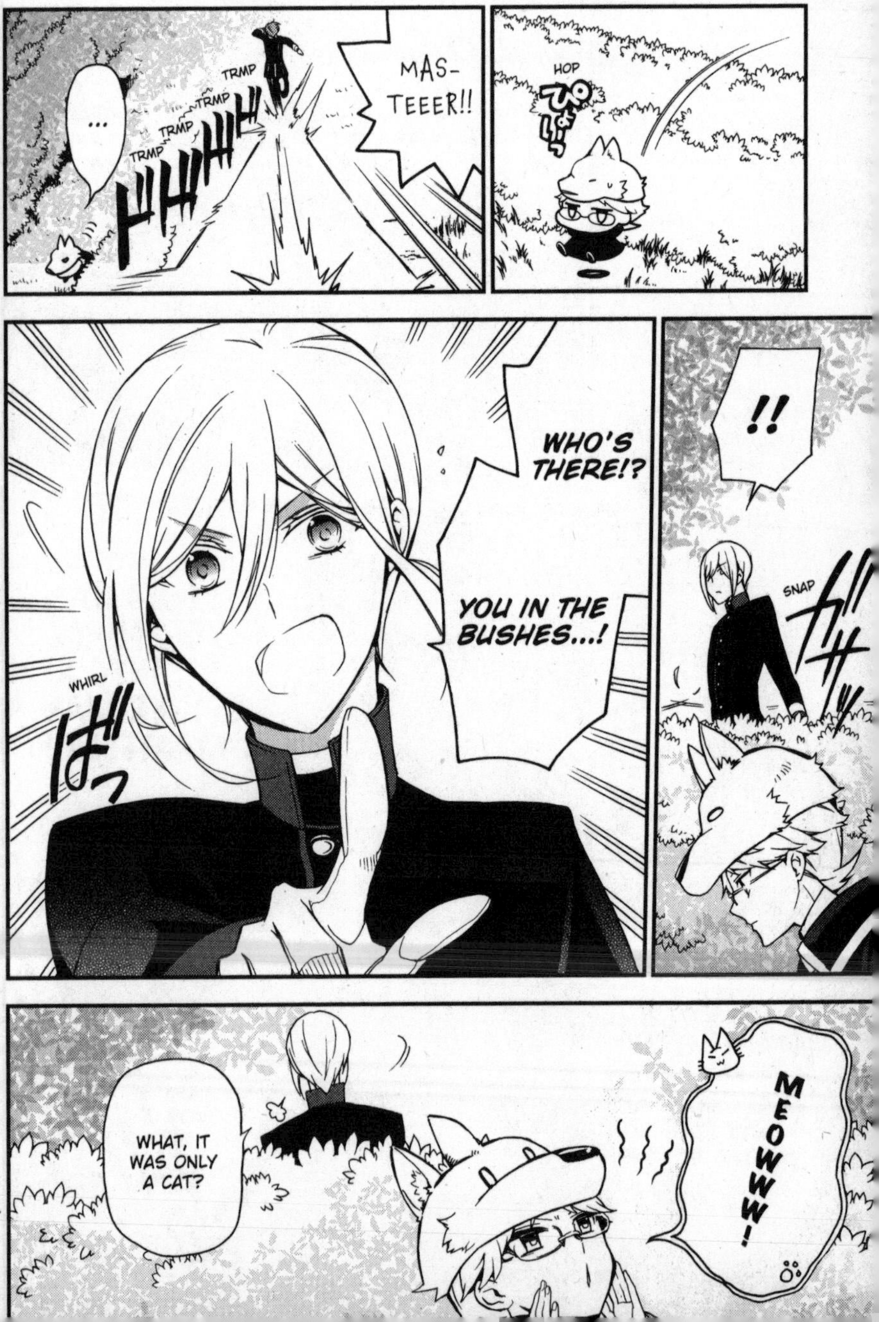
HOP
MAS-
TEEER!!
TRMP
TRMP
TRMP
TRMP
...
!!
SNAP
WHO'S THERE!?
YOU IN THE BUSHES...!
WHIRL
ばっ
MEOWWW!
WHAT, IT WAS ONLY A CAT?

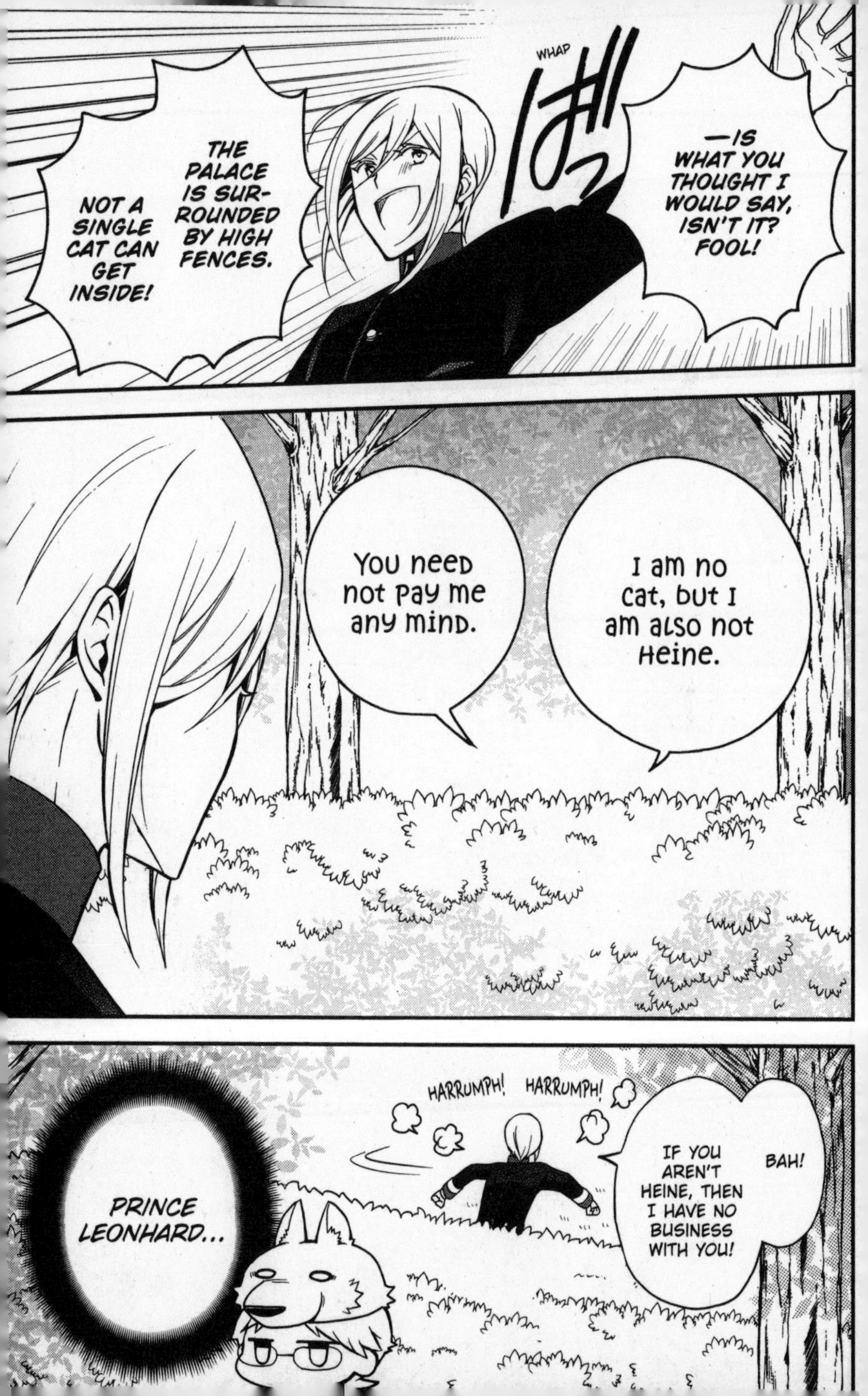
WHAP
—IS WHAT YOU THOUGHT I WOULD SAY, ISN'T IT? FOOL!
THE PALACE IS SUR-ROUNDED BY HIGH FENCES.
NOT A SINGLE CAT CAN GET INSIDE!
I am no cat, but I am also not Heine.
You need not pay me any mind.
BAH!
IF YOU AREN'T HEINE, THEN I HAVE NO BUSINESS WITH YOU!
HARRUMPH! HARRUMPH!
PRINCE LEONHARD...

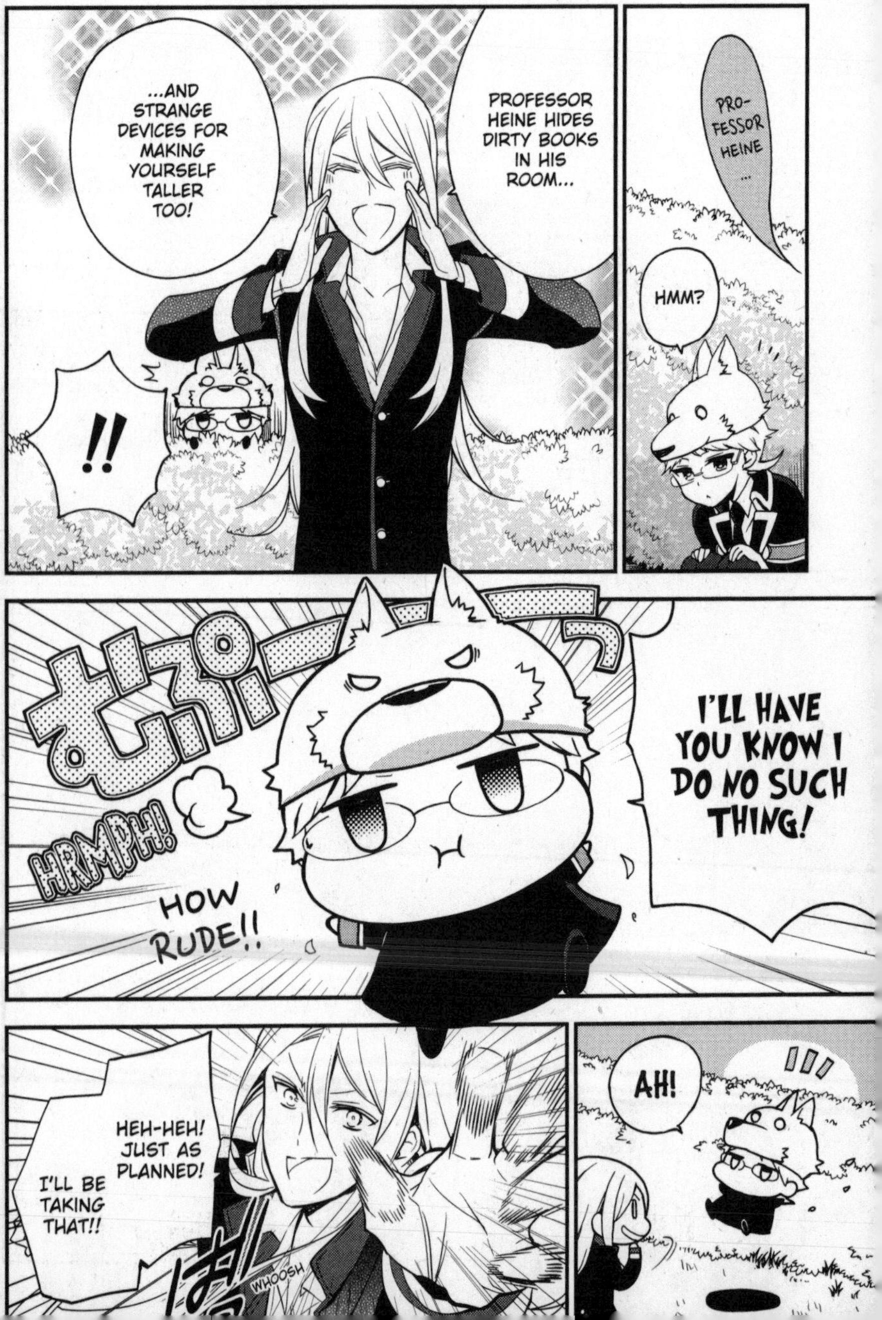
PRO-FESSOR HEINE...
HMM?
PROFESSOR HEINE HIDES DIRTY BOOKS IN HIS ROOM...
...AND STRANGE DEVICES FOR MAKING YOURSELF TALLER TOO!
!!
I'LL HAVE YOU KNOW I DO NO SUCH THING!
HRMPH!
HOW RUDE!!
AH!
HEH-HEH! JUST AS PLANNED!
I'LL BE TAKING THAT!!
WHOOSH

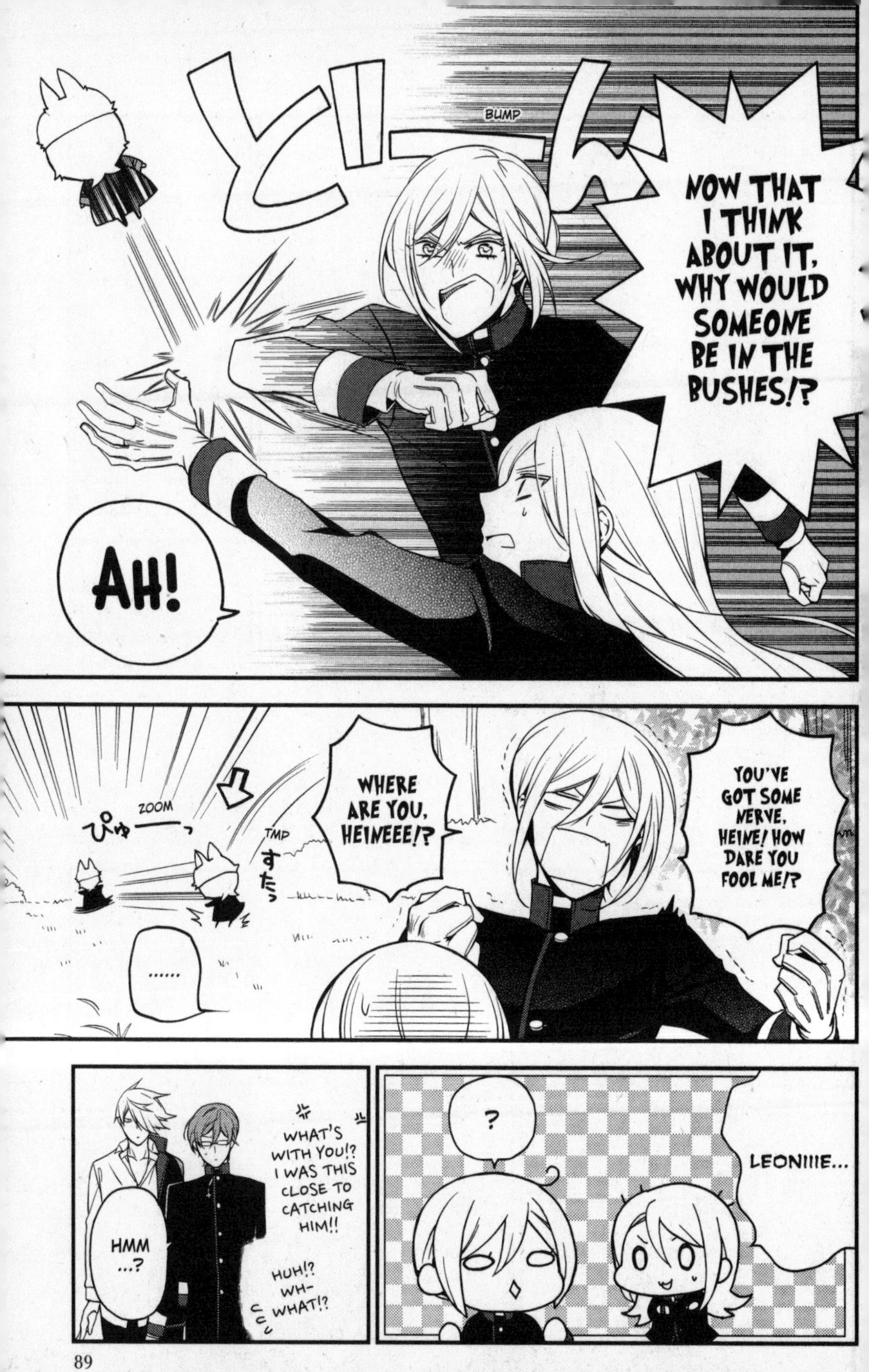
どーん
BUMP
NOW THAT I THINK ABOUT IT, WHY WOULD SOMEONE BE IN THE BUSHES!?
AH!
YOU'VE GOT SOME NERVE, HEINE! HOW DARE YOU FOOL ME!?
WHERE ARE YOU, HEINEEE!?
すたっ
TMP
ぴゅーっ
ZOOM
......
LEONIIIE...
?
WHAT'S WITH YOU!? I WAS THIS CLOSE TO CATCHING HIM!!
HUH!? WH-WHAT!?
HMM ...?

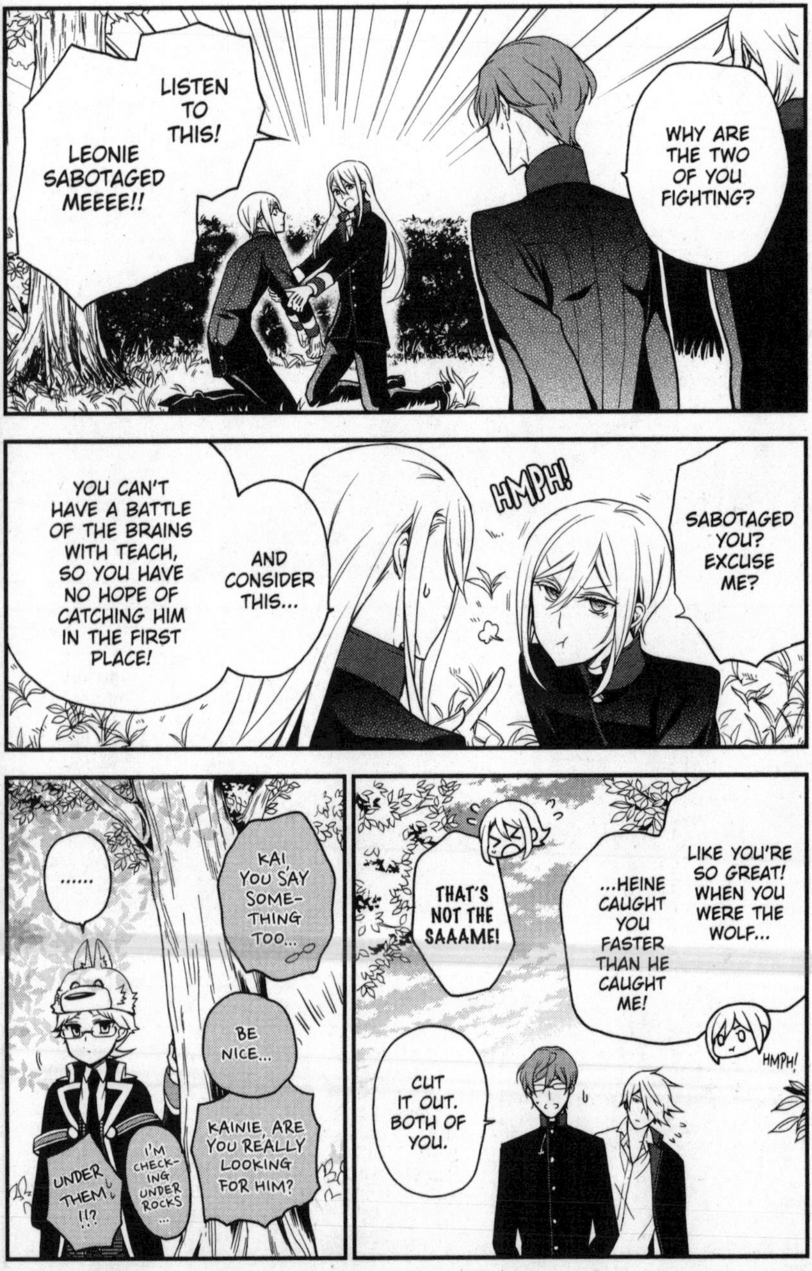
WHY ARE THE TWO OF YOU FIGHTING?
LISTEN TO THIS!
LEONIE SABOTAGED MEEEE!!
SABOTAGED YOU? EXCUSE ME?
HMPH!
AND CONSIDER THIS...
YOU CAN'T HAVE A BATTLE OF THE BRAINS WITH TEACH, SO YOU HAVE NO HOPE OF CATCHING HIM IN THE FIRST PLACE!
LIKE YOU'RE SO GREAT! WHEN YOU WERE THE WOLF...
...HEINE CAUGHT YOU FASTER THAN HE CAUGHT ME!
THAT'S NOT THE SAAAME!
HMPH!
CUT IT OUT. BOTH OF YOU.
KAI, YOU SAY SOME-THING TOO...
......
BE NICE...
KAINIE, ARE YOU REALLY LOOKING FOR HIM?
I'M CHECK-ING UNDER ROCKS...
UNDER THEM!!?

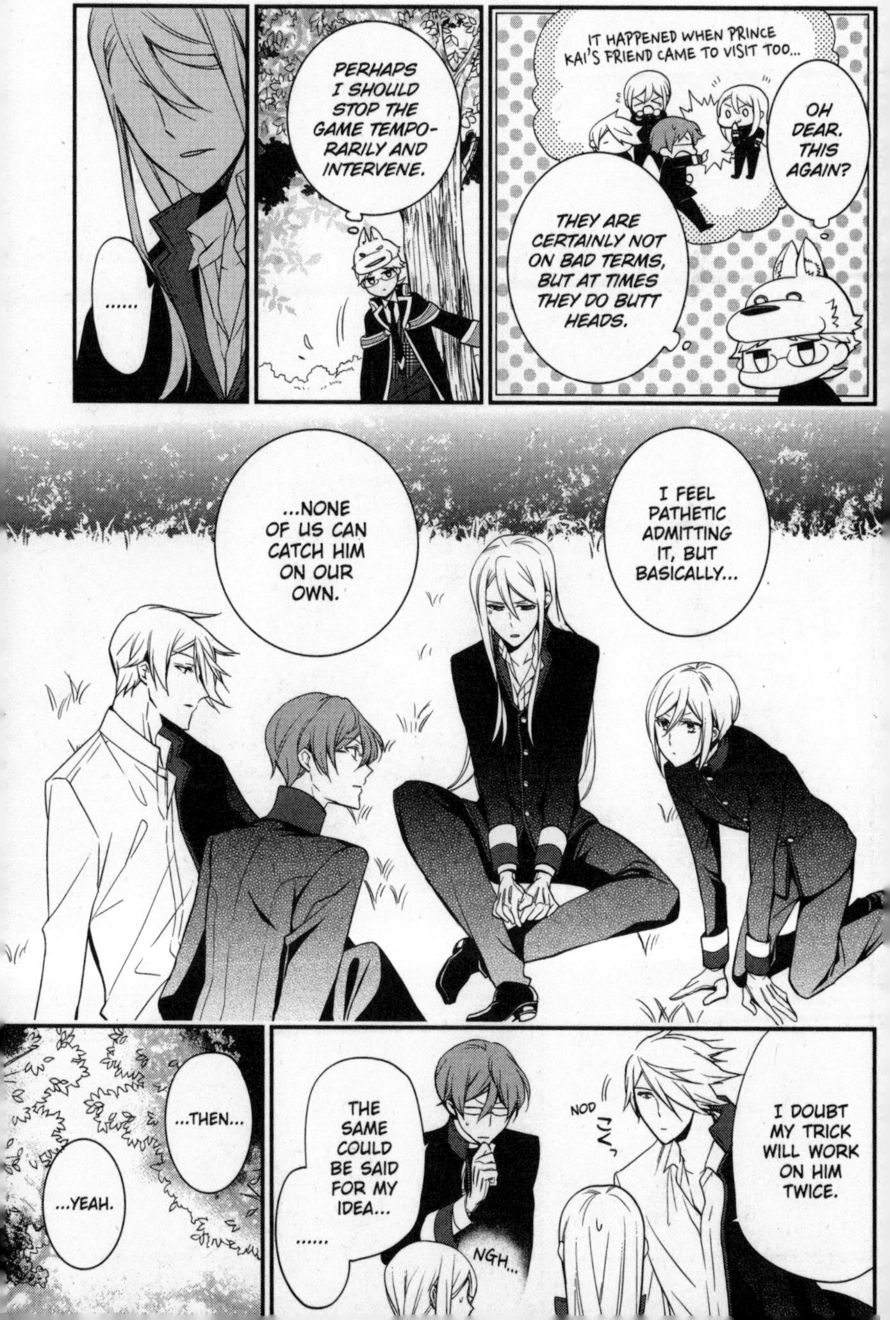
OH DEAR. THIS AGAIN?
IT HAPPENED WHEN PRINCE KAI'S FRIEND CAME TO VISIT TOO...
THEY ARE CERTAINLY NOT ON BAD TERMS, BUT AT TIMES THEY DO BUTT HEADS.
PERHAPS I SHOULD STOP THE GAME TEMPORARILY AND INTERVENE.
......
I FEEL PATHETIC ADMITTING IT, BUT BASICALLY...
...NONE OF US CAN CATCH HIM ON OUR OWN.
I DOUBT MY TRICK WILL WORK ON HIM TWICE.
NOD
THE SAME COULD BE SAID FOR MY IDEA...
NGH...
......
...THEN...
...YEAH.

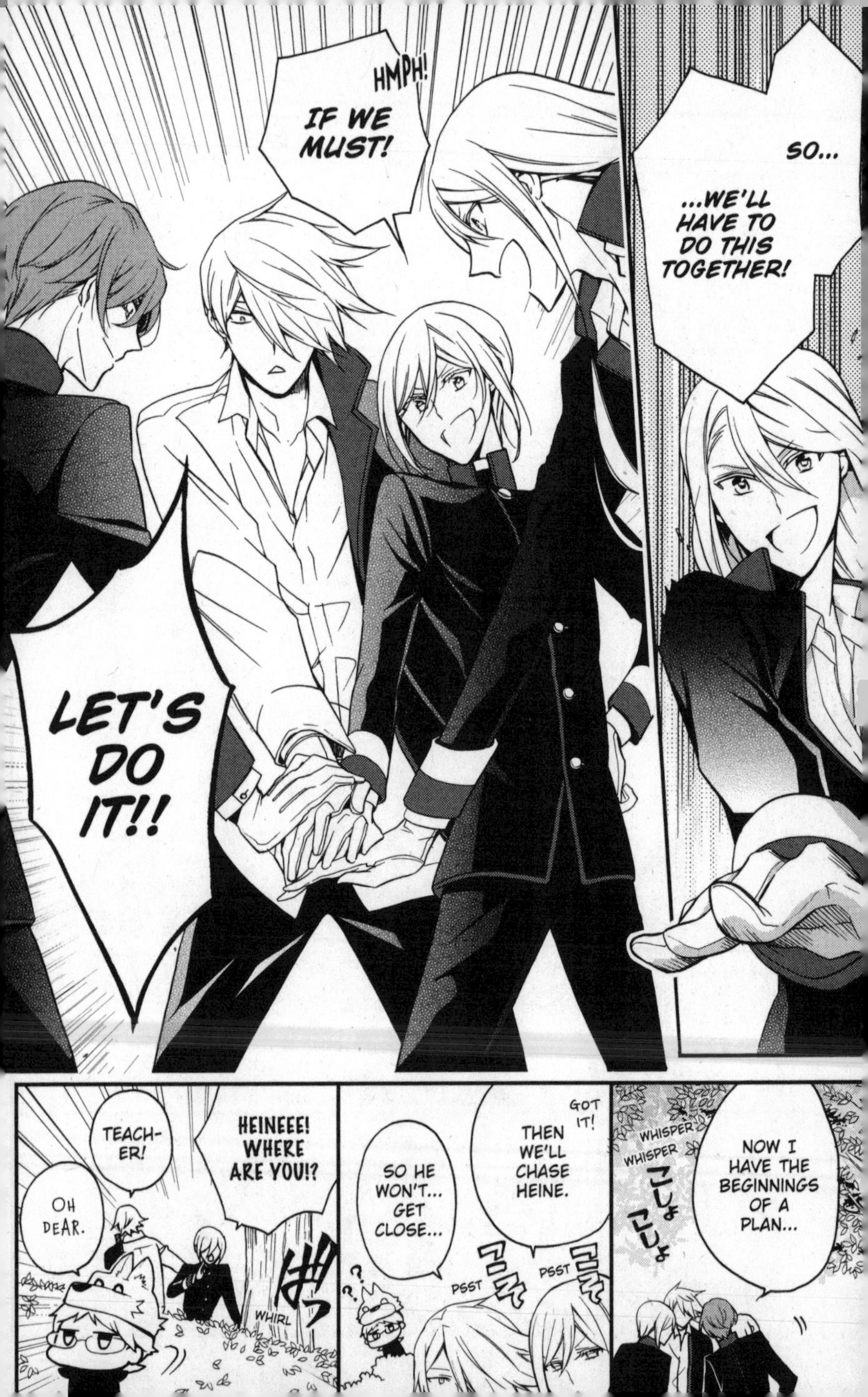
SO...
...WE'LL HAVE TO DO THIS TOGETHER!
HMPH!
IF WE MUST!
LET'S DO IT!!
WHISPER
WHISPER
こしょこしょ
NOW I HAVE THE BEGINNINGS OF A PLAN...
GOT IT!
THEN WE'LL CHASE HEINE.
SO HE WON'T... GET CLOSE...
PSST
PSST
HEINEEE! WHERE ARE YOU!?
TEACH-ER!
OH DEAR.
ばっ
WHIRL

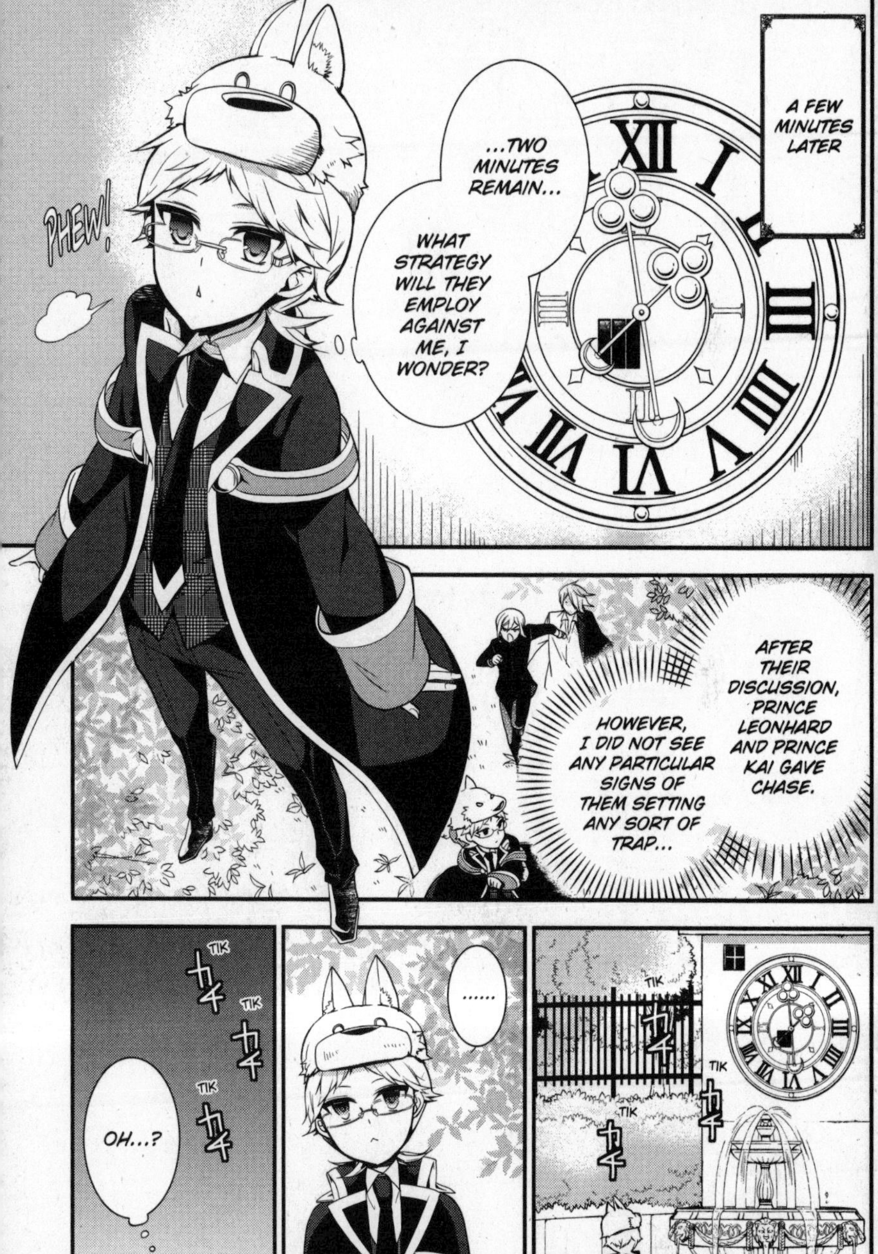
A FEW MINUTES LATER
...TWO MINUTES REMAIN...
WHAT STRATEGY WILL THEY EMPLOY AGAINST ME, I WONDER?
PHEW!
AFTER THEIR DISCUSSION, PRINCE LEONHARD AND PRINCE KAI GAVE CHASE.
HOWEVER, I DID NOT SEE ANY PARTICULAR SIGNS OF THEM SETTING ANY SORT OF TRAP...
TIK
TIK
TIK
......
TIK
TIK
TIK
OH...?

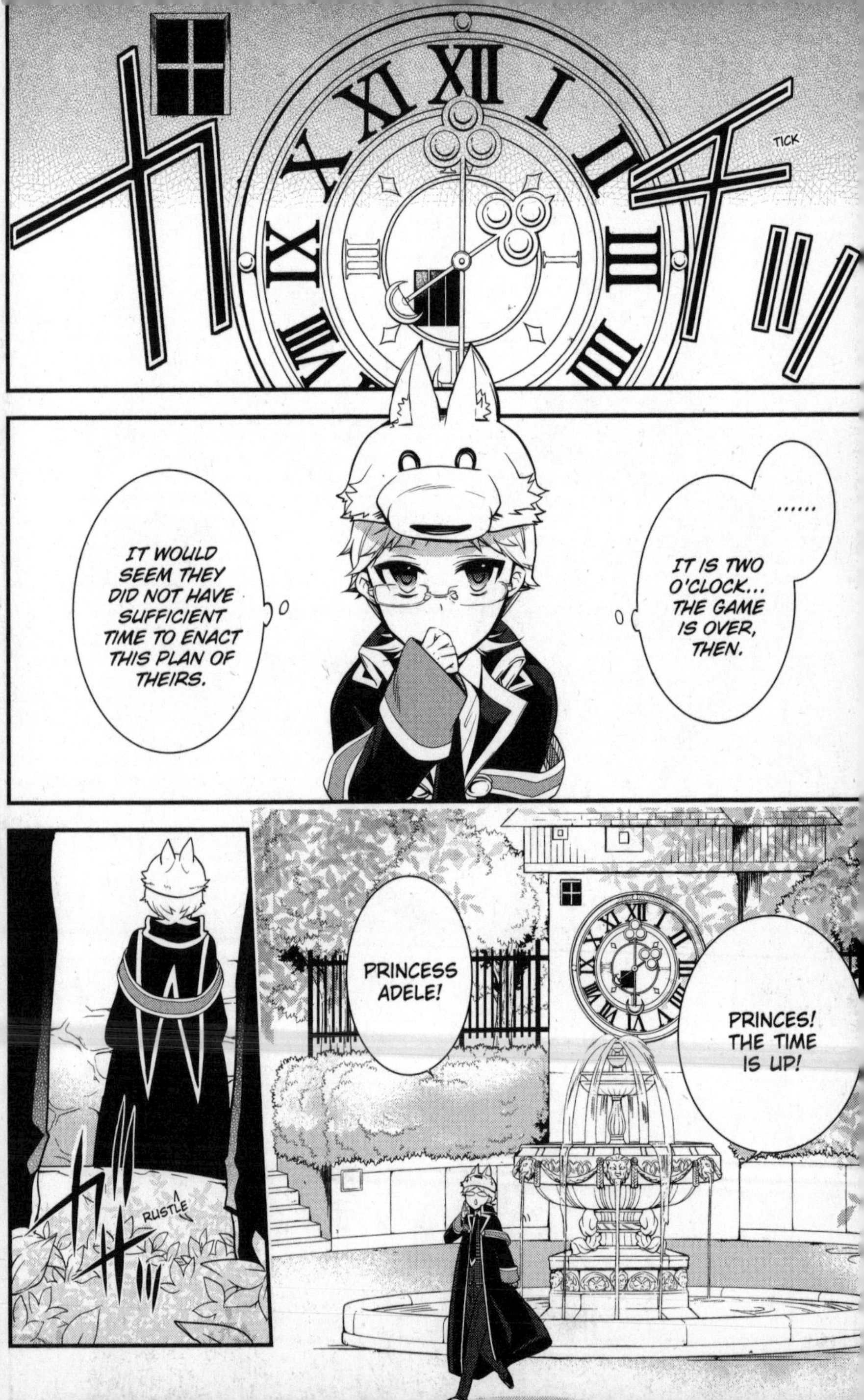
TICK
......
IT IS TWO O'CLOCK... THE GAME IS OVER, THEN.
IT WOULD SEEM THEY DID NOT HAVE SUFFICIENT TIME TO ENACT THIS PLAN OF THEIRS.
PRINCES! THE TIME IS UP!
PRINCESS ADELE!
RUSTLE

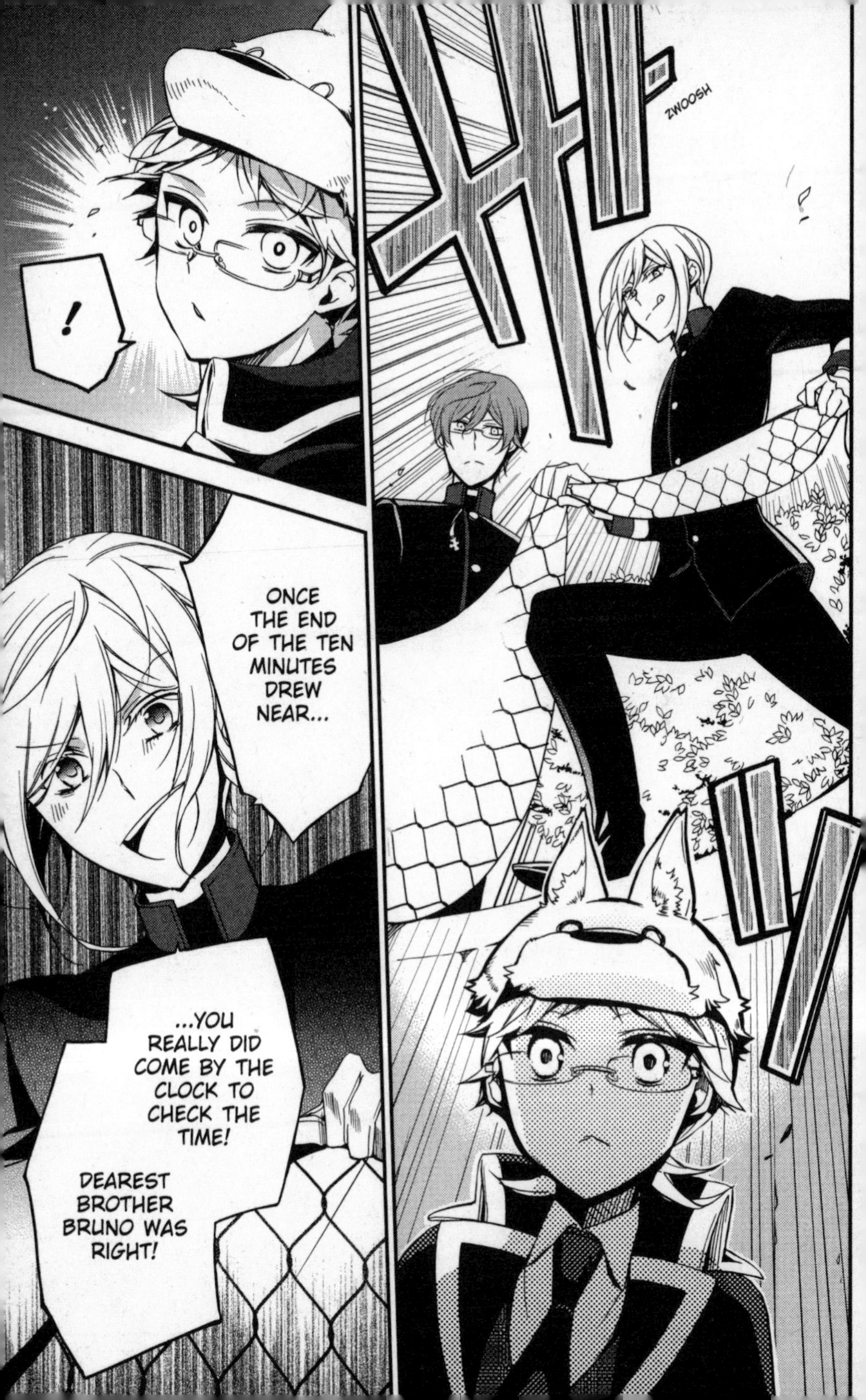
ZWOOSH
!
ONCE THE END OF THE TEN MINUTES DREW NEAR...
...YOU REALLY DID COME BY THE CLOCK TO CHECK THE TIME!
DEAREST BROTHER BRUNO WAS RIGHT!

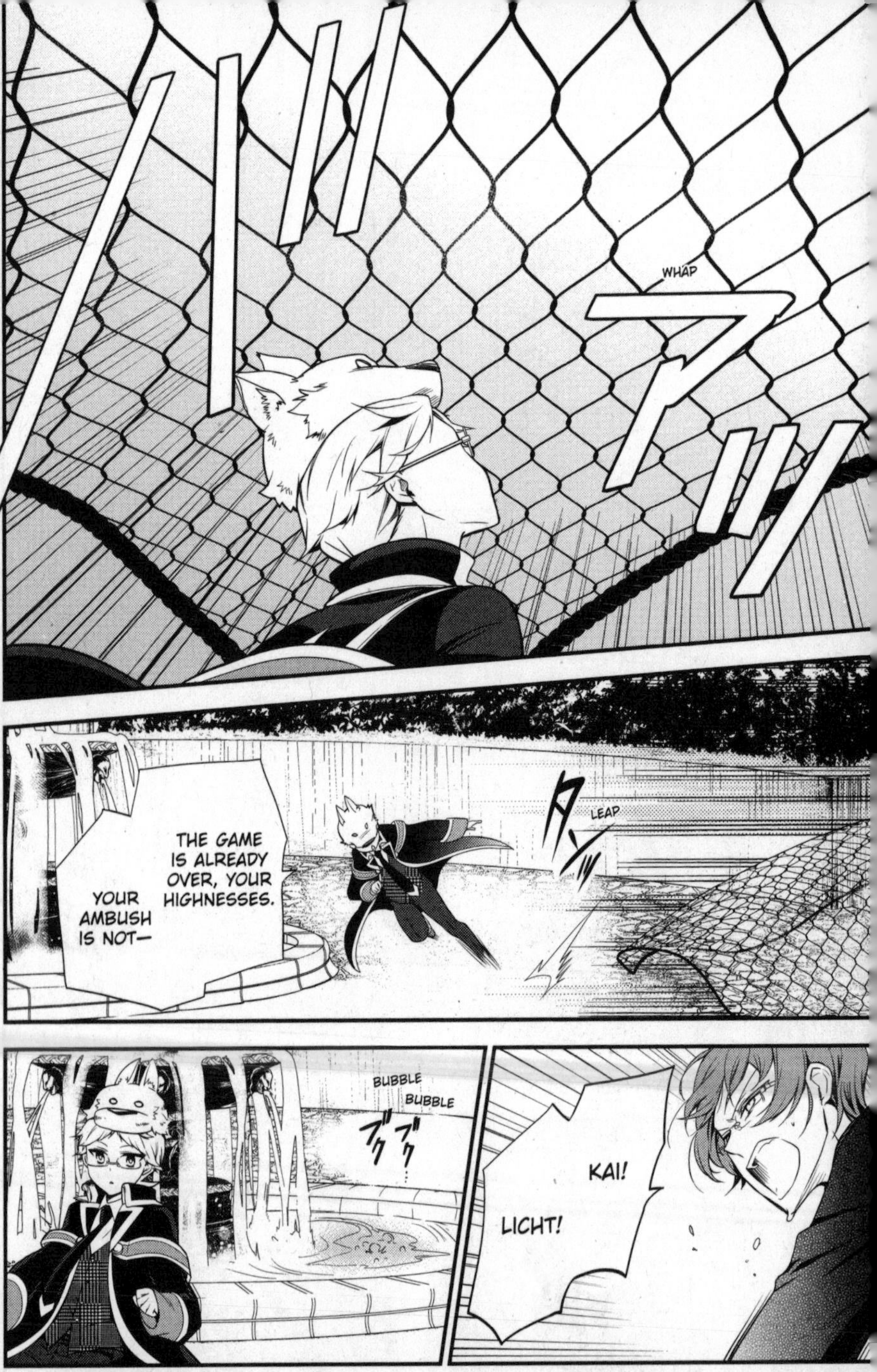
WHAP
THE GAME IS ALREADY OVER, YOUR HIGHNESSES.
YOUR AMBUSH IS NOT—
LEAP
KAI!
LICHT!
BUBBLE
BUBBLE

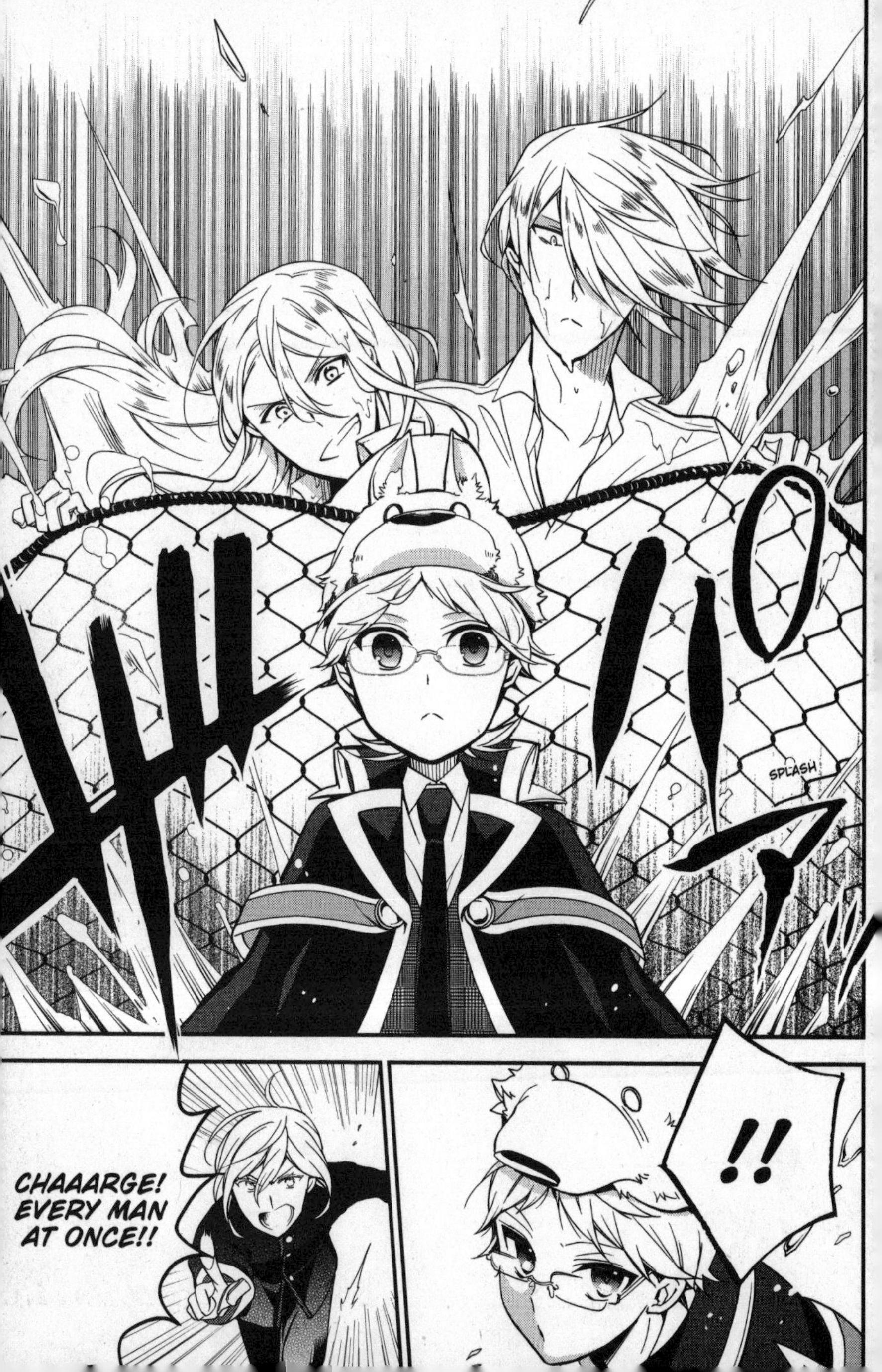
SPLASH
!!
CHAAARGE! EVERY MAN AT ONCE!!

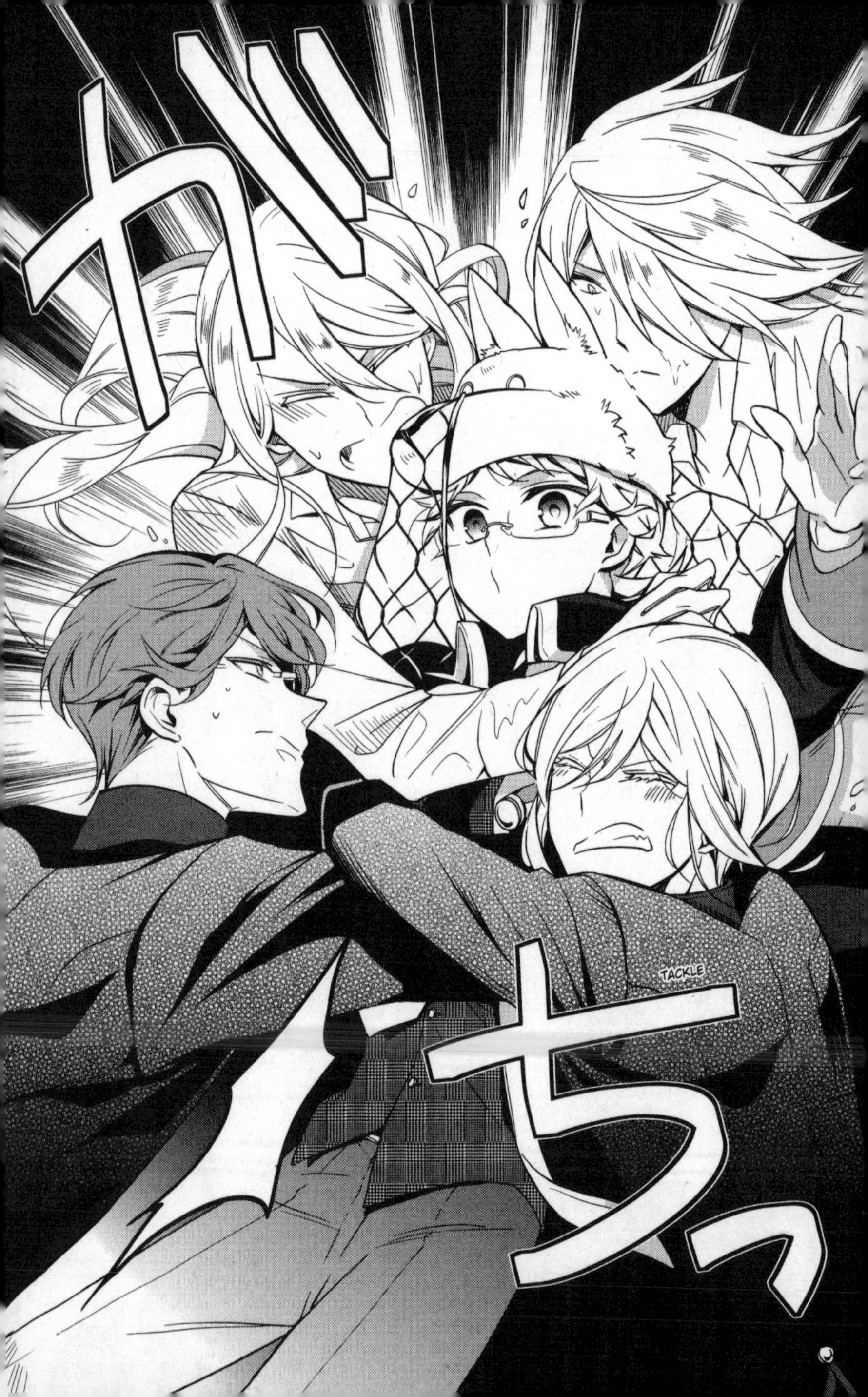
ガッ
TACKLE
ちっ

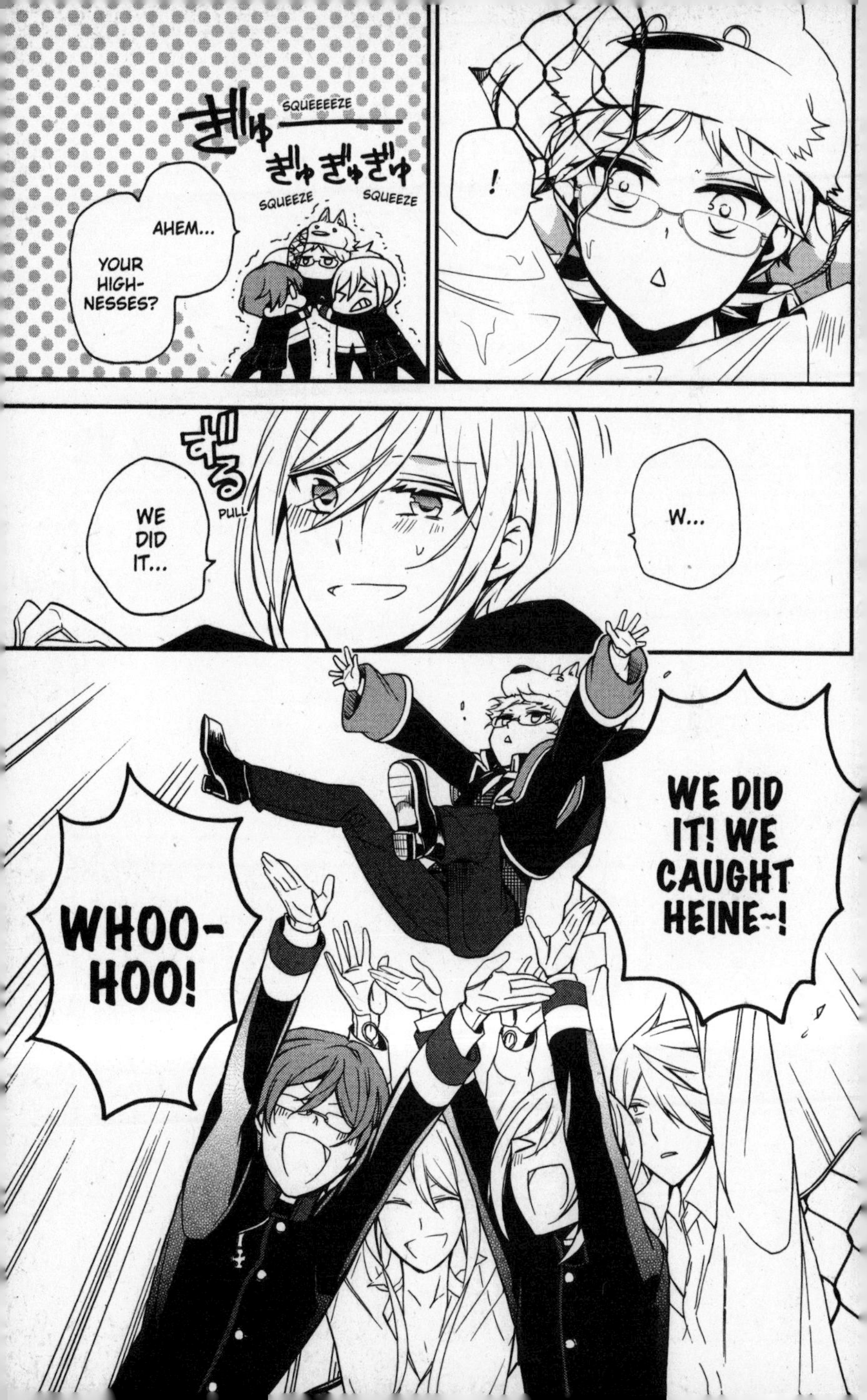
!
ぎゅーーー
SQUEEEEZE
ぎゅぎゅぎゅ
SQUEEZE
SQUEEZE
AHEM...
YOUR HIGHNESSES?
W...
ずる
PULL
WE DID IT...
WE DID IT! WE CAUGHT HEINE~!
WHOO-HOO!

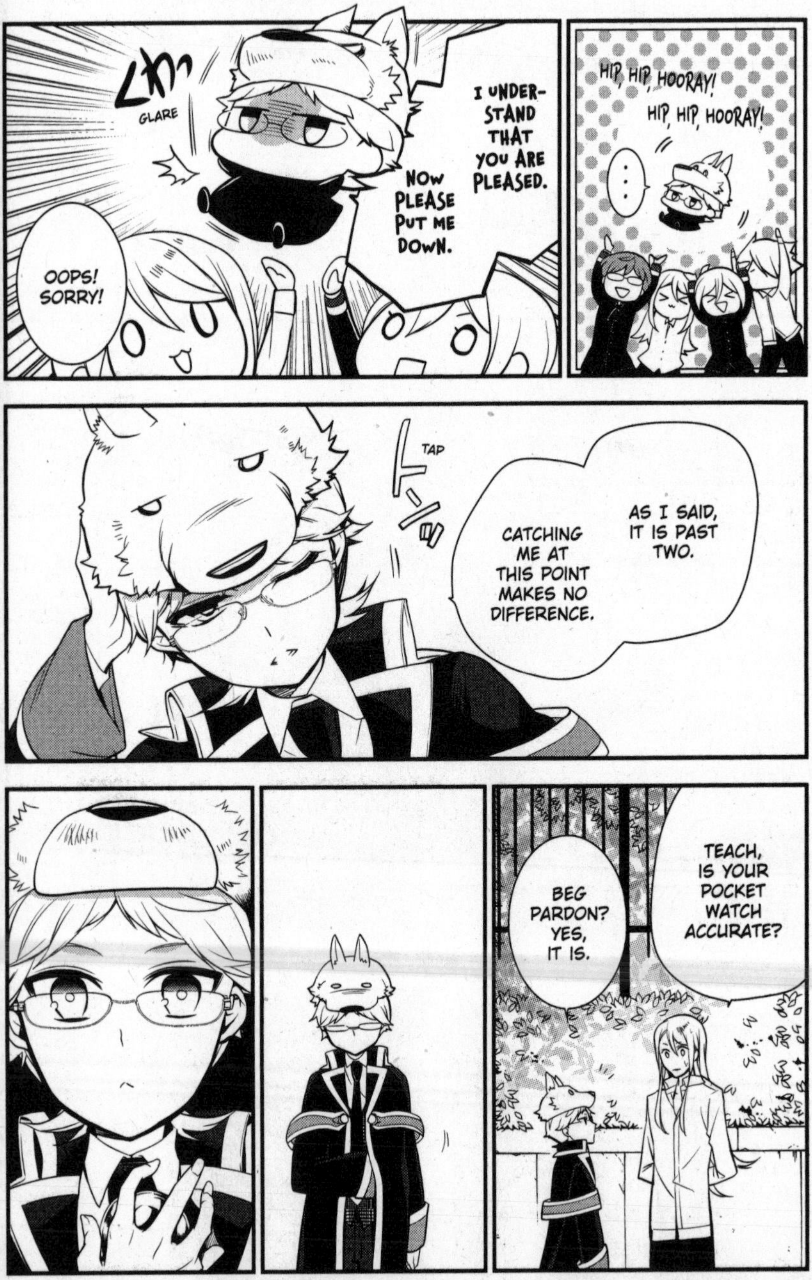
HIP, HIP, HOORAY!
HIP, HIP, HOORAY!
...
I UNDER-STAND THAT YOU ARE PLEASED.
NOW PLEASE PUT ME DOWN.
GLARE
OOPS! SORRY!
TAP
AS I SAID, IT IS PAST TWO.
CATCHING ME AT THIS POINT MAKES NO DIFFERENCE.
TEACH, IS YOUR POCKET WATCH ACCURATE?
BEG PARDON? YES, IT IS.

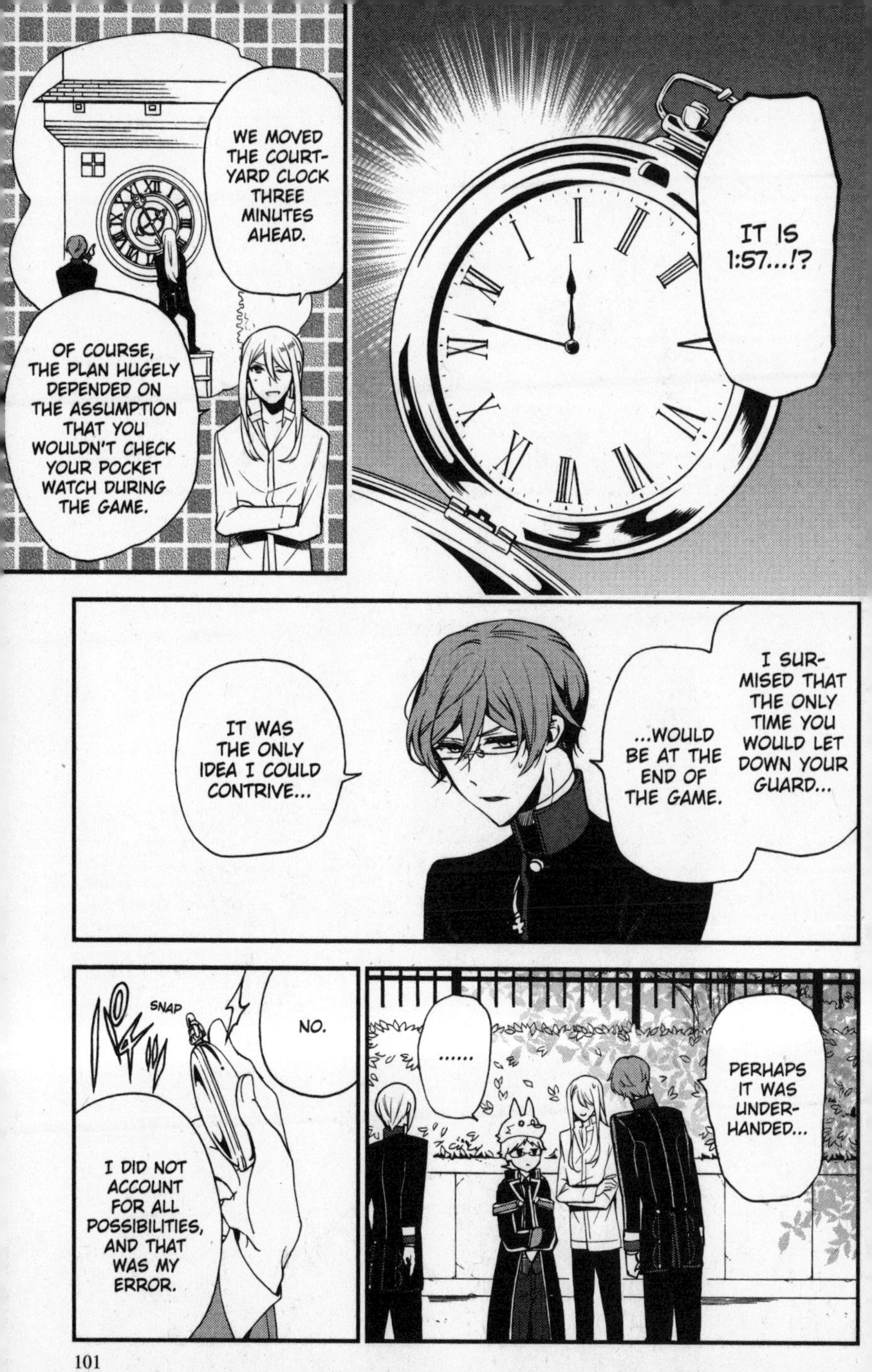
IT IS 1:57...!?
WE MOVED THE COURT-YARD CLOCK THREE MINUTES AHEAD.
OF COURSE, THE PLAN HUGELY DEPENDED ON THE ASSUMPTION THAT YOU WOULDN'T CHECK YOUR POCKET WATCH DURING THE GAME.
I SUR-MISED THAT THE ONLY TIME YOU WOULD LET DOWN YOUR GUARD...
...WOULD BE AT THE END OF THE GAME.
IT WAS THE ONLY IDEA I COULD CONTRIVE...
PERHAPS IT WAS UNDER-HANDED...
......
NO.
SNAP
I DID NOT ACCOUNT FOR ALL POSSIBILITIES, AND THAT WAS MY ERROR.

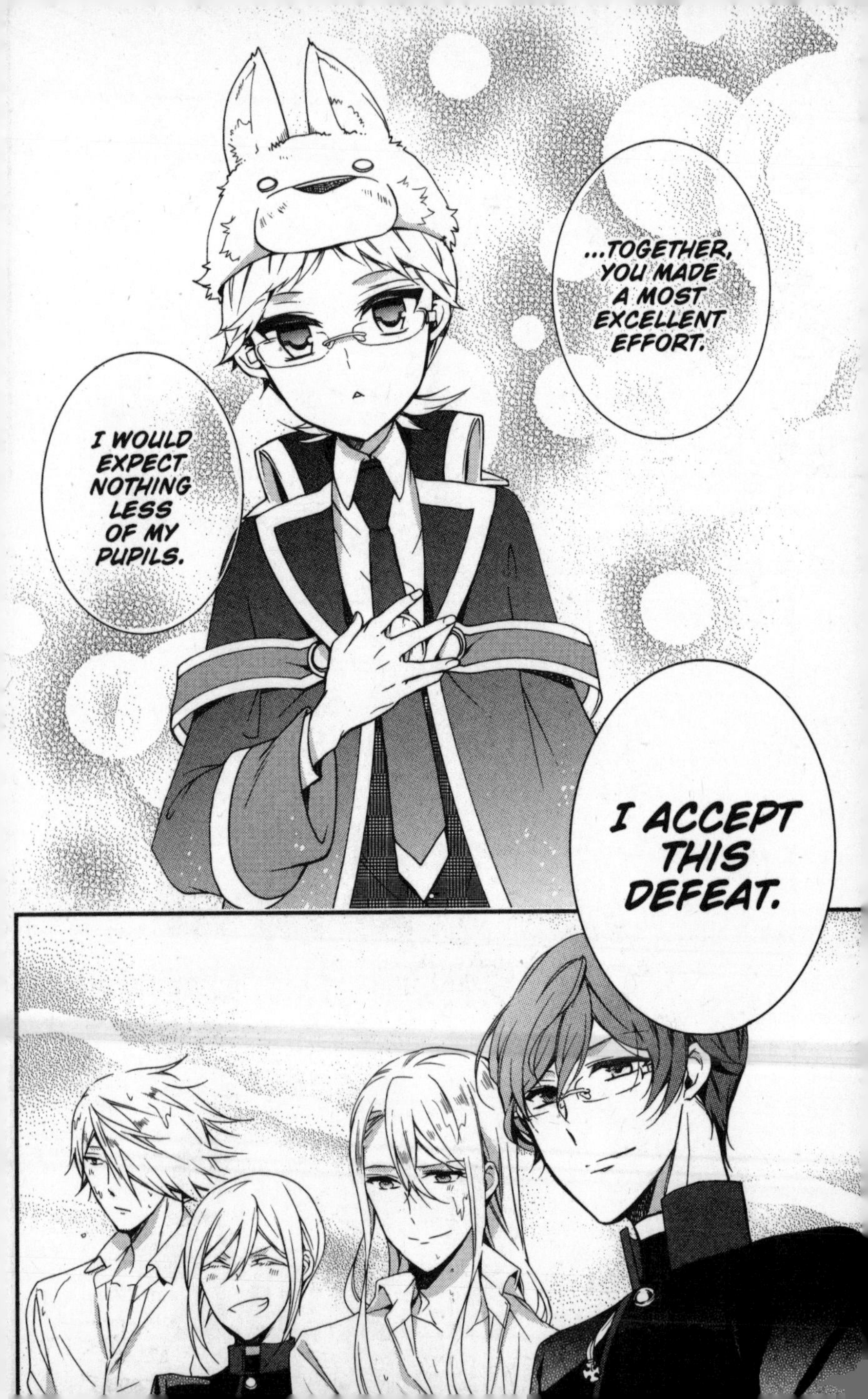
...TOGETHER, YOU MADE A MOST EXCELLENT EFFORT.
I WOULD EXPECT NOTHING LESS OF MY PUPILS.
I ACCEPT THIS DEFEAT.

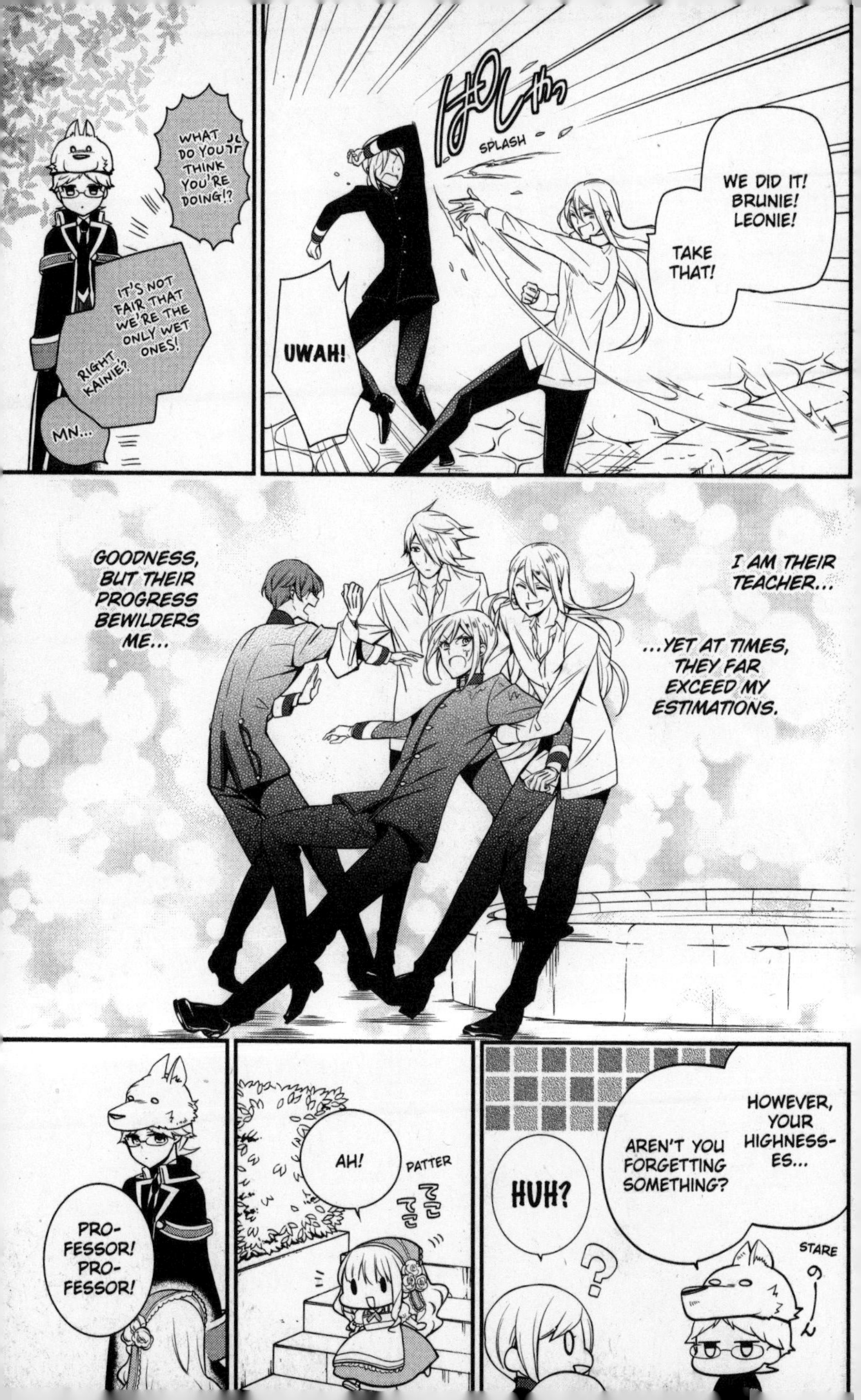
SPLASH
WE DID IT! BRUNIE! LEONIE!
TAKE THAT!
UWAH!
WHAT DO YOU THINK YOU'RE DOING!?
IT'S NOT FAIR THAT WE'RE THE ONLY WET ONES! RIGHT, KAINIE?
MN...
I AM THEIR TEACHER...
...YET AT TIMES, THEY FAR EXCEED MY ESTIMATIONS.
GOODNESS, BUT THEIR PROGRESS BEWILDERS ME...
HOWEVER, YOUR HIGHNESS-ES...
AREN'T YOU FORGETTING SOMETHING?
STARE
HUH?
AH!
PATTER
PRO-FESSOR! PRO-FESSOR!

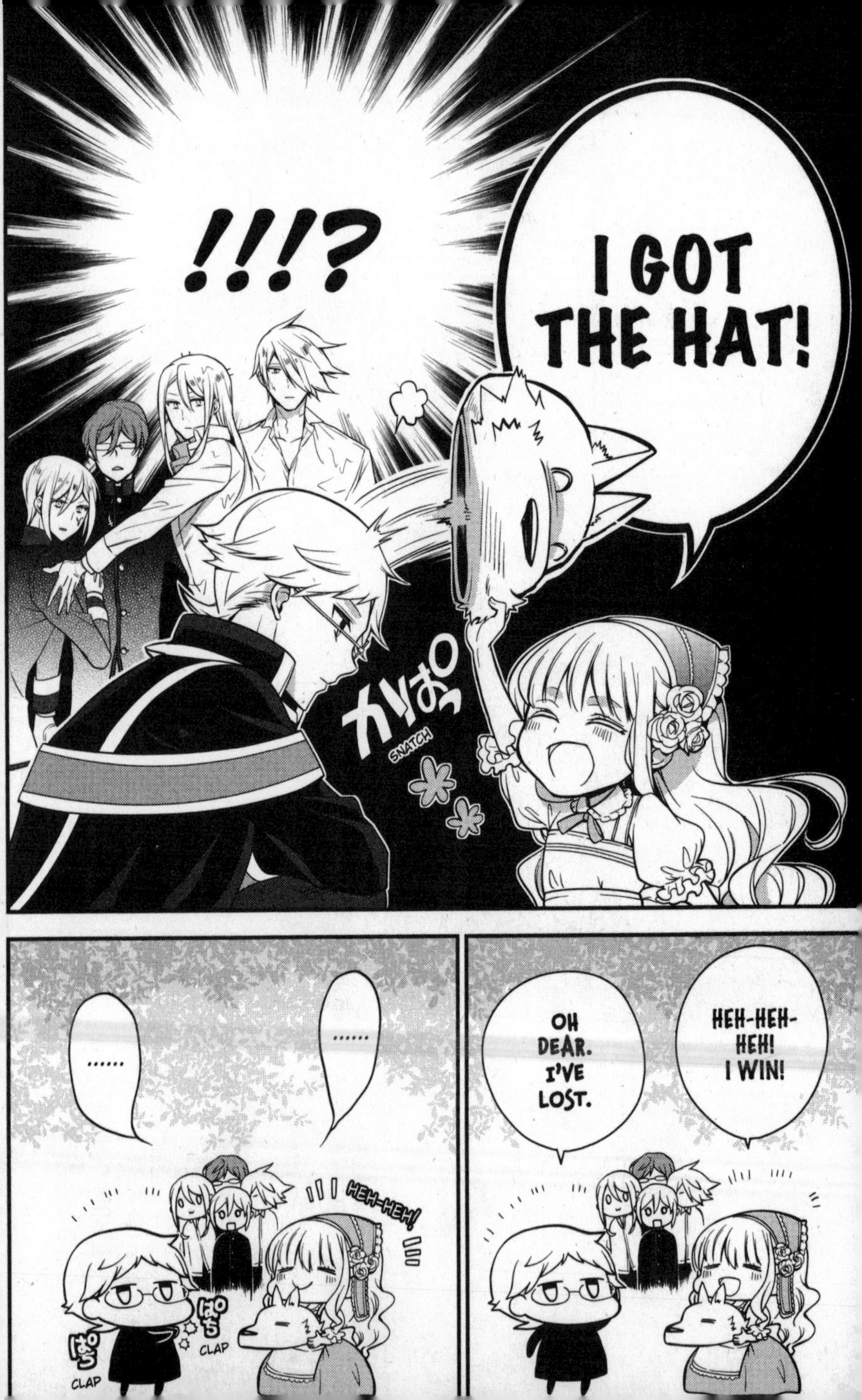
I GOT THE HAT!
!!!?
SNATCH
HEH-HEH-HEH! I WIN!
OH DEAR. I'VE LOST.
......
......
HEH-HEH!
CLAP
CLAP

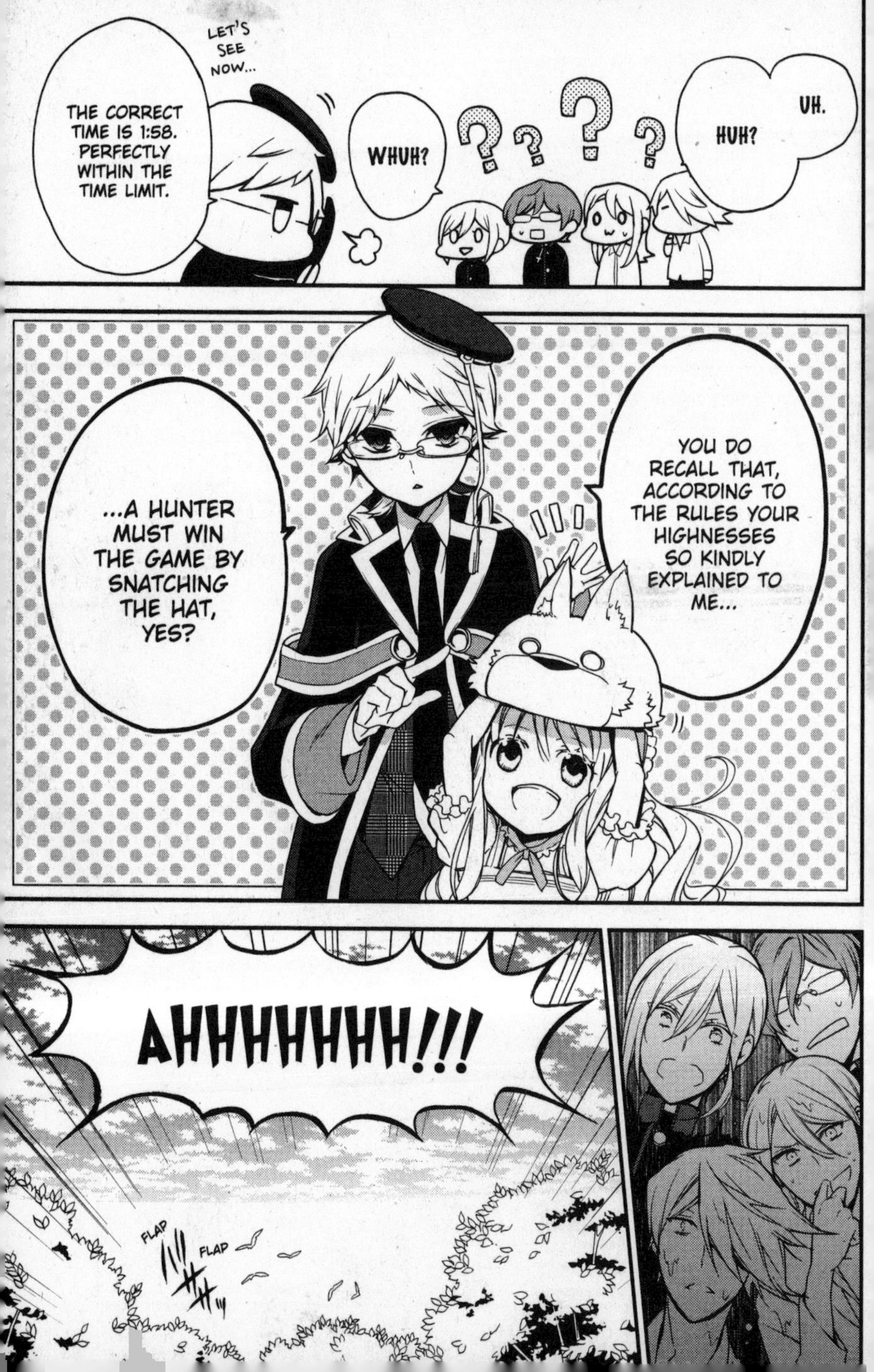
UH. HUH?
WHUH?
LET'S SEE NOW...
THE CORRECT TIME IS 1:58. PERFECTLY WITHIN THE TIME LIMIT.
YOU DO RECALL THAT, ACCORDING TO THE RULES YOUR HIGHNESSES SO KINDLY EXPLAINED TO ME...
...A HUNTER MUST WIN THE GAME BY SNATCHING THE HAT, YES?
AHHHHHHH!!!
FLAP
FLAP

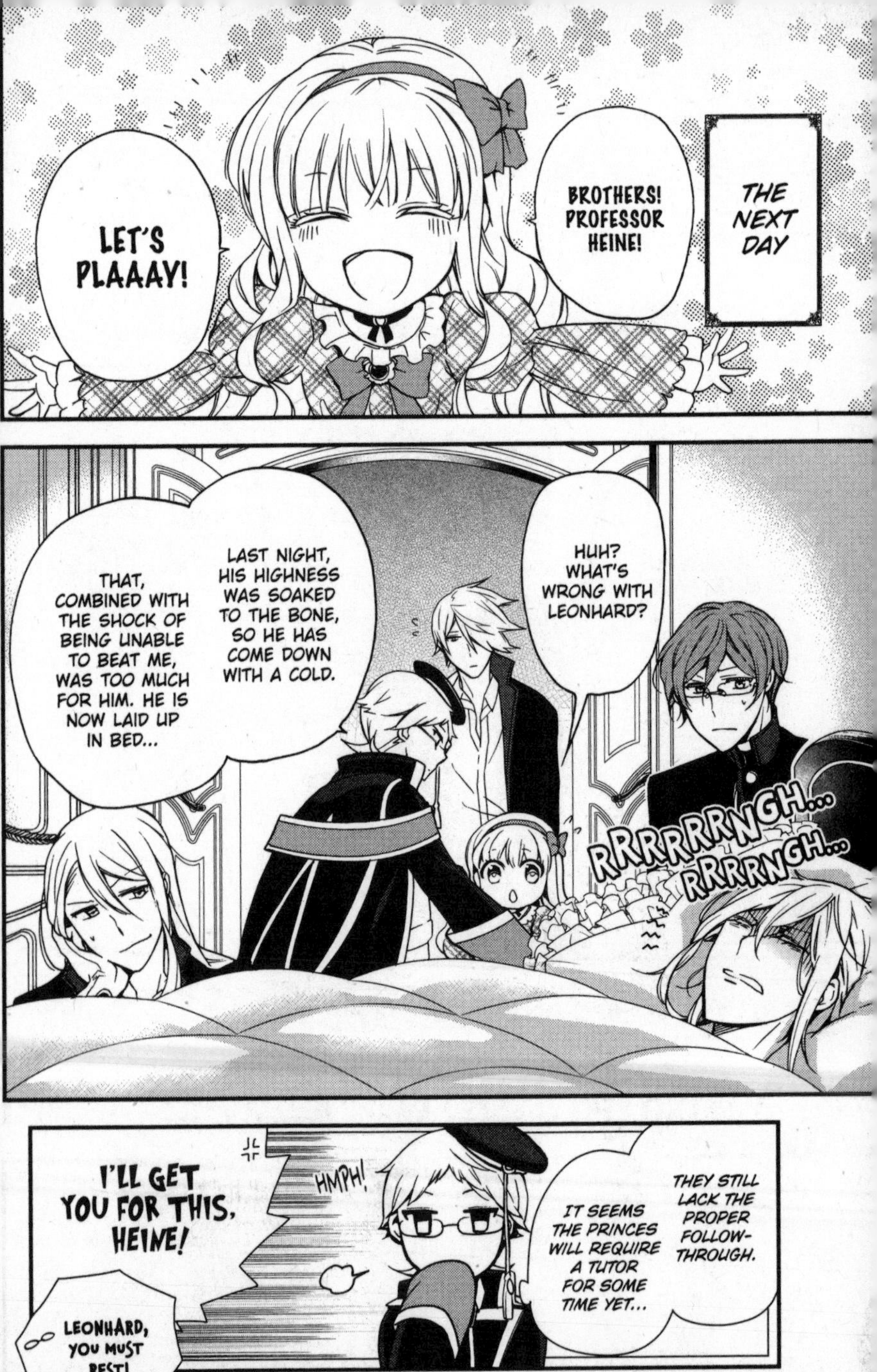
THE NEXT DAY
BROTHERS! PROFESSOR HEINE!
LET'S PLAAAY!
HUH? WHAT'S WRONG WITH LEONHARD?
LAST NIGHT, HIS HIGHNESS WAS SOAKED TO THE BONE, SO HE HAS COME DOWN WITH A COLD.
THAT, COMBINED WITH THE SHOCK OF BEING UNABLE TO BEAT ME, WAS TOO MUCH FOR HIM. HE IS NOW LAID UP IN BED...
RRRRRRNGH... RRRRNGH...
THEY STILL LACK THE PROPER FOLLOW-THROUGH.
IT SEEMS THE PRINCES WILL REQUIRE A TUTOR FOR SOME TIME YET...
HMPH!
I'LL GET YOU FOR THIS, HEINE!
LEONHARD, YOU MUST REST!

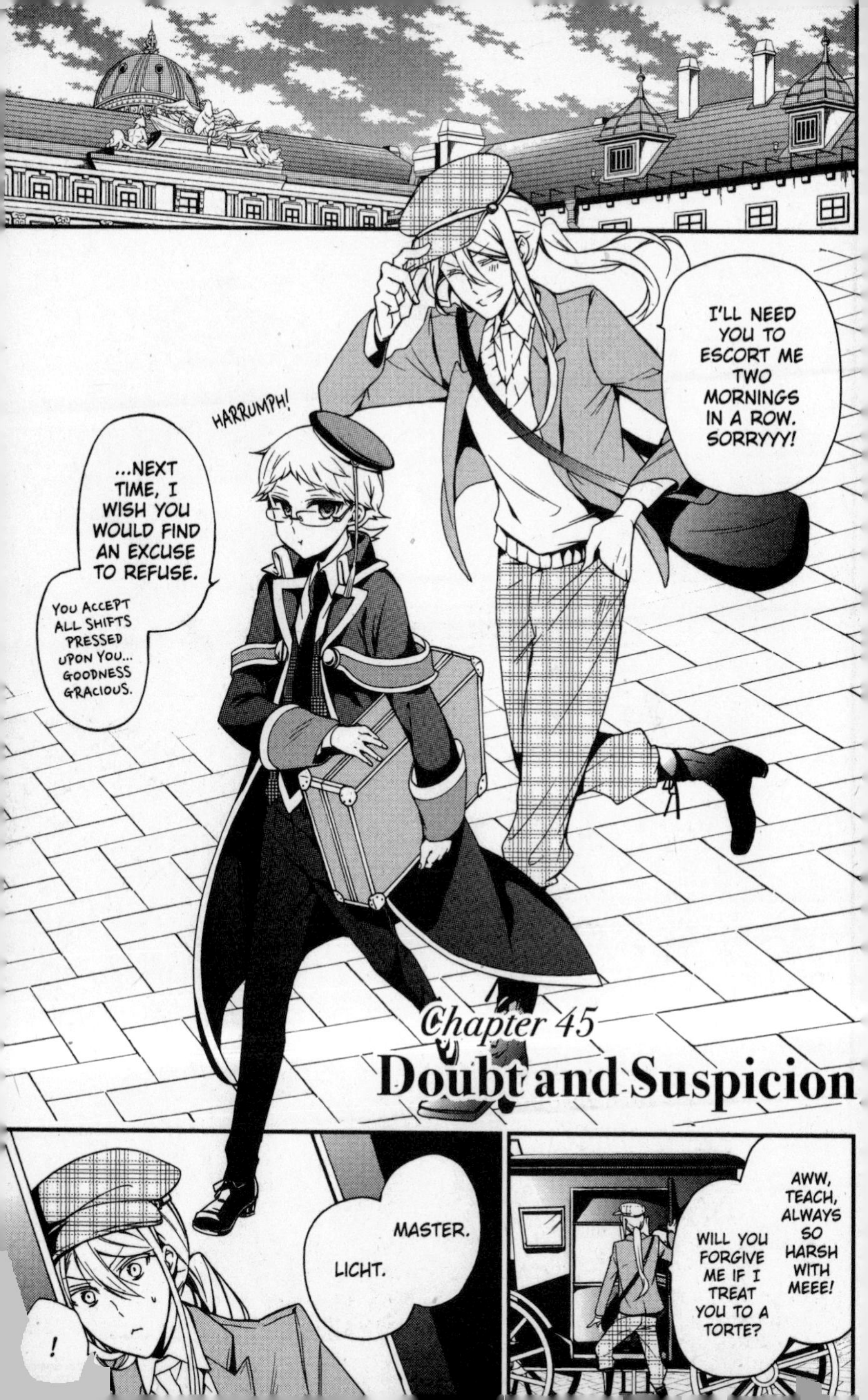
I'LL NEED YOU TO ESCORT ME TWO MORNINGS IN A ROW. SORRYYY!
HARRUMPH!
...NEXT TIME, I WISH YOU WOULD FIND AN EXCUSE TO REFUSE.
YOU ACCEPT ALL SHIFTS PRESSED UPON YOU... GOODNESS GRACIOUS.
Chapter 45
Doubt and Suspicion
AWW, TEACH, ALWAYS SO HARSH WITH MEEE!
WILL YOU FORGIVE ME IF I TREAT YOU TO A TORTE?
MASTER.
LICHT.
!

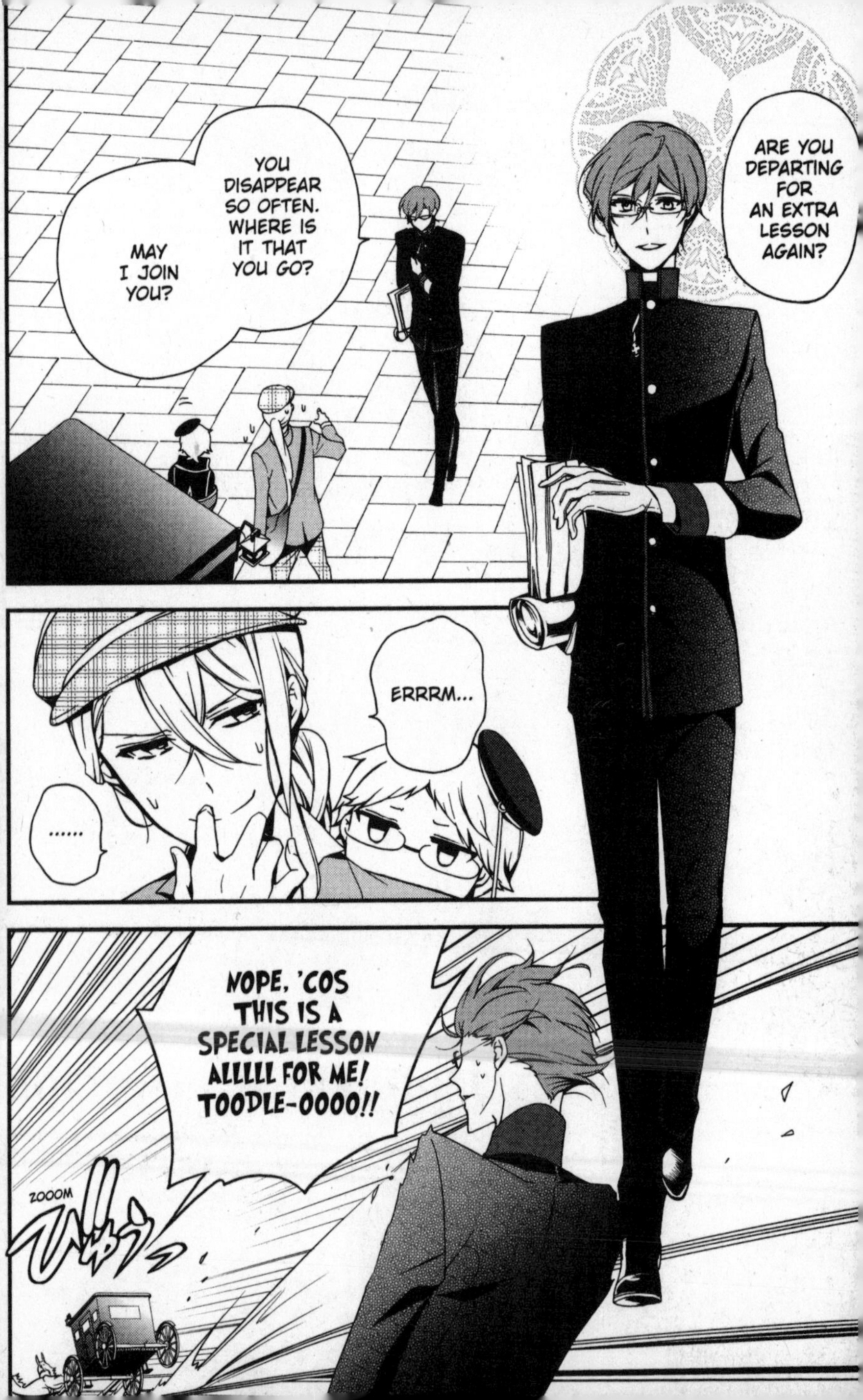
ARE YOU DEPARTING FOR AN EXTRA LESSON AGAIN?
YOU DISAPPEAR SO OFTEN. WHERE IS IT THAT YOU GO?
MAY I JOIN YOU?
ERRRM...
......
NOPE, 'COS THIS IS A SPECIAL LESSON ALLLLL FOR ME! TOODLE-OOOO!!
ZOOOM

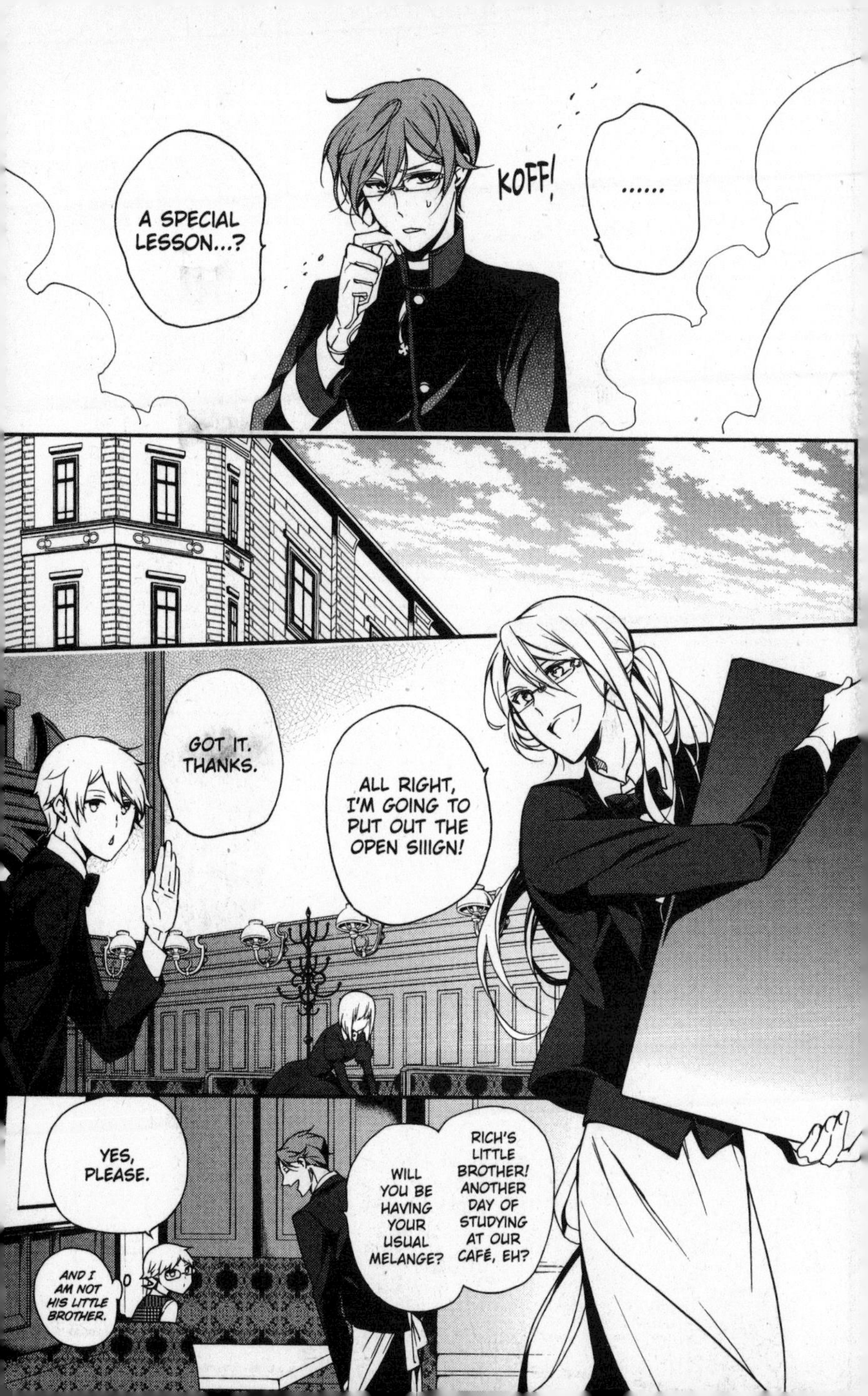
......
KOFF!
A SPECIAL LESSON...?
ALL RIGHT, I'M GOING TO PUT OUT THE OPEN SIIIGN!
GOT IT. THANKS.
RICH'S LITTLE BROTHER! ANOTHER DAY OF STUDYING AT OUR CAFÉ, EH?
WILL YOU BE HAVING YOUR USUAL MELANGE?
YES, PLEASE.
AND I AM NOT HIS LITTLE BROTHER.

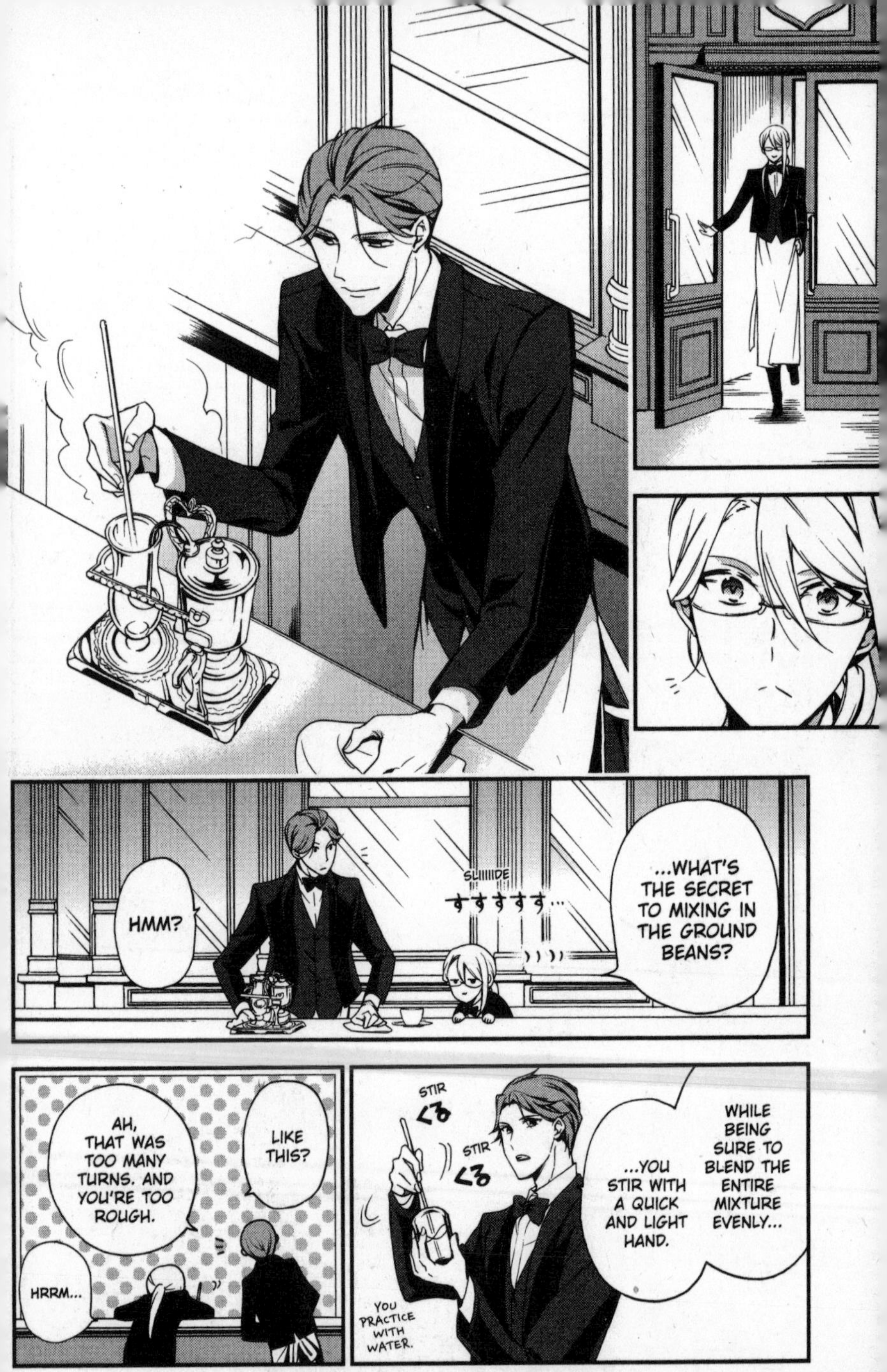
...WHAT'S THE SECRET TO MIXING IN THE GROUND BEANS?
SLIIIIDE
すすすすす…
HMM?
WHILE BEING SURE TO BLEND THE ENTIRE MIXTURE EVENLY...
...YOU STIR WITH A QUICK AND LIGHT HAND.
STIR
くる
STIR
くる
YOU PRACTICE WITH WATER.
LIKE THIS?
AH, THAT WAS TOO MANY TURNS. AND YOU'RE TOO ROUGH.
HRRM...

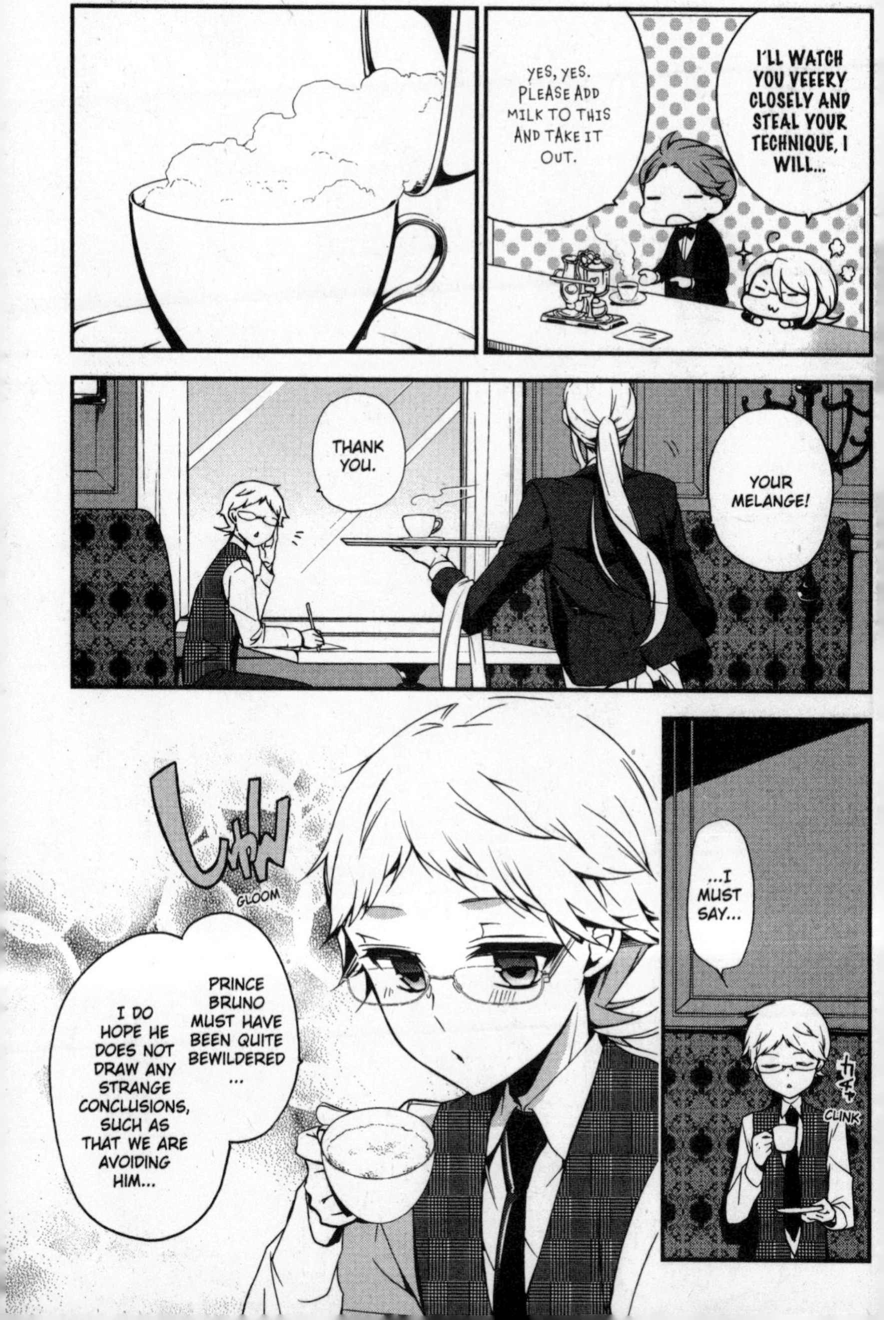
I'LL WATCH YOU VEEERY CLOSELY AND STEAL YOUR TECHNIQUE, I WILL...
YES, YES. PLEASE ADD MILK TO THIS AND TAKE IT OUT.
YOUR MELANGE!
THANK YOU.
...I MUST SAY...
CLINK
PRINCE BRUNO MUST HAVE BEEN QUITE BEWILDERED...
I DO HOPE HE DOES NOT DRAW ANY STRANGE CONCLUSIONS, SUCH AS THAT WE ARE AVOIDING HIM...
GLOOM

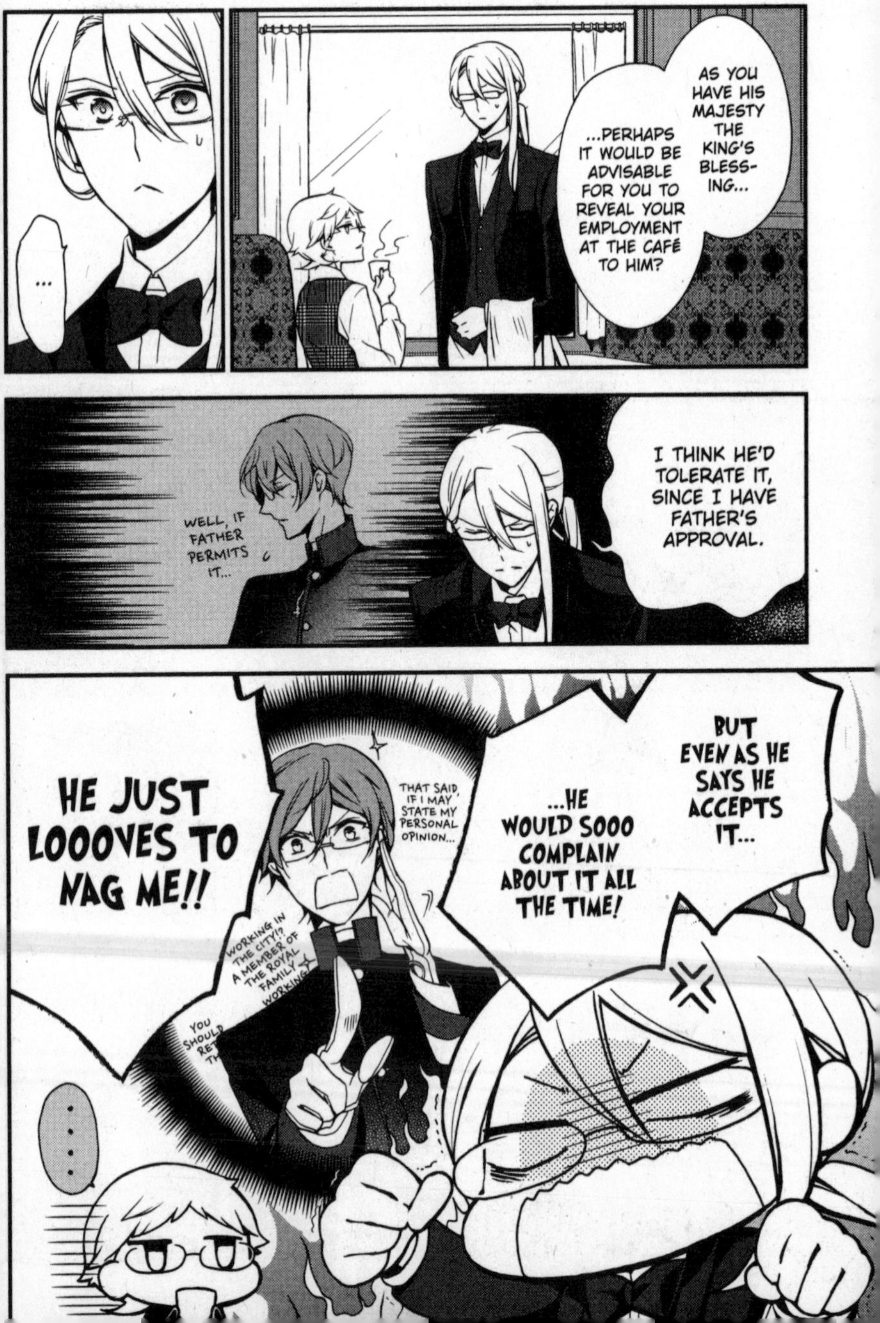
AS YOU HAVE HIS MAJESTY THE KING'S BLESSING...
...PERHAPS IT WOULD BE ADVISABLE FOR YOU TO REVEAL YOUR EMPLOYMENT AT THE CAFÉ TO HIM?
...
I THINK HE'D TOLERATE IT, SINCE I HAVE FATHER'S APPROVAL.
WELL, IF FATHER PERMITS IT...
BUT EVEN AS HE SAYS HE ACCEPTS IT...
...HE WOULD SOOO COMPLAIN ABOUT IT ALL THE TIME!
THAT SAID, IF I MAY STATE MY PERSONAL OPINION...
HE JUST LOOOVES TO NAG ME!!
WORKING IN THE CITY!? A MEMBER OF THE ROYAL FAMILY WORKING
YOU SHOULD
...

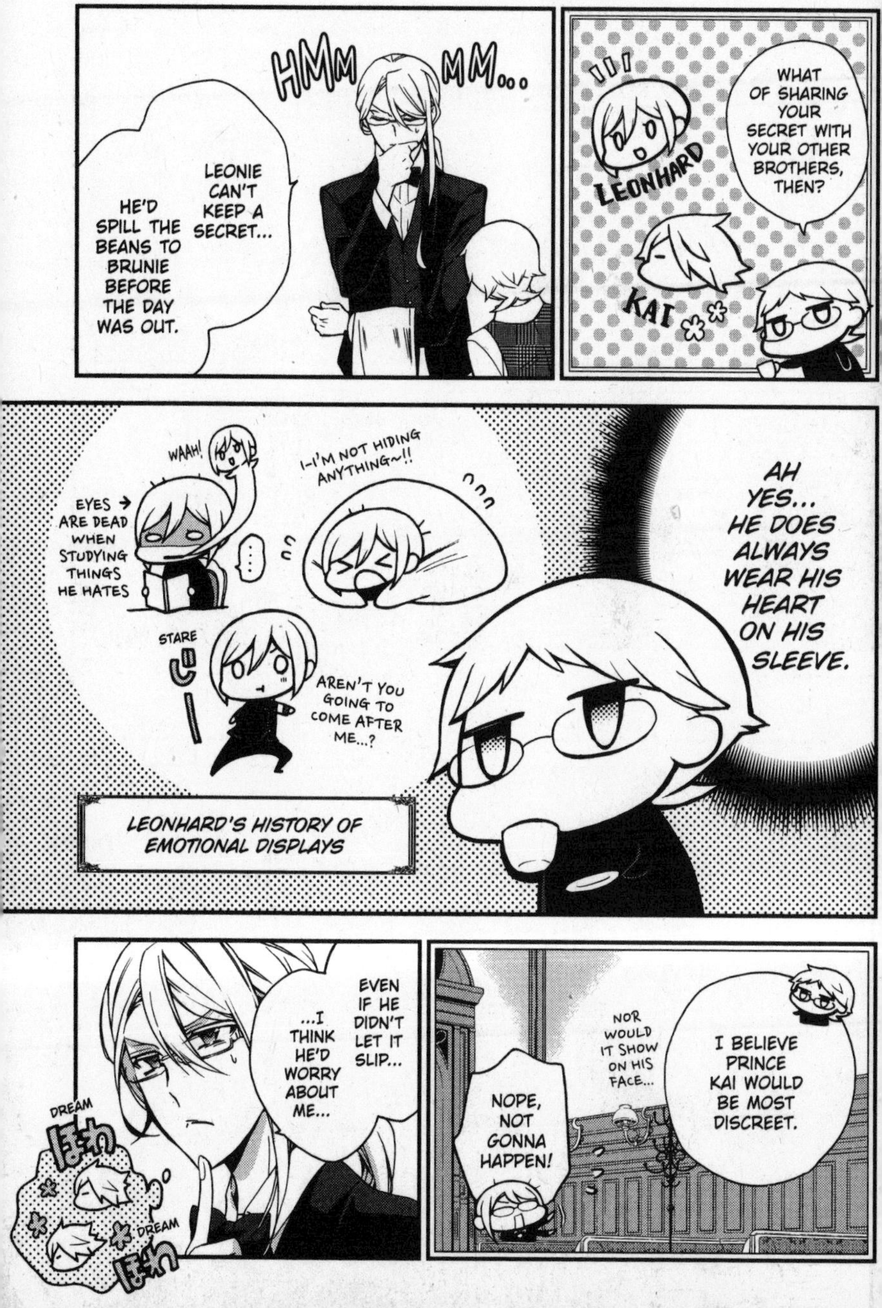
WHAT OF SHARING YOUR SECRET WITH YOUR OTHER BROTHERS, THEN?
LEONHARD
KAI
HMMMM...
LEONIE CAN'T KEEP A SECRET...
HE'D SPILL THE BEANS TO BRUNIE BEFORE THE DAY WAS OUT.
AH YES... HE DOES ALWAYS WEAR HIS HEART ON HIS SLEEVE.
I-I'M NOT HIDING ANYTHING~!!
WAAH!
EYES → ARE DEAD WHEN STUDYING THINGS HE HATES
...
STARE
AREN'T YOU GOING TO COME AFTER ME...?
LEONHARD'S HISTORY OF EMOTIONAL DISPLAYS
I BELIEVE PRINCE KAI WOULD BE MOST DISCREET.
NOR WOULD IT SHOW ON HIS FACE...
NOPE, NOT GONNA HAPPEN!
EVEN IF HE DIDN'T LET IT SLIP...
...I THINK HE'D WORRY ABOUT ME...
DREAM
DREAM

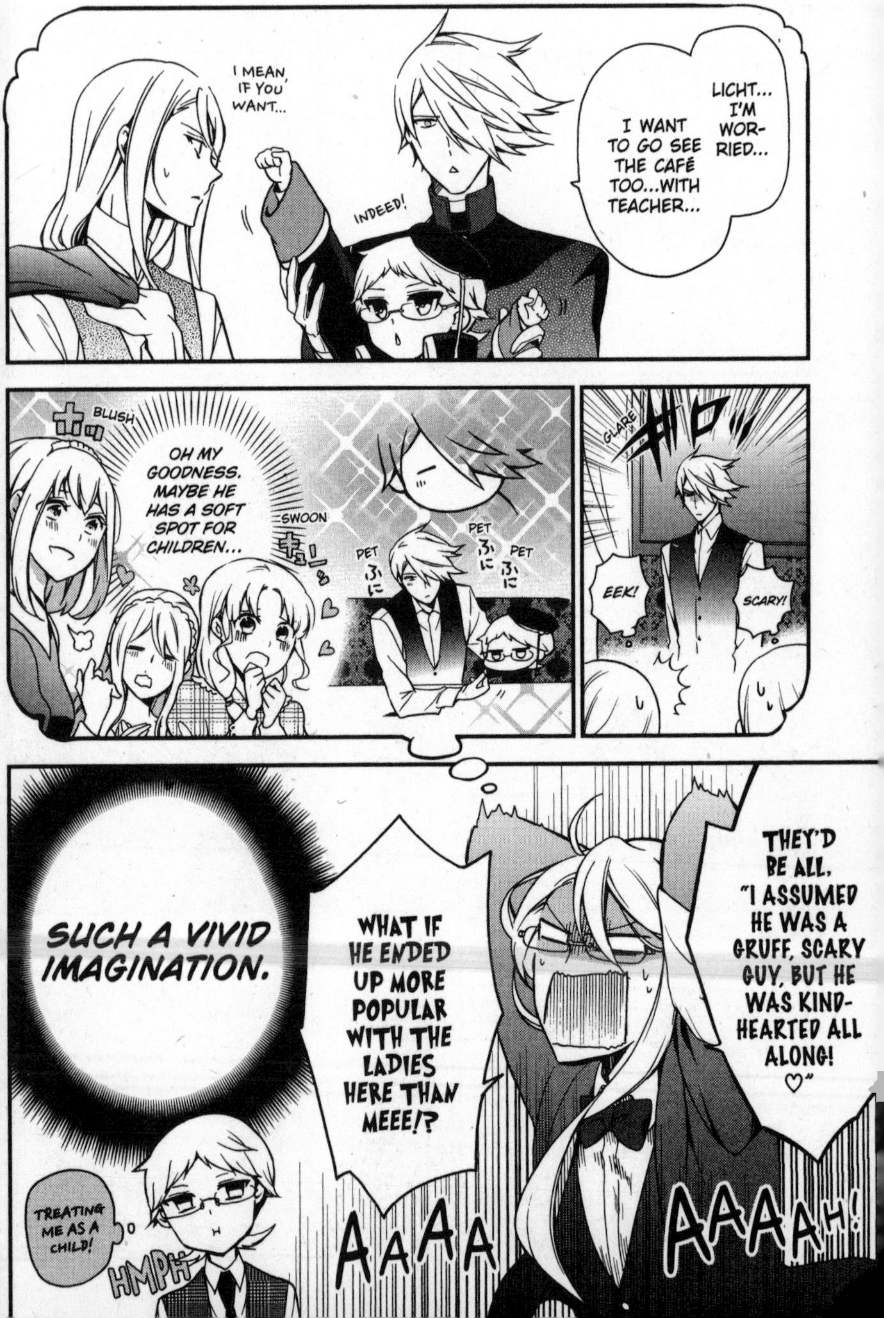
LICHT... I'M WOR-RIED...
I WANT TO GO SEE THE CAFÉ TOO...WITH TEACHER...
INDEED!
I MEAN, IF YOU WANT...
GLARE
EEK!
SCARY!
BLUSH
OH MY GOODNESS. MAYBE HE HAS A SOFT SPOT FOR CHILDREN...
SWOON
PET ふに
PET ふに
PET ふに
THEY'D BE ALL, "I ASSUMED HE WAS A GRUFF, SCARY GUY, BUT HE WAS KIND-HEARTED ALL ALONG! ♡"
AAAAH!
WHAT IF HE ENDED UP MORE POPULAR WITH THE LADIES HERE THAN MEEE!?
AAAA
SUCH A VIVID IMAGINATION.
TREATING ME AS A CHILD!
HMPH

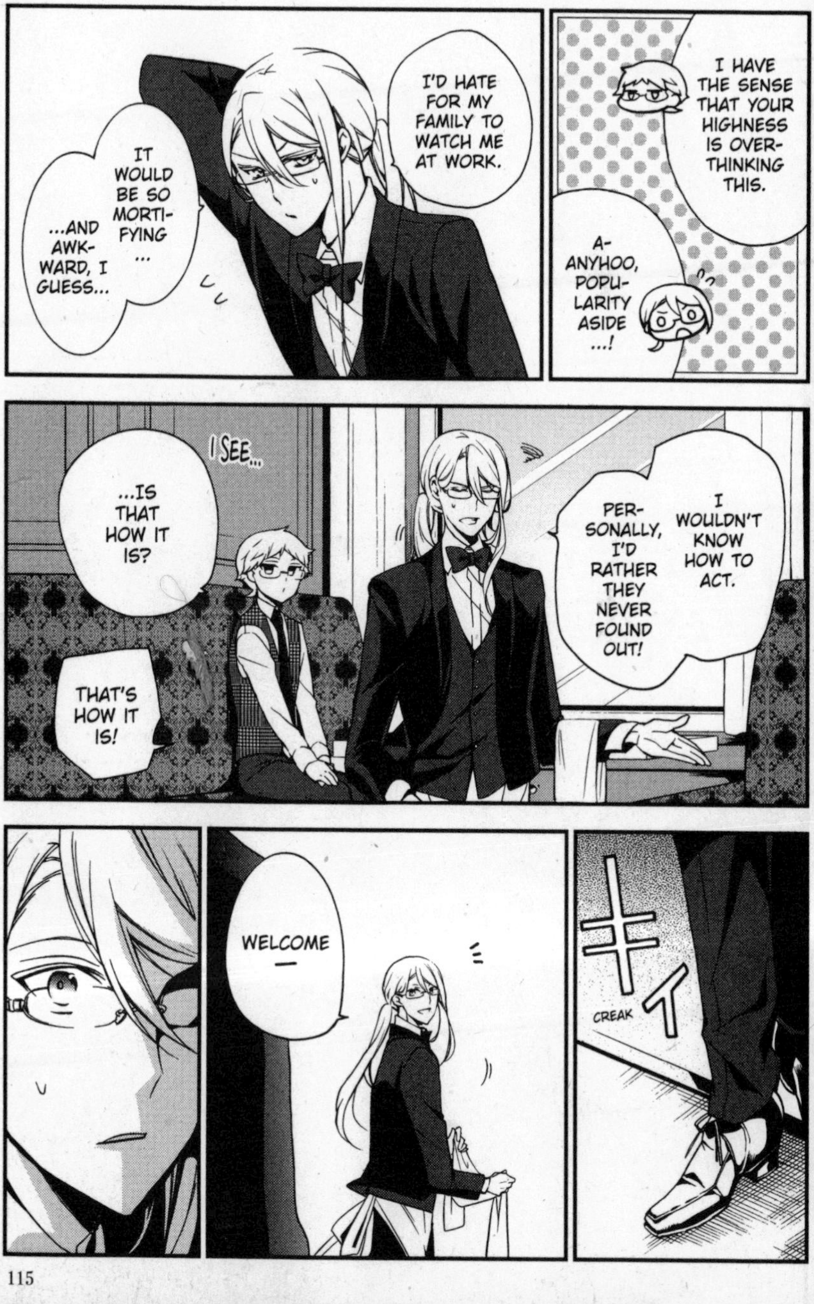
I HAVE THE SENSE THAT YOUR HIGHNESS IS OVER-THINKING THIS.
A-ANYHOO, POPU-LARITY ASIDE ...!
I'D HATE FOR MY FAMILY TO WATCH ME AT WORK.
IT WOULD BE SO MORTI-FYING ...
...AND AWK-WARD, I GUESS...
I WOULDN'T KNOW HOW TO ACT.
PER-SONALLY, I'D RATHER THEY NEVER FOUND OUT!
I SEE...
...IS THAT HOW IT IS?
THAT'S HOW IT IS!
CREAK
WELCOME—

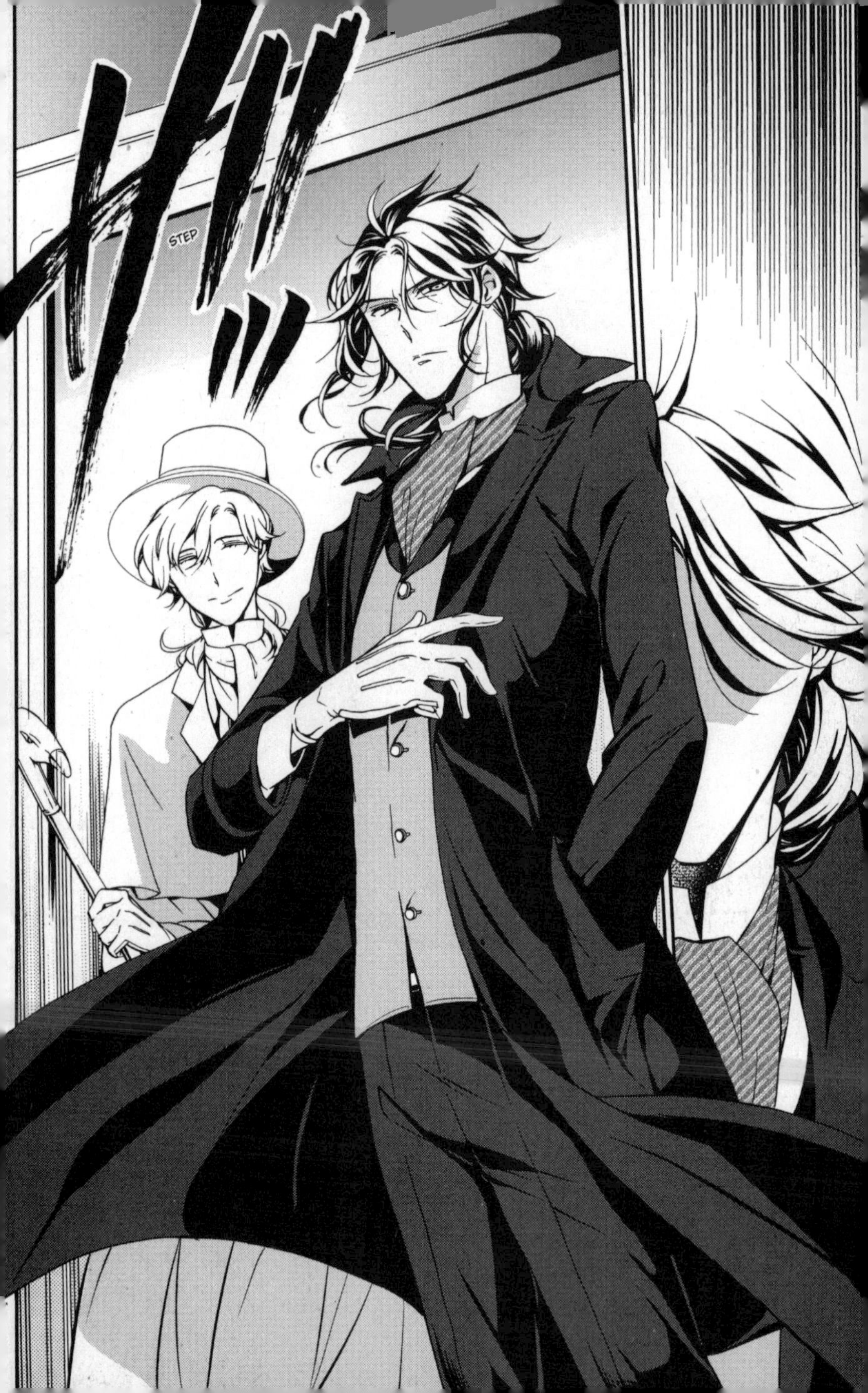
STEP

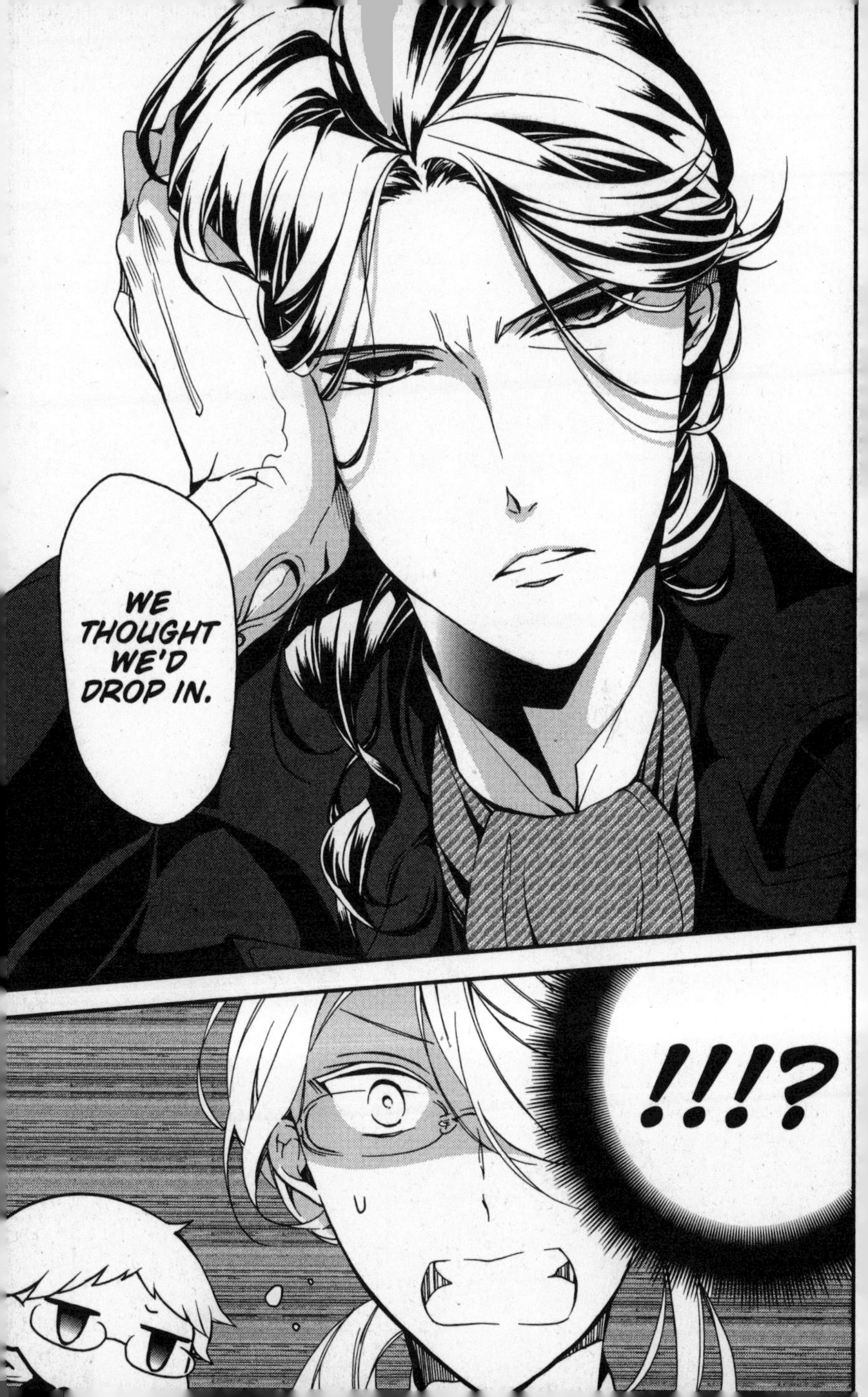
WE THOUGHT WE'D DROP IN.
!!!?

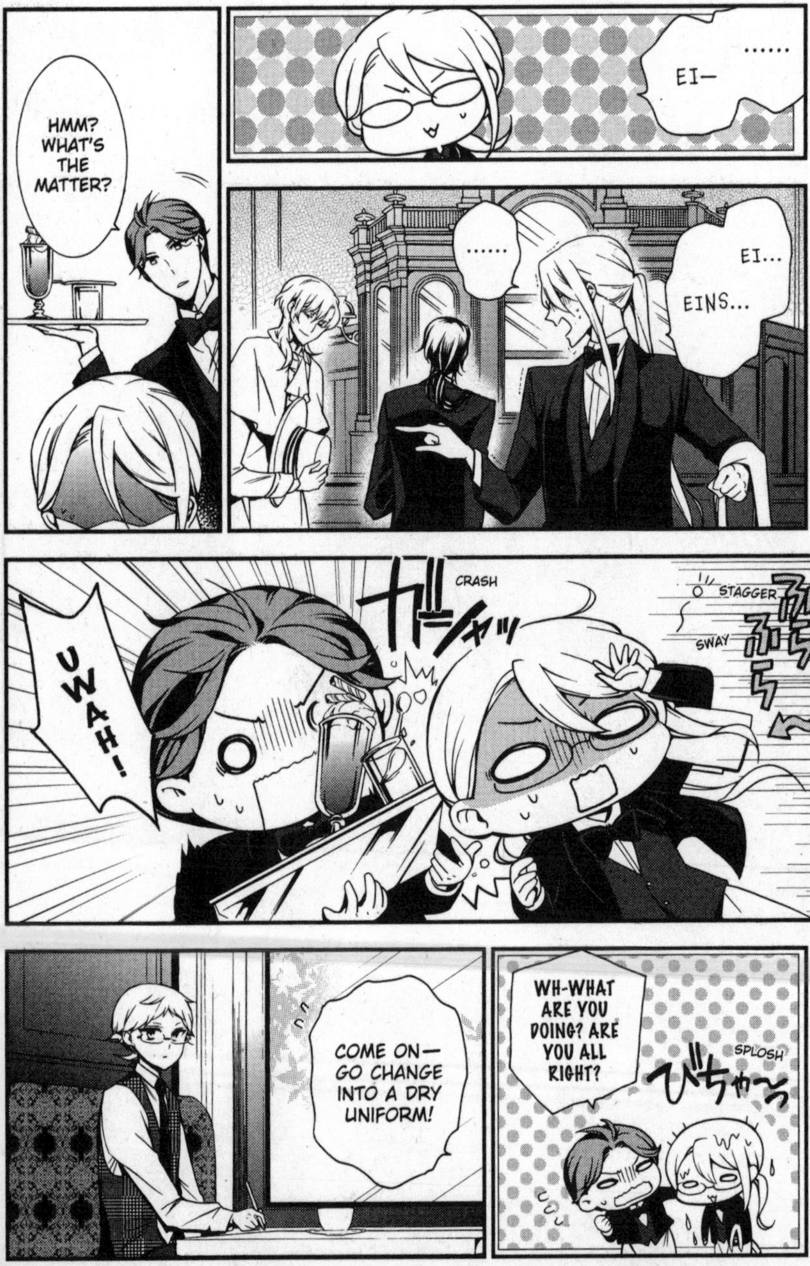
......
EI—
EI... EINS...
......
HMM? WHAT'S THE MATTER?
STAGGER
SWAY
CRASH
UWAH!
SPLOSH
WH-WHAT ARE YOU DOING? ARE YOU ALL RIGHT?
COME ON— GO CHANGE INTO A DRY UNIFORM!

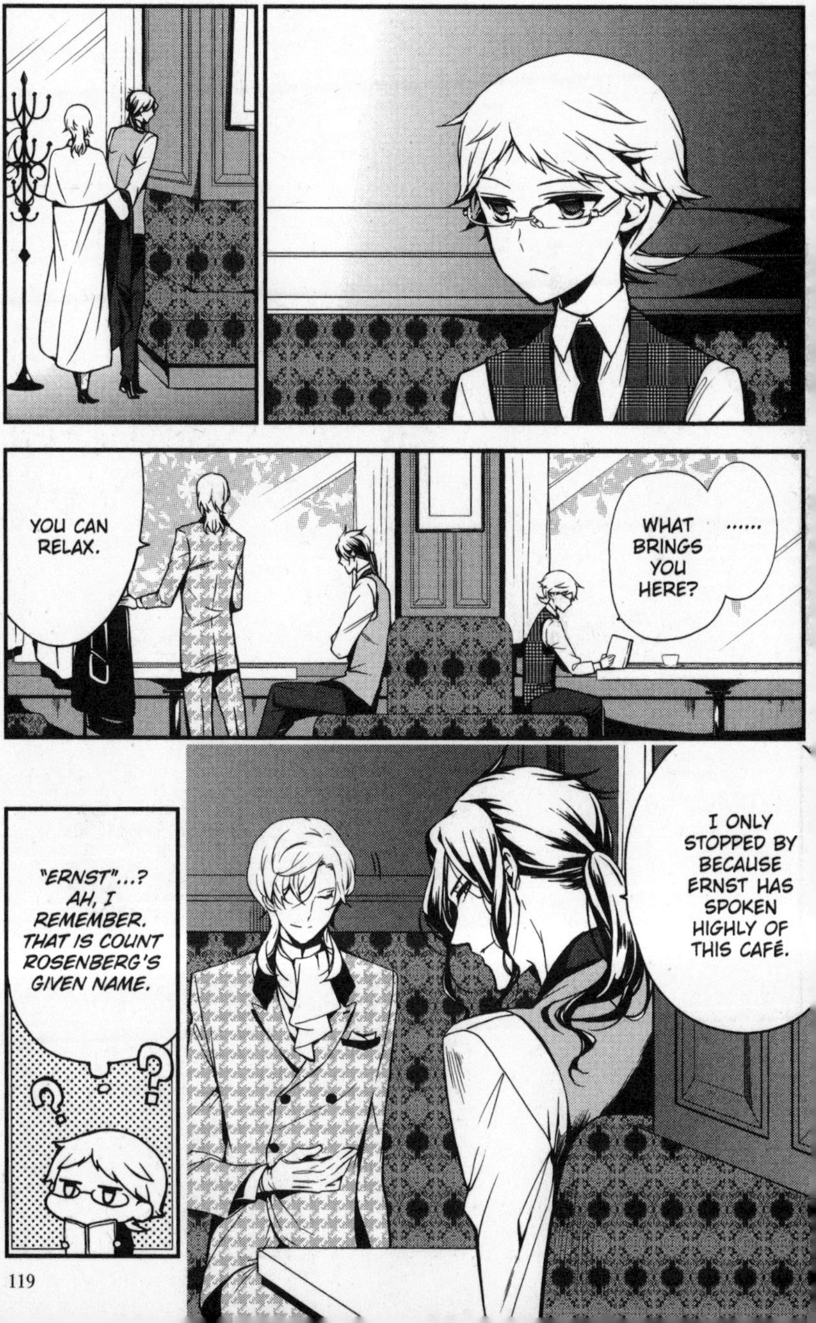
......
WHAT BRINGS YOU HERE?
YOU CAN RELAX.
I ONLY STOPPED BY BECAUSE ERNST HAS SPOKEN HIGHLY OF THIS CAFÉ.
"ERNST"...? AH, I REMEMBER. THAT IS COUNT ROSENBERG'S GIVEN NAME.

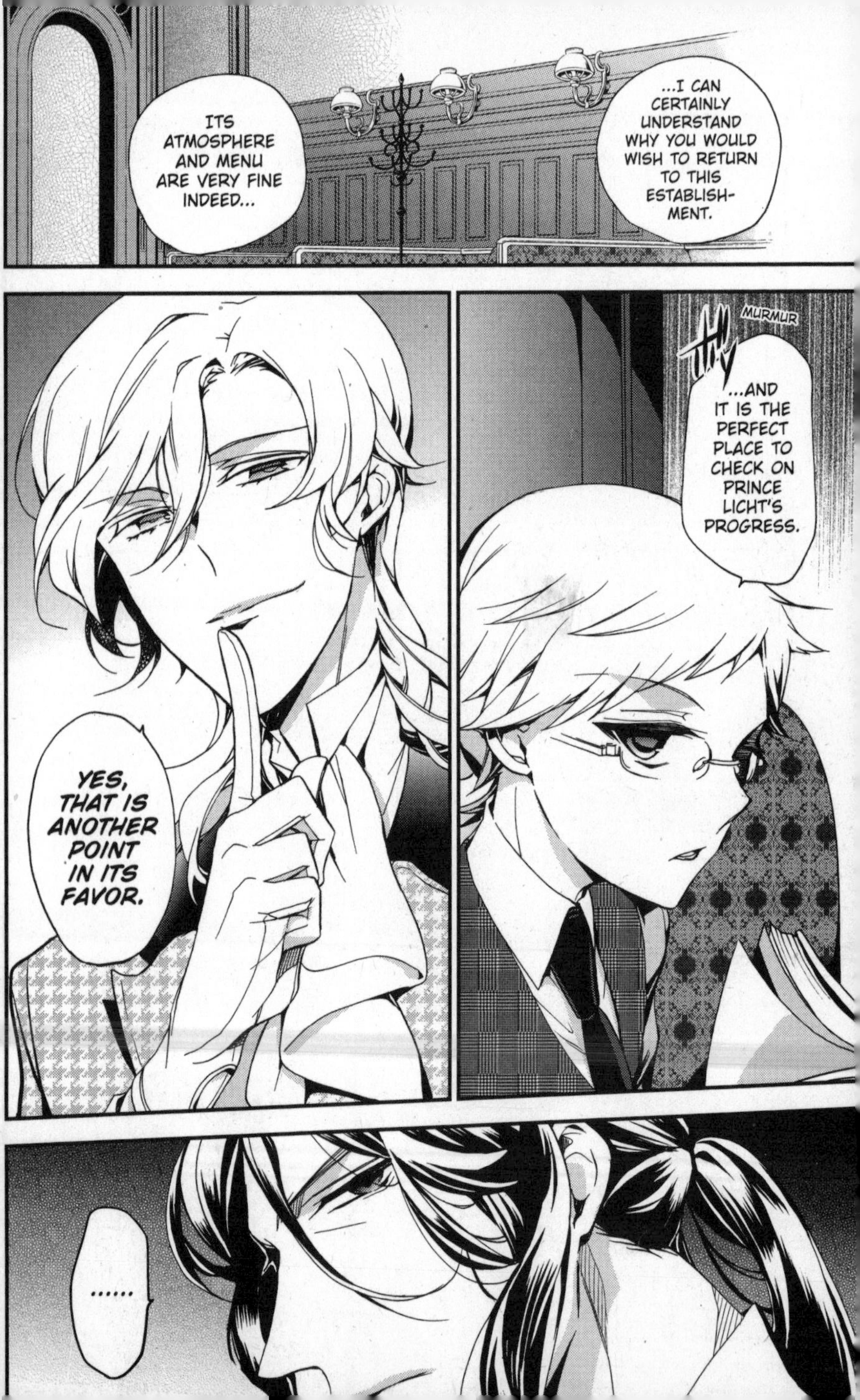
...I CAN CERTAINLY UNDERSTAND WHY YOU WOULD WISH TO RETURN TO THIS ESTABLISH-MENT.
ITS ATMOSPHERE AND MENU ARE VERY FINE INDEED...
MURMUR
...AND IT IS THE PERFECT PLACE TO CHECK ON PRINCE LICHT'S PROGRESS.
YES, THAT IS ANOTHER POINT IN ITS FAVOR.
......

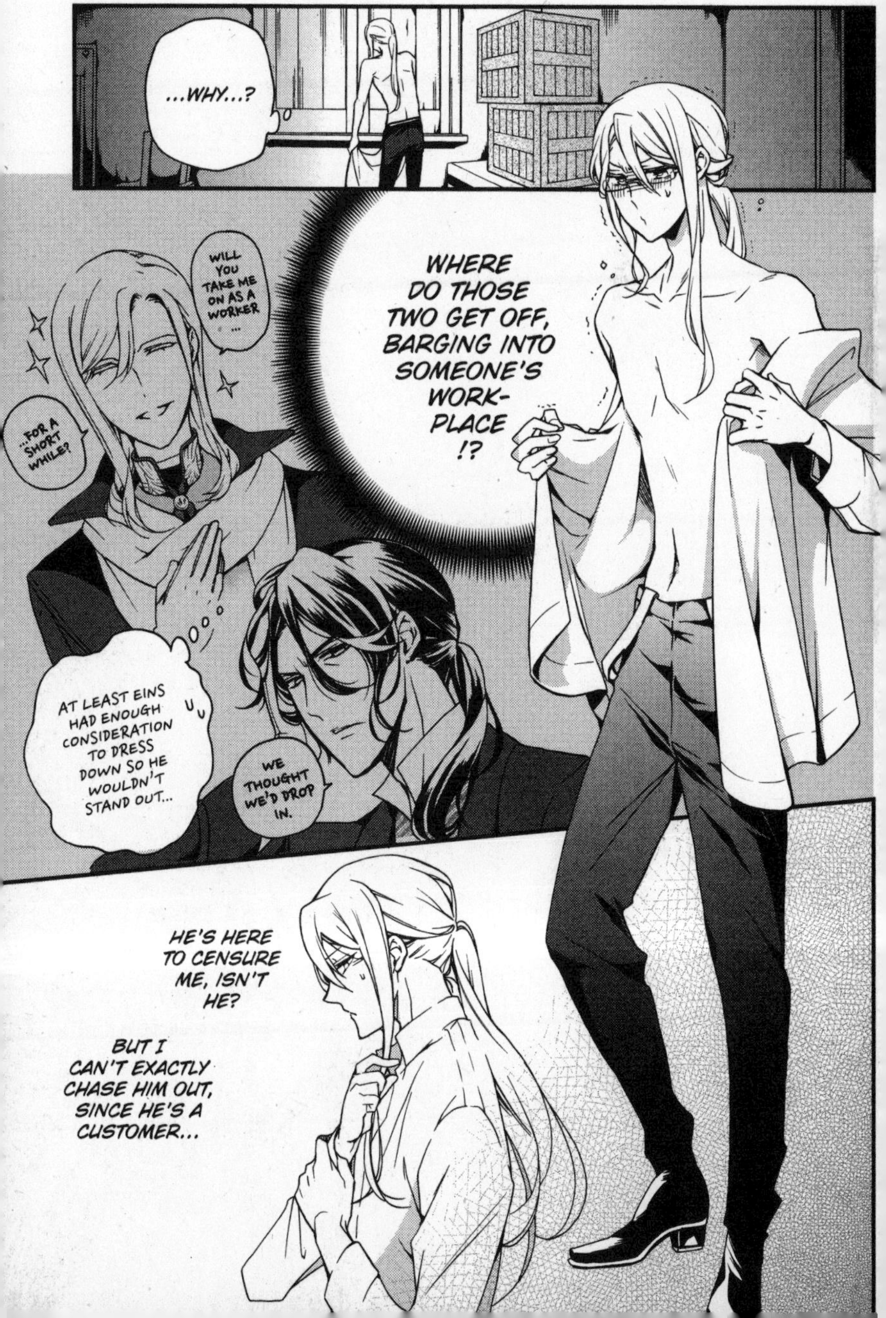
...WHY...?
WHERE DO THOSE TWO GET OFF, BARGING INTO SOMEONE'S WORK-PLACE !?
WILL YOU TAKE ME ON AS A WORKER ...
...FOR A SHORT WHILE?
WE THOUGHT WE'D DROP IN.
AT LEAST EINS HAD ENOUGH CONSIDERATION TO DRESS DOWN SO HE WOULDN'T STAND OUT...
HE'S HERE TO CENSURE ME, ISN'T HE?
BUT I CAN'T EXACTLY CHASE HIM OUT, SINCE HE'S A CUSTOMER...

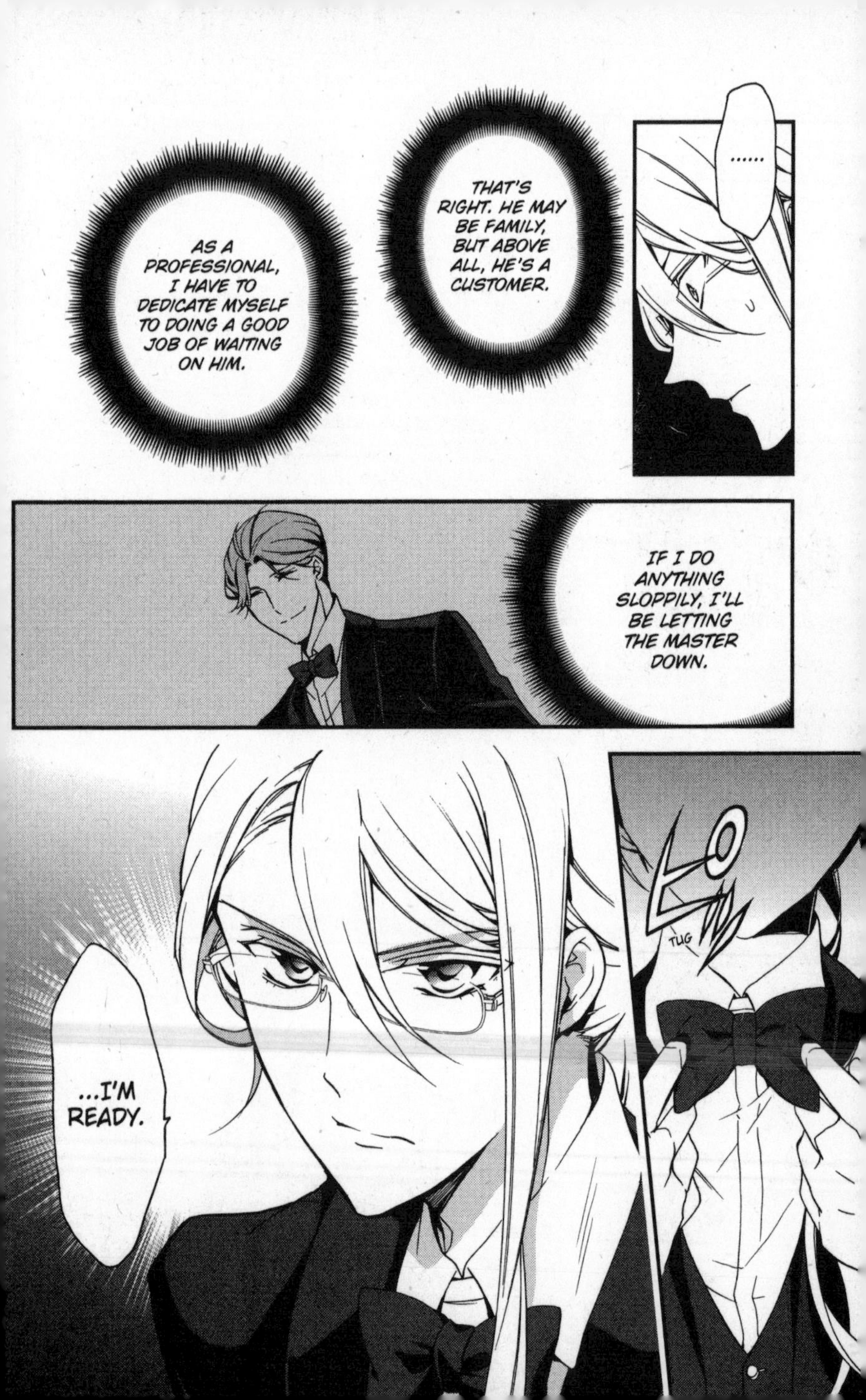
......
THAT'S RIGHT. HE MAY BE FAMILY, BUT ABOVE ALL, HE'S A CUSTOMER.
AS A PROFESSIONAL, I HAVE TO DEDICATE MYSELF TO DOING A GOOD JOB OF WAITING ON HIM.
IF I DO ANYTHING SLOPPILY, I'LL BE LETTING THE MASTER DOWN.
TUG
...I'M READY.

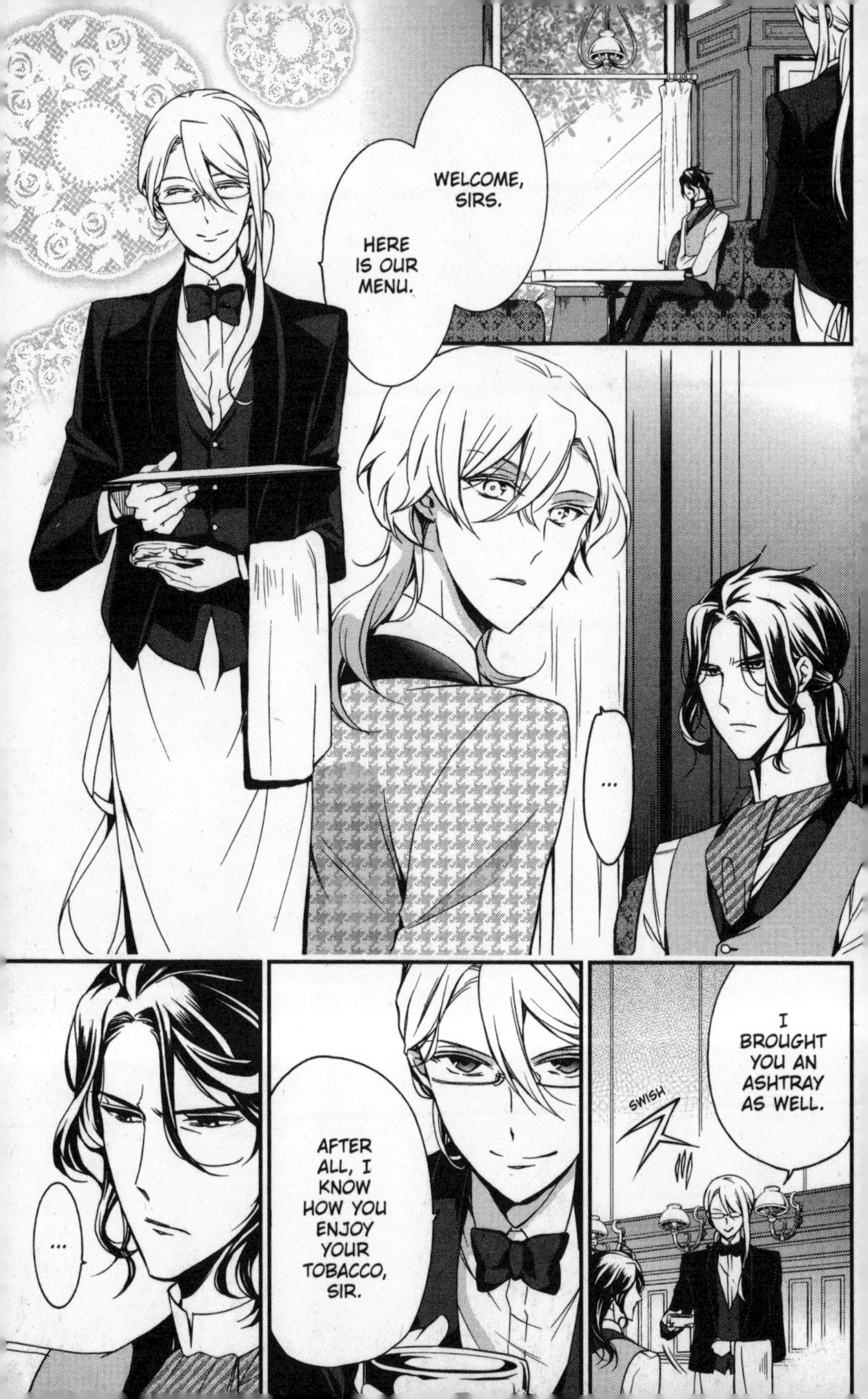
WELCOME, SIRS.
HERE IS OUR MENU.
...
I BROUGHT YOU AN ASHTRAY AS WELL.
SWISH
AFTER ALL, I KNOW HOW YOU ENJOY YOUR TOBACCO, SIR.
...

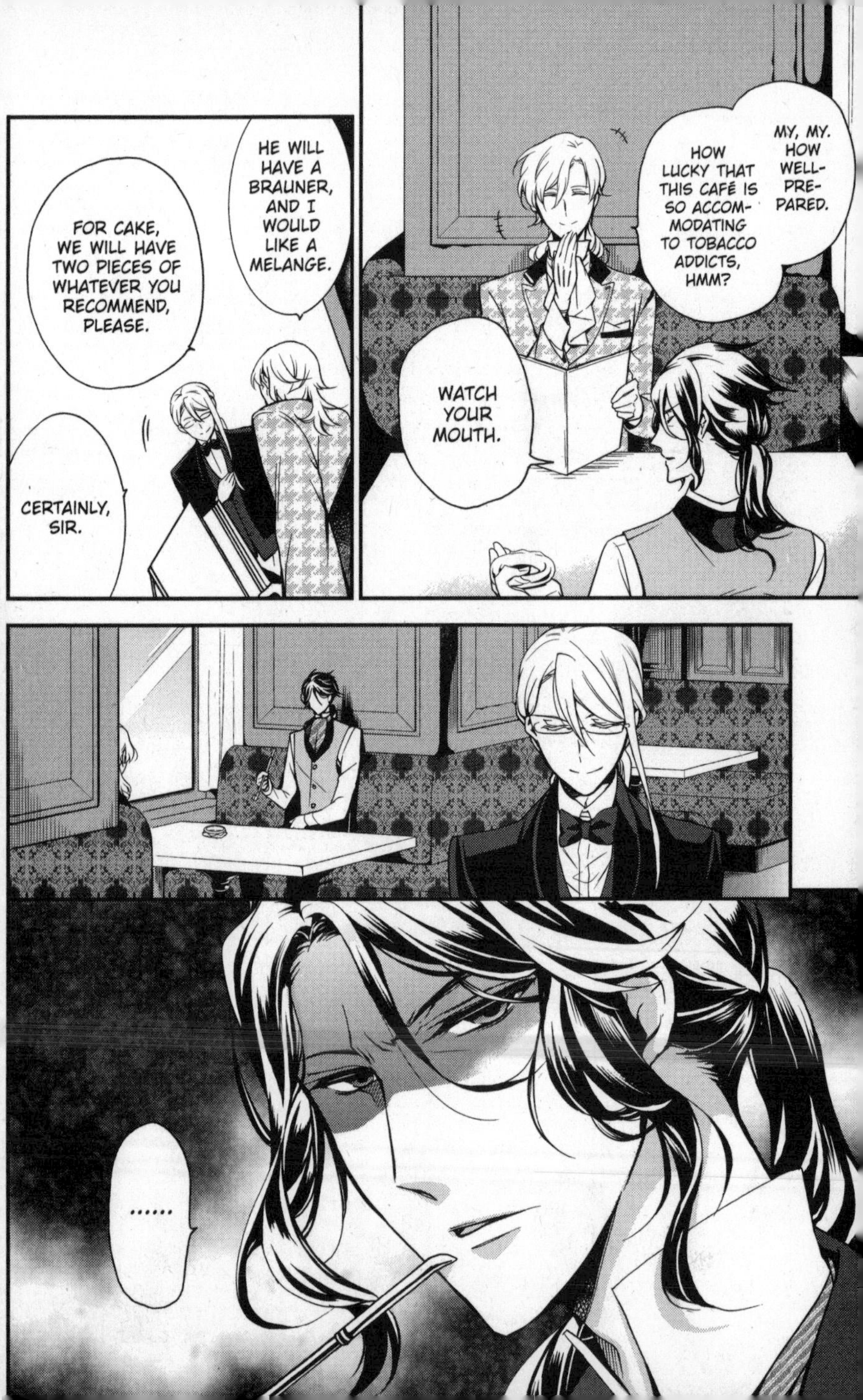
MY, MY. HOW WELL-PREPARED.
HOW LUCKY THAT THIS CAFÉ IS SO ACCOMMODATING TO TOBACCO ADDICTS, HMM?
WATCH YOUR MOUTH.
HE WILL HAVE A BRAUNER, AND I WOULD LIKE A MELANGE.
FOR CAKE, WE WILL HAVE TWO PIECES OF WHATEVER YOU RECOMMEND, PLEASE.
CERTAINLY, SIR.
......

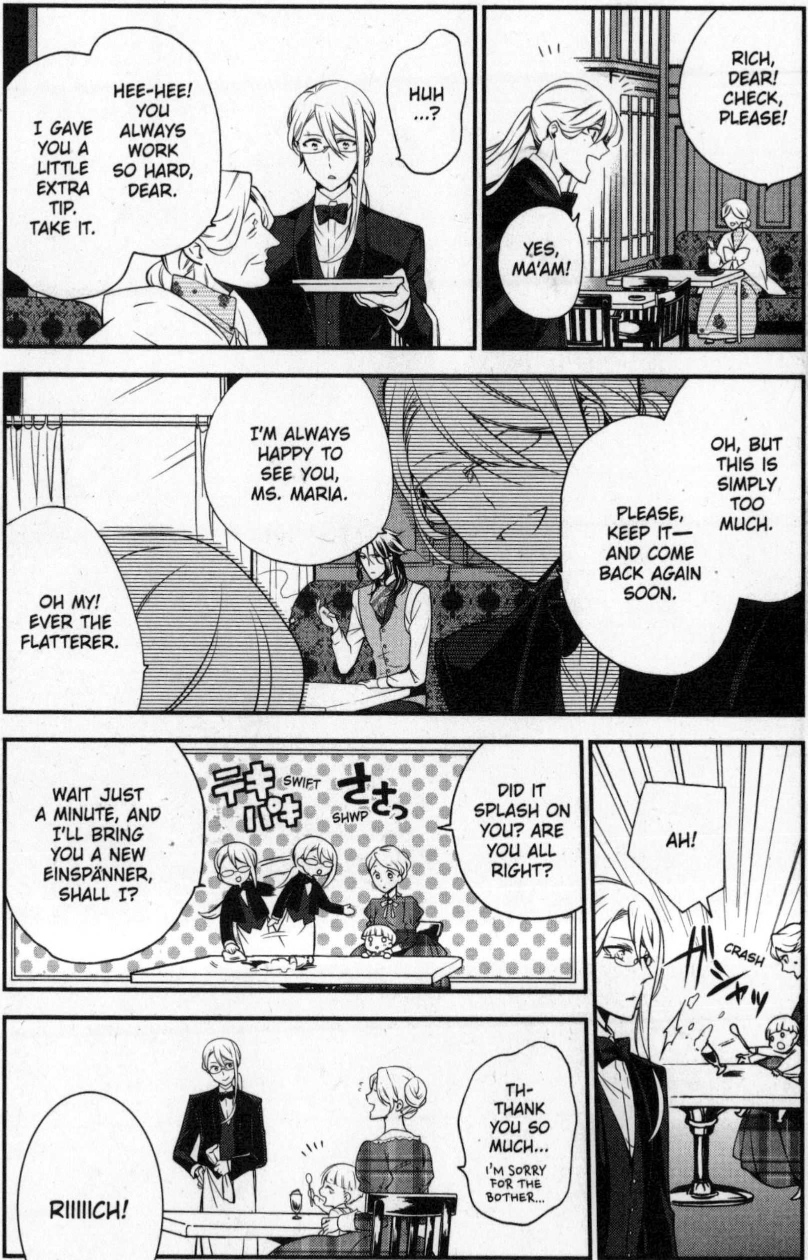
RICH, DEAR! CHECK, PLEASE!
YES, MA'AM!
HUH ...?
HEE-HEE! YOU ALWAYS WORK SO HARD, DEAR.
I GAVE YOU A LITTLE EXTRA TIP. TAKE IT.
OH, BUT THIS IS SIMPLY TOO MUCH.
PLEASE, KEEP IT— AND COME BACK AGAIN SOON.
I'M ALWAYS HAPPY TO SEE YOU, MS. MARIA.
OH MY! EVER THE FLATTERER.
AH!
CRASH
DID IT SPLASH ON YOU? ARE YOU ALL RIGHT?
SHWP
SWIFT
WAIT JUST A MINUTE, AND I'LL BRING YOU A NEW EINSPÄNNER, SHALL I?
TH-THANK YOU SO MUCH...
I'M SORRY FOR THE BOTHER...
RIIIIICH!

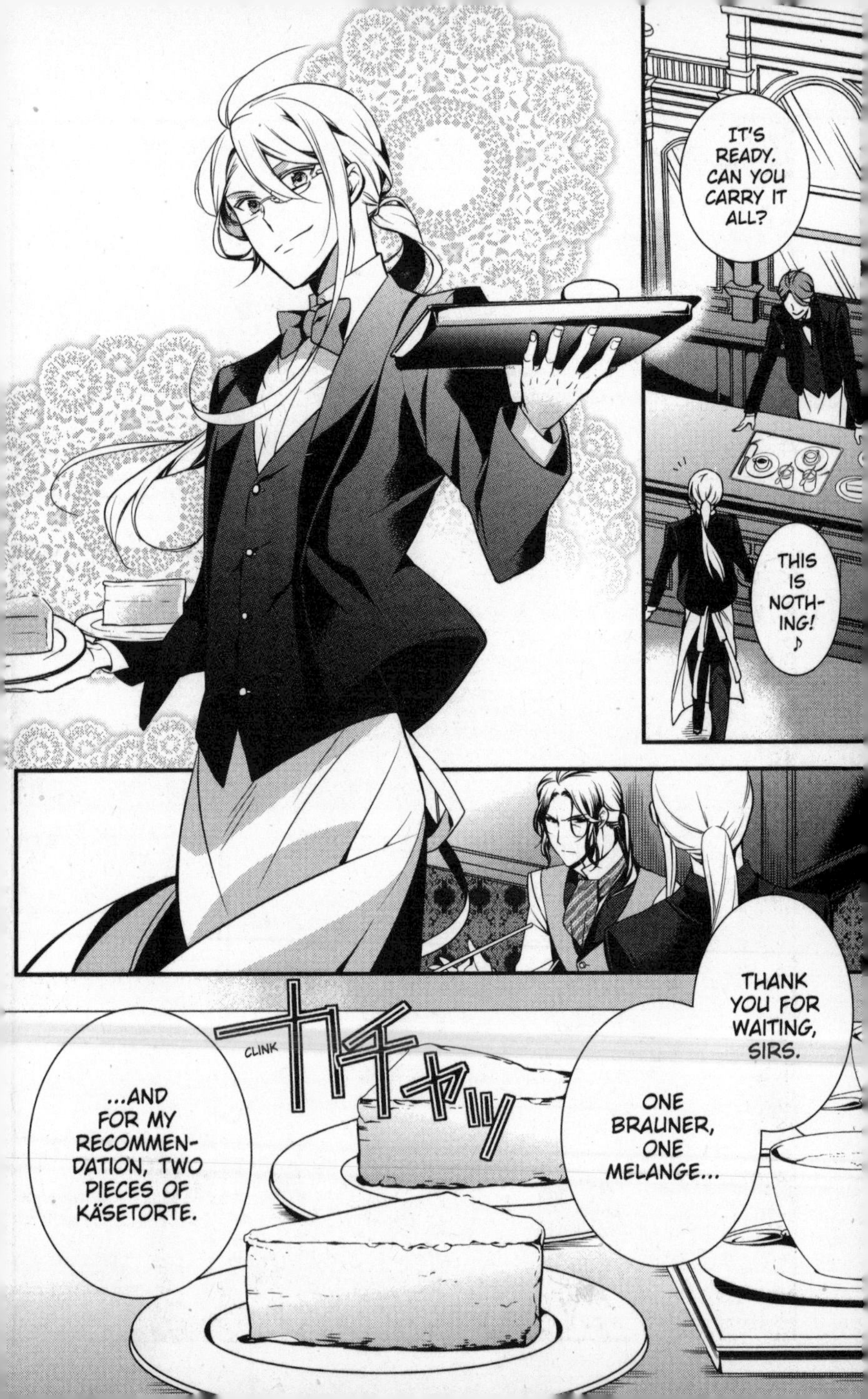
IT'S READY. CAN YOU CARRY IT ALL?
THIS IS NOTHING! ♪
THANK YOU FOR WAITING, SIRS.
ONE BRAUNER, ONE MELANGE...
カチャッ
CLINK
...AND FOR MY RECOMMENDATION, TWO PIECES OF KÄSETORTE.

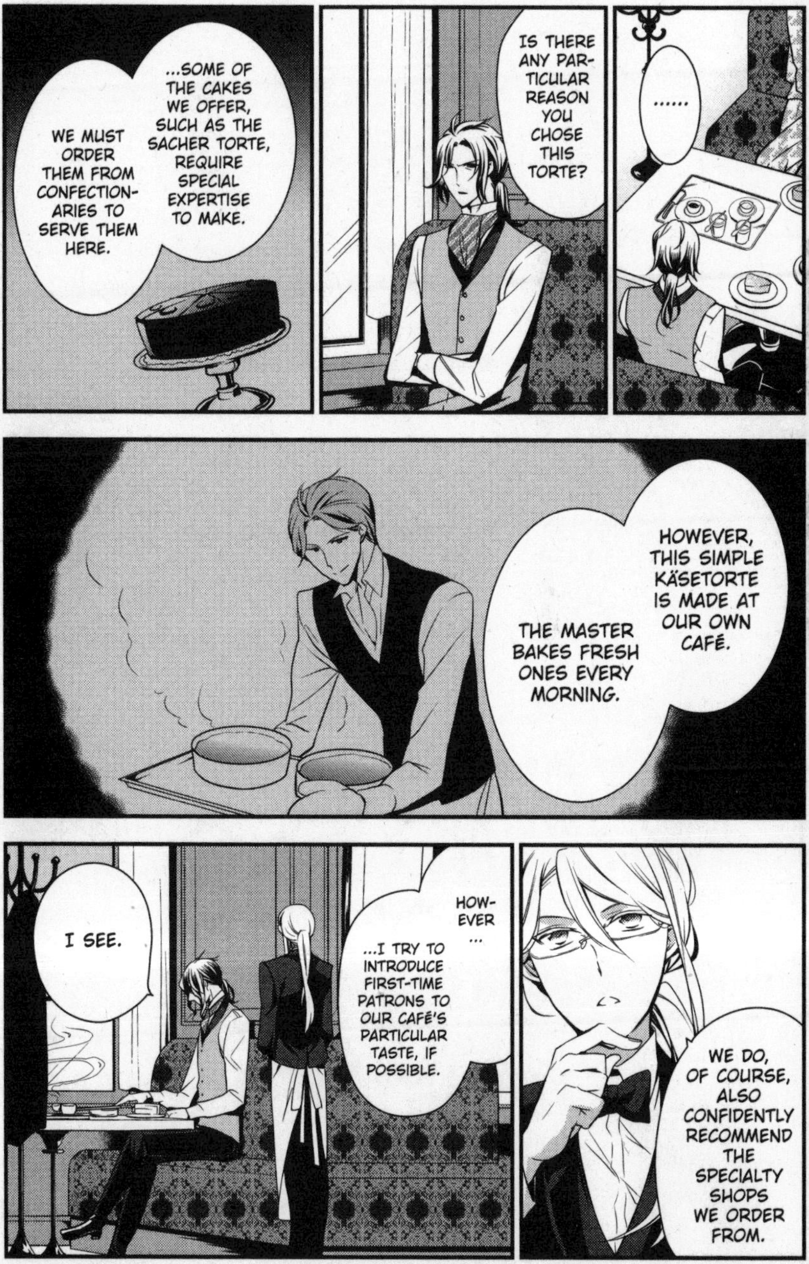
......
IS THERE ANY PARTICULAR REASON YOU CHOSE THIS TORTE?
...SOME OF THE CAKES WE OFFER, SUCH AS THE SACHER TORTE, REQUIRE SPECIAL EXPERTISE TO MAKE.
WE MUST ORDER THEM FROM CONFECTIONARIES TO SERVE THEM HERE.
HOWEVER, THIS SIMPLE KÄSETORTE IS MADE AT OUR OWN CAFÉ.
THE MASTER BAKES FRESH ONES EVERY MORNING.
WE DO, OF COURSE, ALSO CONFIDENTLY RECOMMEND THE SPECIALTY SHOPS WE ORDER FROM.
HOWEVER...
...I TRY TO INTRODUCE FIRST-TIME PATRONS TO OUR CAFÉ'S PARTICULAR TASTE, IF POSSIBLE.
I SEE.

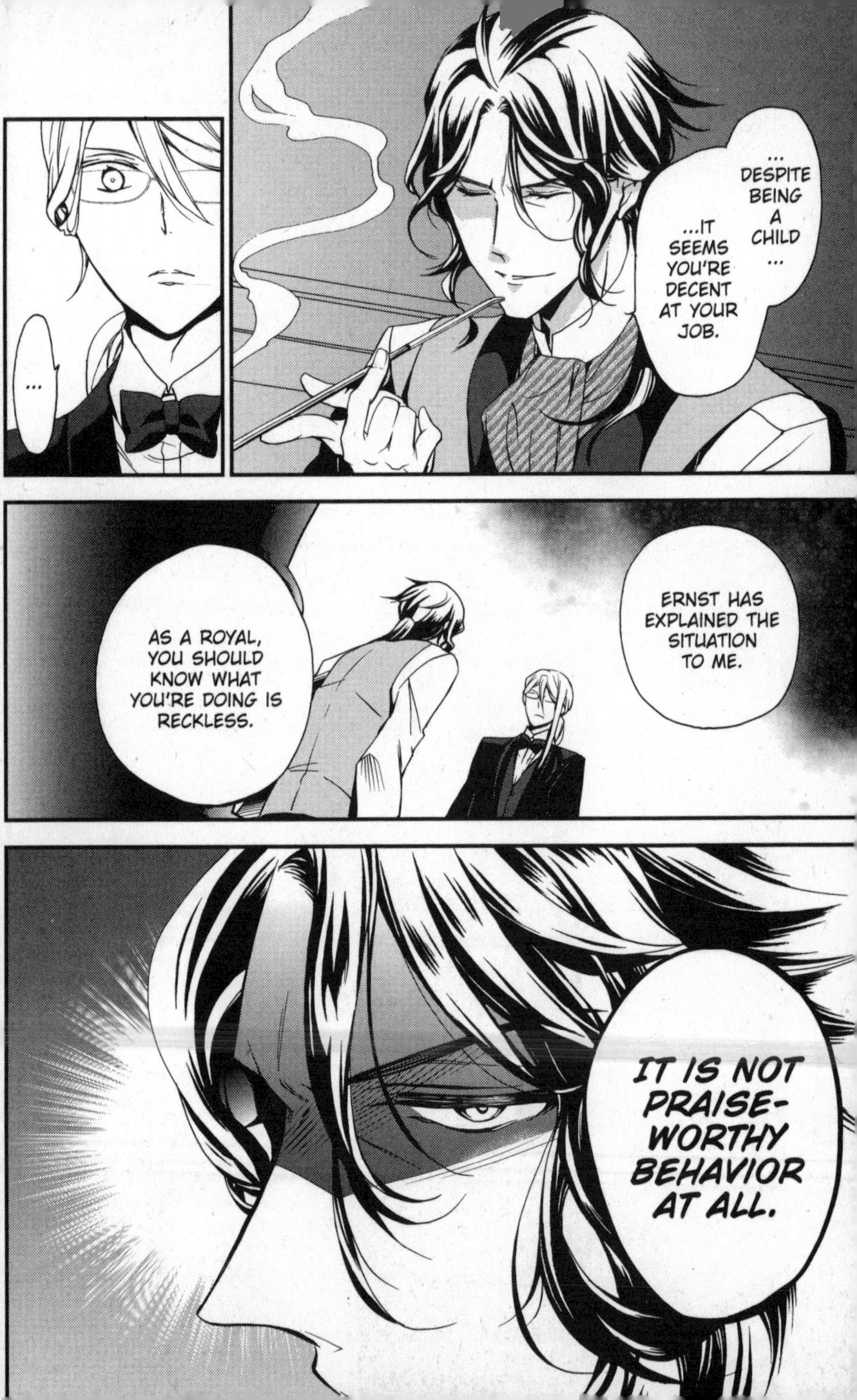
... DESPITE BEING A CHILD ...
...IT SEEMS YOU'RE DECENT AT YOUR JOB.
...
ERNST HAS EXPLAINED THE SITUATION TO ME.
AS A ROYAL, YOU SHOULD KNOW WHAT YOU'RE DOING IS RECKLESS.
IT IS NOT PRAISE-WORTHY BEHAVIOR AT ALL.

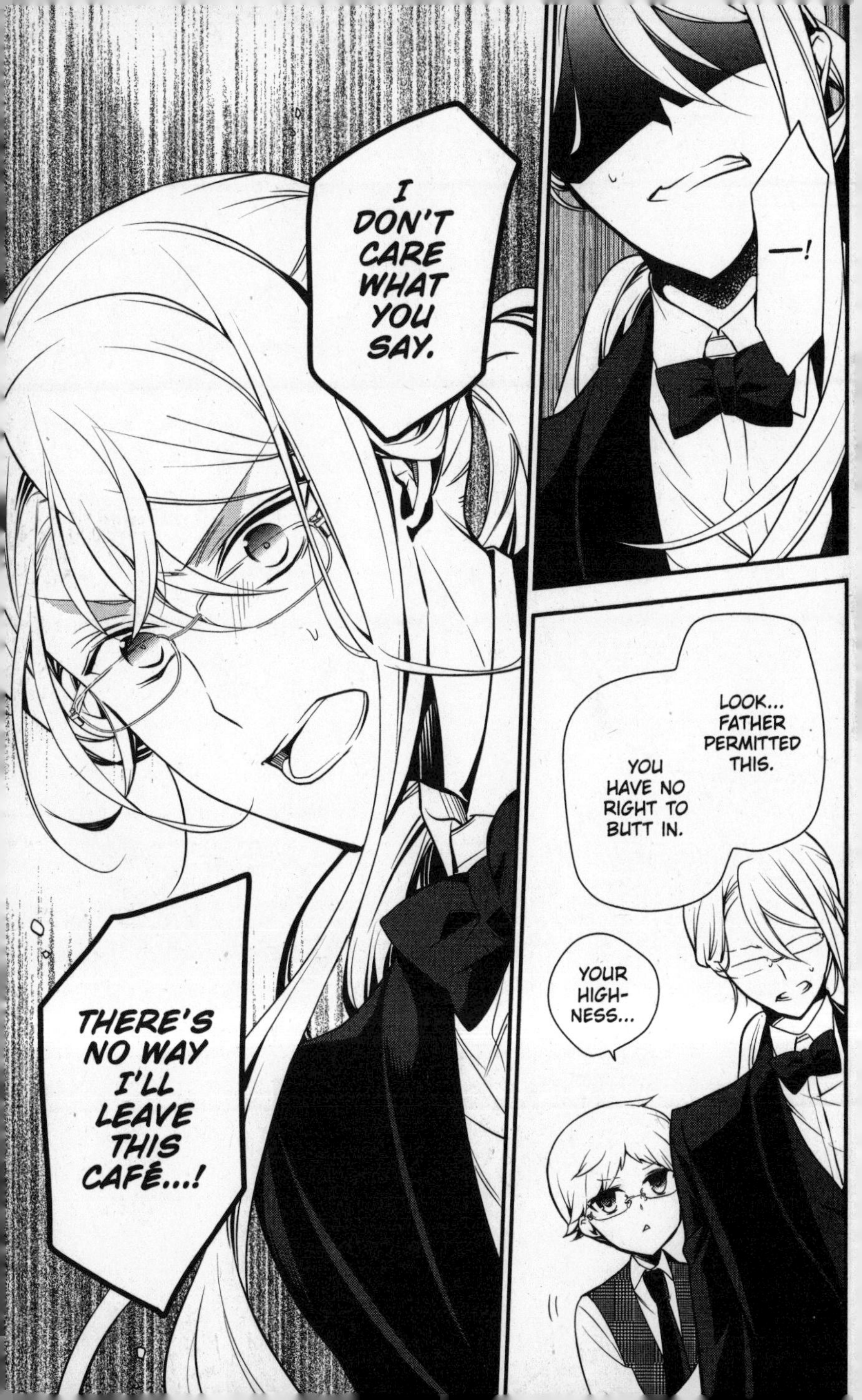
—!
LOOK... FATHER PERMITTED THIS.
YOU HAVE NO RIGHT TO BUTT IN.
YOUR HIGH-NESS...
I DON'T CARE WHAT YOU SAY.
THERE'S NO WAY I'LL LEAVE THIS CAFÉ...!

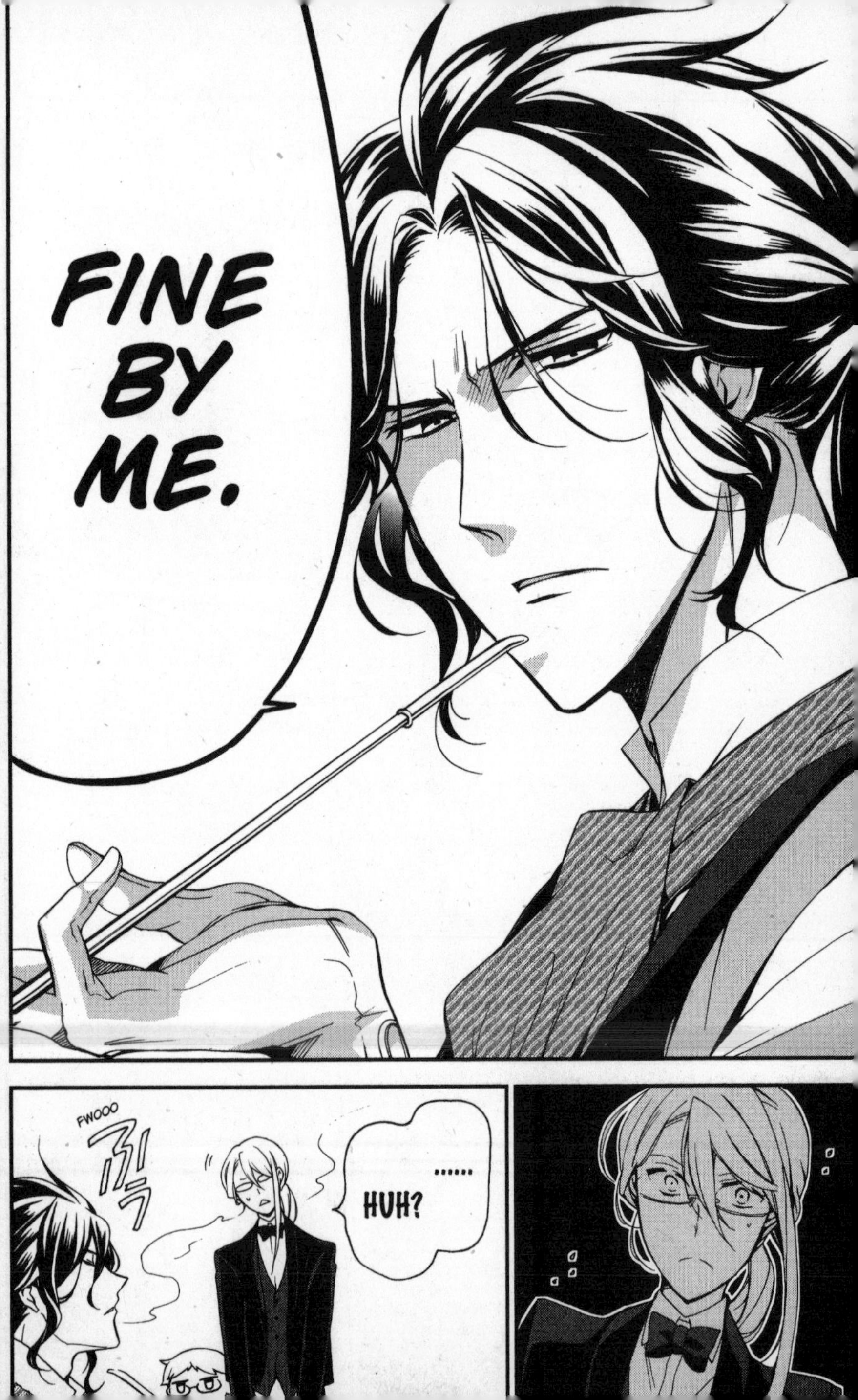
FINE BY ME.
......
HUH?
FWOOO

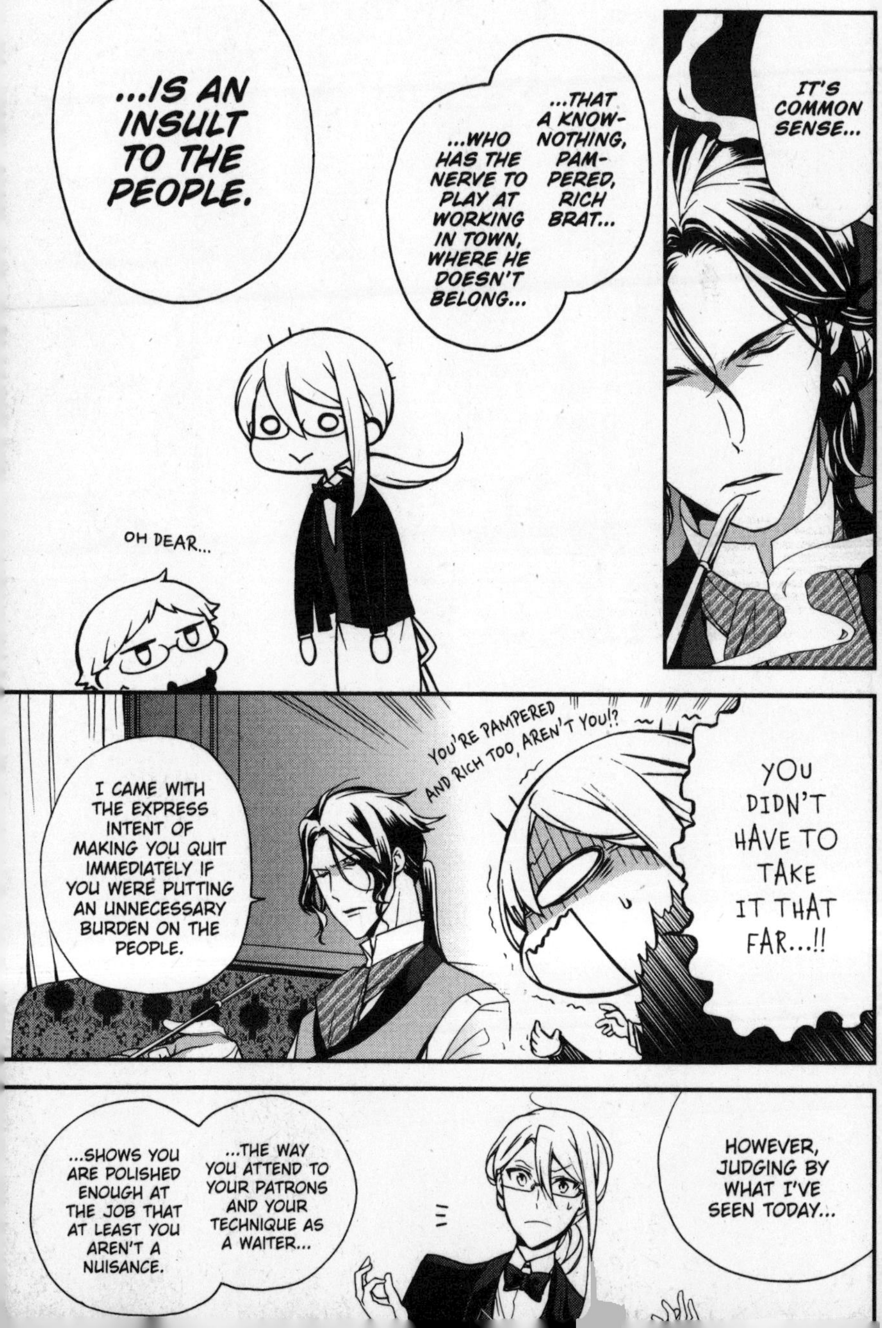
IT'S COMMON SENSE...
...THAT A KNOW-NOTHING, PAMPERED, RICH BRAT...
...WHO HAS THE NERVE TO PLAY AT WORKING IN TOWN, WHERE HE DOESN'T BELONG...
...IS AN INSULT TO THE PEOPLE.
OH DEAR...
YOU DIDN'T HAVE TO TAKE IT THAT FAR...!!
YOU'RE PAMPERED AND RICH TOO, AREN'T YOU!?
I CAME WITH THE EXPRESS INTENT OF MAKING YOU QUIT IMMEDIATELY IF YOU WERE PUTTING AN UNNECESSARY BURDEN ON THE PEOPLE.
HOWEVER, JUDGING BY WHAT I'VE SEEN TODAY...
...THE WAY YOU ATTEND TO YOUR PATRONS AND YOUR TECHNIQUE AS A WAITER...
...SHOWS YOU ARE POLISHED ENOUGH AT THE JOB THAT AT LEAST YOU AREN'T A NUISANCE.

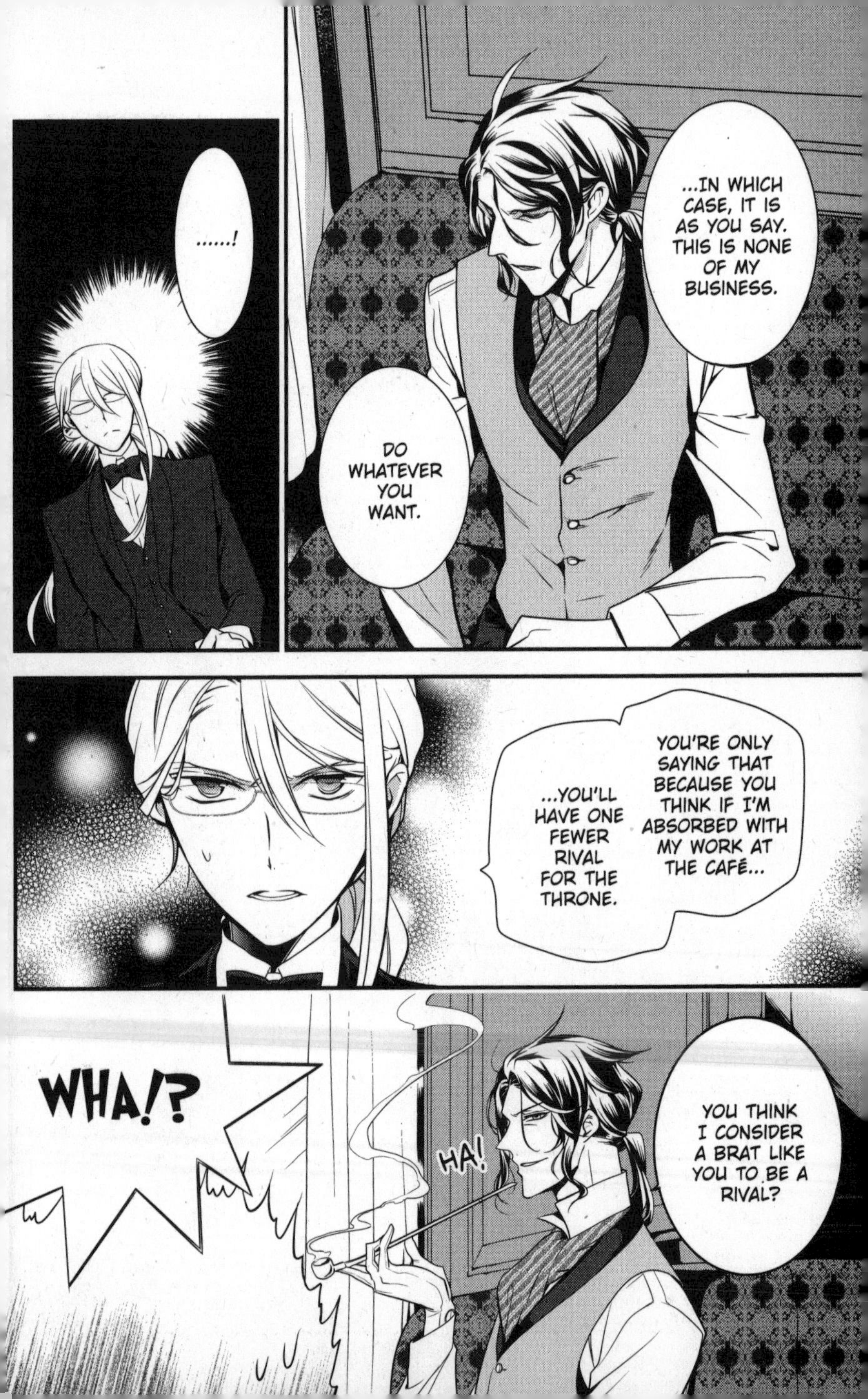
...IN WHICH CASE, IT IS AS YOU SAY. THIS IS NONE OF MY BUSINESS.
DO WHATEVER YOU WANT.
......!
YOU'RE ONLY SAYING THAT BECAUSE YOU THINK IF I'M ABSORBED WITH MY WORK AT THE CAFÉ...
...YOU'LL HAVE ONE FEWER RIVAL FOR THE THRONE.
YOU THINK I CONSIDER A BRAT LIKE YOU TO BE A RIVAL?
HA!
WHA!?

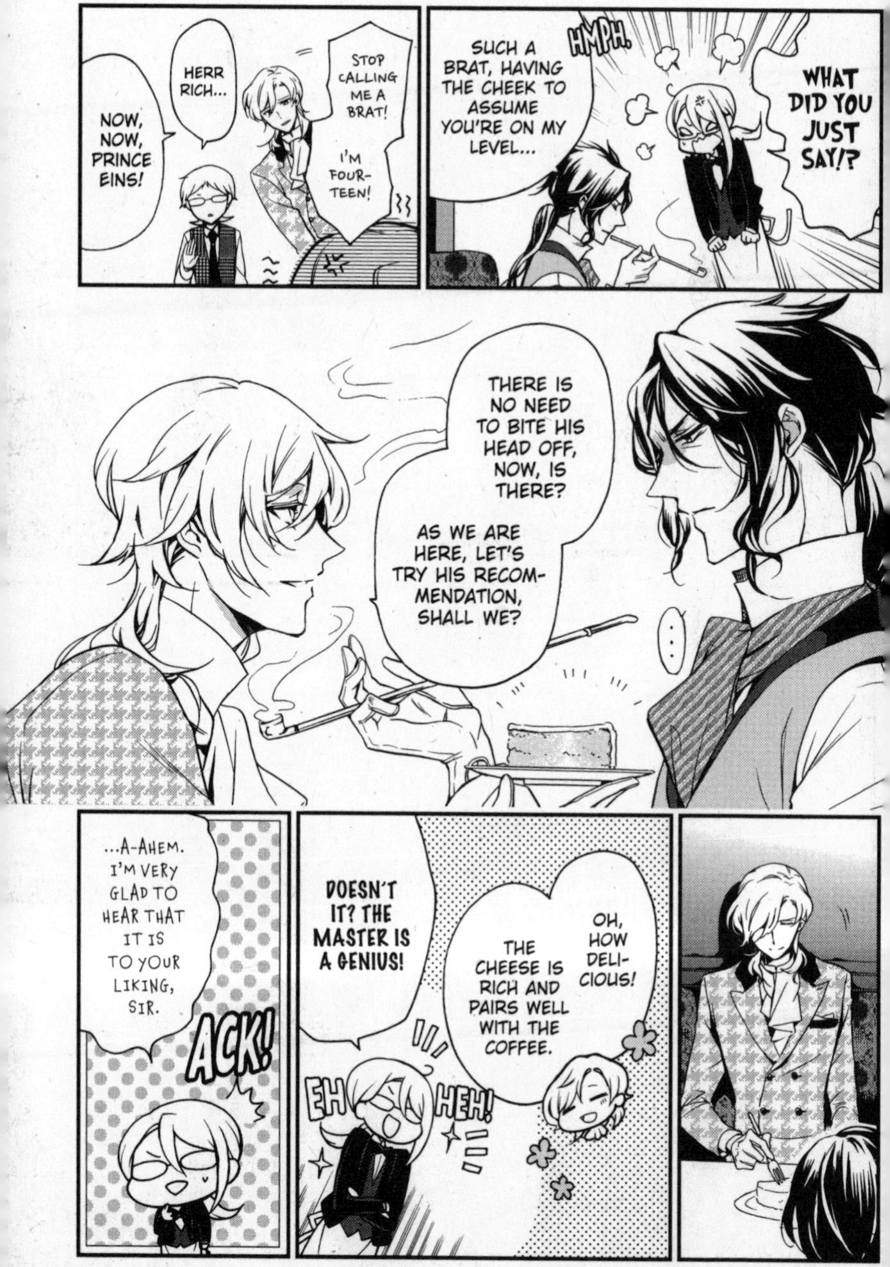
HMPH.
SUCH A BRAT, HAVING THE CHEEK TO ASSUME YOU'RE ON MY LEVEL...
WHAT DID YOU JUST SAY!?
STOP CALLING ME A BRAT!
I'M FOUR-TEEN!
HERR RICH...
NOW, NOW, PRINCE EINS!
THERE IS NO NEED TO BITE HIS HEAD OFF, NOW, IS THERE?
AS WE ARE HERE, LET'S TRY HIS RECOM-MENDATION, SHALL WE?
...
OH, HOW DELI-CIOUS!
THE CHEESE IS RICH AND PAIRS WELL WITH THE COFFEE.
DOESN'T IT? THE MASTER IS A GENIUS!
EH HEH!
...A-AHEM. I'M VERY GLAD TO HEAR THAT IT IS TO YOUR LIKING, SIR.
ACK!

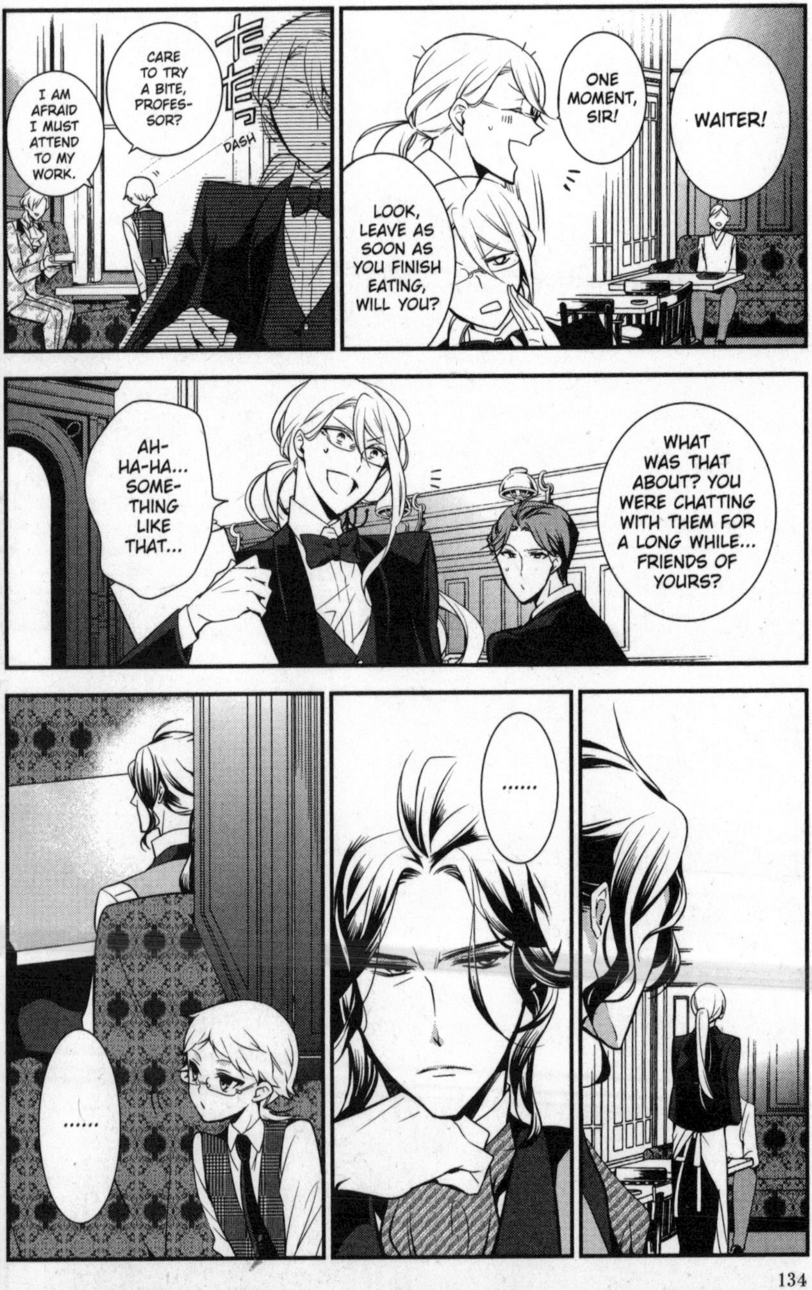
WAITER!
ONE MOMENT, SIR!
LOOK, LEAVE AS SOON AS YOU FINISH EATING, WILL YOU?
CARE TO TRY A BITE, PROFESSOR?
I AM AFRAID I MUST ATTEND TO MY WORK.
DASH
WHAT WAS THAT ABOUT? YOU WERE CHATTING WITH THEM FOR A LONG WHILE... FRIENDS OF YOURS?
AH-HA-HA... SOMETHING LIKE THAT...
......
......

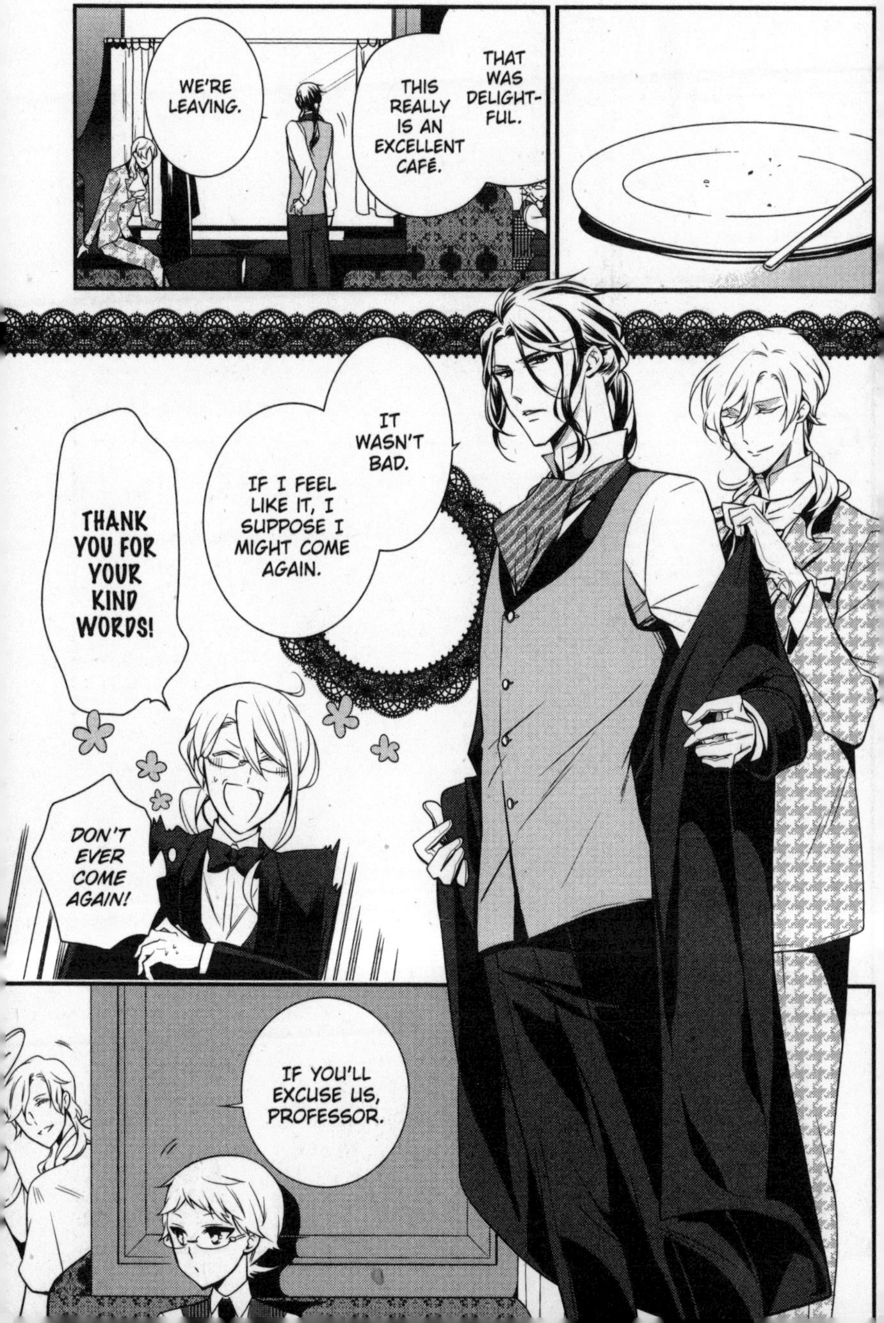
THAT WAS DELIGHTFUL.
THIS REALLY IS AN EXCELLENT CAFÉ.
WE'RE LEAVING.
IT WASN'T BAD.
IF I FEEL LIKE IT, I SUPPOSE I MIGHT COME AGAIN.
THANK YOU FOR YOUR KIND WORDS!
DON'T EVER COME AGAIN!
IF YOU'LL EXCUSE US, PROFESSOR.

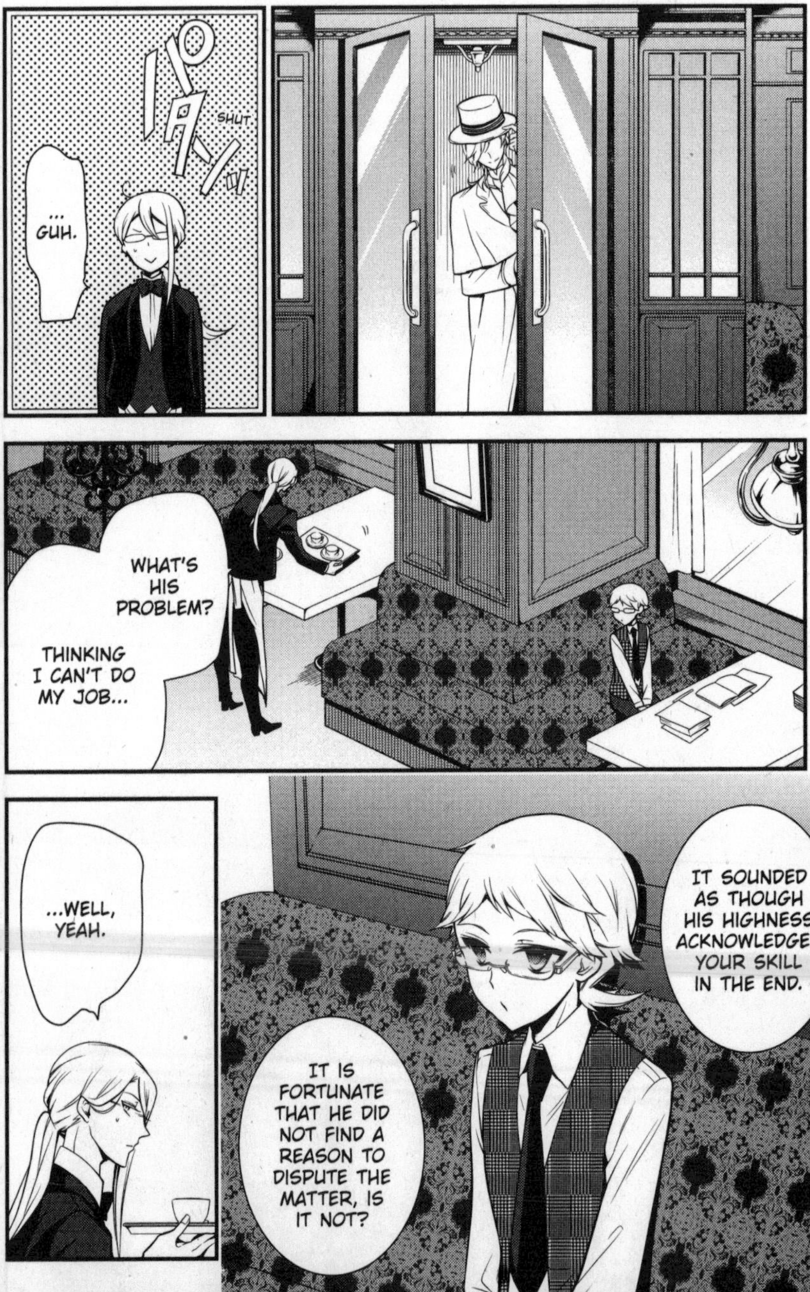
SHUT
... GUH.
WHAT'S HIS PROBLEM?
THINKING I CAN'T DO MY JOB...
IT SOUNDED AS THOUGH HIS HIGHNESS ACKNOWLEDGED YOUR SKILL IN THE END.
IT IS FORTUNATE THAT HE DID NOT FIND A REASON TO DISPUTE THE MATTER, IS IT NOT?
...WELL, YEAH.

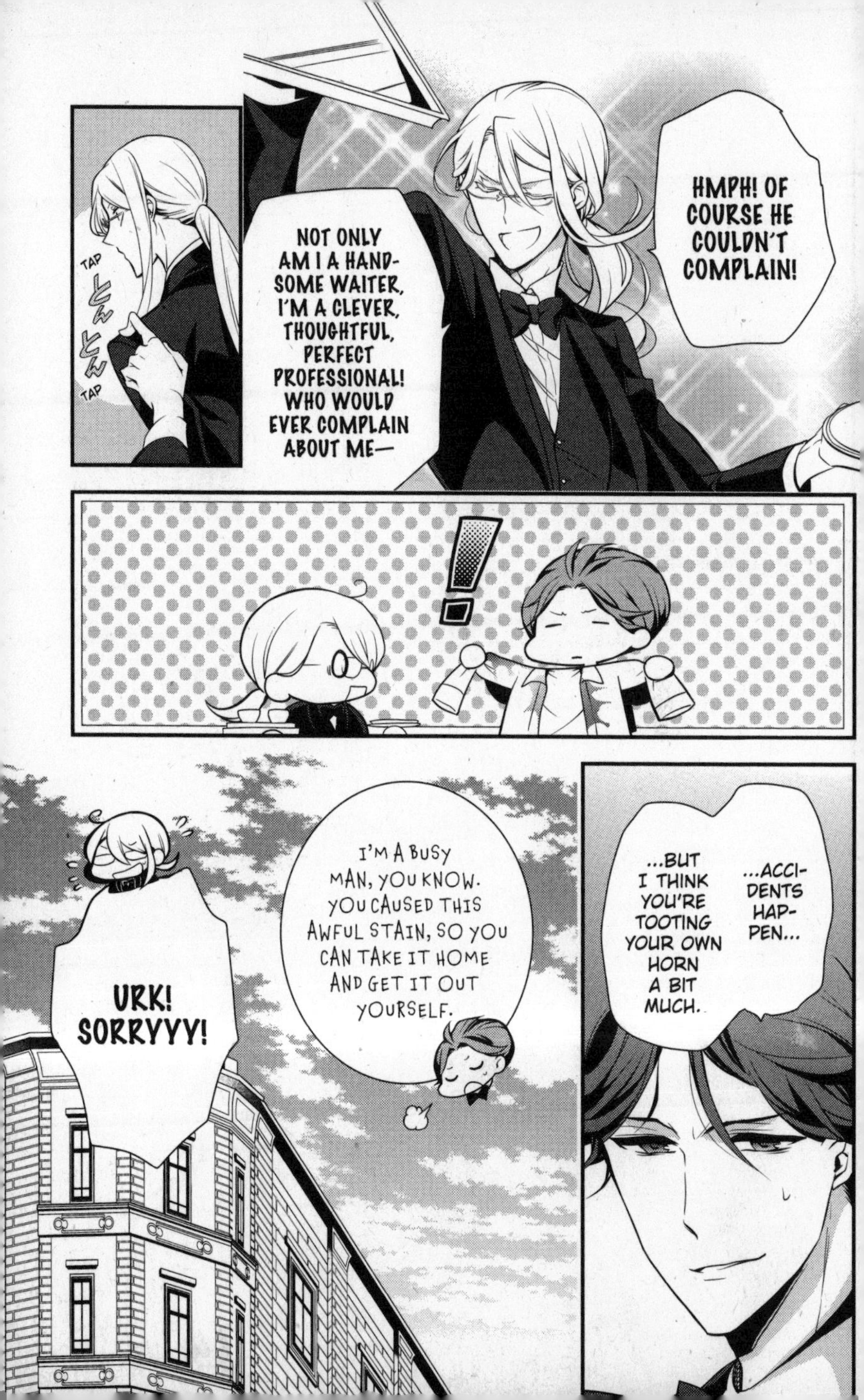
HMPH! OF COURSE HE COULDN'T COMPLAIN!
NOT ONLY AM I A HAND-SOME WAITER, I'M A CLEVER, THOUGHTFUL, PERFECT PROFESSIONAL! WHO WOULD EVER COMPLAIN ABOUT ME—
TAP
とんとん
TAP
!
...ACCI-DENTS HAP-PEN...
...BUT I THINK YOU'RE TOOTING YOUR OWN HORN A BIT MUCH.
I'M A BUSY MAN, YOU KNOW. YOU CAUSED THIS AWFUL STAIN, SO YOU CAN TAKE IT HOME AND GET IT OUT YOURSELF.
URK! SORRYYY!

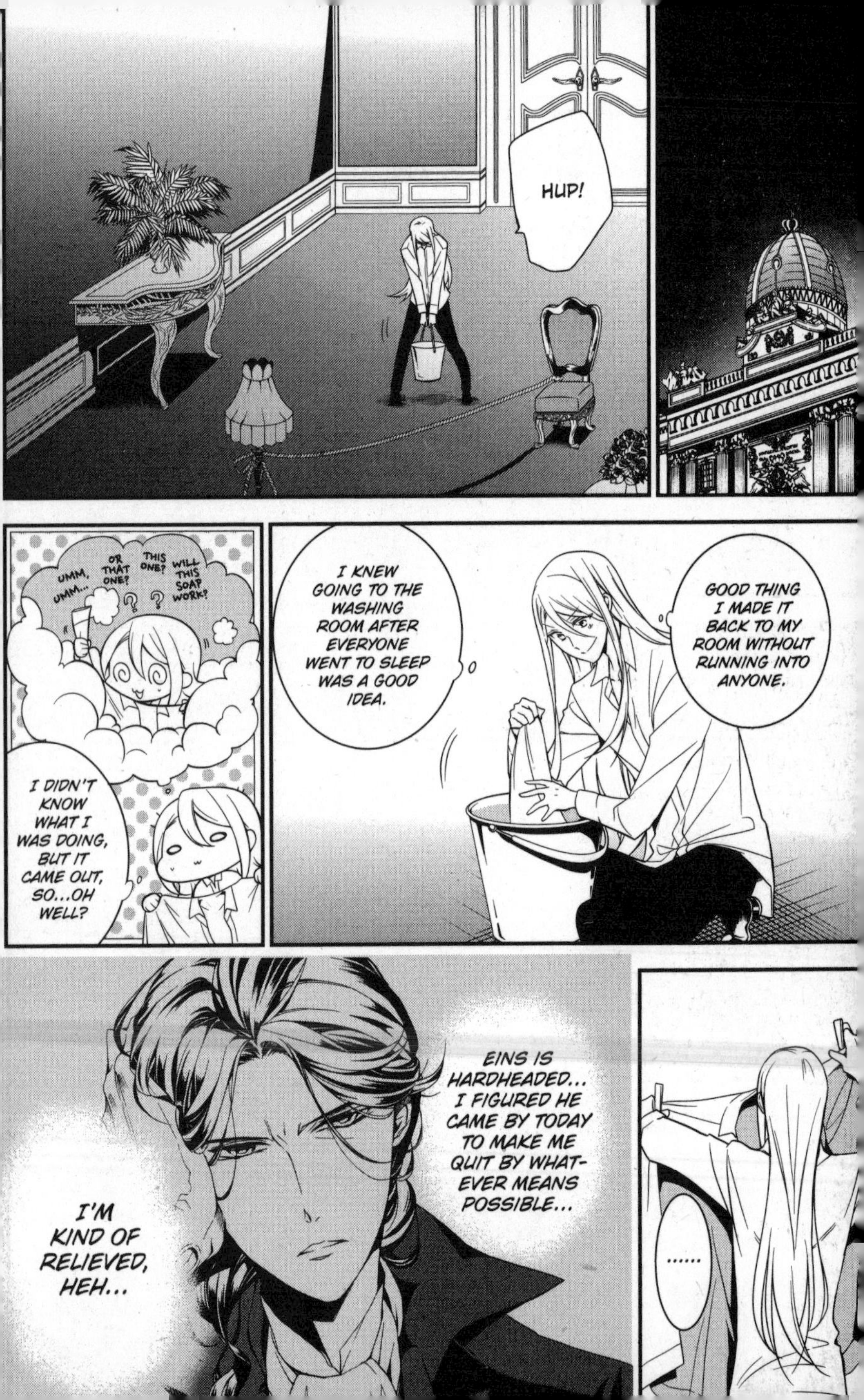
HUP!
GOOD THING I MADE IT BACK TO MY ROOM WITHOUT RUNNING INTO ANYONE.
I KNEW GOING TO THE WASHING ROOM AFTER EVERYONE WENT TO SLEEP WAS A GOOD IDEA.
UMM, UMM...
THIS ONE?
OR THAT ONE?
WILL THIS SOAP WORK?
I DIDN'T KNOW WHAT I WAS DOING, BUT IT CAME OUT, SO...OH WELL?
......
EINS IS HARDHEADED... I FIGURED HE CAME BY TODAY TO MAKE ME QUIT BY WHATEVER MEANS POSSIBLE...
I'M KIND OF RELIEVED, HEH...

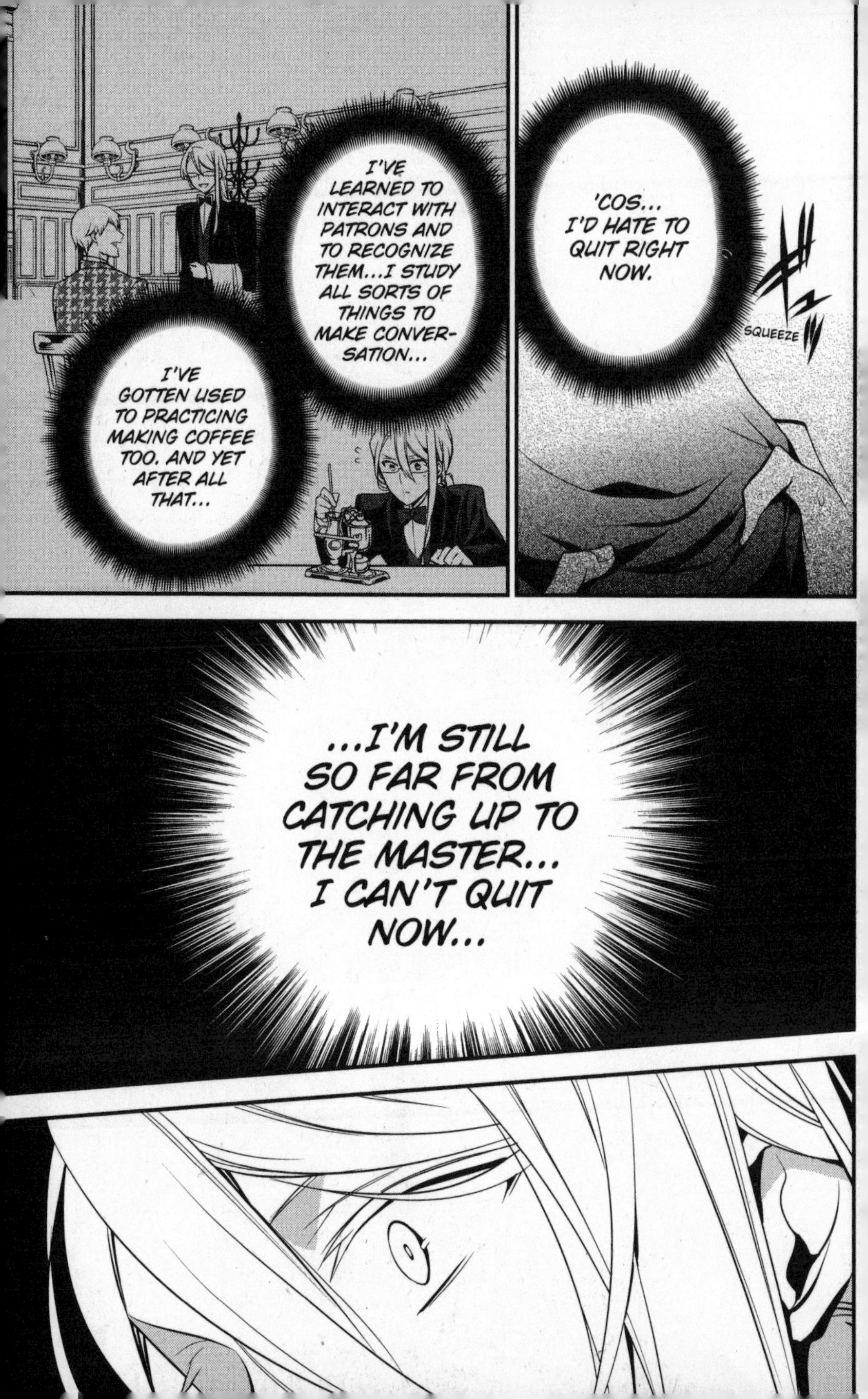
'COS... I'D HATE TO QUIT RIGHT NOW.
SQUEEZE
I'VE LEARNED TO INTERACT WITH PATRONS AND TO RECOGNIZE THEM...I STUDY ALL SORTS OF THINGS TO MAKE CONVER-SATION...
I'VE GOTTEN USED TO PRACTICING MAKING COFFEE TOO. AND YET AFTER ALL THAT...
...I'M STILL SO FAR FROM CATCHING UP TO THE MASTER... I CAN'T QUIT NOW...

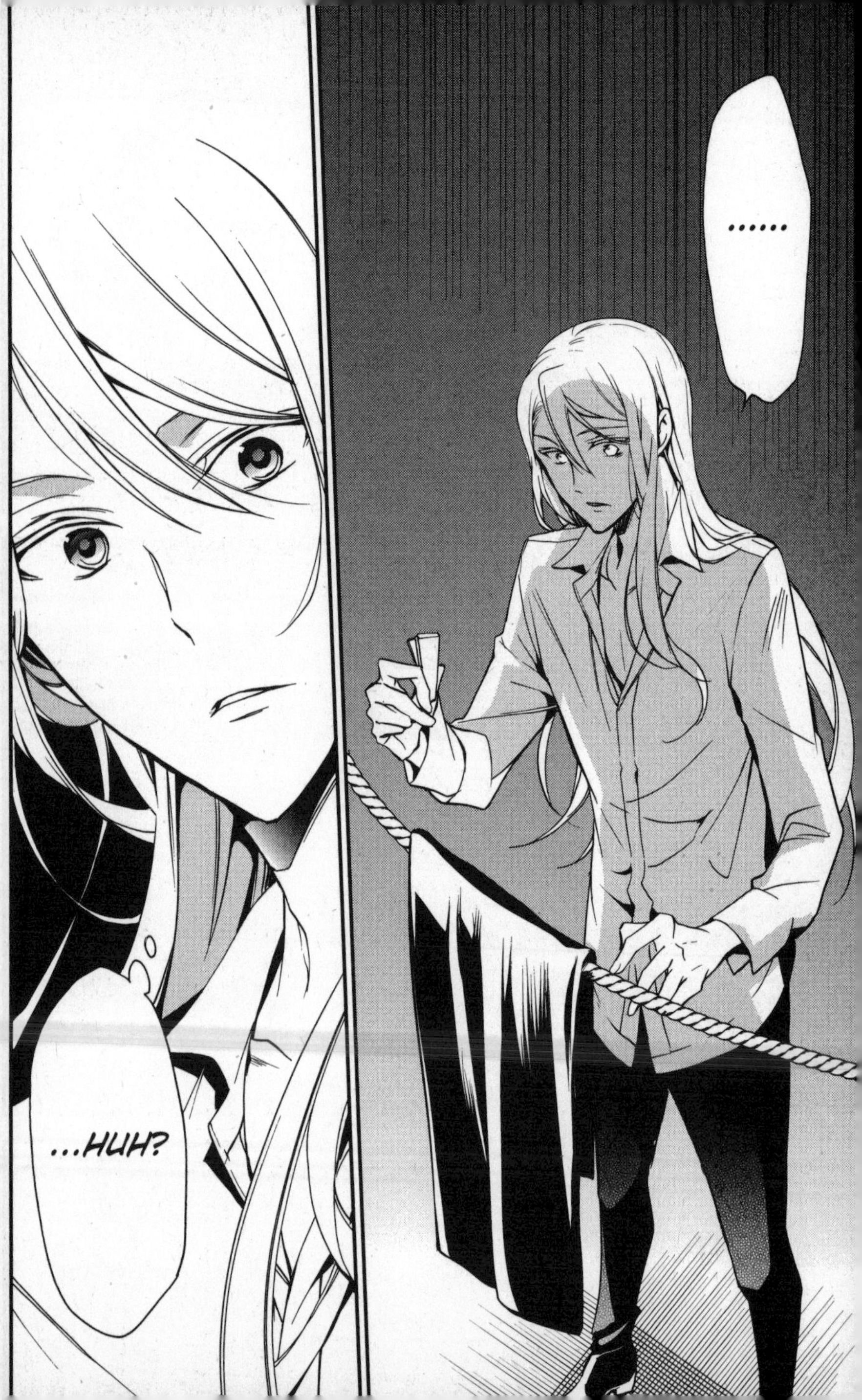
......
...HUH?

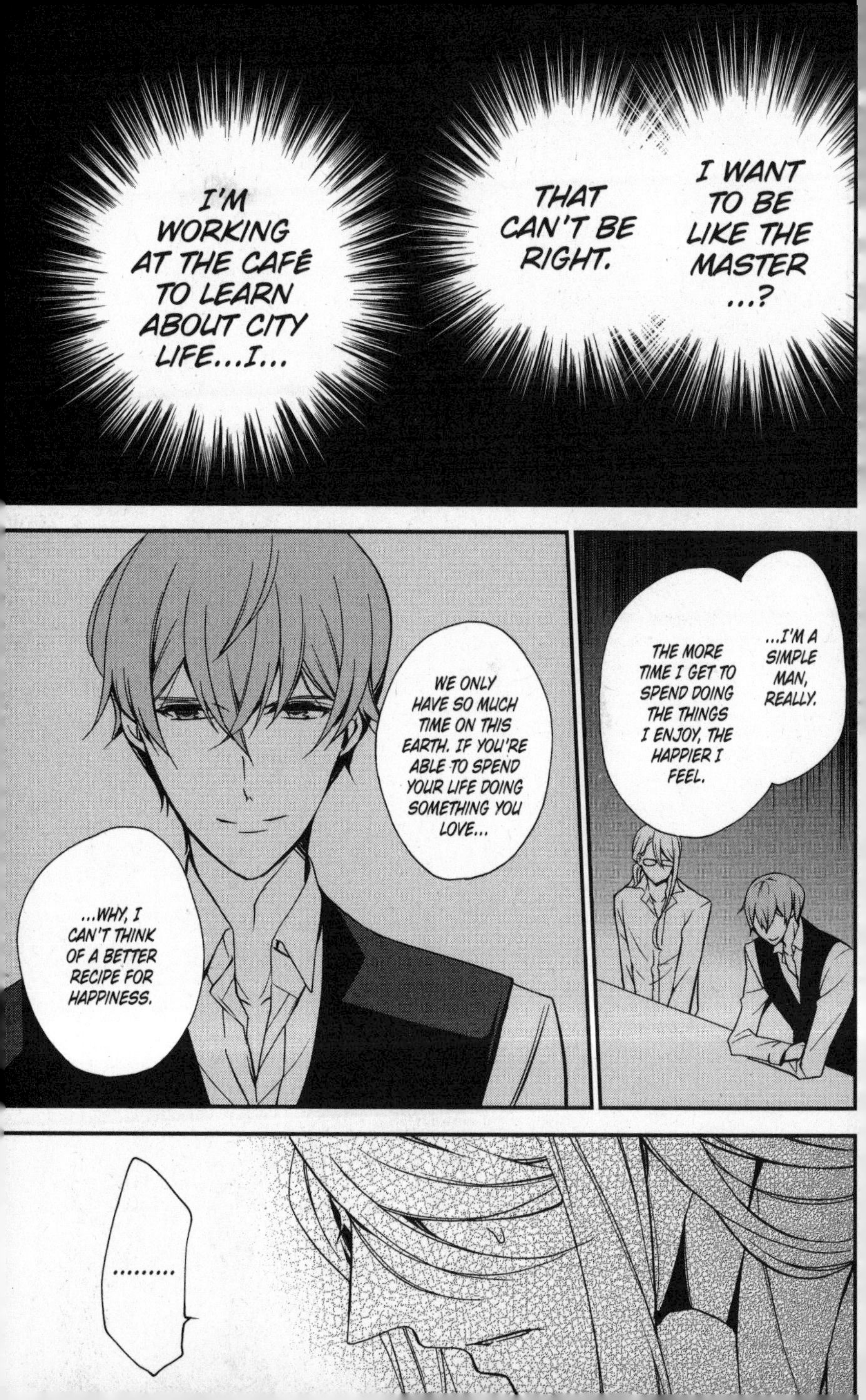
I WANT TO BE LIKE THE MASTER ...?
THAT CAN'T BE RIGHT.
I'M WORKING AT THE CAFÉ TO LEARN ABOUT CITY LIFE...I...
...I'M A SIMPLE MAN, REALLY.
THE MORE TIME I GET TO SPEND DOING THE THINGS I ENJOY, THE HAPPIER I FEEL.
WE ONLY HAVE SO MUCH TIME ON THIS EARTH. IF YOU'RE ABLE TO SPEND YOUR LIFE DOING SOMETHING YOU LOVE...
...WHY, I CAN'T THINK OF A BETTER RECIPE FOR HAPPINESS.
....

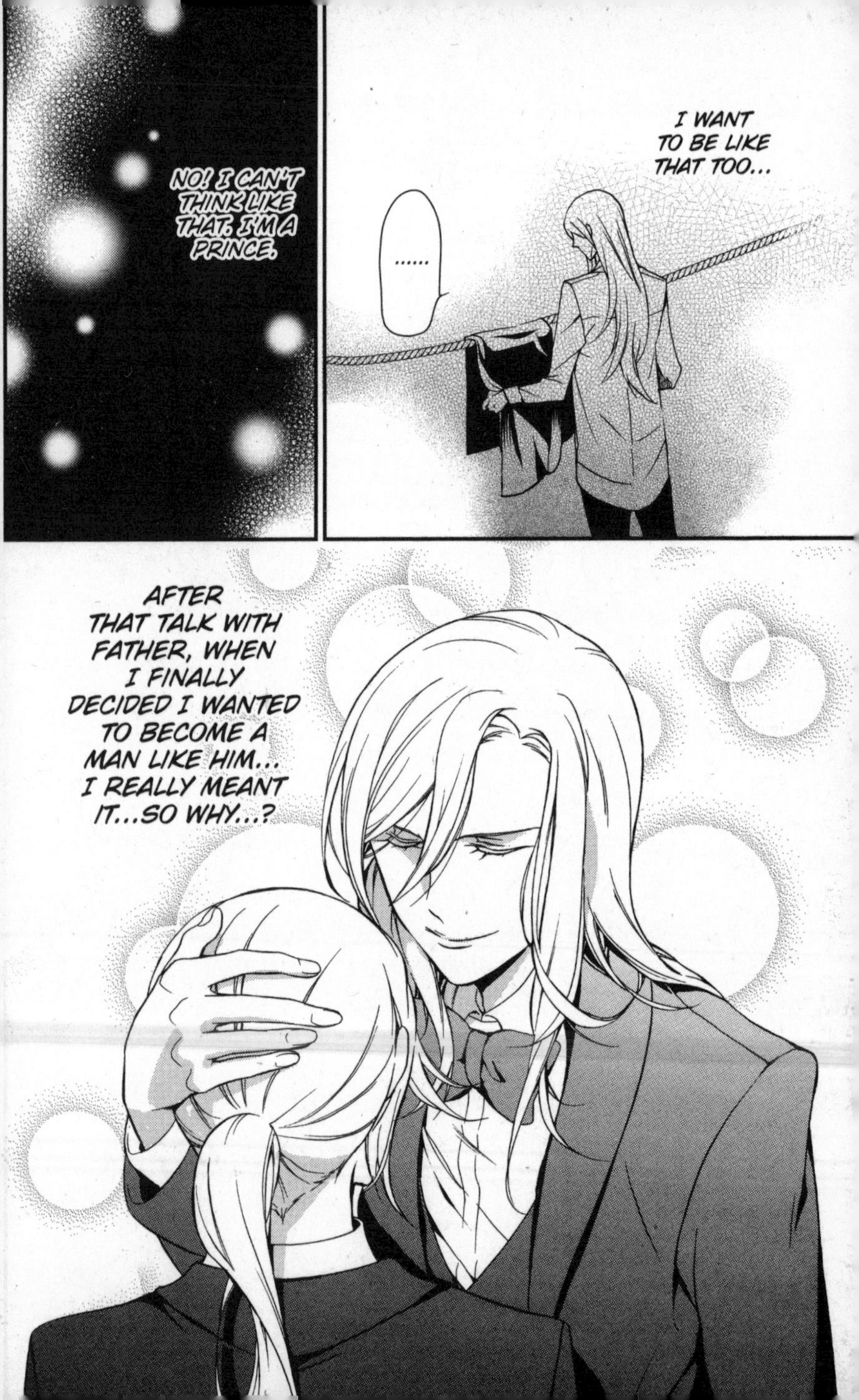
I WANT TO BE LIKE THAT TOO...
......
NO! I CAN'T THINK LIKE THAT. I'M A PRINCE.
AFTER THAT TALK WITH FATHER, WHEN I FINALLY DECIDED I WANTED TO BECOME A MAN LIKE HIM... I REALLY MEANT IT...SO WHY...?

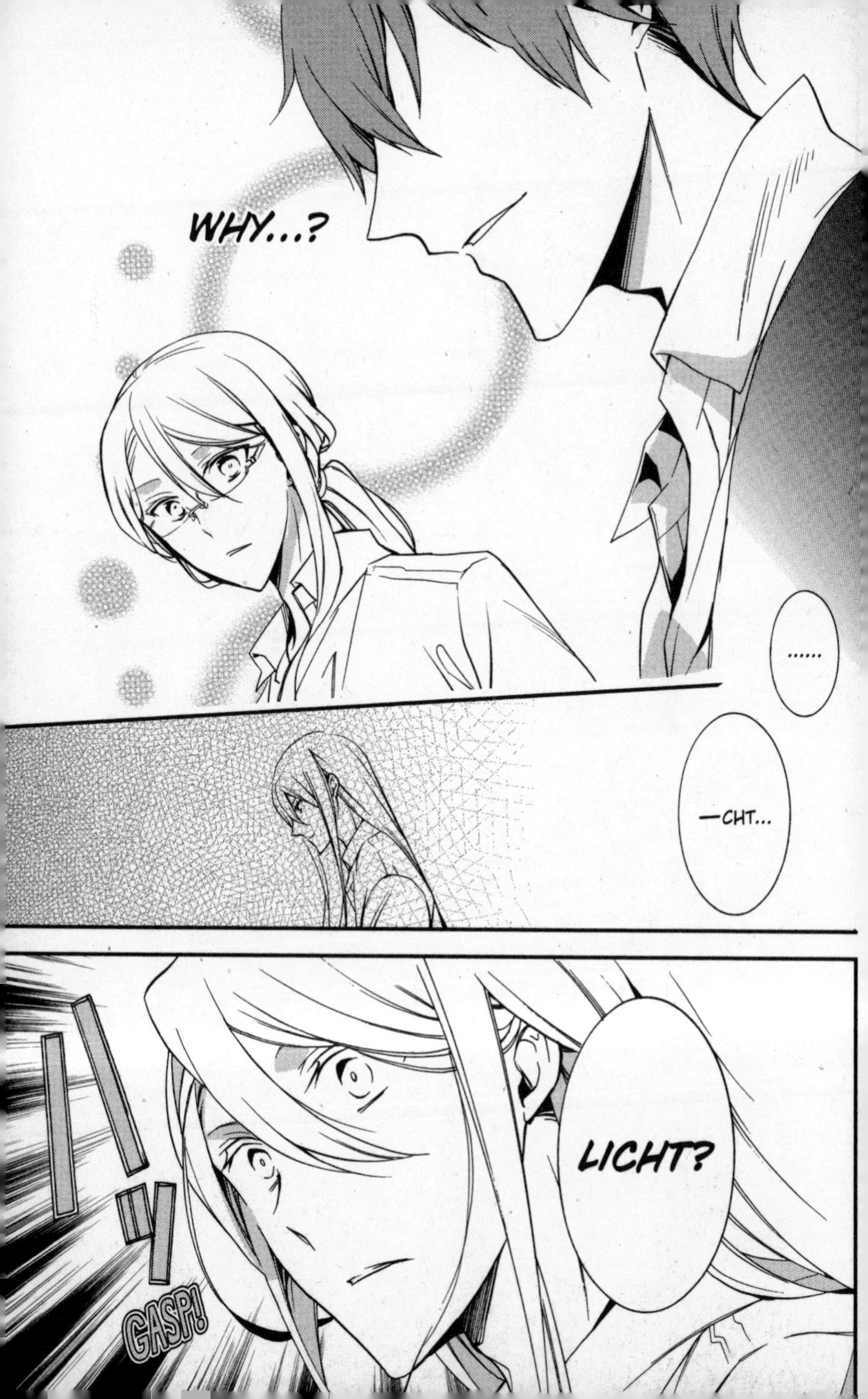
WHY...?
......
—CHT...
LICHT?
GASP!

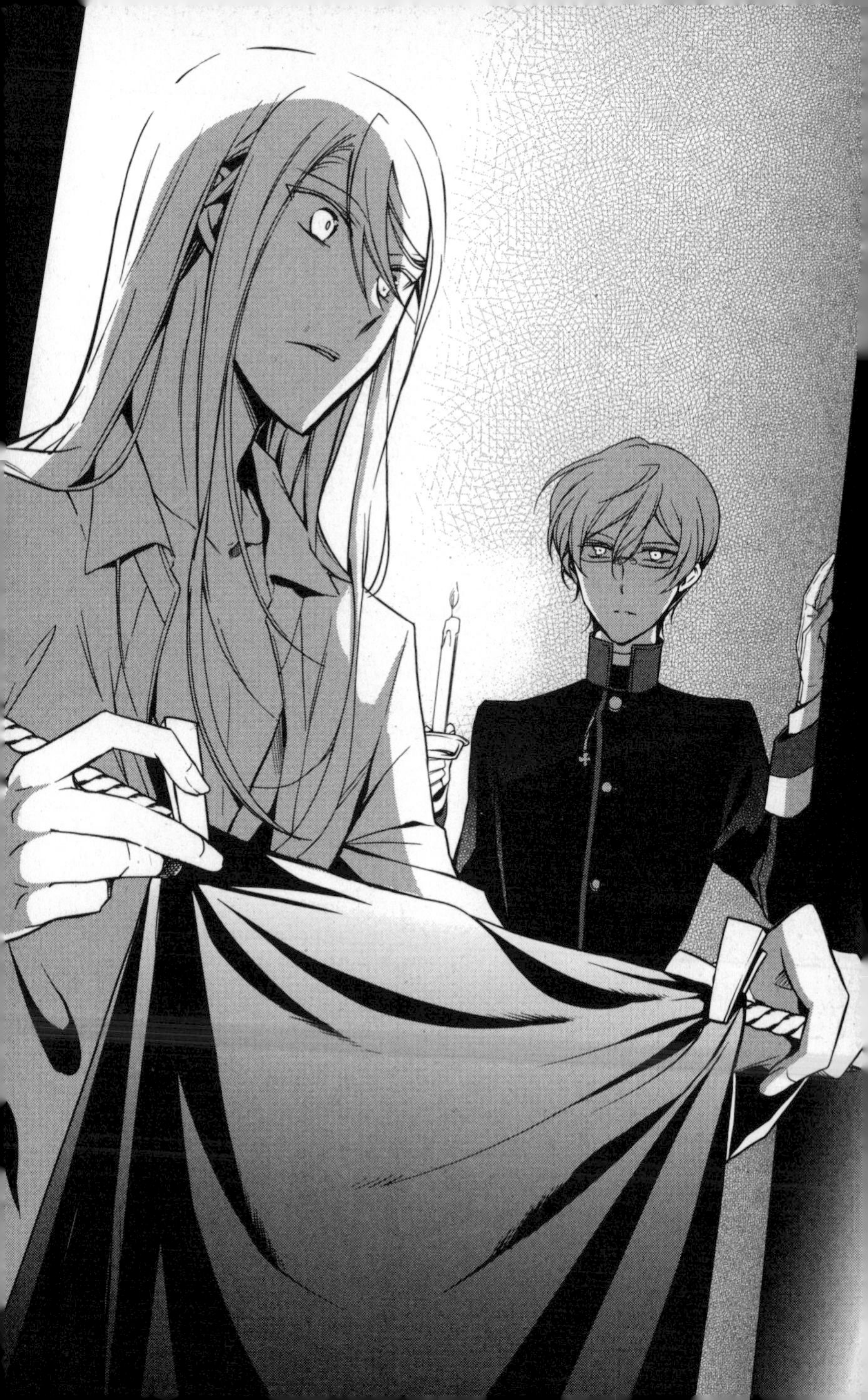

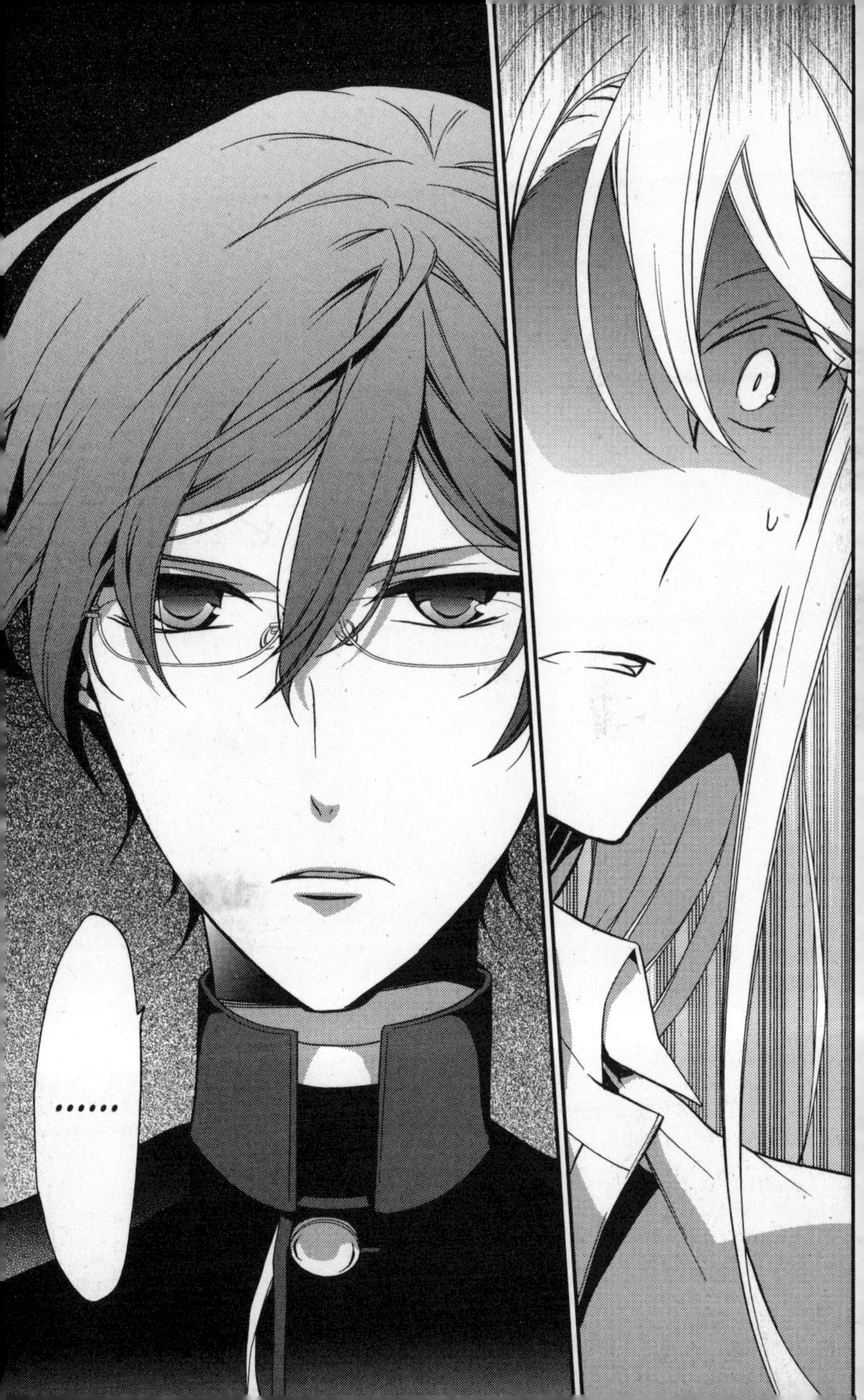
……

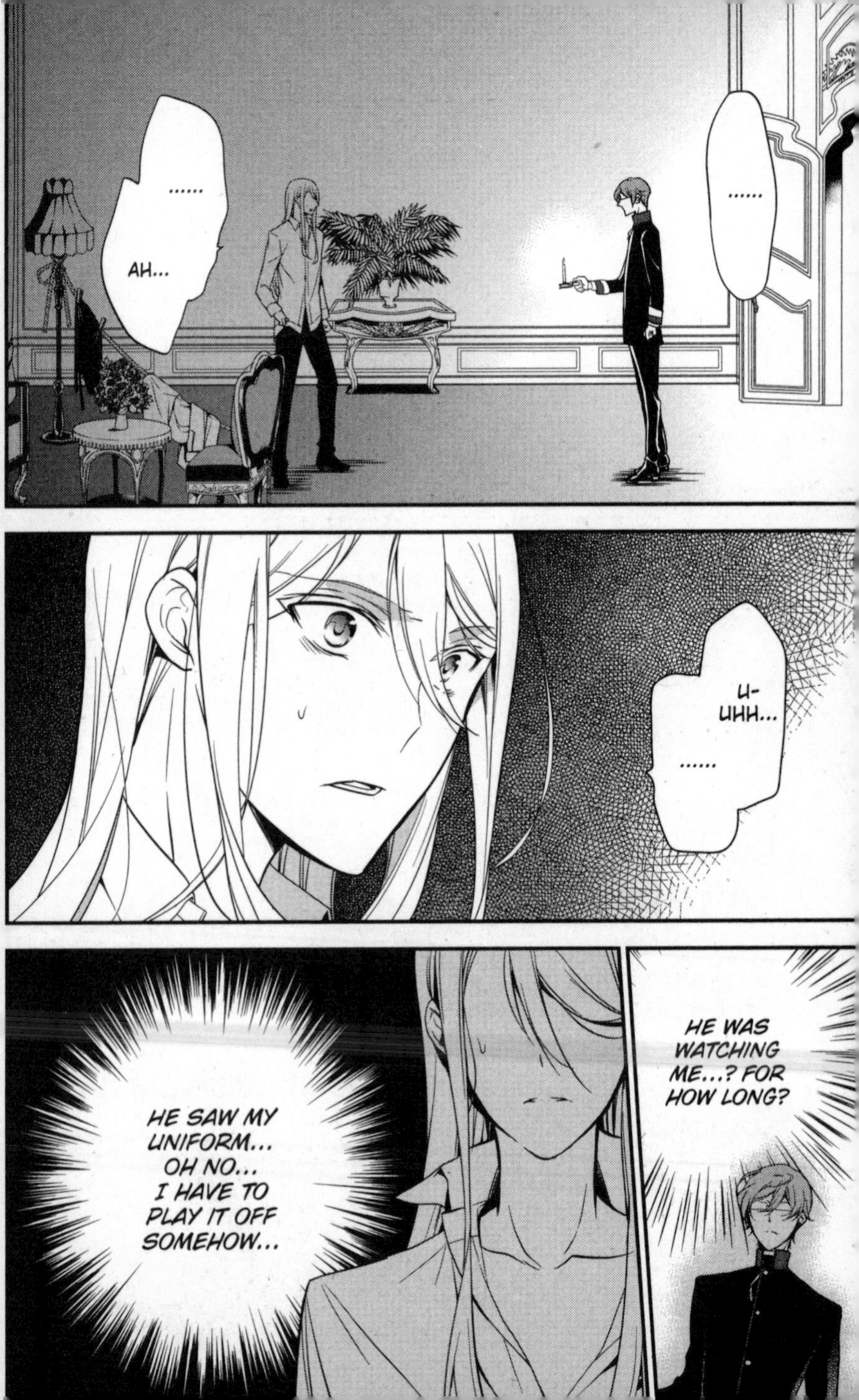
......
......
AH...
U-UHH...
......
HE WAS WATCHING ME...? FOR HOW LONG?
HE SAW MY UNIFORM... OH NO... I HAVE TO PLAY IT OFF SOMEHOW...

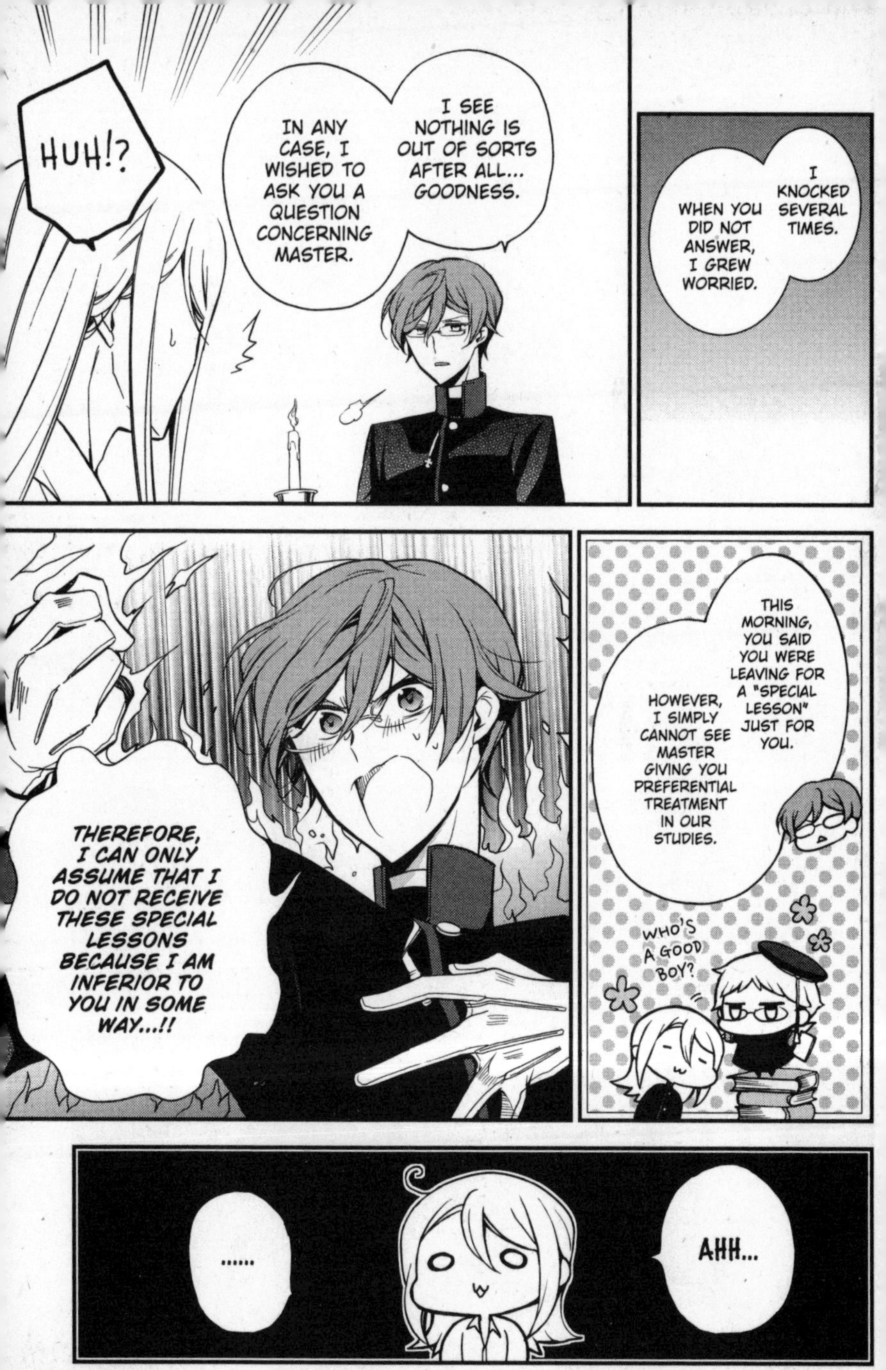
I KNOCKED SEVERAL TIMES.
WHEN YOU DID NOT ANSWER, I GREW WORRIED.
I SEE NOTHING IS OUT OF SORTS AFTER ALL... GOODNESS.
IN ANY CASE, I WISHED TO ASK YOU A QUESTION CONCERNING MASTER.
HUH!?
THIS MORNING, YOU SAID YOU WERE LEAVING FOR A "SPECIAL LESSON" JUST FOR YOU.
HOWEVER, I SIMPLY CANNOT SEE MASTER GIVING YOU PREFERENTIAL TREATMENT IN OUR STUDIES.
WHO'S A GOOD BOY?
THEREFORE, I CAN ONLY ASSUME THAT I DO NOT RECEIVE THESE SPECIAL LESSONS BECAUSE I AM INFERIOR TO YOU IN SOME WAY...!!
AHH...
......

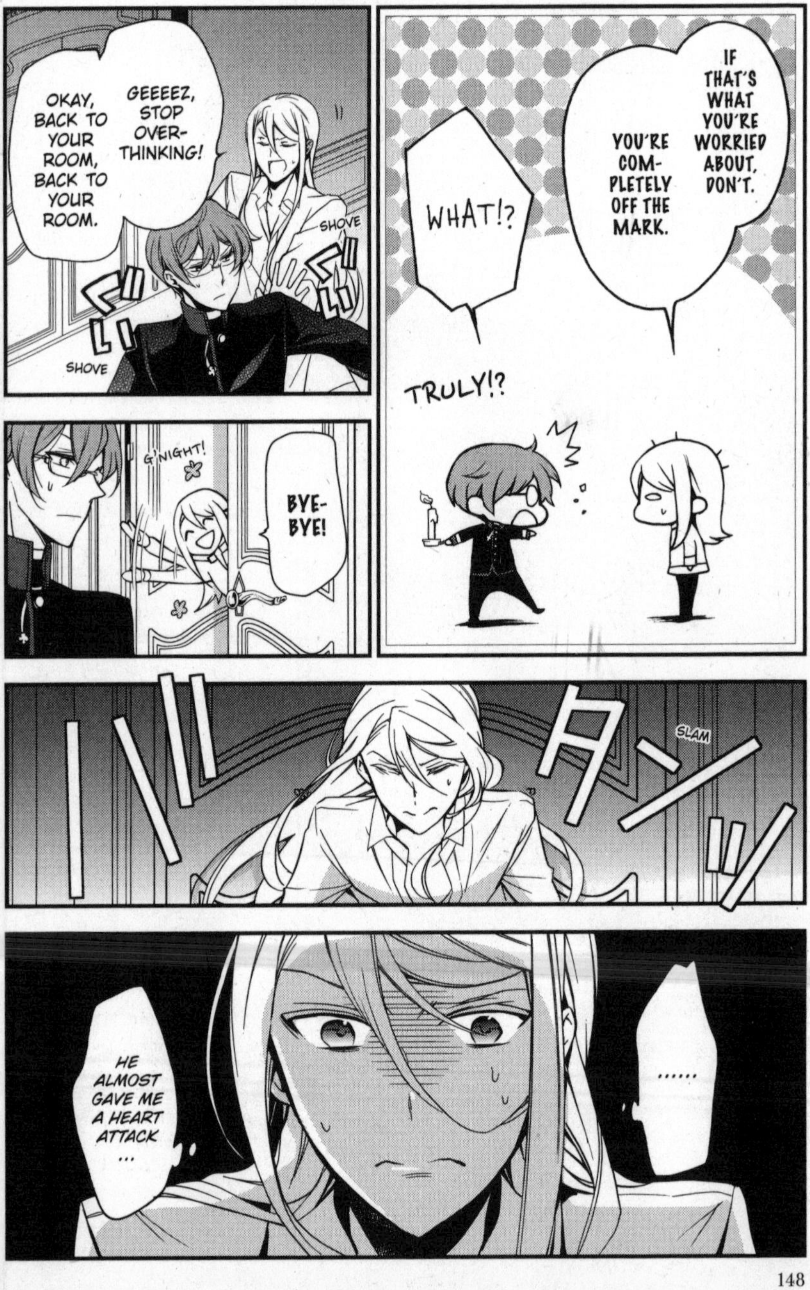
IF THAT'S WHAT YOU'RE WORRIED ABOUT, DON'T.
YOU'RE COM-PLETELY OFF THE MARK.
WHAT!?
TRULY!?
GEEEEZ, STOP OVER-THINKING!
OKAY, BACK TO YOUR ROOM, BACK TO YOUR ROOM.
SHOVE
SHOVE
BYE-BYE!
G'NIGHT!
SLAM
......
HE ALMOST GAVE ME A HEART ATTACK...

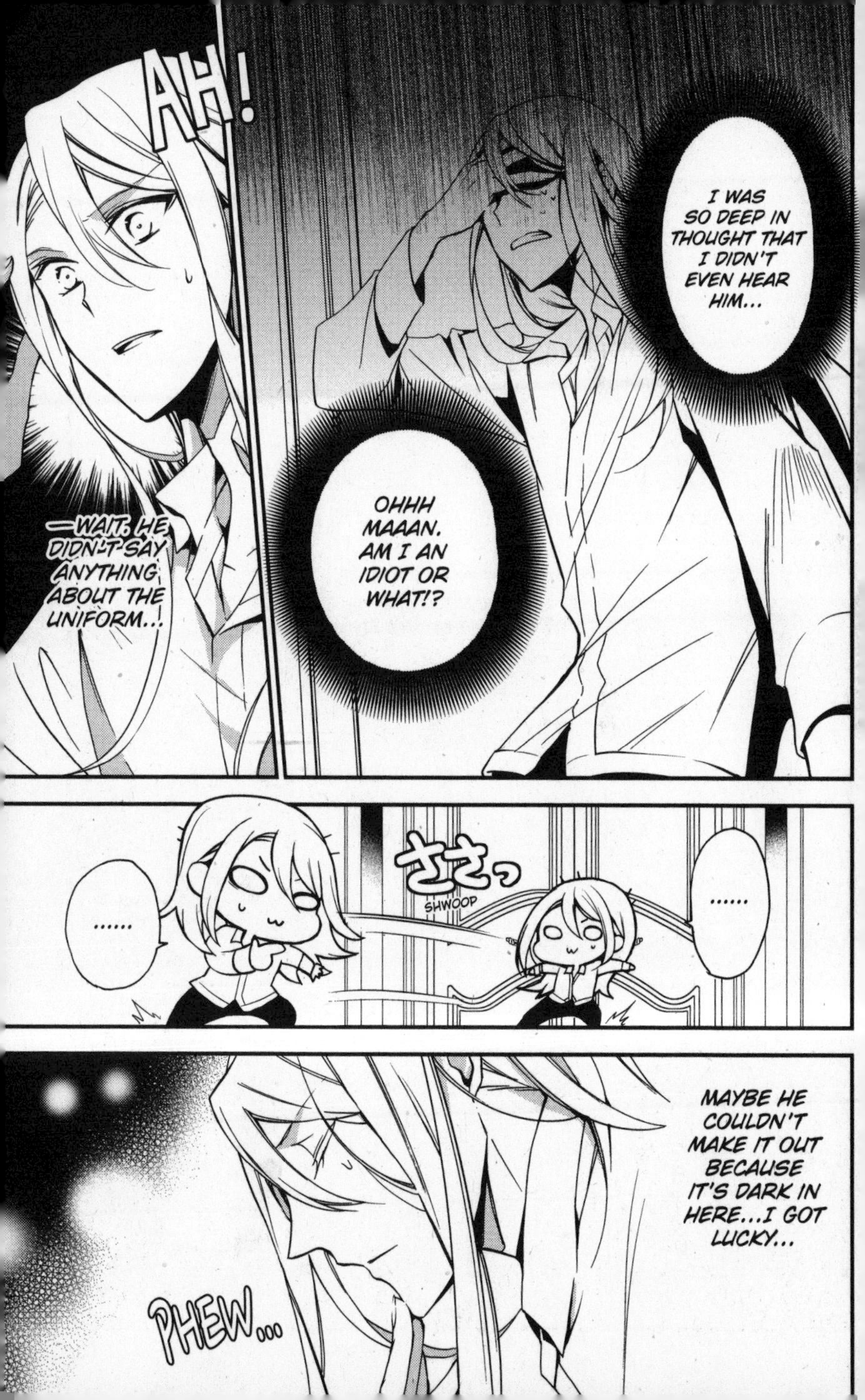
I WAS SO DEEP IN THOUGHT THAT I DIDN'T EVEN HEAR HIM...
OHHH MAAAN. AM I AN IDIOT OR WHAT!?
AH!
—WAIT. HE DIDN'T SAY ANYTHING ABOUT THE UNIFORM...
......
ささっ
SHWOOP
......
MAYBE HE COULDN'T MAKE IT OUT BECAUSE IT'S DARK IN HERE...I GOT LUCKY...
PHEW...

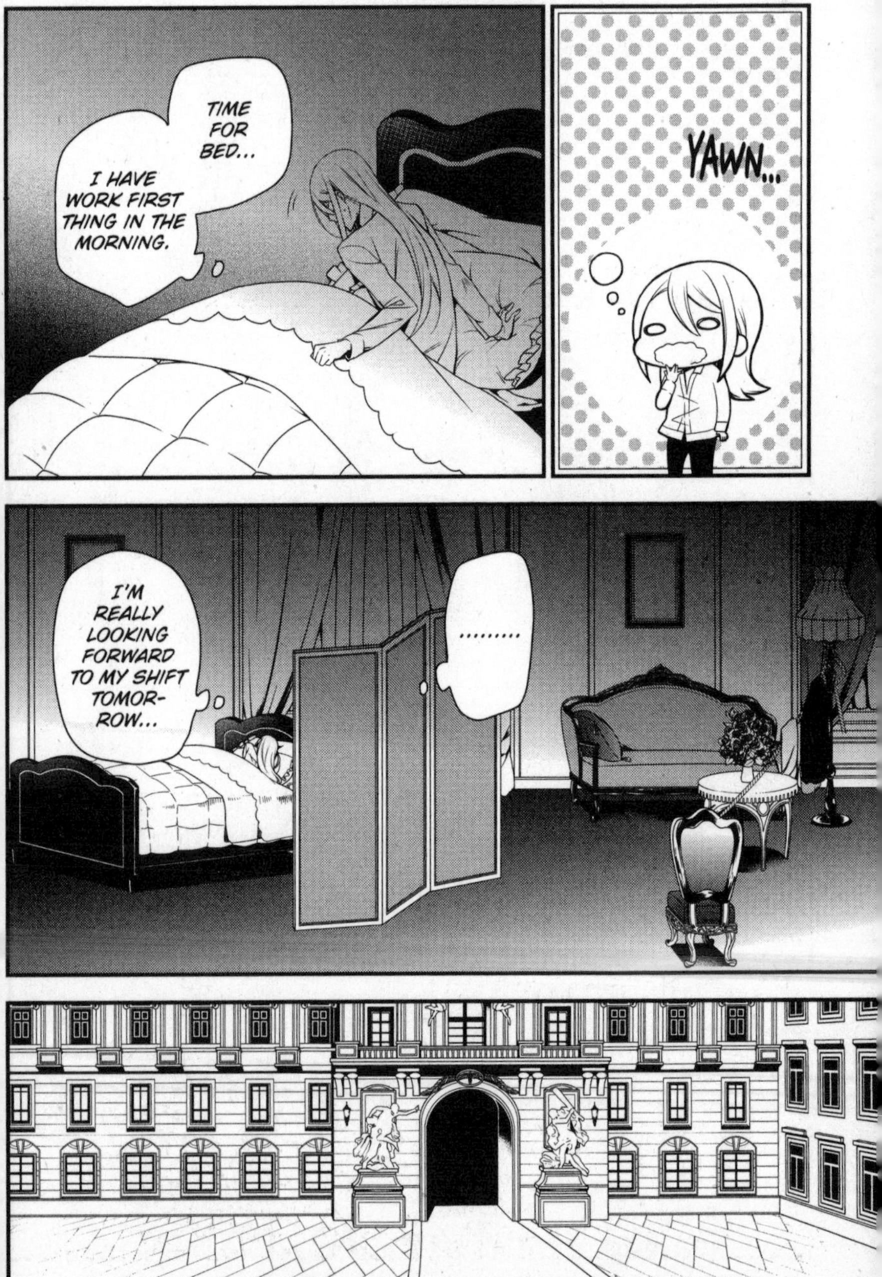
YAWN...
TIME FOR BED...
I HAVE WORK FIRST THING IN THE MORNING.
....
I'M REALLY LOOKING FORWARD TO MY SHIFT TOMOR-ROW...

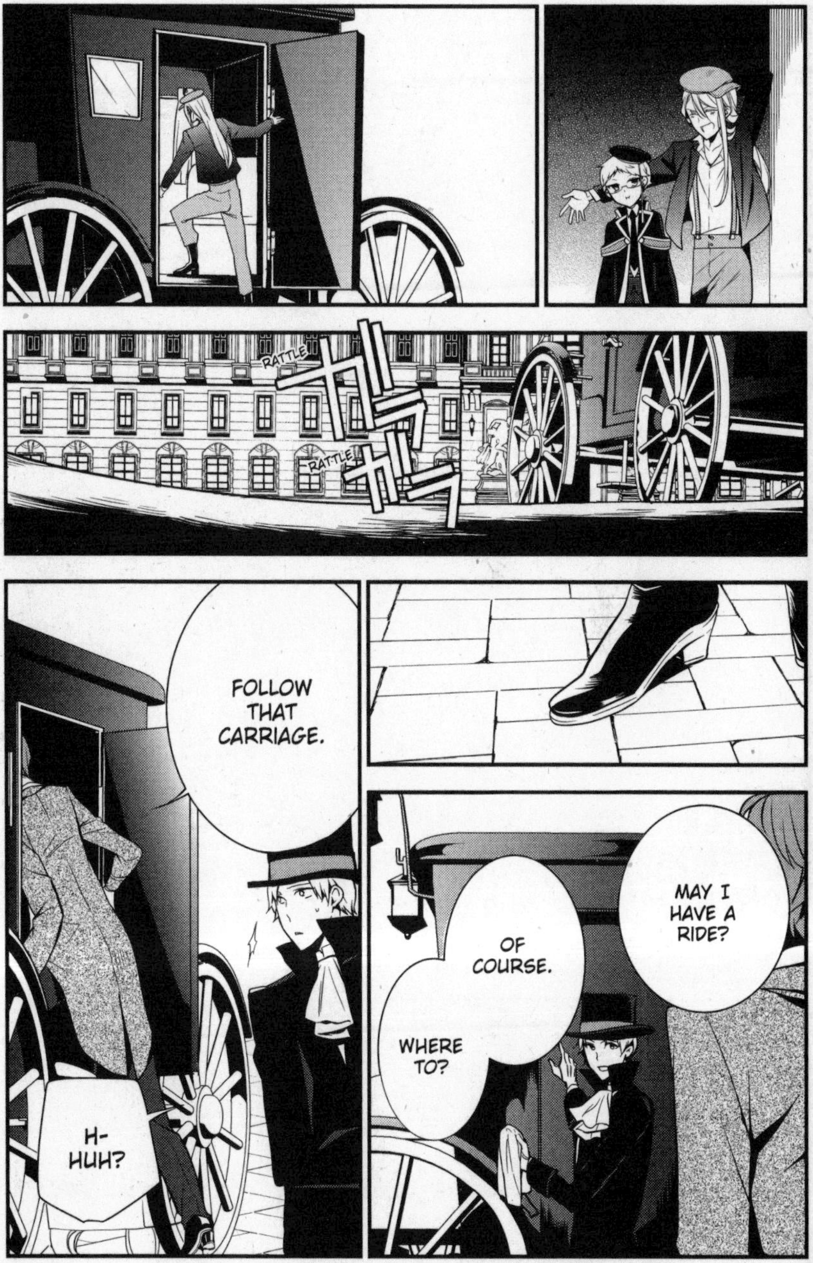
RATTLE
RATTLE
MAY I HAVE A RIDE?
OF COURSE.
WHERE TO?
FOLLOW THAT CARRIAGE.
H-HUH?

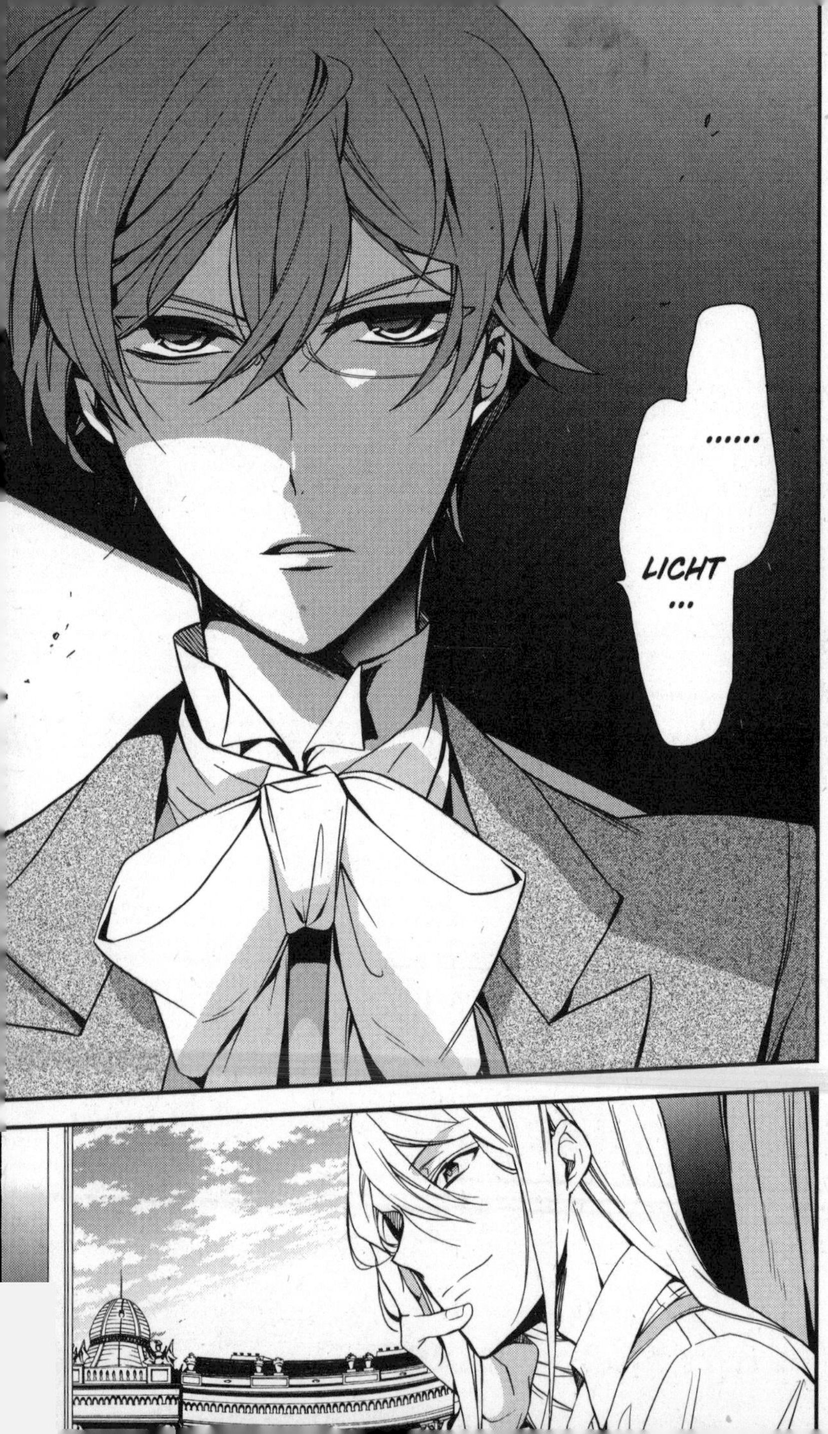
……
LICHT …

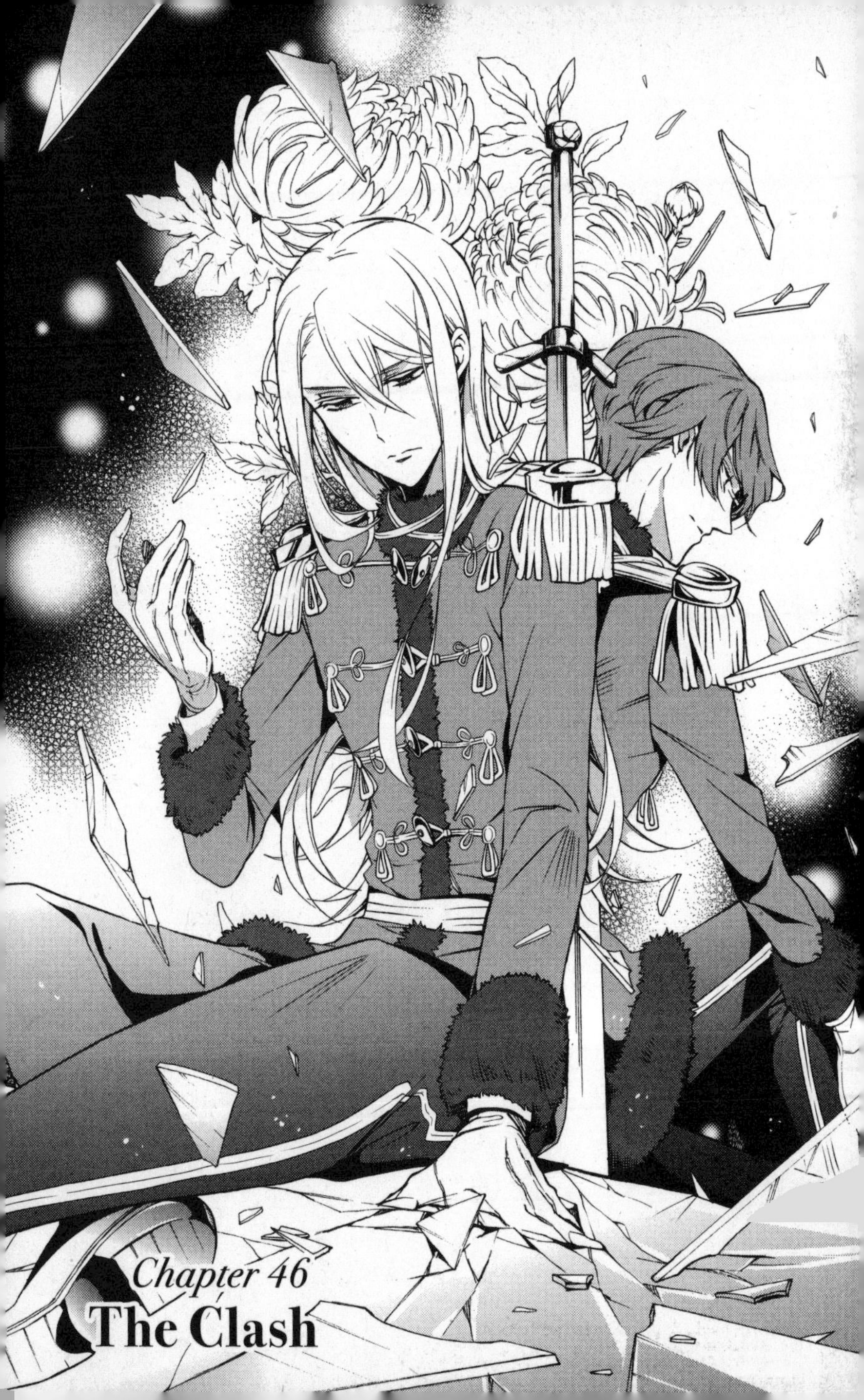

Chapter 46
The Clash

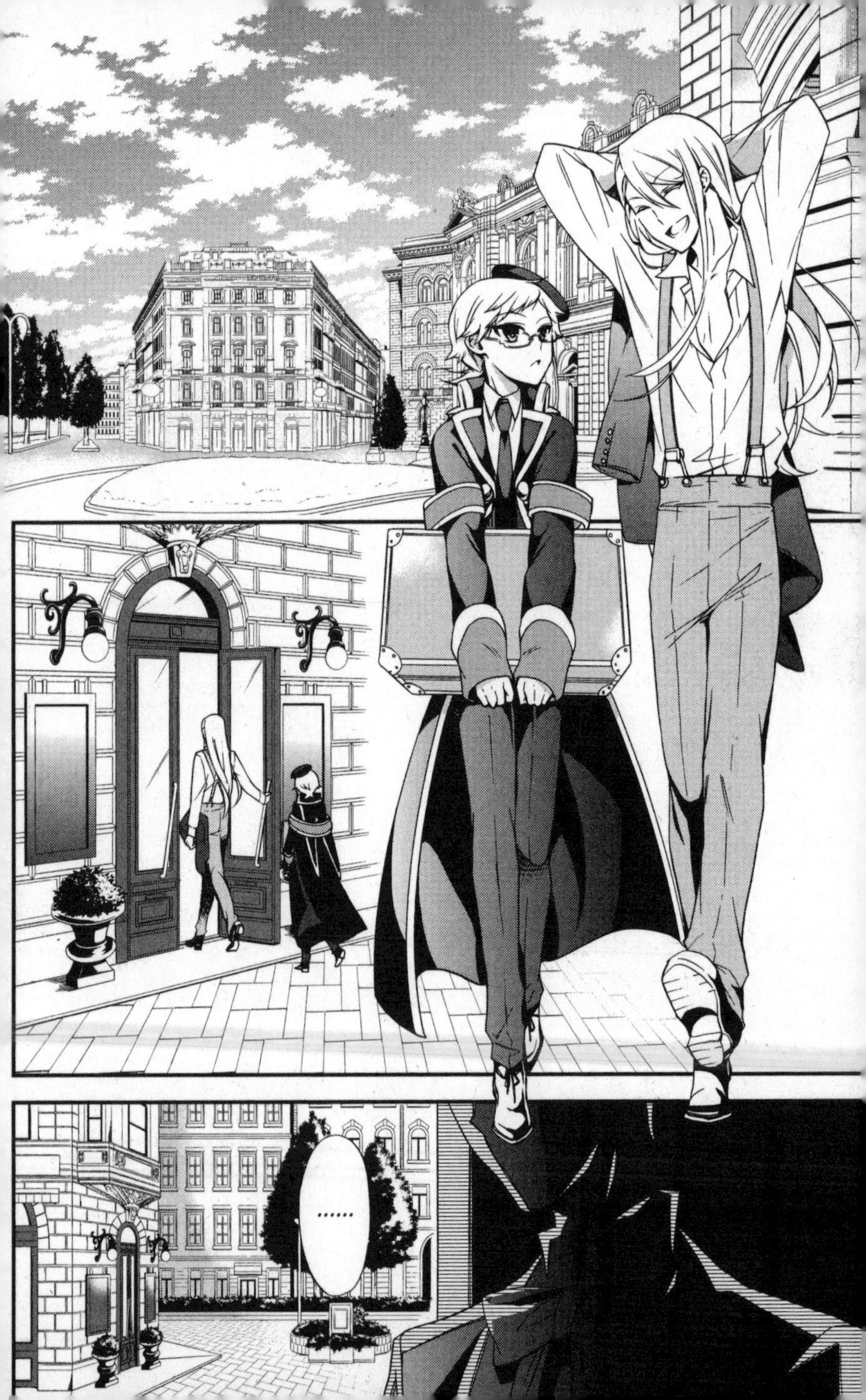
......

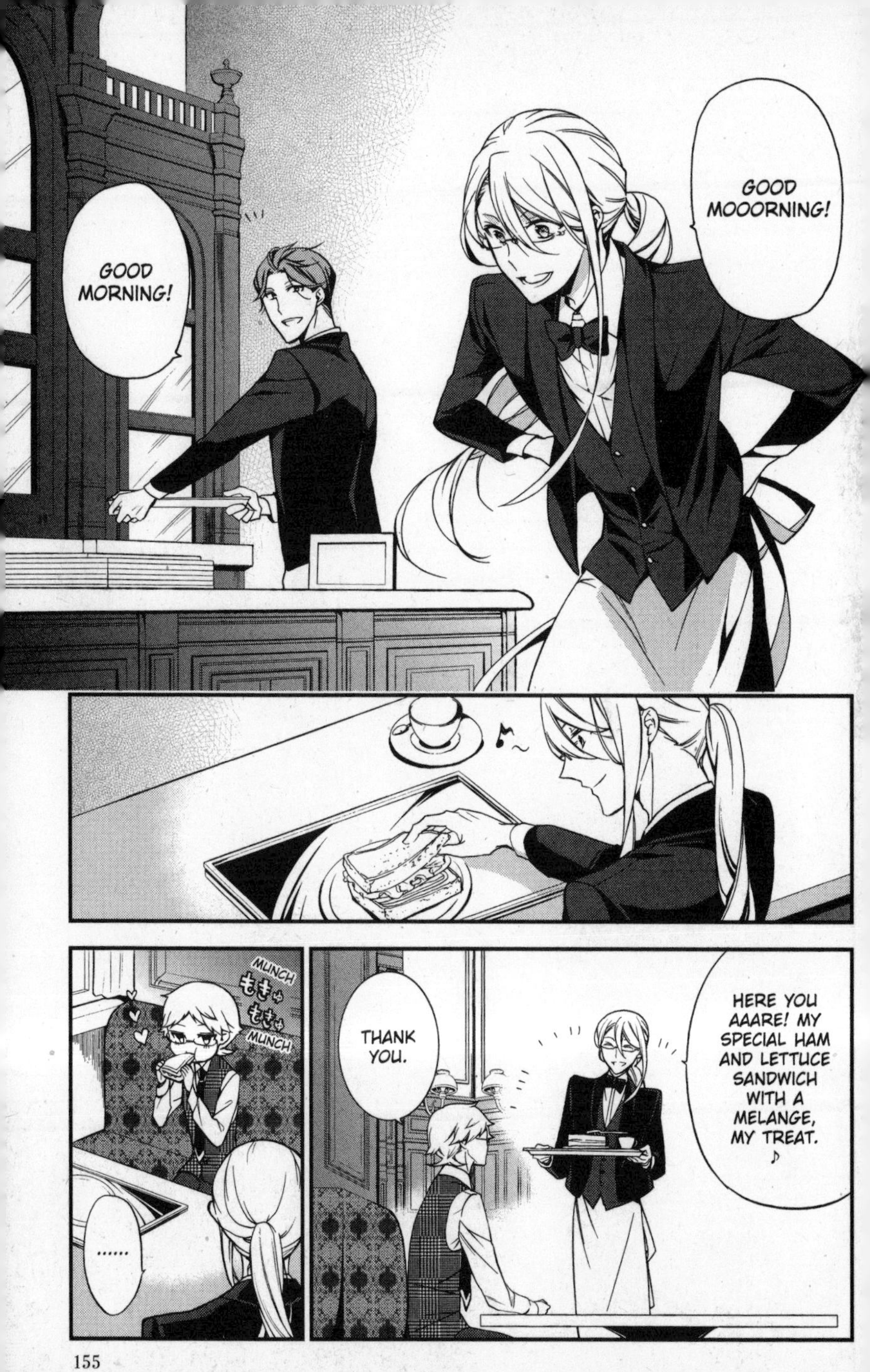
GOOD MOOORNING!
GOOD MORNING!
HERE YOU AAARE! MY SPECIAL HAM AND LETTUCE SANDWICH WITH A MELANGE, MY TREAT. ♪
THANK YOU.
MUNCH もきゅもきゅ MUNCH
......

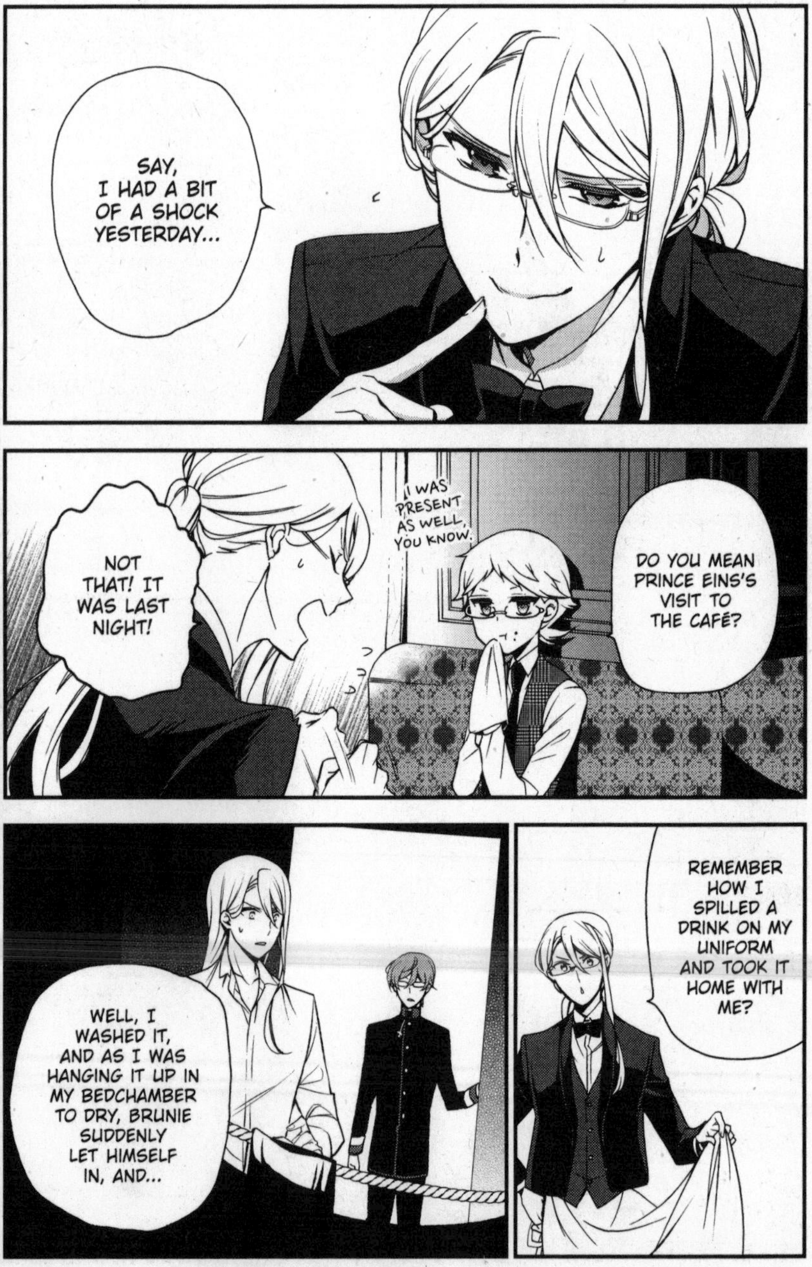
SAY, I HAD A BIT OF A SHOCK YESTERDAY...
DO YOU MEAN PRINCE EINS'S VISIT TO THE CAFÉ?
I WAS PRESENT AS WELL, YOU KNOW.
NOT THAT! IT WAS LAST NIGHT!
REMEMBER HOW I SPILLED A DRINK ON MY UNIFORM AND TOOK IT HOME WITH ME?
WELL, I WASHED IT, AND AS I WAS HANGING IT UP IN MY BEDCHAMBER TO DRY, BRUNIE SUDDENLY LET HIMSELF IN, AND...

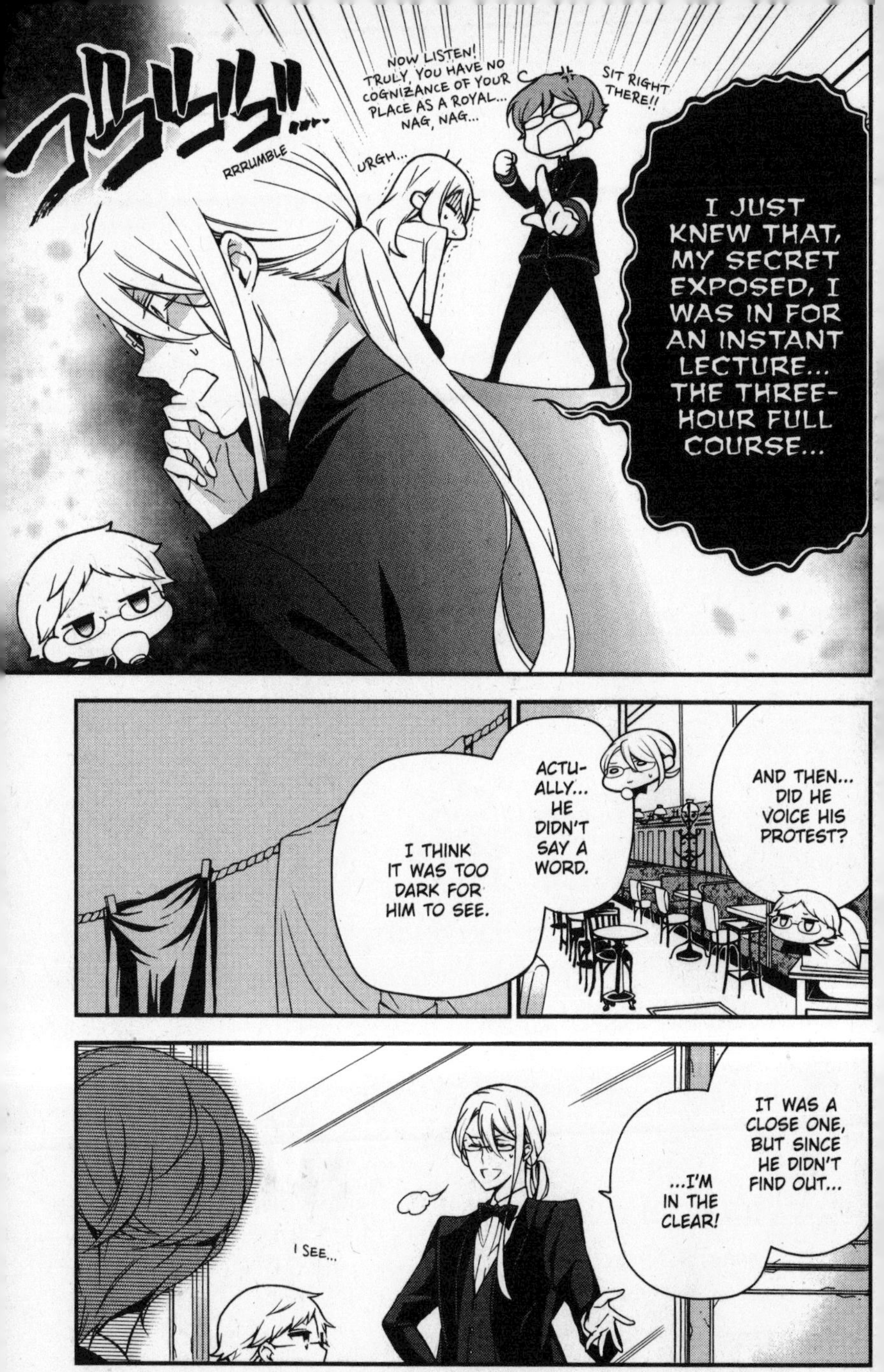
I JUST KNEW THAT, MY SECRET EXPOSED, I WAS IN FOR AN INSTANT LECTURE... THE THREE-HOUR FULL COURSE...
SIT RIGHT THERE!!
NOW LISTEN! TRULY, YOU HAVE NO COGNIZANCE OF YOUR PLACE AS A ROYAL... NAG, NAG...
URGH...
RRRUMBLE
AND THEN... DID HE VOICE HIS PROTEST?
ACTU-ALLY... HE DIDN'T SAY A WORD.
I THINK IT WAS TOO DARK FOR HIM TO SEE.
IT WAS A CLOSE ONE, BUT SINCE HE DIDN'T FIND OUT...
...I'M IN THE CLEAR!
I SEE...

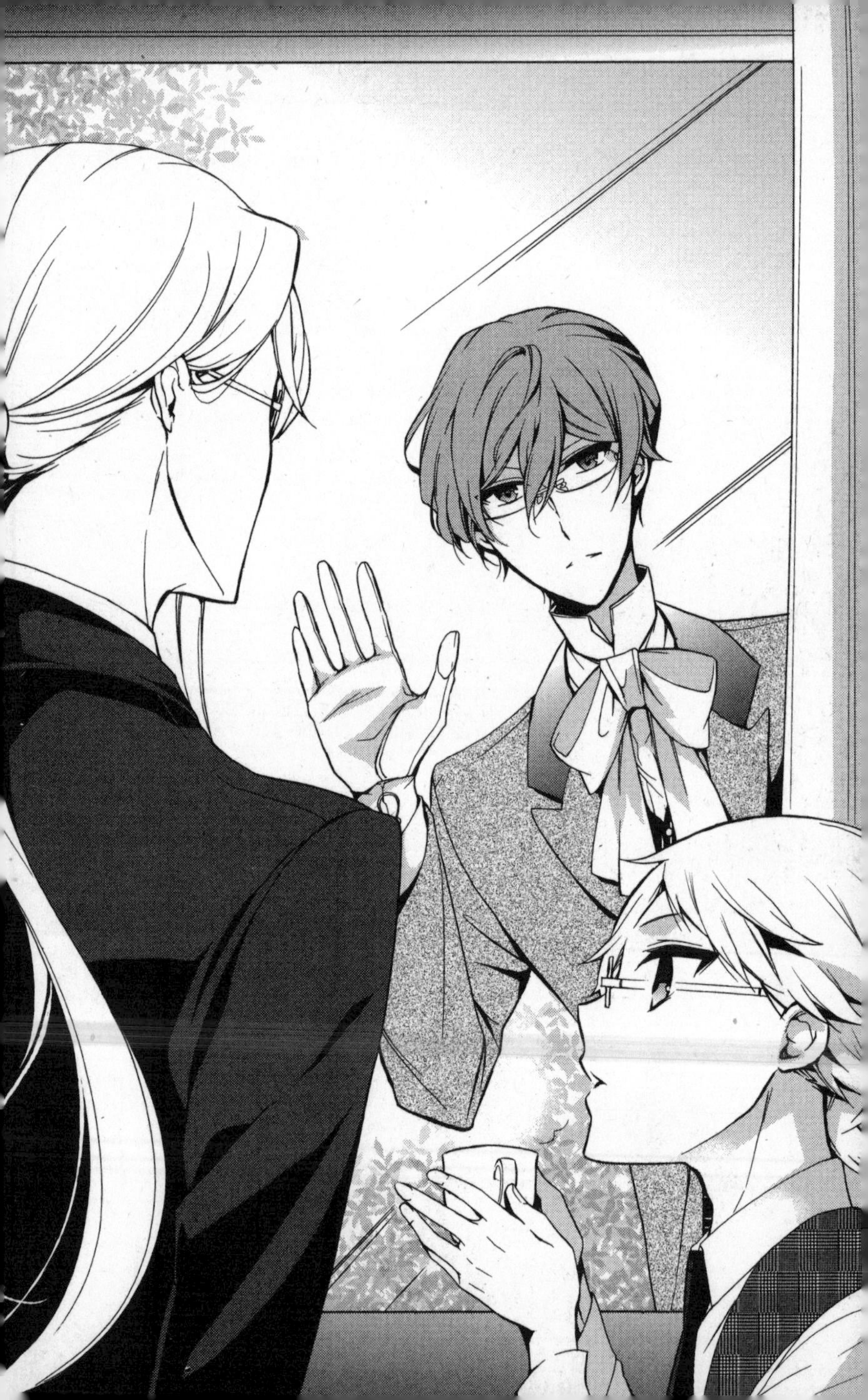

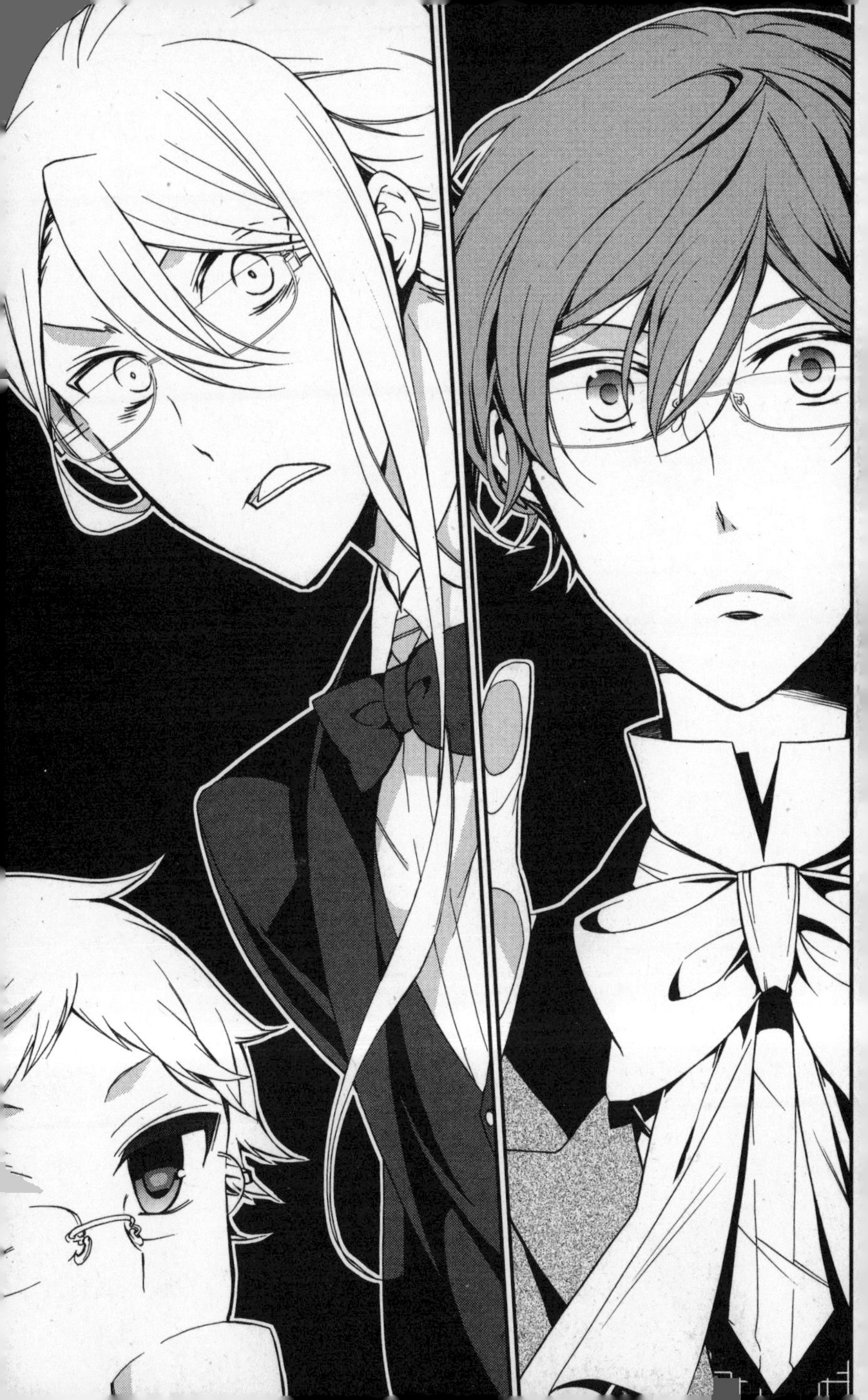

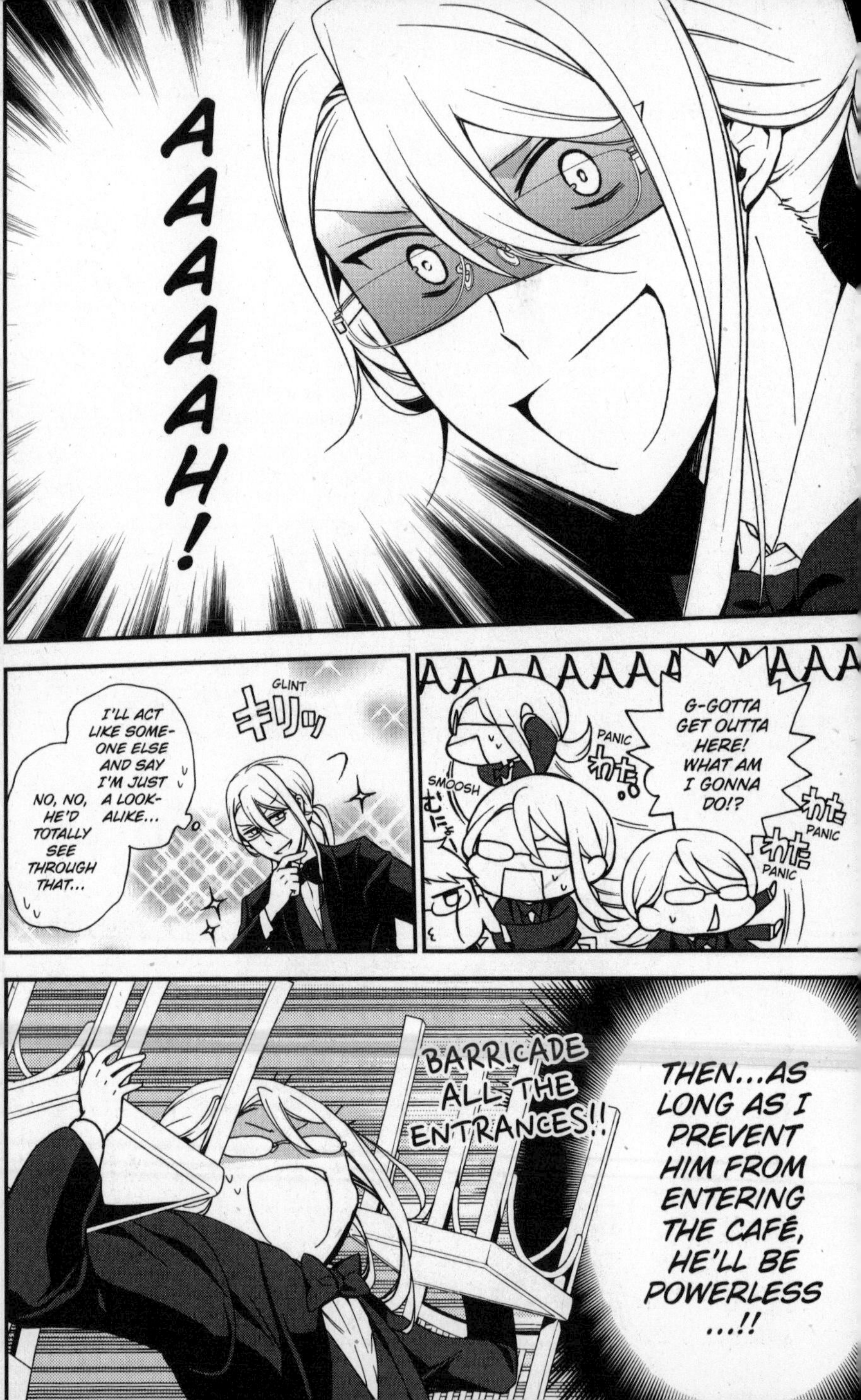
AAAAAH!
AAAAAAAAAAAAAA
G-GOTTA GET OUTTA HERE! WHAT AM I GONNA DO!?
PANIC
PANIC
PANIC
SMOOSH
GLINT
キリッ
I'LL ACT LIKE SOME-ONE ELSE AND SAY I'M JUST A LOOK-ALIKE...
NO, NO, HE'D TOTALLY SEE THROUGH THAT...
THEN...AS LONG AS I PREVENT HIM FROM ENTERING THE CAFÉ, HE'LL BE POWERLESS ...!!
BARRICADE ALL THE ENTRANCES!!

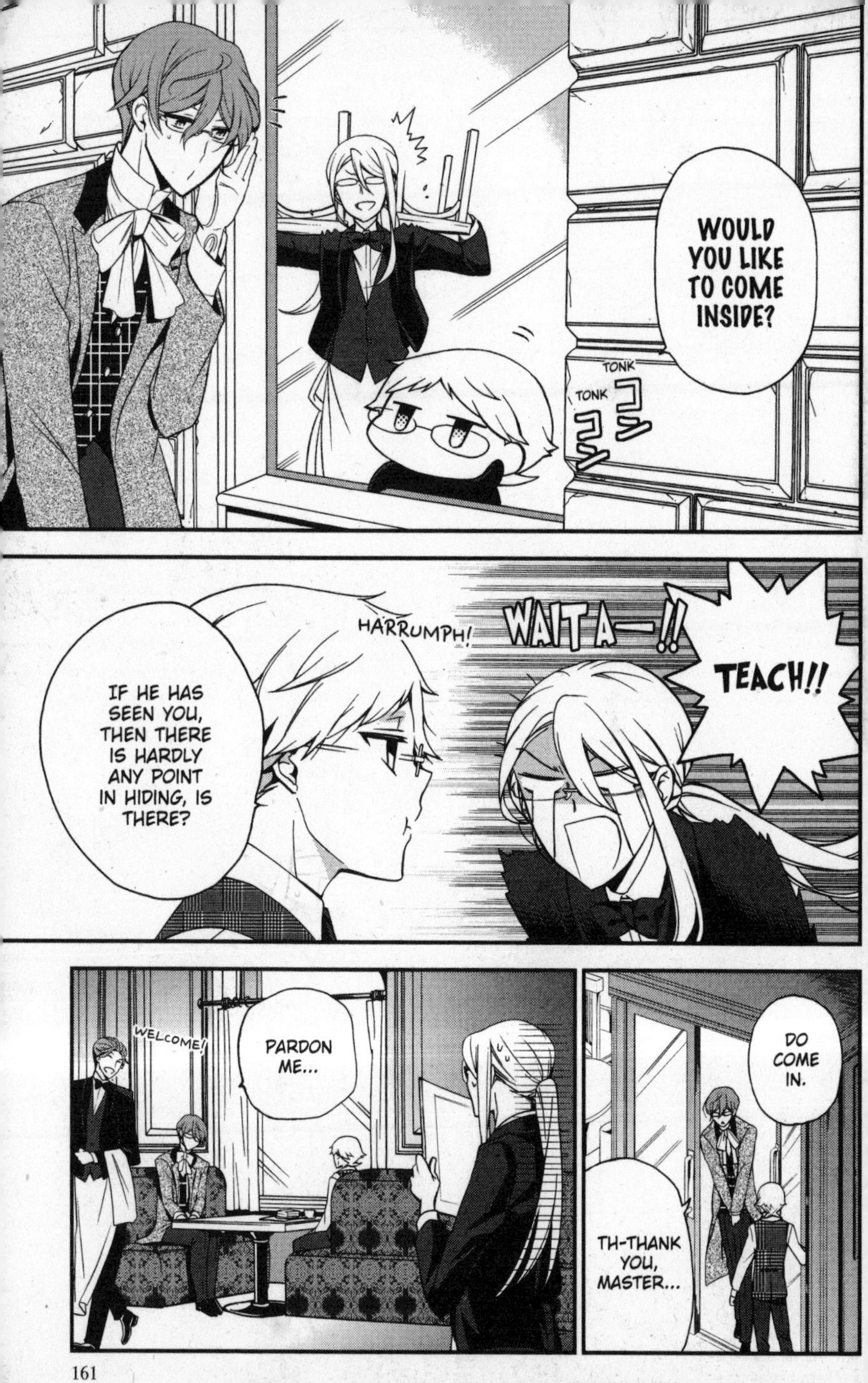
WOULD YOU LIKE TO COME INSIDE?
TONK
TONK
WAIT A—!!
TEACH!!
HARRUMPH!
IF HE HAS SEEN YOU, THEN THERE IS HARDLY ANY POINT IN HIDING, IS THERE?
DO COME IN.
TH-THANK YOU, MASTER...
PARDON ME...
WELCOME!

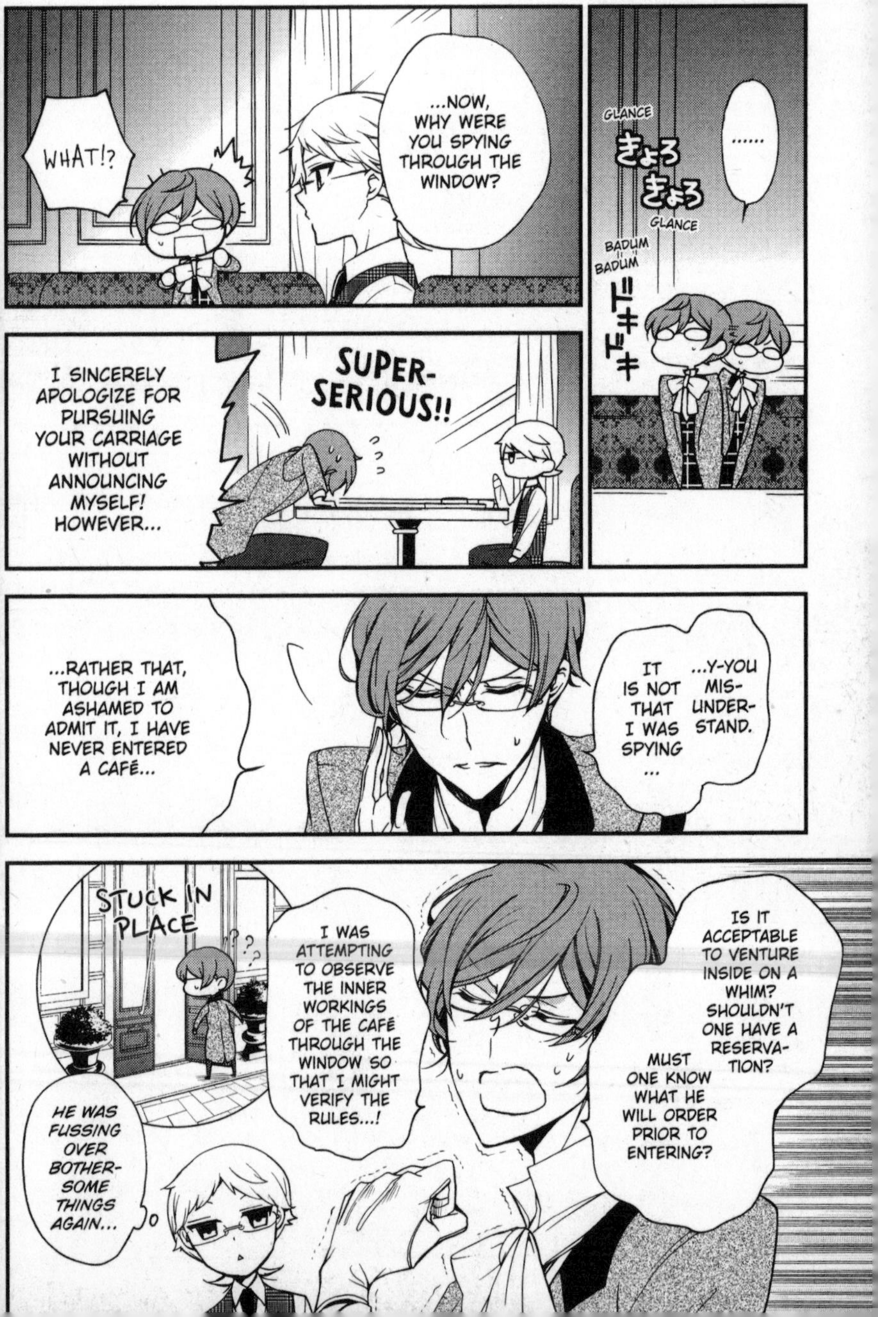
......
GLANCE
きょろきょろ
GLANCE
BADUM BADUM
ドキドキ
...NOW, WHY WERE YOU SPYING THROUGH THE WINDOW?
WHAT!?
SUPER-SERIOUS!!
I SINCERELY APOLOGIZE FOR PURSUING YOUR CARRIAGE WITHOUT ANNOUNCING MYSELF! HOWEVER...
...Y-YOU MISUNDERSTAND.
IT IS NOT THAT I WAS SPYING...
...RATHER THAT, THOUGH I AM ASHAMED TO ADMIT IT, I HAVE NEVER ENTERED A CAFÉ...
IS IT ACCEPTABLE TO VENTURE INSIDE ON A WHIM? SHOULDN'T ONE HAVE A RESERVATION?
MUST ONE KNOW WHAT HE WILL ORDER PRIOR TO ENTERING?
I WAS ATTEMPTING TO OBSERVE THE INNER WORKINGS OF THE CAFÉ THROUGH THE WINDOW SO THAT I MIGHT VERIFY THE RULES...!
STUCK IN PLACE
HE WAS FUSSING OVER BOTHERSOME THINGS AGAIN...

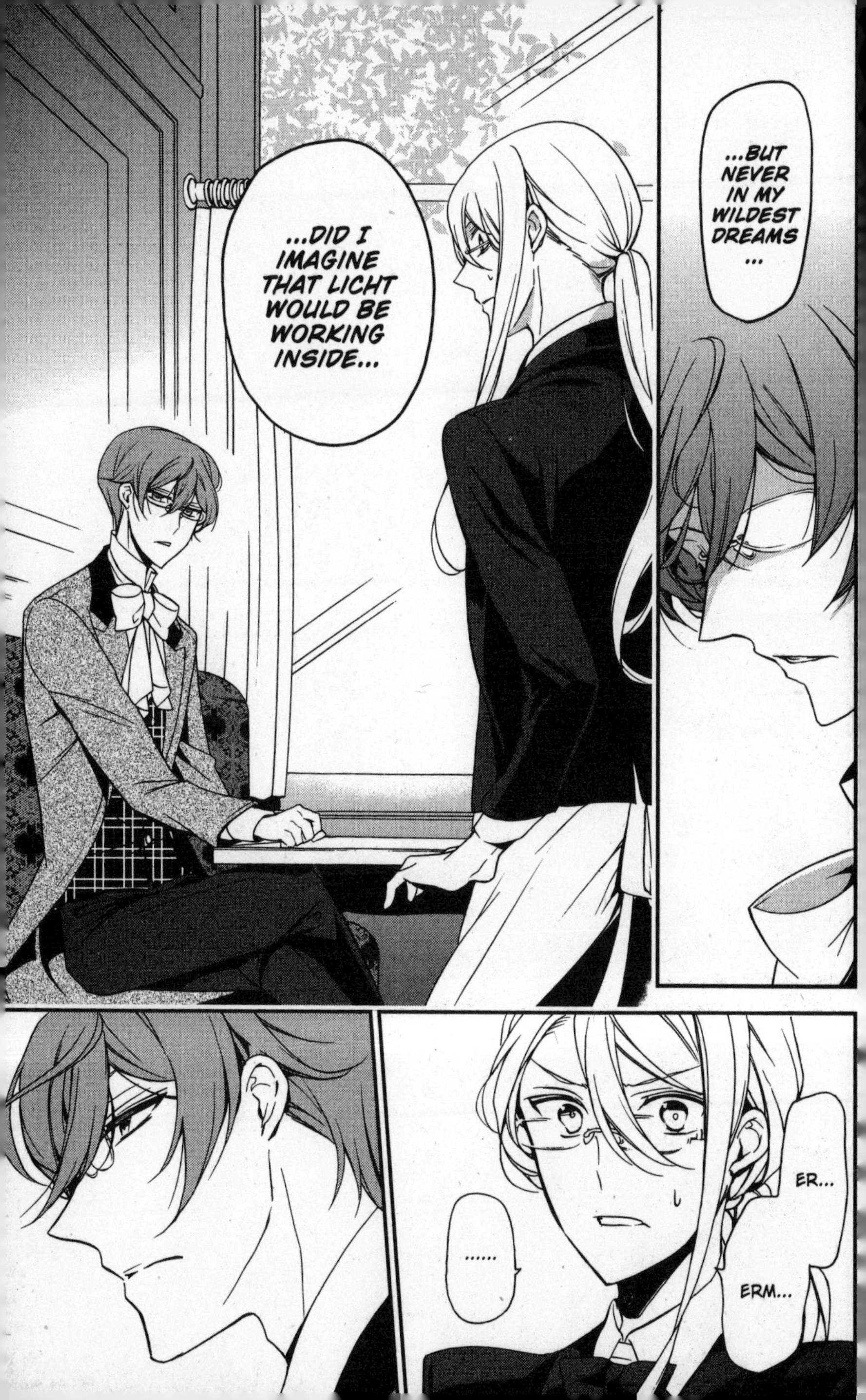
...BUT NEVER IN MY WILDEST DREAMS...
...DID I IMAGINE THAT LICHT WOULD BE WORKING INSIDE...
ER...
......
ERM...

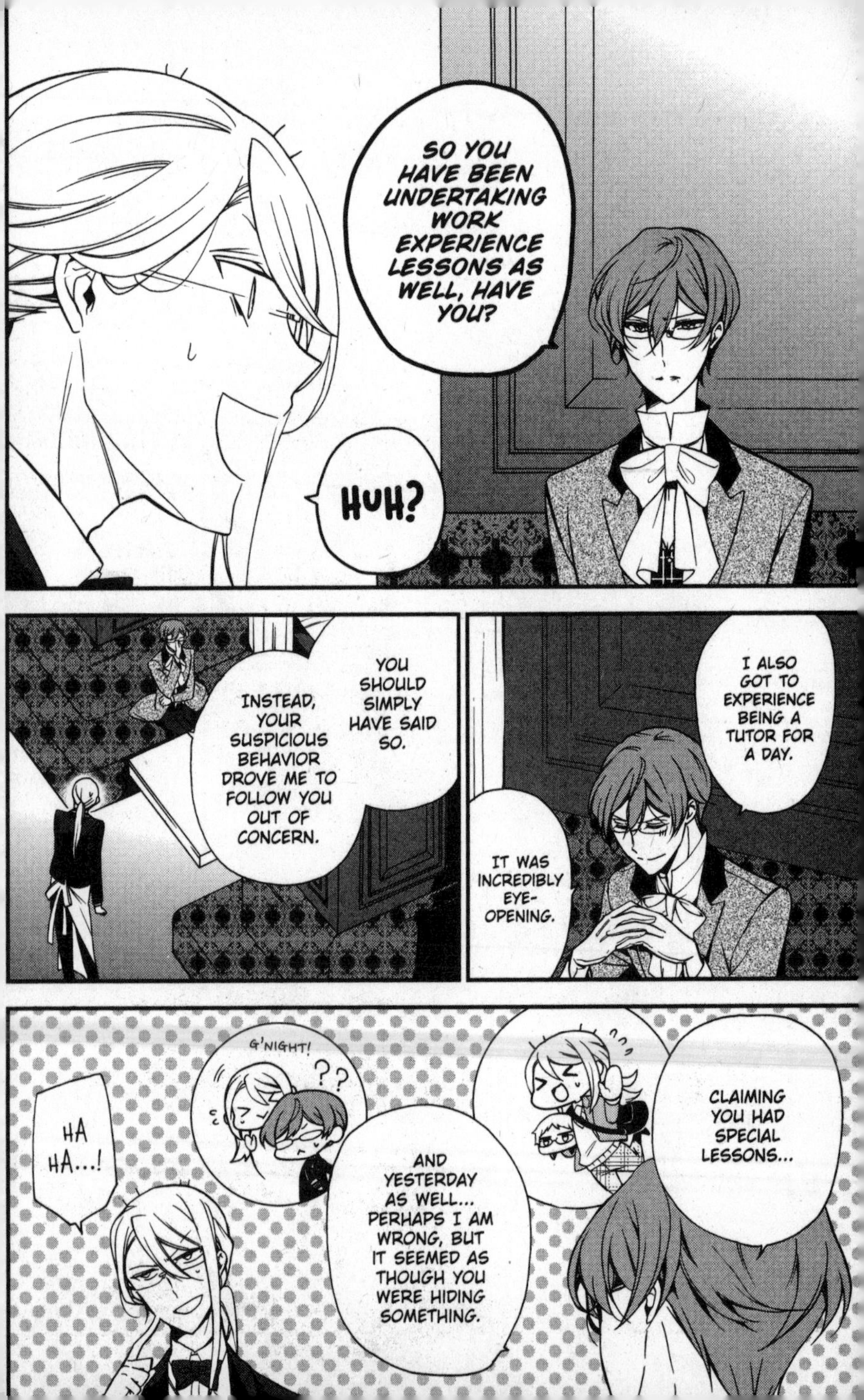
SO YOU HAVE BEEN UNDERTAKING WORK EXPERIENCE LESSONS AS WELL, HAVE YOU?
HUH?
I ALSO GOT TO EXPERIENCE BEING A TUTOR FOR A DAY.
IT WAS INCREDIBLY EYE-OPENING.
YOU SHOULD SIMPLY HAVE SAID SO.
INSTEAD, YOUR SUSPICIOUS BEHAVIOR DROVE ME TO FOLLOW YOU OUT OF CONCERN.
CLAIMING YOU HAD SPECIAL LESSONS...
G'NIGHT!
AND YESTERDAY AS WELL... PERHAPS I AM WRONG, BUT IT SEEMED AS THOUGH YOU WERE HIDING SOMETHING.
HA HA...!

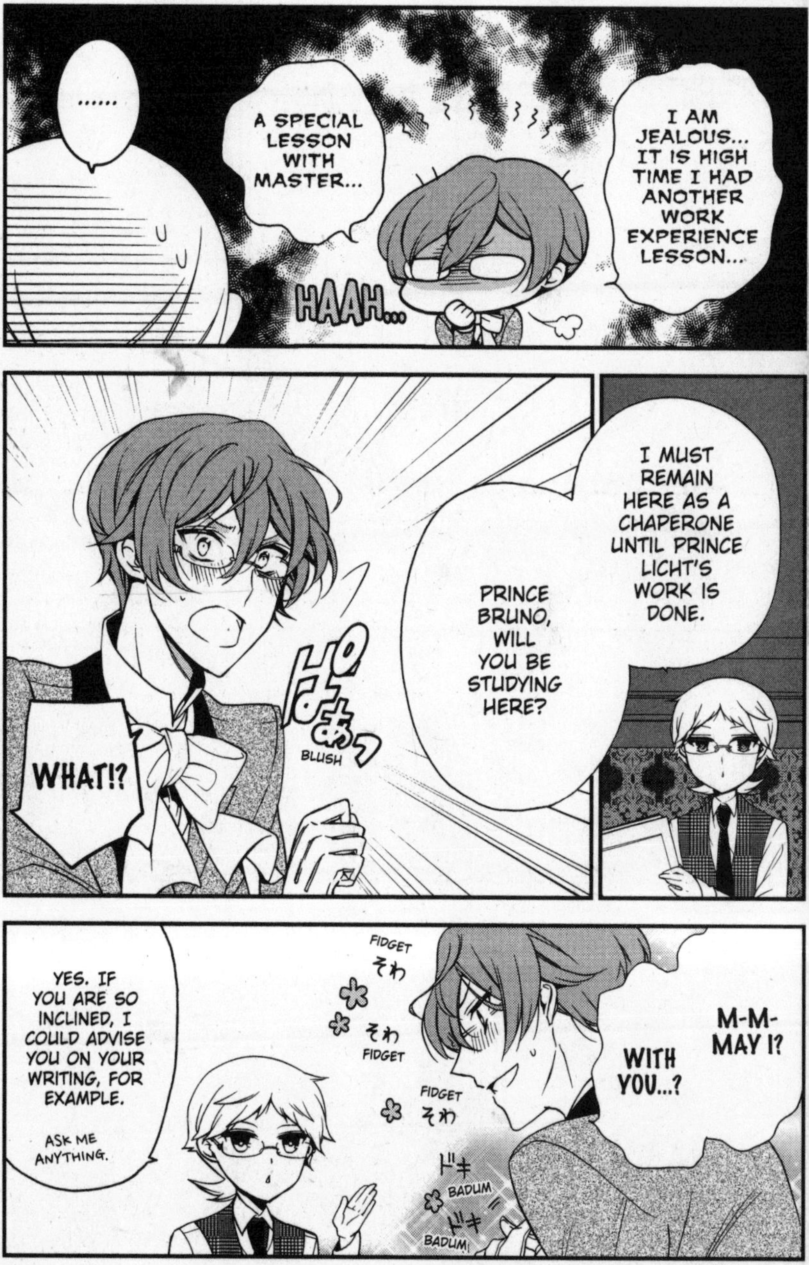

I AM JEALOUS... IT IS HIGH TIME I HAD ANOTHER WORK EXPERIENCE LESSON...
A SPECIAL LESSON WITH MASTER...
HAAH...
......
I MUST REMAIN HERE AS A CHAPERONE UNTIL PRINCE LICHT'S WORK IS DONE.
PRINCE BRUNO, WILL YOU BE STUDYING HERE?
ぱあっ
BLUSH
WHAT!?
M-M-MAY I?
WITH YOU...?
FIDGET
そわ
そわ
FIDGET
FIDGET
そわ
ドキ
BADUM
ドキ
BADUM
YES. IF YOU ARE SO INCLINED, I COULD ADVISE YOU ON YOUR WRITING, FOR EXAMPLE.
ASK ME ANYTHING.

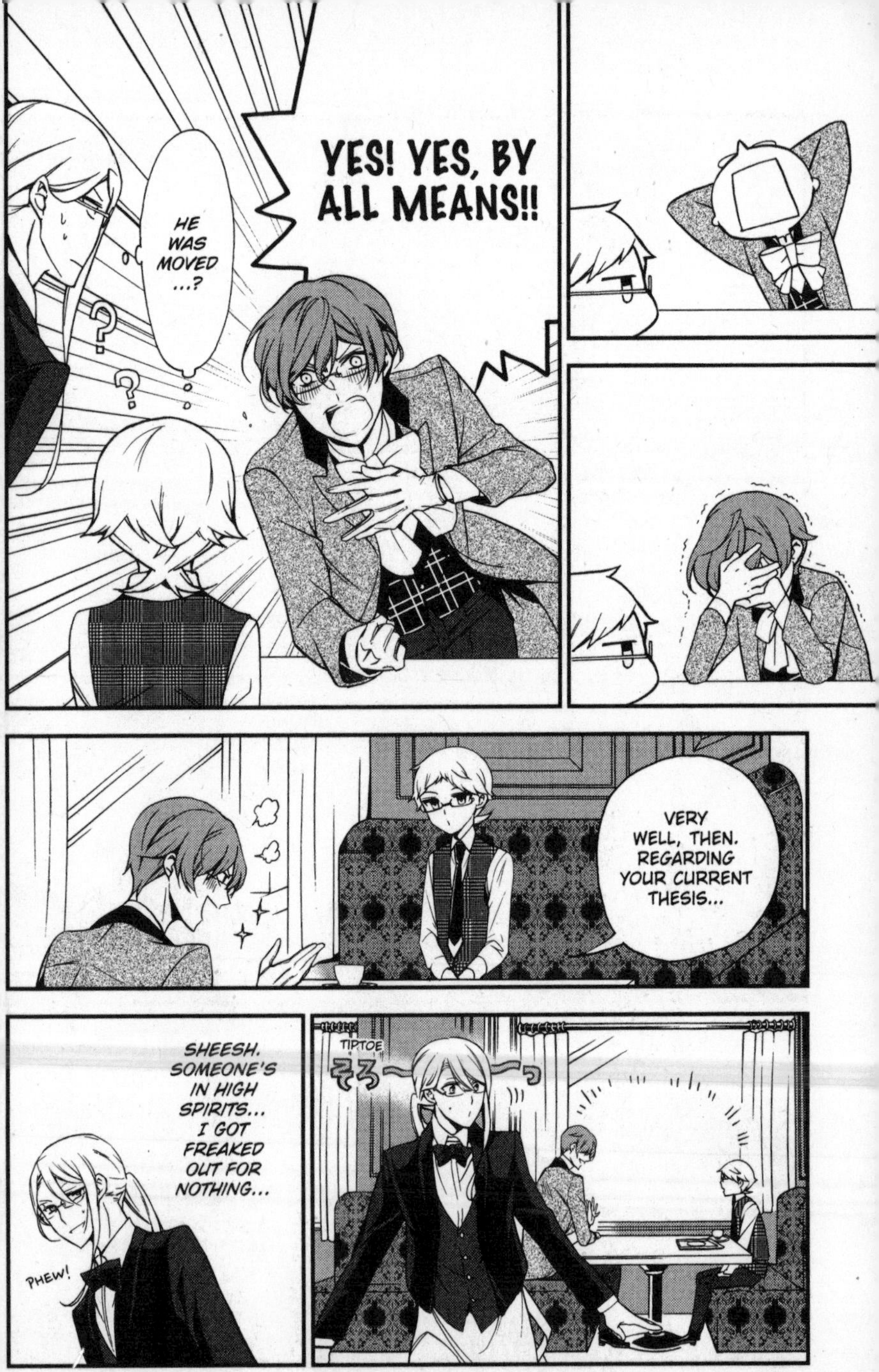
YES! YES, BY ALL MEANS!!
HE WAS MOVED ...?
VERY WELL, THEN. REGARDING YOUR CURRENT THESIS...
TIPTOE
そろ〜〜っ
SHEESH. SOMEONE'S IN HIGH SPIRITS... I GOT FREAKED OUT FOR NOTHING...
PHEW!

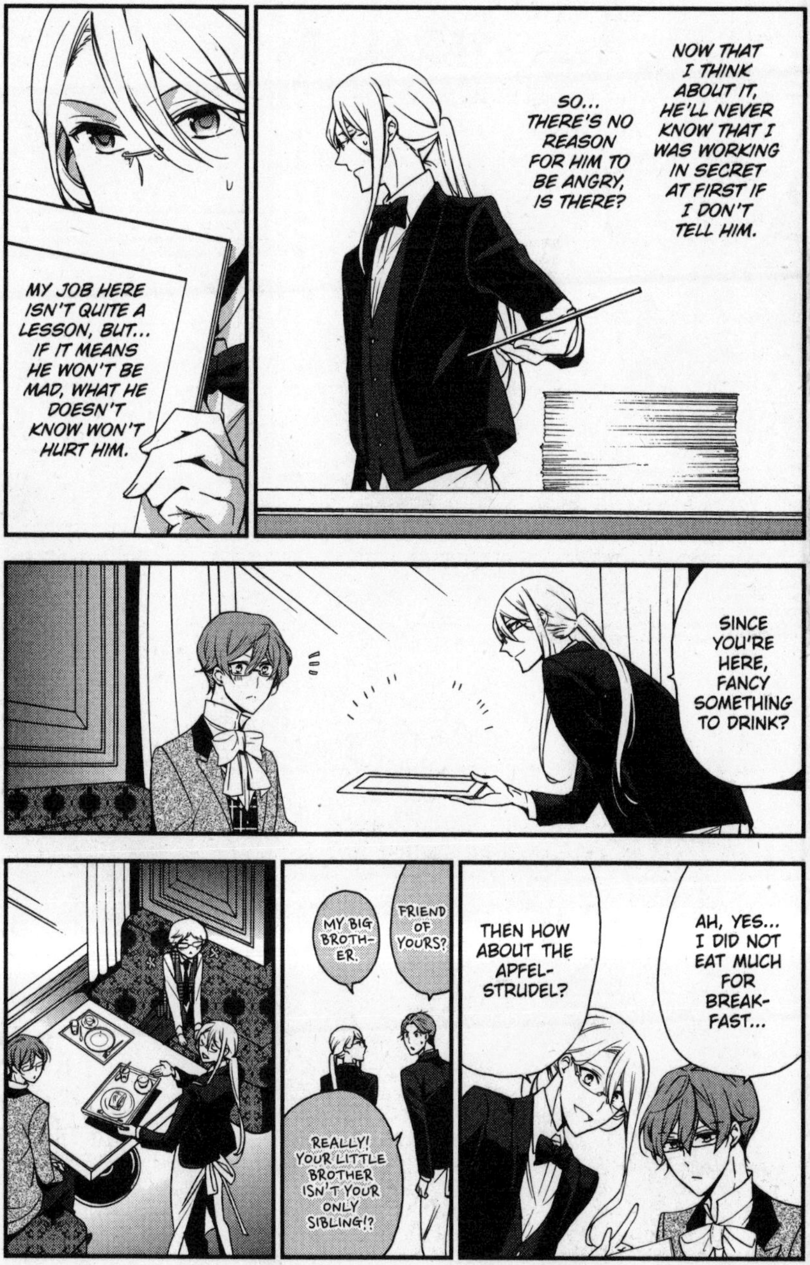
NOW THAT I THINK ABOUT IT, HE'LL NEVER KNOW THAT I WAS WORKING IN SECRET AT FIRST IF I DON'T TELL HIM.
SO... THERE'S NO REASON FOR HIM TO BE ANGRY, IS THERE?
MY JOB HERE ISN'T QUITE A LESSON, BUT... IF IT MEANS HE WON'T BE MAD, WHAT HE DOESN'T KNOW WON'T HURT HIM.
SINCE YOU'RE HERE, FANCY SOMETHING TO DRINK?
AH, YES... I DID NOT EAT MUCH FOR BREAK-FAST...
THEN HOW ABOUT THE APFEL-STRUDEL?
FRIEND OF YOURS?
MY BIG BROTH-ER.
REALLY! YOUR LITTLE BROTHER ISN'T YOUR ONLY SIBLING!?

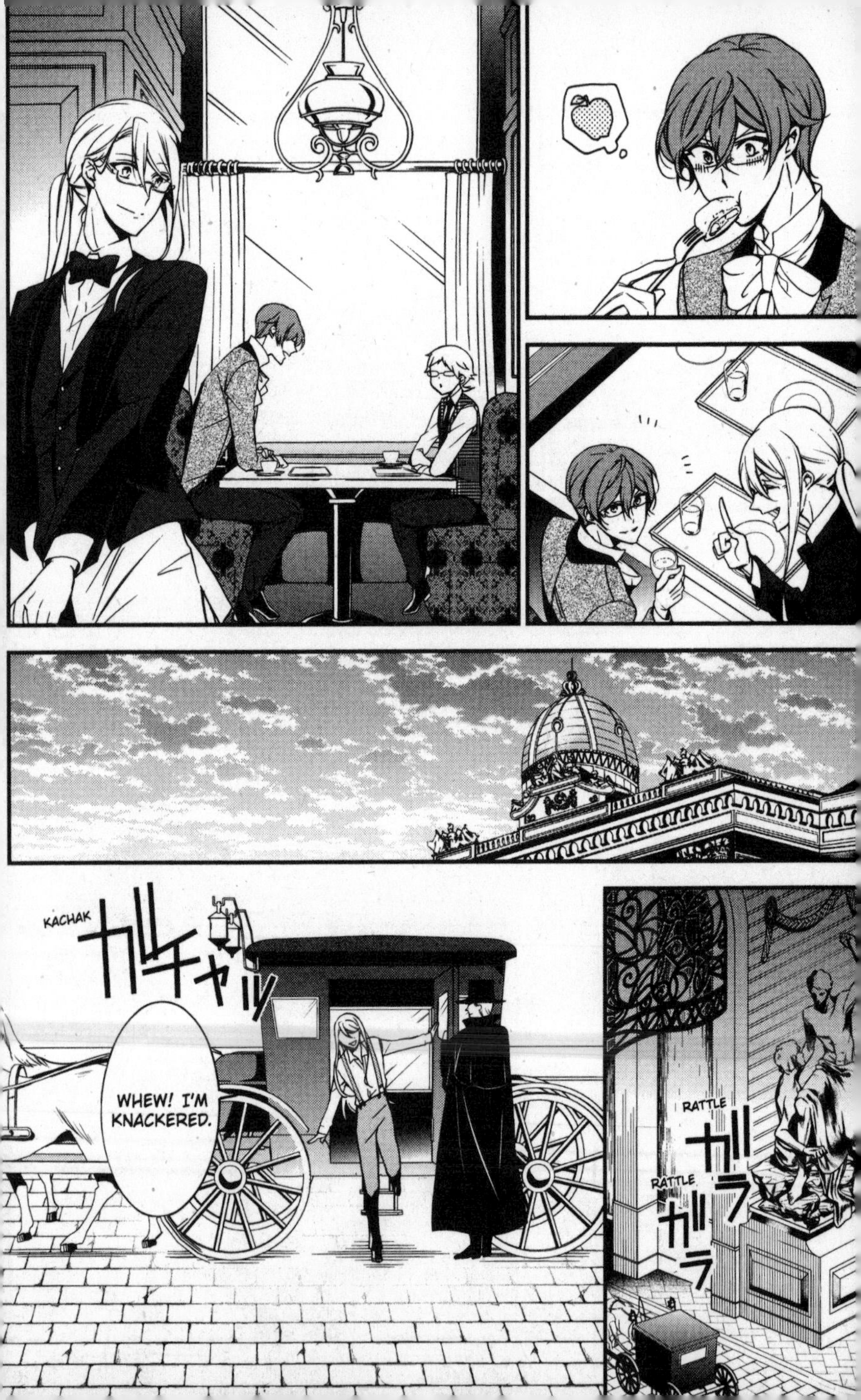
RATTLE
RATTLE
KACHAK
WHEW! I'M KNACKERED.

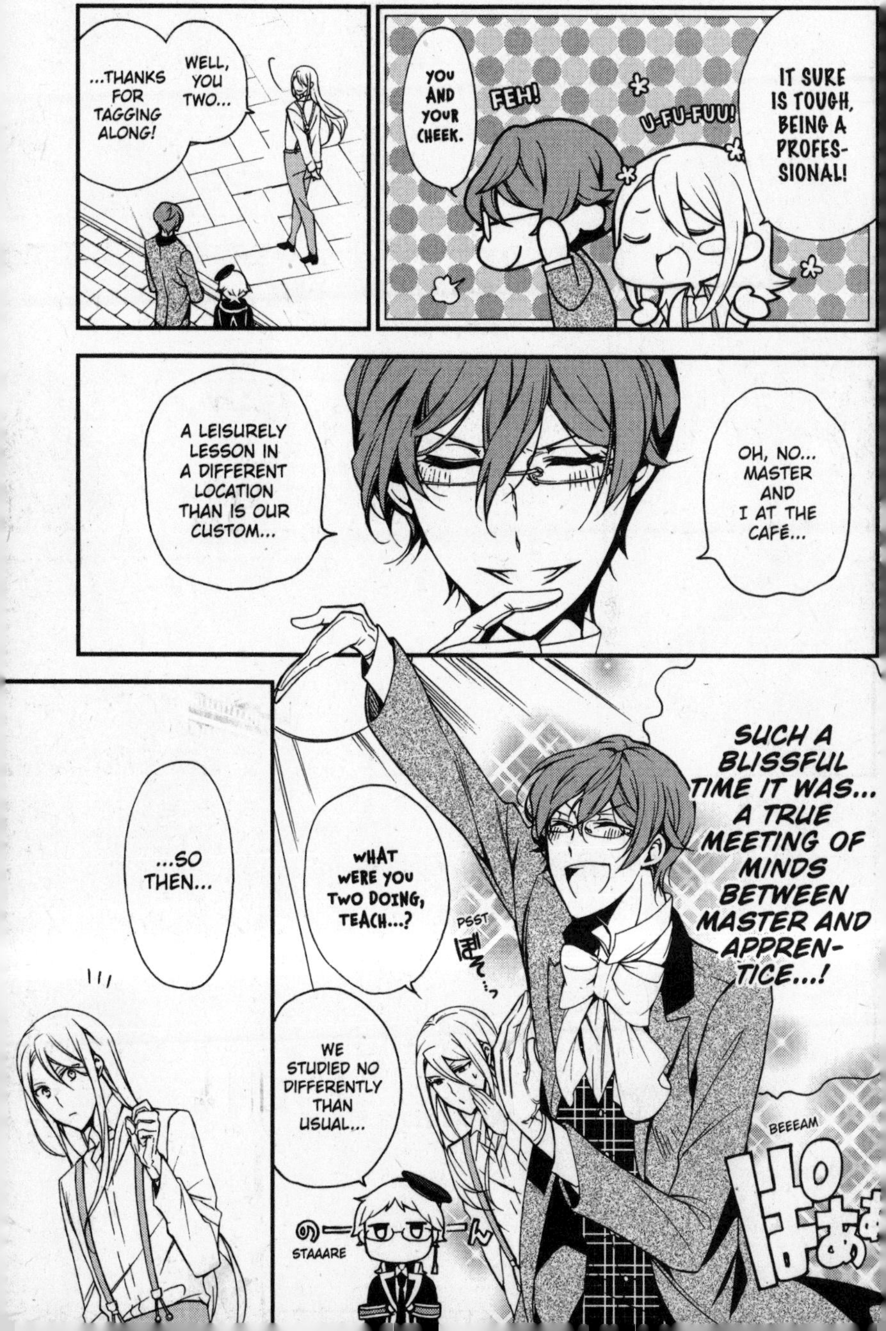
IT SURE IS TOUGH, BEING A PROFES-SIONAL!
U-FU-FUU!
FEH!
YOU AND YOUR CHEEK.
WELL, YOU TWO...
...THANKS FOR TAGGING ALONG!
OH, NO... MASTER AND I AT THE CAFÉ...
A LEISURELY LESSON IN A DIFFERENT LOCATION THAN IS OUR CUSTOM...
SUCH A BLISSFUL TIME IT WAS... A TRUE MEETING OF MINDS BETWEEN MASTER AND APPREN-TICE...!
BEEEAM
PSST
WHAT WERE YOU TWO DOING, TEACH...?
WE STUDIED NO DIFFERENTLY THAN USUAL...
STAAARE
...SO THEN...

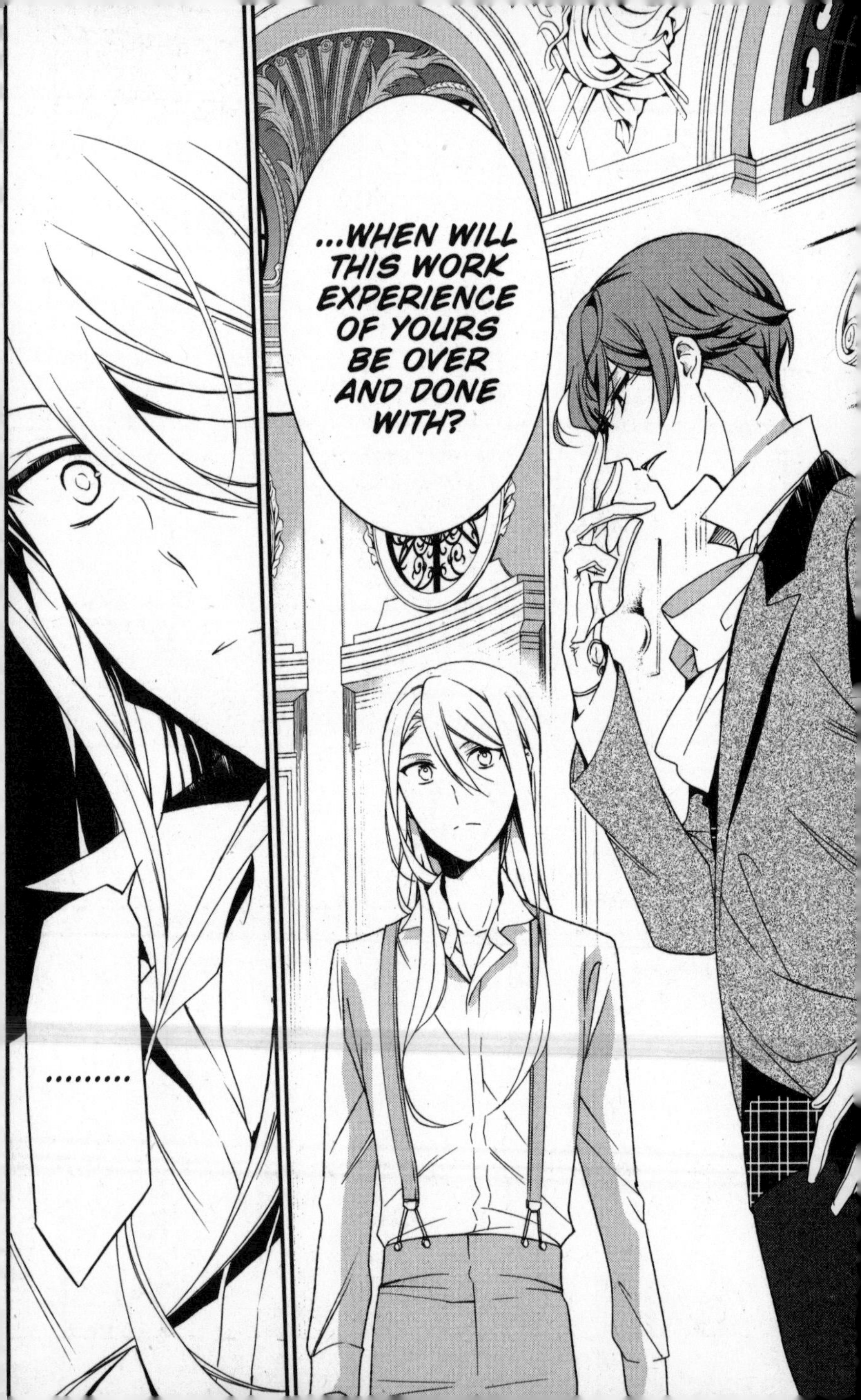
...WHEN WILL THIS WORK EXPERIENCE OF YOURS BE OVER AND DONE WITH?
....

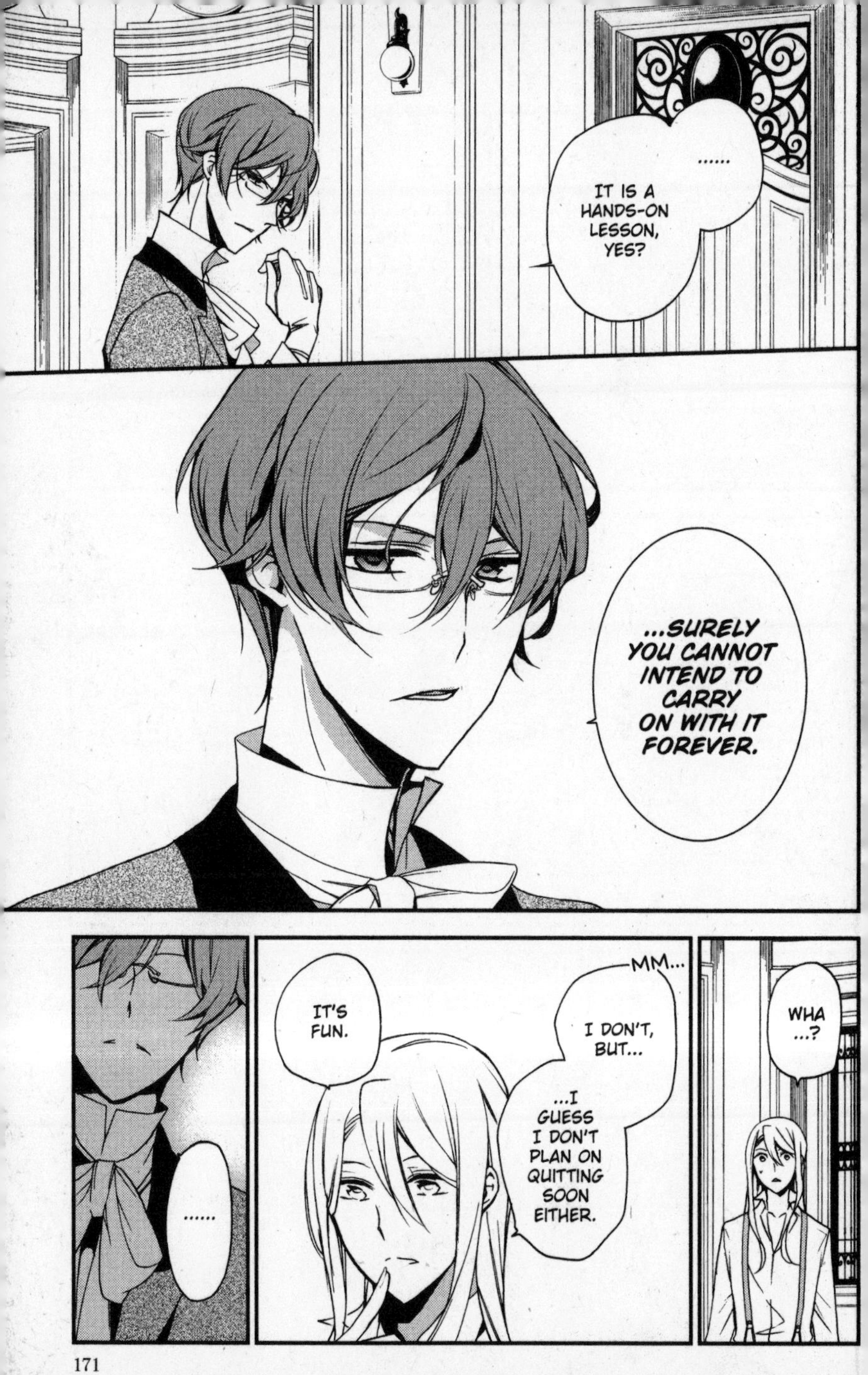
......
IT IS A HANDS-ON LESSON, YES?
...SURELY YOU CANNOT INTEND TO CARRY ON WITH IT FOREVER.
WHA ...?
MM...
I DON'T, BUT...
...I GUESS I DON'T PLAN ON QUITTING SOON EITHER.
IT'S FUN.
......

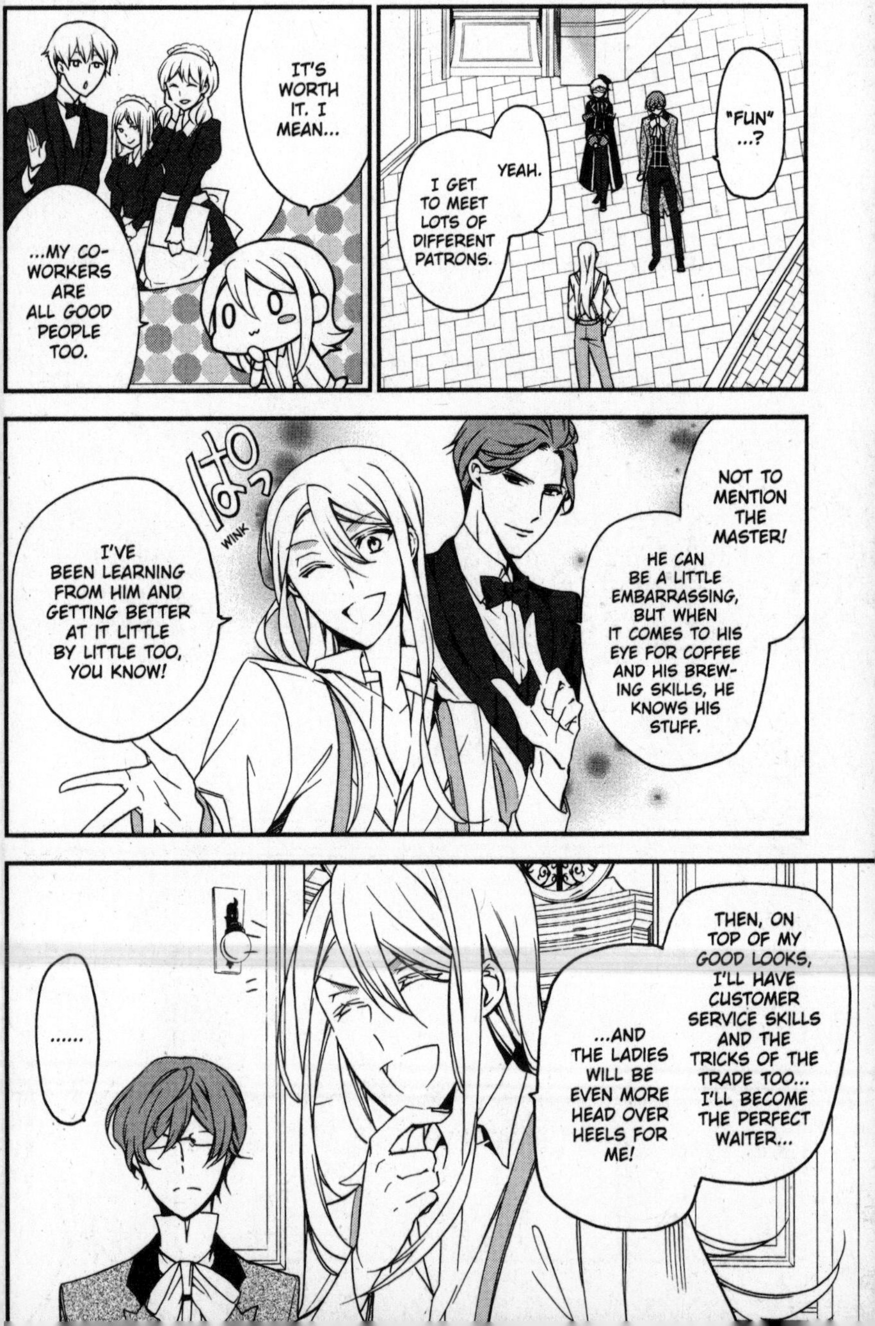
"FUN" ...?
YEAH.
I GET TO MEET LOTS OF DIFFERENT PATRONS.
IT'S WORTH IT. I MEAN...
...MY CO-WORKERS ARE ALL GOOD PEOPLE TOO.
NOT TO MENTION THE MASTER!
HE CAN BE A LITTLE EMBARRASSING, BUT WHEN IT COMES TO HIS EYE FOR COFFEE AND HIS BREWING SKILLS, HE KNOWS HIS STUFF.
ぱっ
WINK
I'VE BEEN LEARNING FROM HIM AND GETTING BETTER AT IT LITTLE BY LITTLE TOO, YOU KNOW!
THEN, ON TOP OF MY GOOD LOOKS, I'LL HAVE CUSTOMER SERVICE SKILLS AND THE TRICKS OF THE TRADE TOO... I'LL BECOME THE PERFECT WAITER...
...AND THE LADIES WILL BE EVEN MORE HEAD OVER HEELS FOR ME!
......

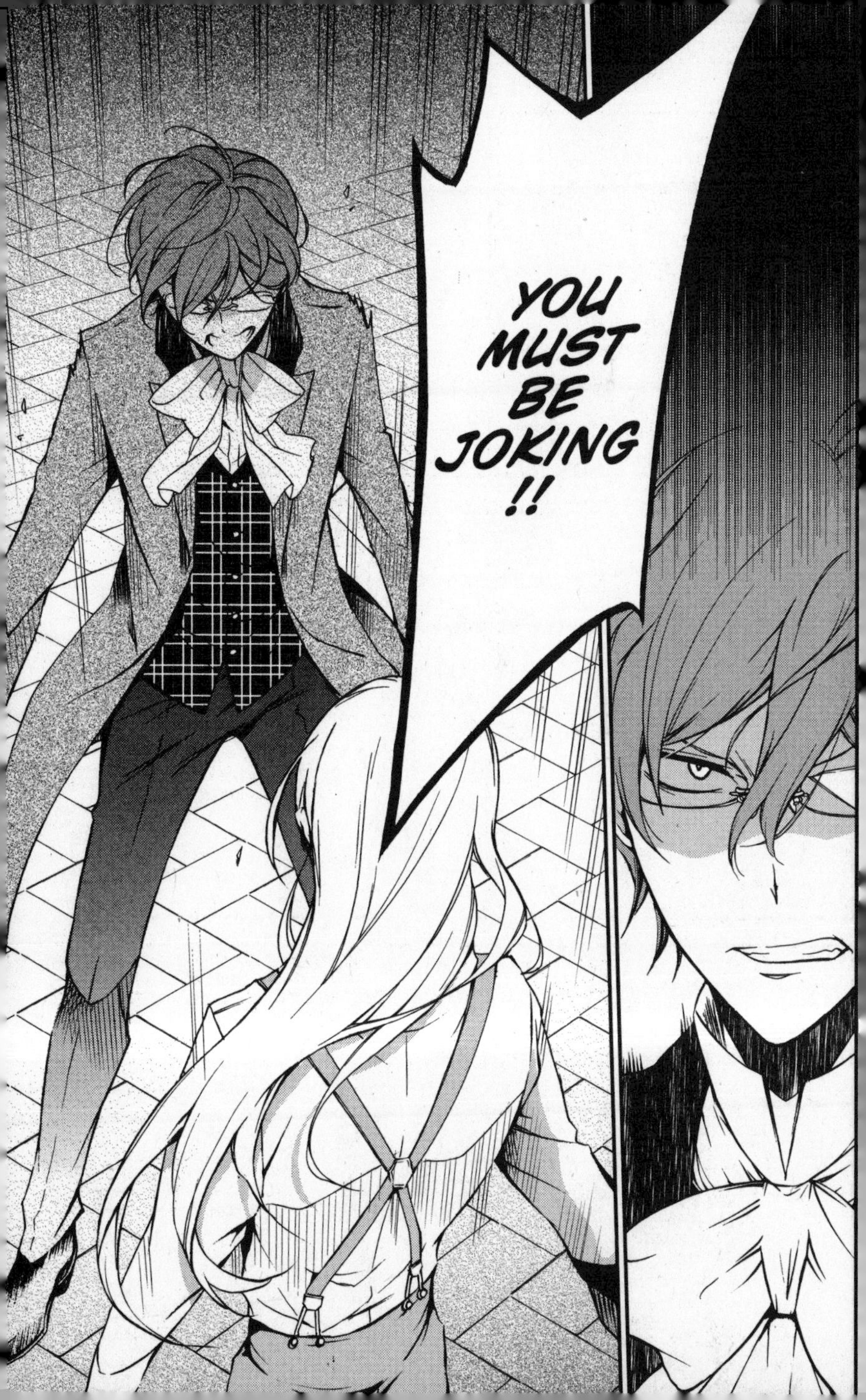
YOU MUST BE JOKING !!

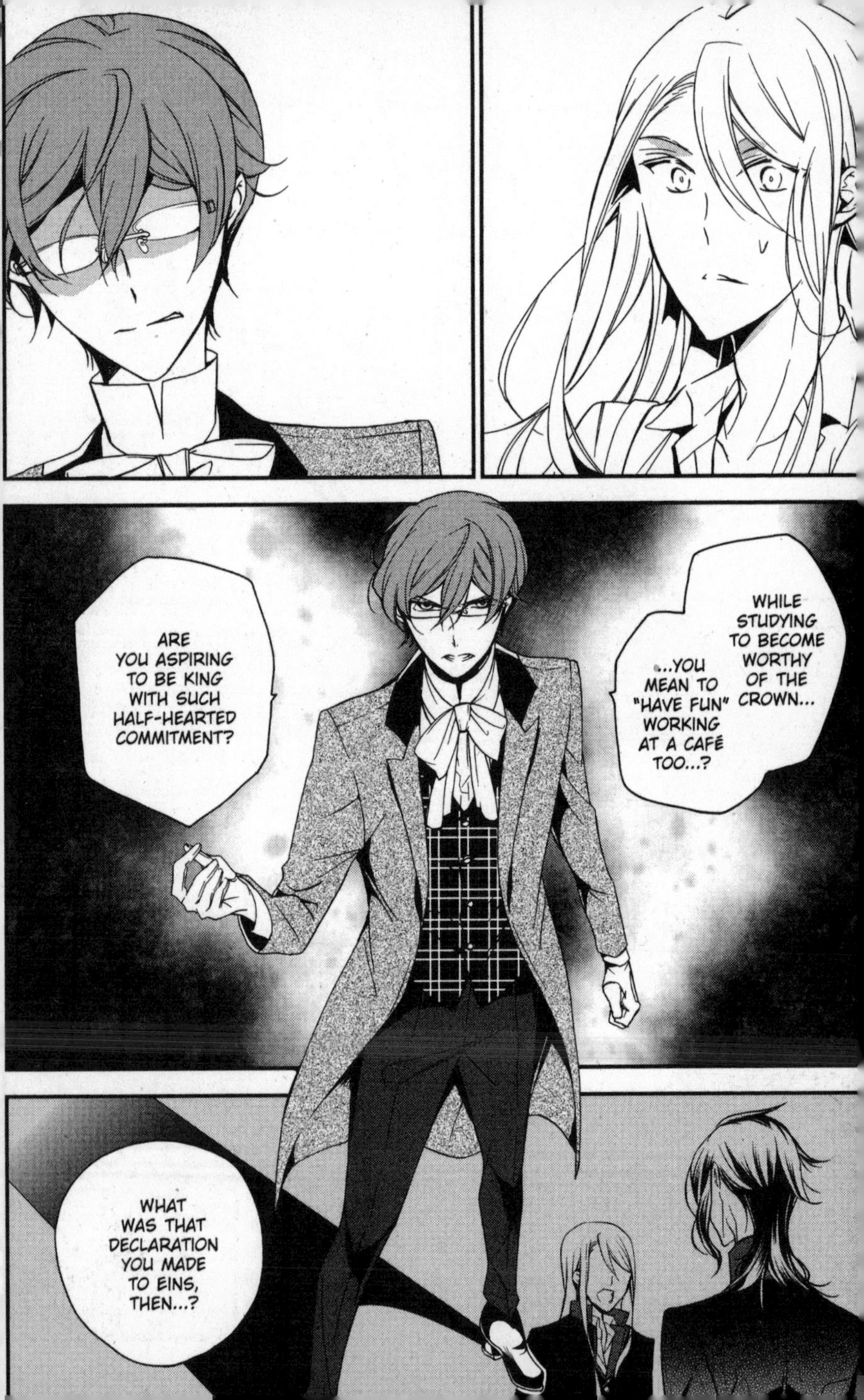
WHILE STUDYING TO BECOME WORTHY OF THE CROWN...
...YOU MEAN TO "HAVE FUN" WORKING AT A CAFÉ TOO...?
ARE YOU ASPIRING TO BE KING WITH SUCH HALF-HEARTED COMMITMENT?
WHAT WAS THAT DECLARATION YOU MADE TO EINS, THEN...?

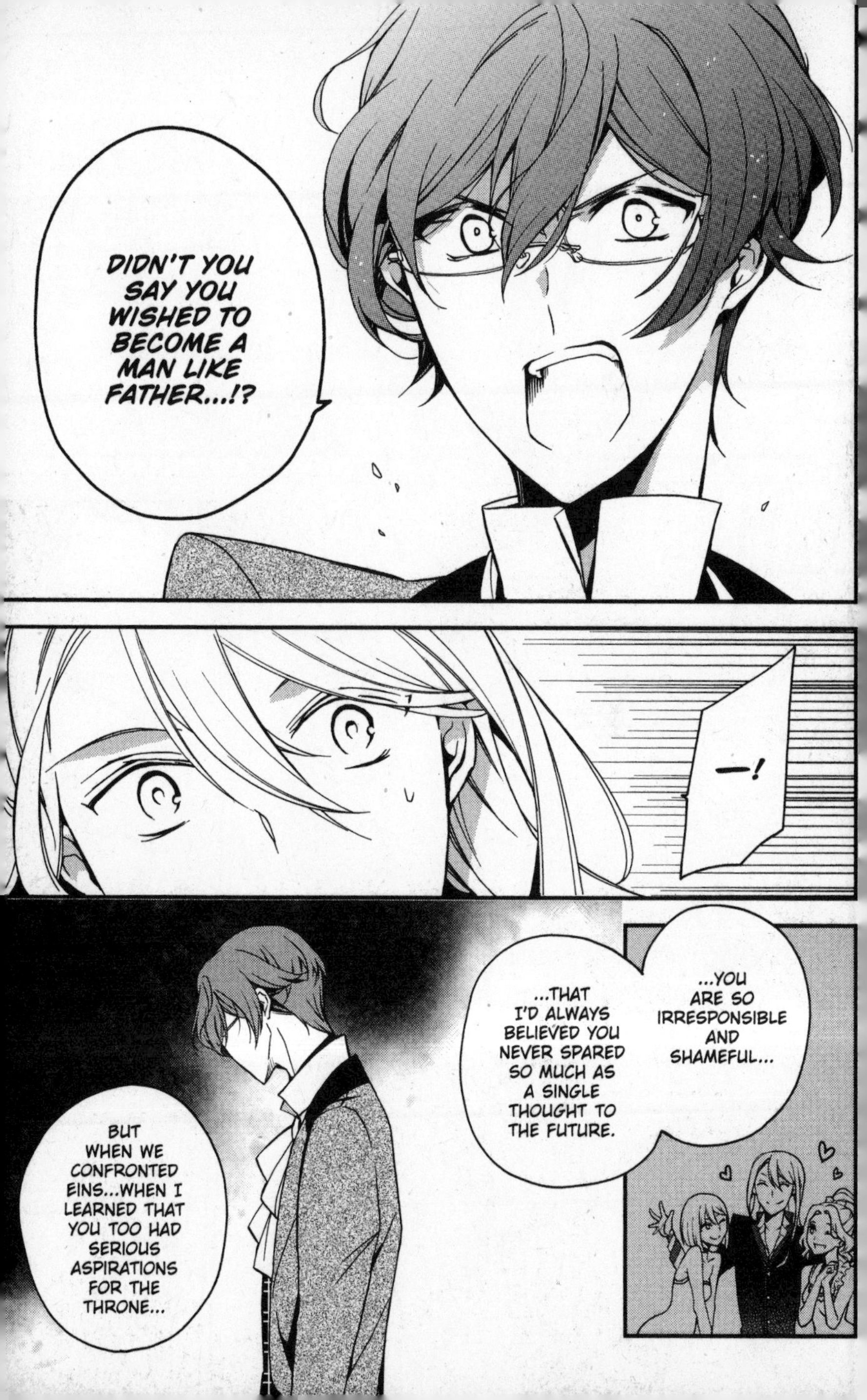
DIDN'T YOU SAY YOU WISHED TO BECOME A MAN LIKE FATHER...!?
—!
...YOU ARE SO IRRESPONSIBLE AND SHAMEFUL...
...THAT I'D ALWAYS BELIEVED YOU NEVER SPARED SO MUCH AS A SINGLE THOUGHT TO THE FUTURE.
BUT WHEN WE CONFRONTED EINS...WHEN I LEARNED THAT YOU TOO HAD SERIOUS ASPIRATIONS FOR THE THRONE...

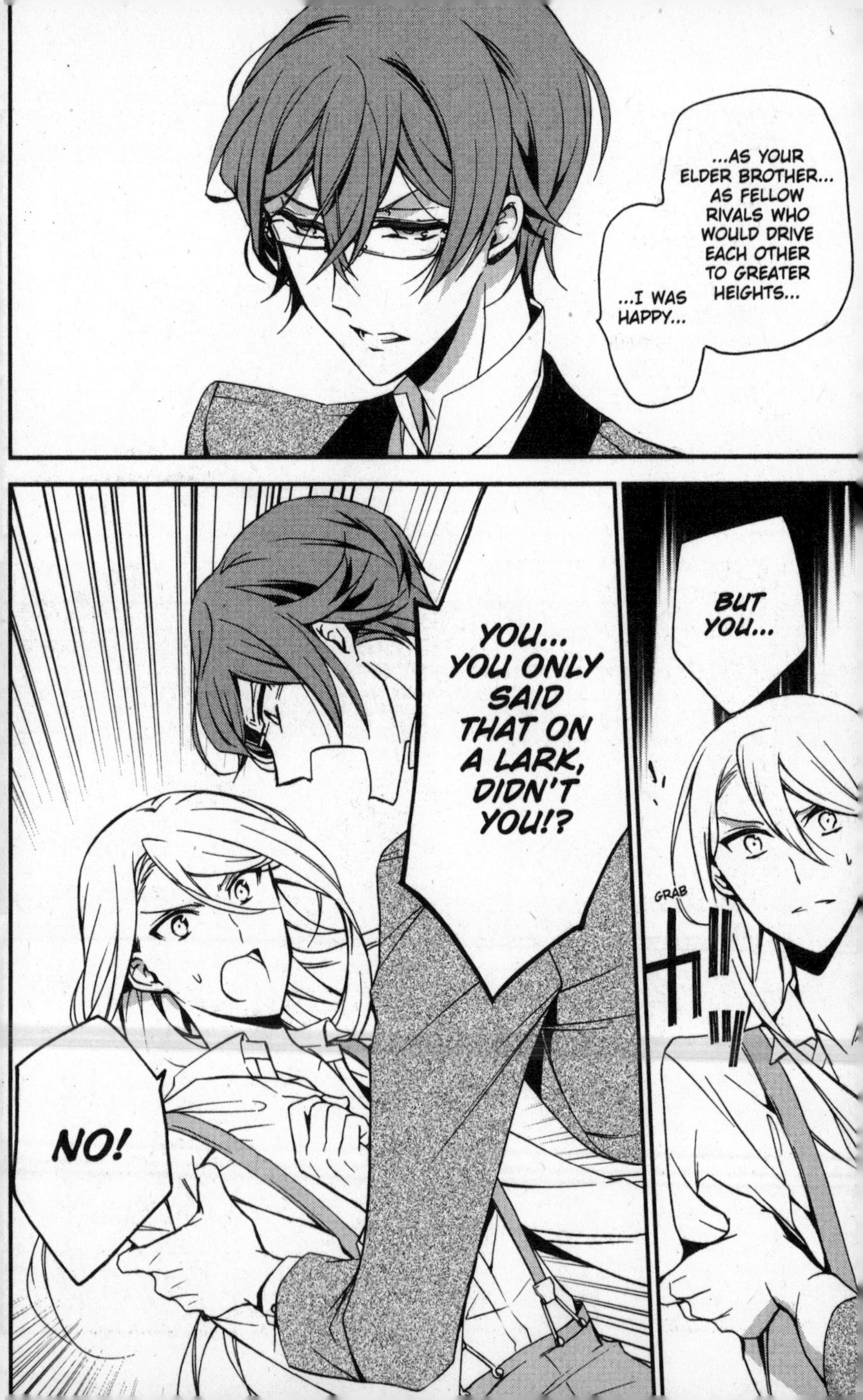
...AS YOUR ELDER BROTHER... AS FELLOW RIVALS WHO WOULD DRIVE EACH OTHER TO GREATER HEIGHTS...
...I WAS HAPPY...
BUT YOU...
GRAB
YOU... YOU ONLY SAID THAT ON A LARK, DIDN'T YOU!?
NO!

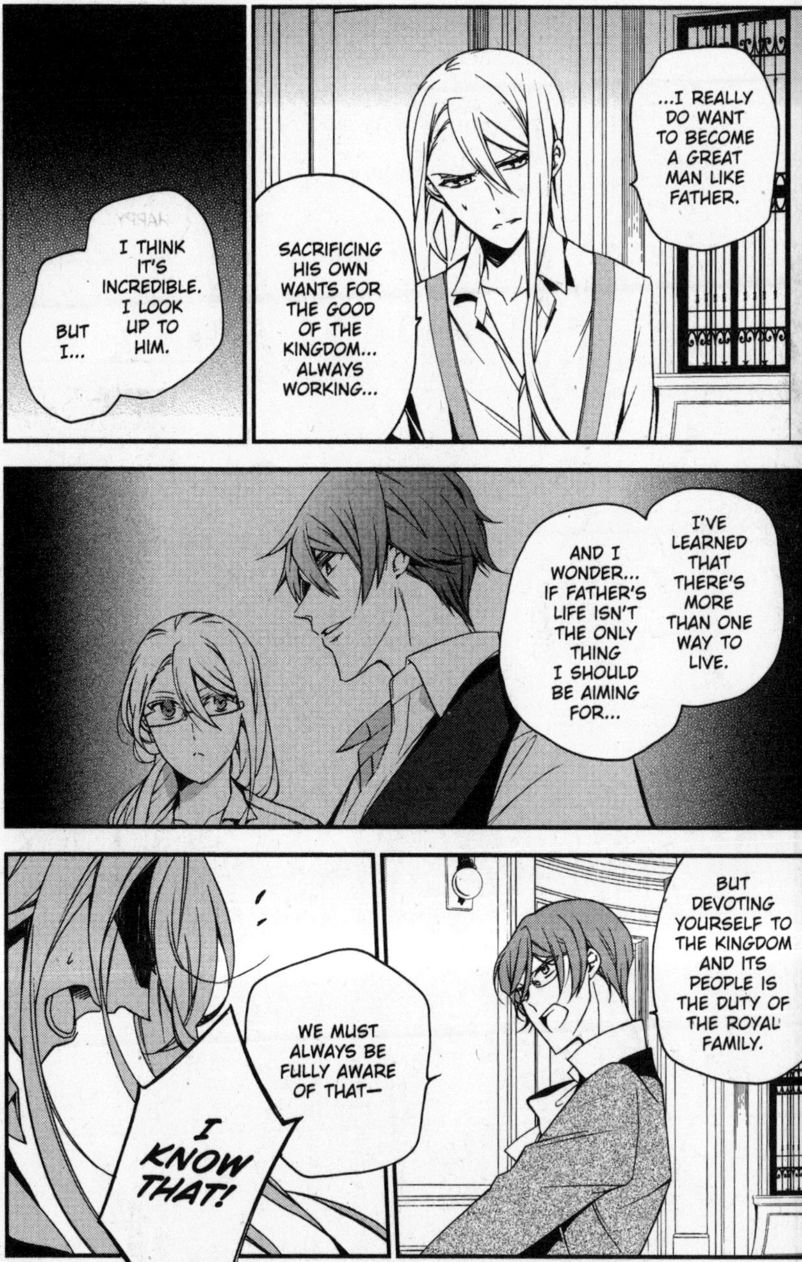
...I REALLY DO WANT TO BECOME A GREAT MAN LIKE FATHER.
SACRIFICING HIS OWN WANTS FOR THE GOOD OF THE KINGDOM... ALWAYS WORKING...
I THINK IT'S INCREDIBLE. I LOOK UP TO HIM.
BUT I...
I'VE LEARNED THAT THERE'S MORE THAN ONE WAY TO LIVE.
AND I WONDER... IF FATHER'S LIFE ISN'T THE ONLY THING I SHOULD BE AIMING FOR...
BUT DEVOTING YOURSELF TO THE KINGDOM AND ITS PEOPLE IS THE DUTY OF THE ROYAL FAMILY.
WE MUST ALWAYS BE FULLY AWARE OF THAT—
!
I KNOW THAT!

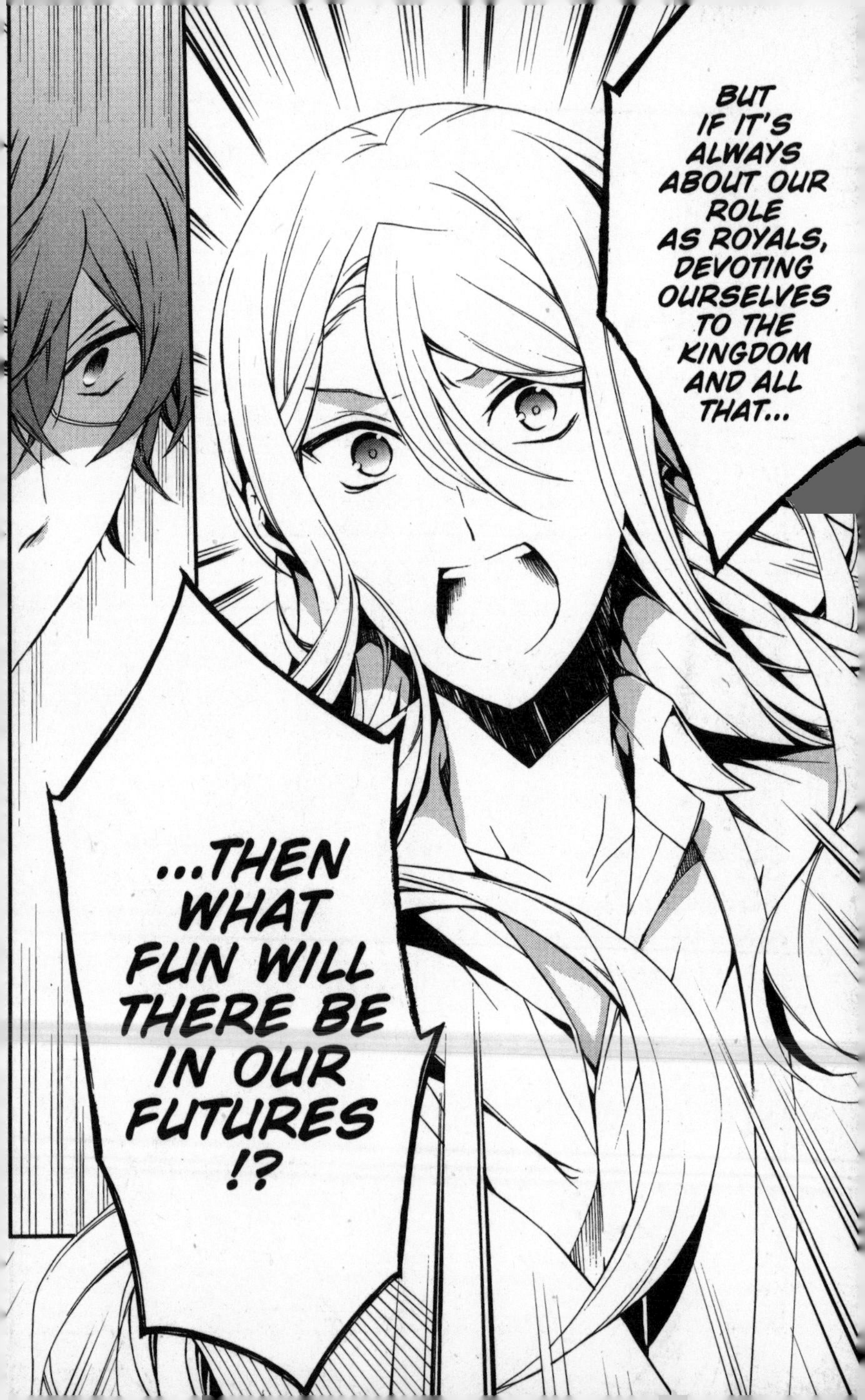
BUT IF IT'S ALWAYS ABOUT OUR ROLE AS ROYALS, DEVOTING OURSELVES TO THE KINGDOM AND ALL THAT...
...THEN WHAT FUN WILL THERE BE IN OUR FUTURES !?

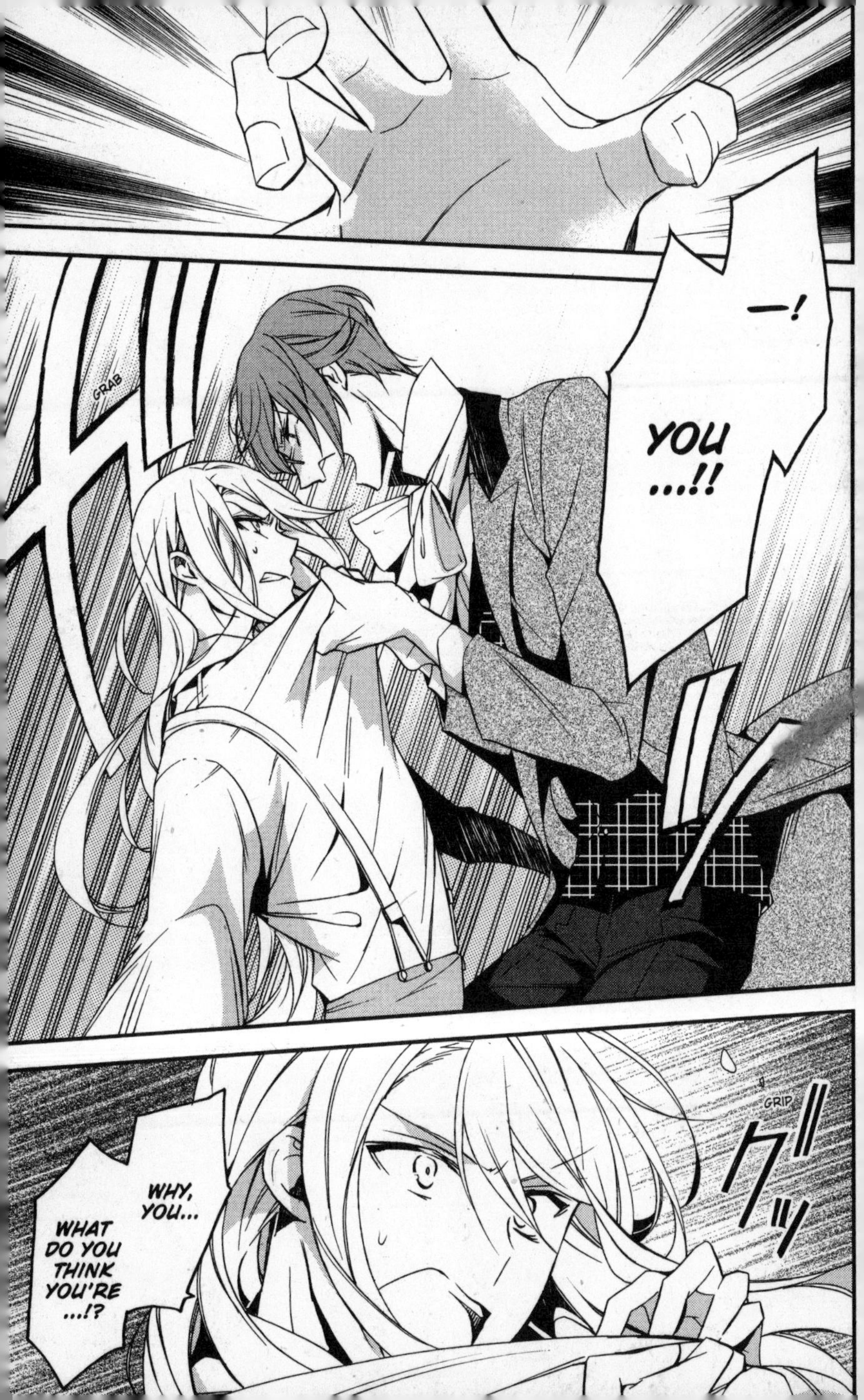
—!
YOU ...!!
GRAB
GRIP
グッ
WHY, YOU...
WHAT DO YOU THINK YOU'RE ...!?

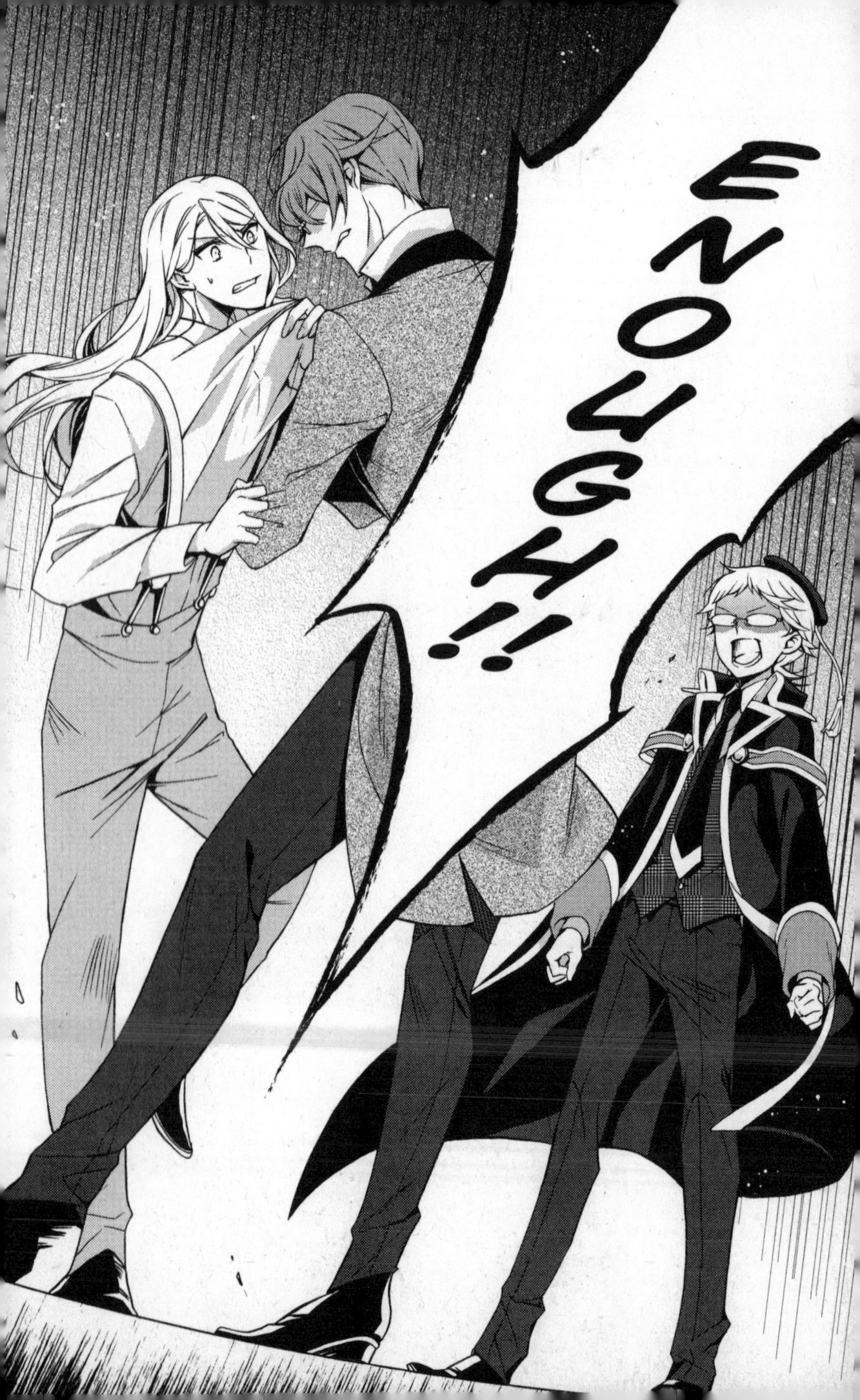
ENOUGH!!

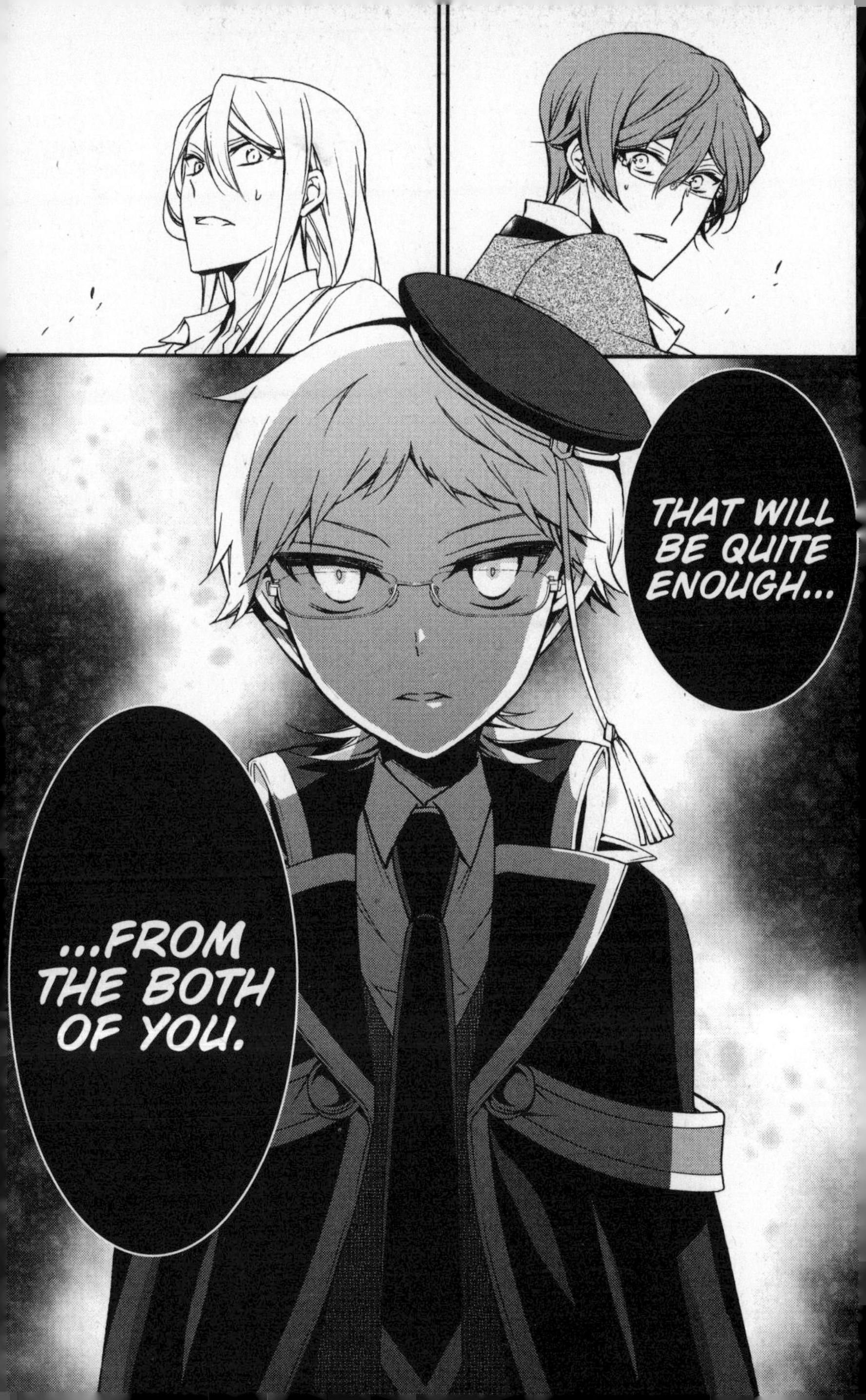
THAT WILL BE QUITE ENOUGH...
...FROM THE BOTH OF YOU.

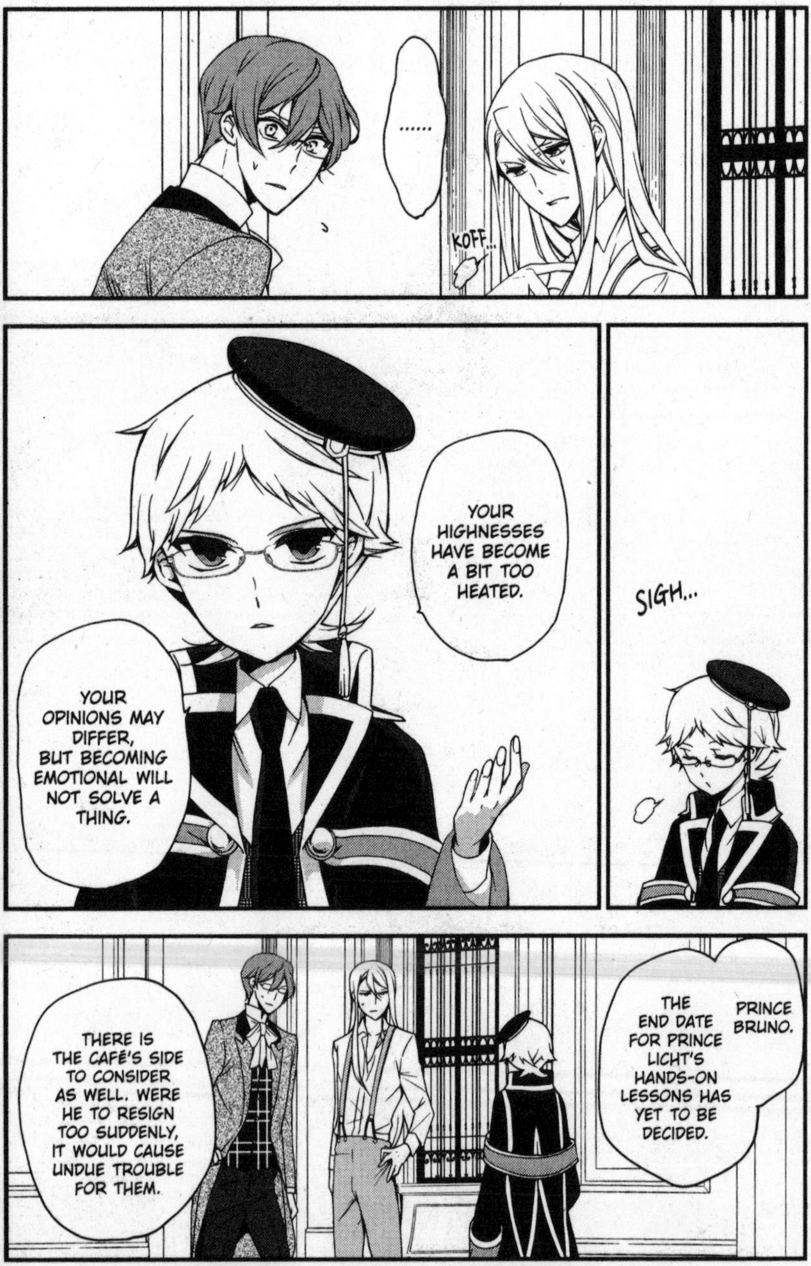
......
KOFF...
SIGH...
YOUR HIGHNESSES HAVE BECOME A BIT TOO HEATED.
YOUR OPINIONS MAY DIFFER, BUT BECOMING EMOTIONAL WILL NOT SOLVE A THING.
PRINCE BRUNO.
THE END DATE FOR PRINCE LICHT'S HANDS-ON LESSONS HAS YET TO BE DECIDED.
THERE IS THE CAFÉ'S SIDE TO CONSIDER AS WELL. WERE HE TO RESIGN TOO SUDDENLY, IT WOULD CAUSE UNDUE TROUBLE FOR THEM.

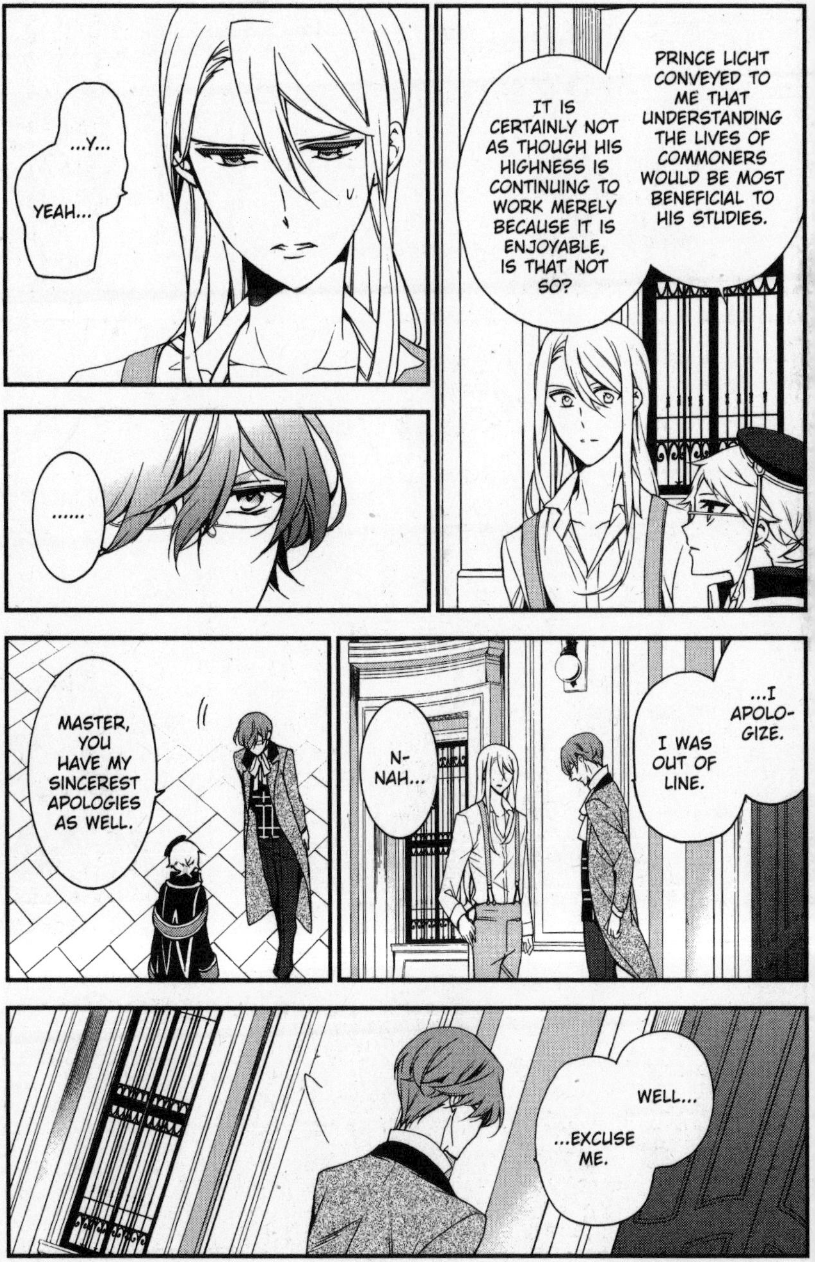
PRINCE LICHT CONVEYED TO ME THAT UNDERSTANDING THE LIVES OF COMMONERS WOULD BE MOST BENEFICIAL TO HIS STUDIES.
IT IS CERTAINLY NOT AS THOUGH HIS HIGHNESS IS CONTINUING TO WORK MERELY BECAUSE IT IS ENJOYABLE, IS THAT NOT SO?
...Y... YEAH...
......
...I APOLOGIZE.
I WAS OUT OF LINE.
N-NAH...
MASTER, YOU HAVE MY SINCEREST APOLOGIES AS WELL.
WELL...
...EXCUSE ME.

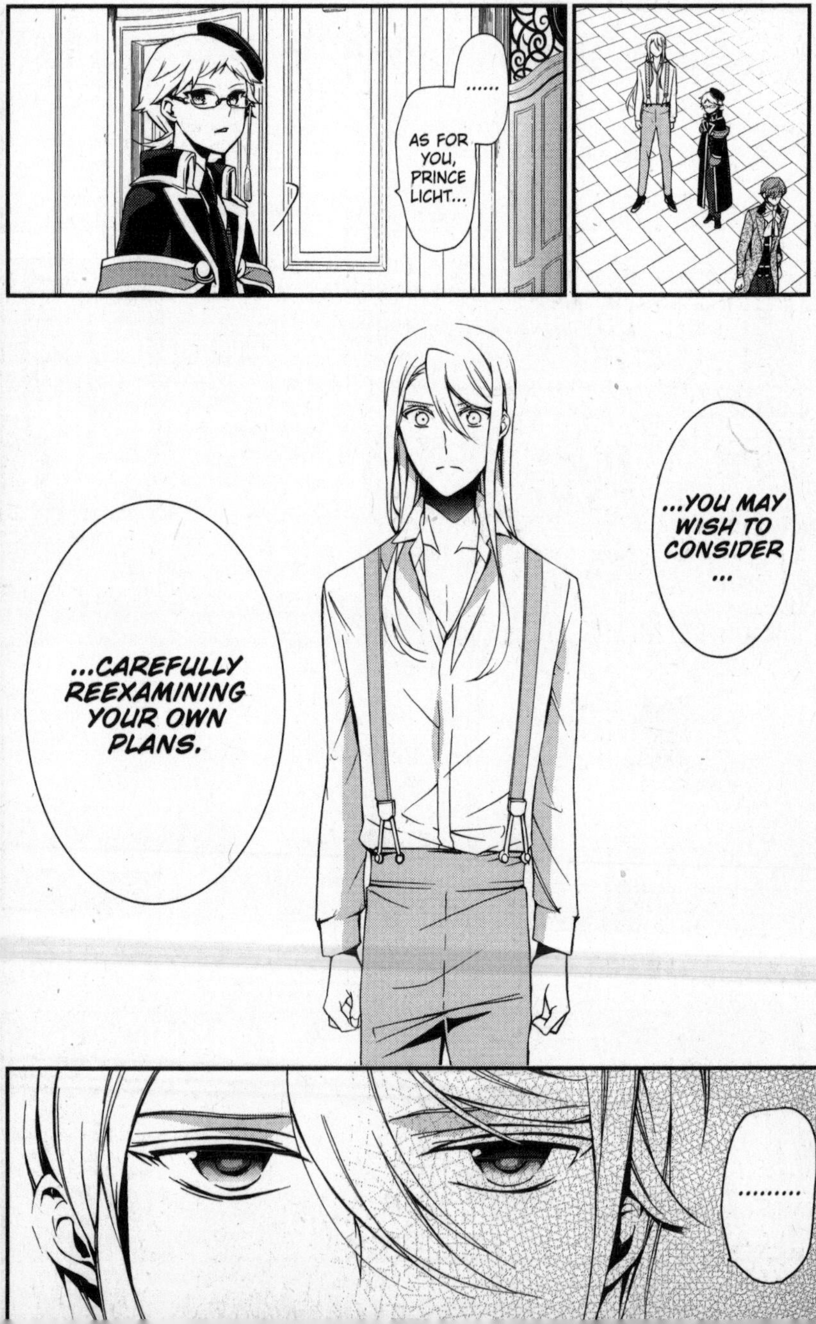
......
AS FOR YOU, PRINCE LICHT...
...YOU MAY WISH TO CONSIDER ...
...CAREFULLY REEXAMINING YOUR OWN PLANS.
....

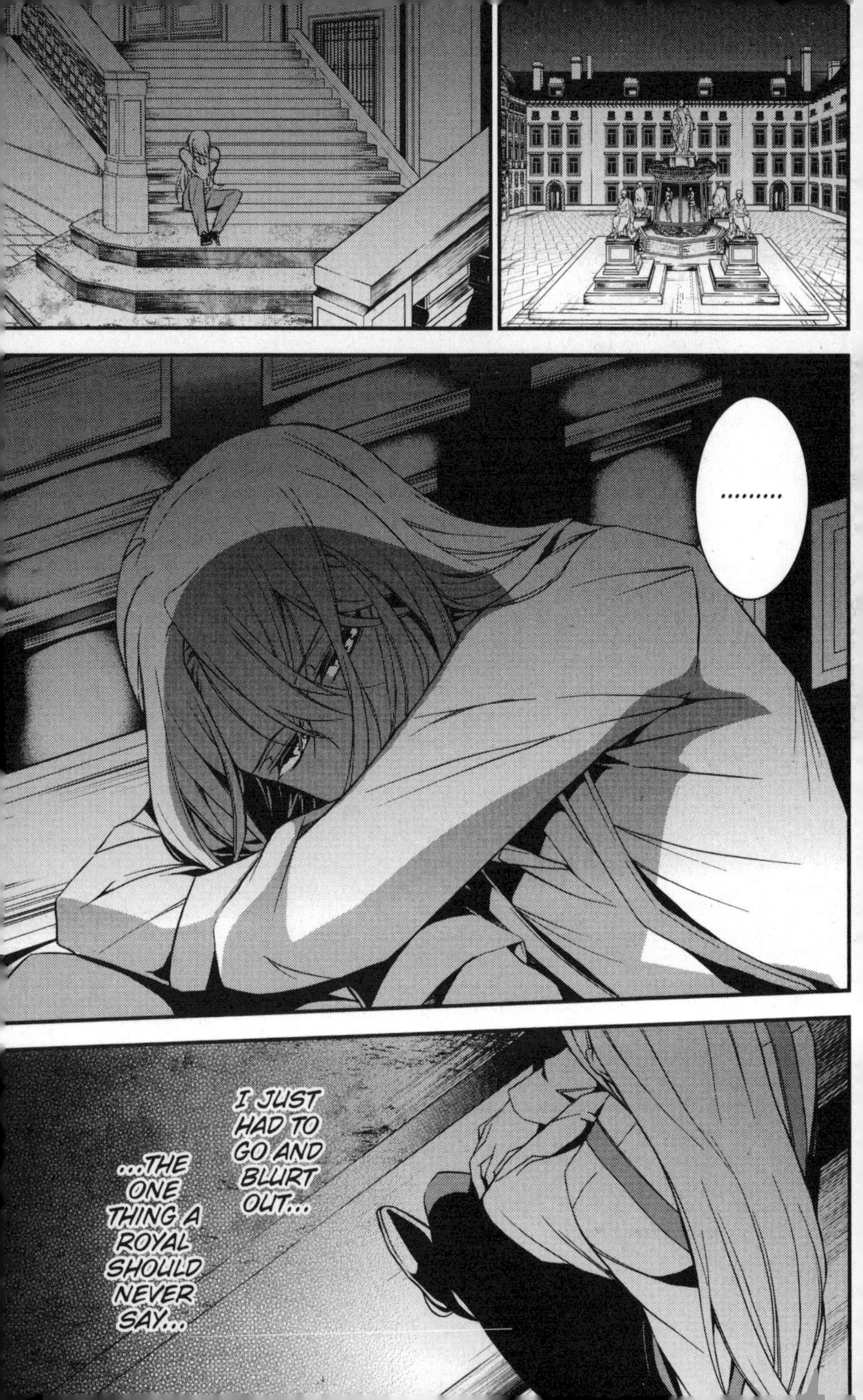
....
I JUST HAD TO GO AND BLURT OUT...
...THE ONE THING A ROYAL SHOULD NEVER SAY...

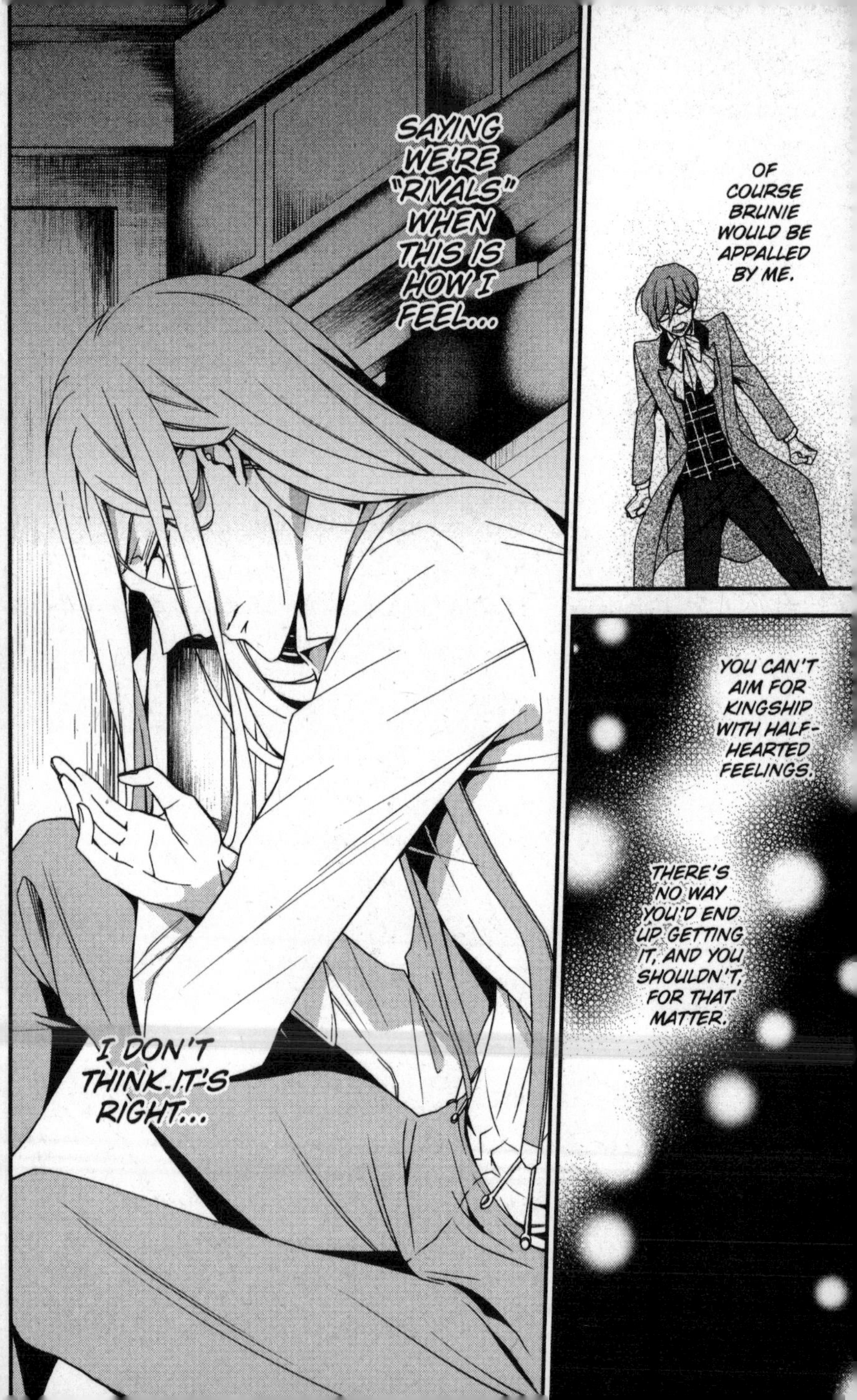
OF COURSE BRUNIE WOULD BE APPALLED BY ME.
YOU CAN'T AIM FOR KINGSHIP WITH HALF-HEARTED FEELINGS.
THERE'S NO WAY YOU'D END UP GETTING IT, AND YOU SHOULDN'T, FOR THAT MATTER.
SAYING WE'RE "RIVALS" WHEN THIS IS HOW I FEEL...
I DON'T THINK IT'S RIGHT...

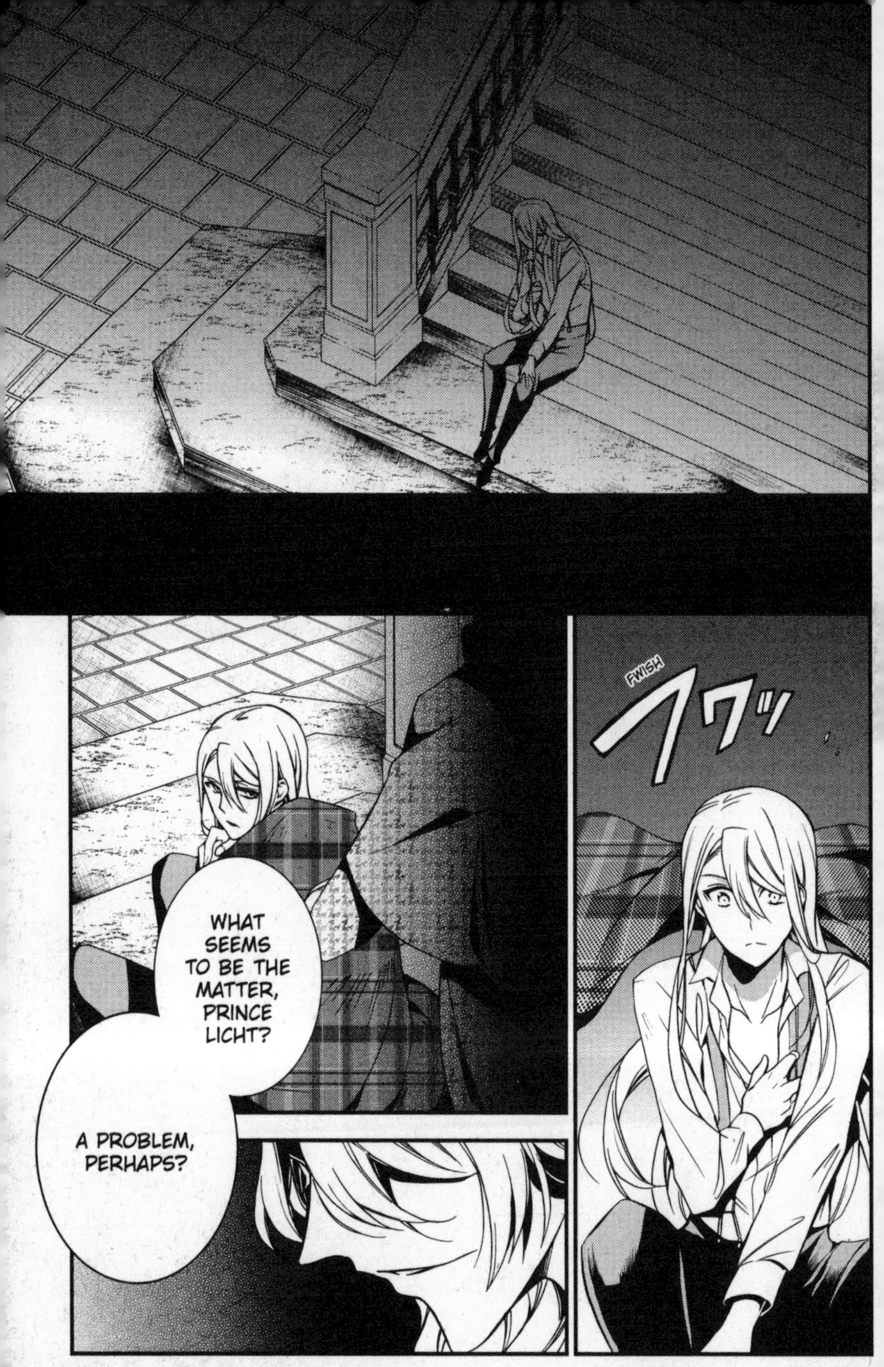
FWISH
フワッ
WHAT SEEMS TO BE THE MATTER, PRINCE LICHT?
A PROBLEM, PERHAPS?

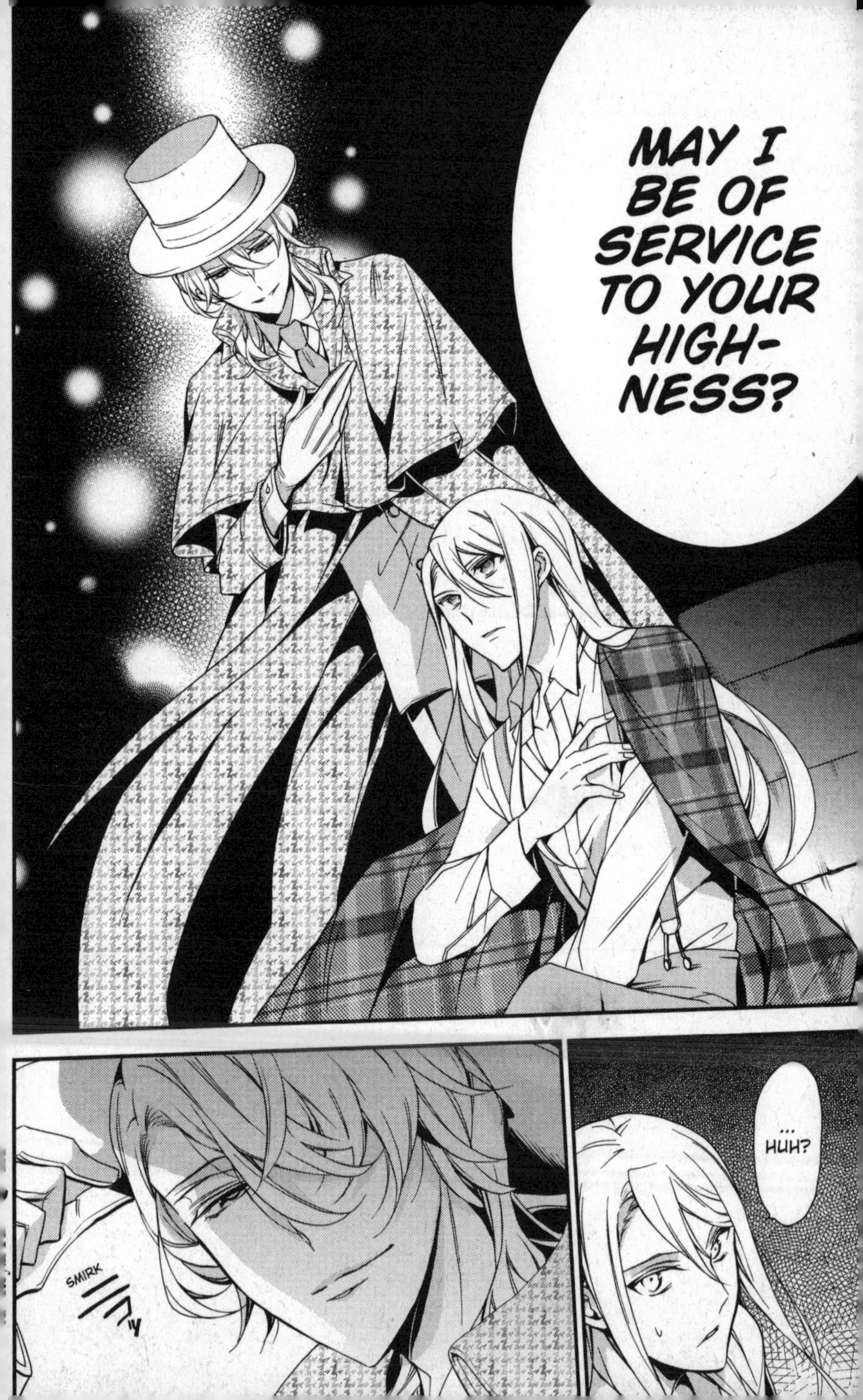
MAY I BE OF SERVICE TO YOUR HIGH-NESS?
...HUH?
SMIRK

VIII

SPECIAL THANKS

YOSHI KOUJU-SAN

CHIMURA-SAN

OOMORI-SAN

MY EDITOR, AKIYAMA-SAN

EXTRA

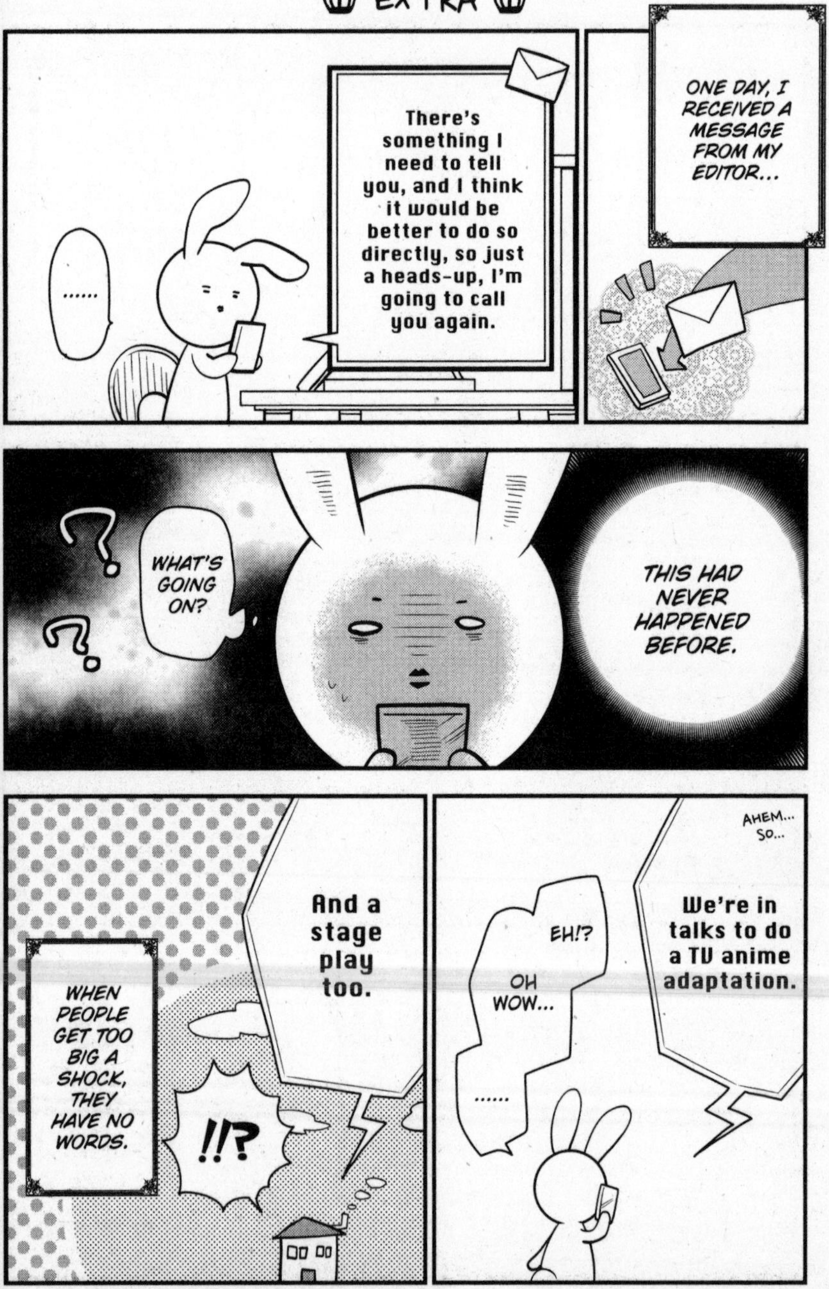
ONE DAY, I RECEIVED A MESSAGE FROM MY EDITOR...
There's something I need to tell you, and I think it would be better to do so directly, so just a heads-up, I'm going to call you again.
......
THIS HAD NEVER HAPPENED BEFORE.
WHAT'S GOING ON?
AHEM... SO...
We're in talks to do a TV anime adaptation.
EH!?
OH WOW...
......
And a stage play too.
!!?
WHEN PEOPLE GET TOO BIG A SHOCK, THEY HAVE NO WORDS.

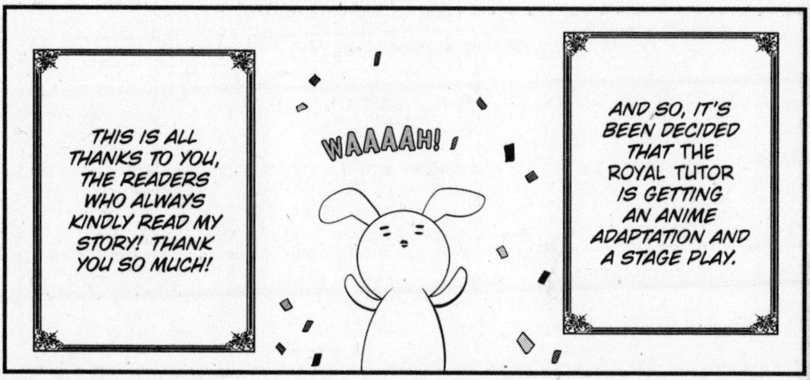
AND SO, IT'S BEEN DECIDED THAT THE ROYAL TUTOR IS GETTING AN ANIME ADAPTATION AND A STAGE PLAY.
WAAAAH!
THIS IS ALL THANKS TO YOU, THE READERS WHO ALWAYS KINDLY READ MY STORY! THANK YOU SO MUCH!

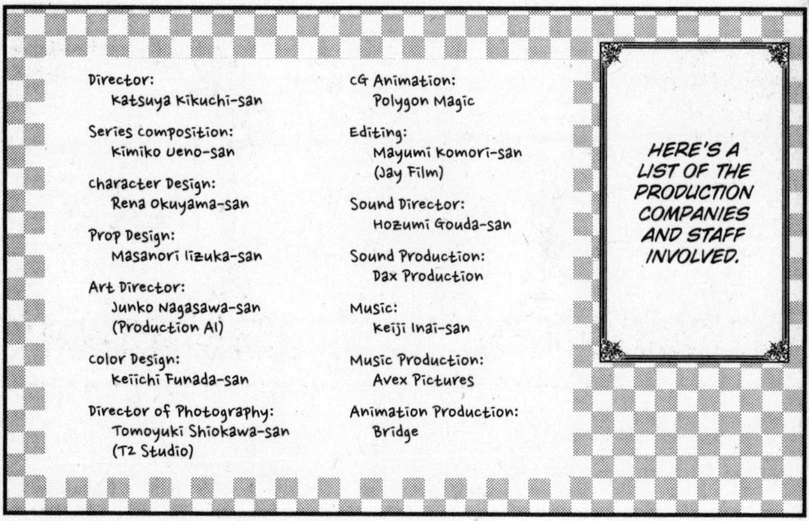
HERE'S A LIST OF THE PRODUCTION COMPANIES AND STAFF INVOLVED.
Director: Katsuya Kikuchi-san
Series composition: Kimiko Ueno-san
Character Design: Rena Okuyama-san
Prop Design: Masanori Iizuka-san
Art Director: Junko Nagasawa-san (Production AI)
Color Design: Keiichi Funada-san
Director of Photography: Tomoyuki Shiokawa-san (T2 Studio)
CG Animation: Polygon Magic
Editing: Mayumi Komori-san (Jay Film)
Sound Director: Hozumi Gouda-san
Sound Production: Dax Production
Music: Keiji Inai-san
Music Production: Avex Pictures
Animation Production: Bridge

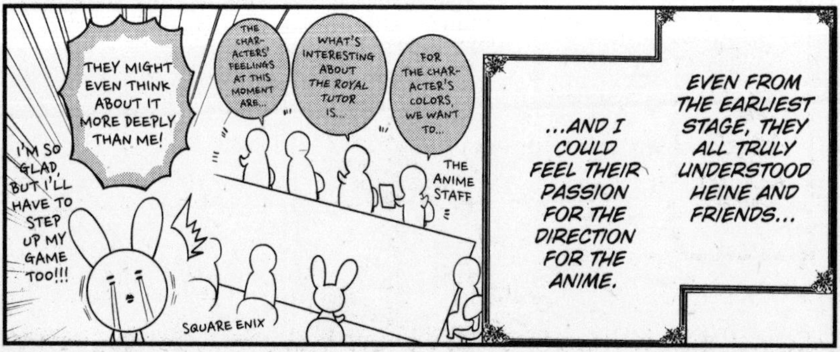
EVEN FROM THE EARLIEST STAGE, THEY ALL TRULY UNDERSTOOD HEINE AND FRIENDS...
...AND I COULD FEEL THEIR PASSION FOR THE DIRECTION FOR THE ANIME.
FOR THE CHARACTER'S COLORS, WE WANT TO...
THE ANIME STAFF
WHAT'S INTERESTING ABOUT THE ROYAL TUTOR IS...
THE CHARACTERS' FEELINGS AT THIS MOMENT ARE...
THEY MIGHT EVEN THINK ABOUT IT MORE DEEPLY THAN ME!
I'M SO GLAD, BUT I'LL HAVE TO STEP UP MY GAME TOO!!!
SQUARE ENIX

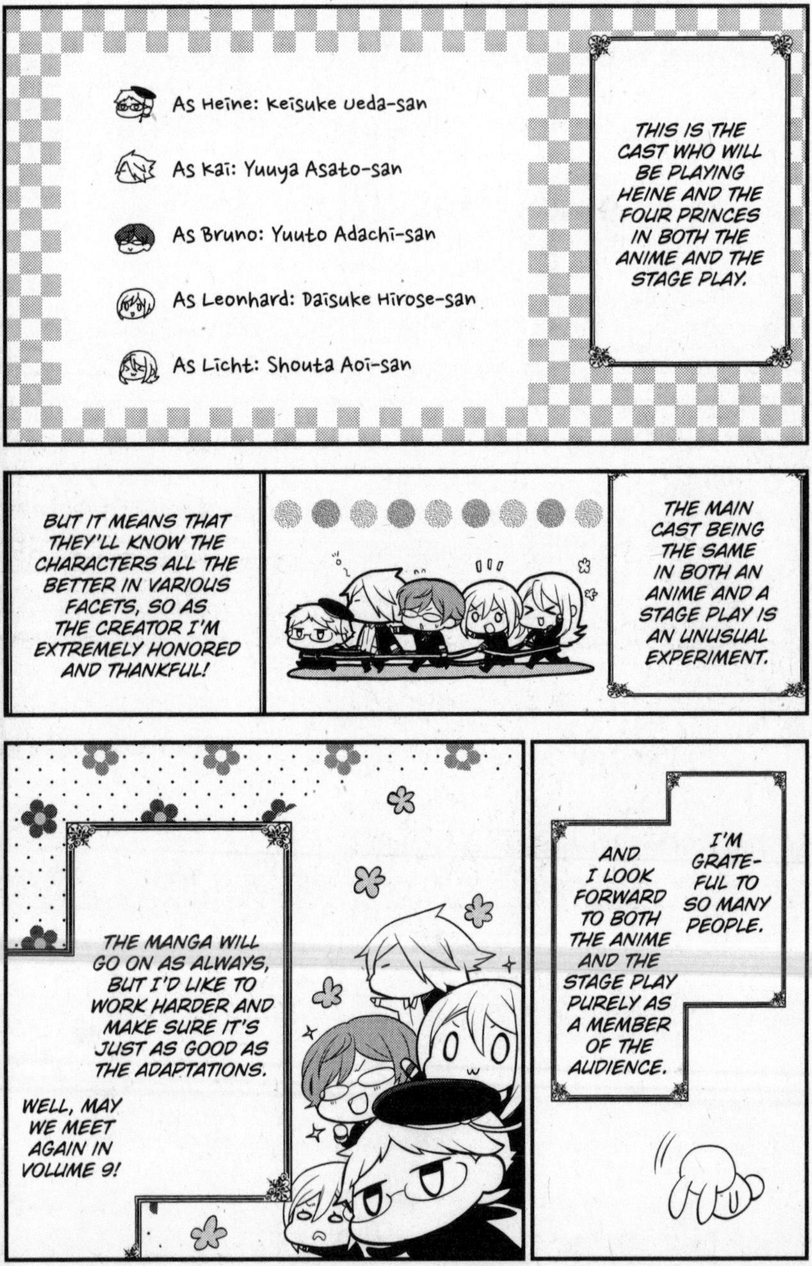
THIS IS THE CAST WHO WILL BE PLAYING HEINE AND THE FOUR PRINCES IN BOTH THE ANIME AND THE STAGE PLAY.
As Heine: Keisuke Ueda-san
As Kai: Yuuya Asato-san
As Bruno: Yuuto Adachi-san
As Leonhard: Daisuke Hirose-san
As Licht: Shouta Aoi-san
THE MAIN CAST BEING THE SAME IN BOTH AN ANIME AND A STAGE PLAY IS AN UNUSUAL EXPERIMENT.
BUT IT MEANS THAT THEY'LL KNOW THE CHARACTERS ALL THE BETTER IN VARIOUS FACETS, SO AS THE CREATOR I'M EXTREMELY HONORED AND THANKFUL!
I'M GRATE-FUL TO SO MANY PEOPLE.
AND I LOOK FORWARD TO BOTH THE ANIME AND THE STAGE PLAY PURELY AS A MEMBER OF THE AUDIENCE.
THE MANGA WILL GO ON AS ALWAYS, BUT I'D LIKE TO WORK HARDER AND MAKE SURE IT'S JUST AS GOOD AS THE ADAPTATIONS.
WELL, MAY WE MEET AGAIN IN VOLUME 9!

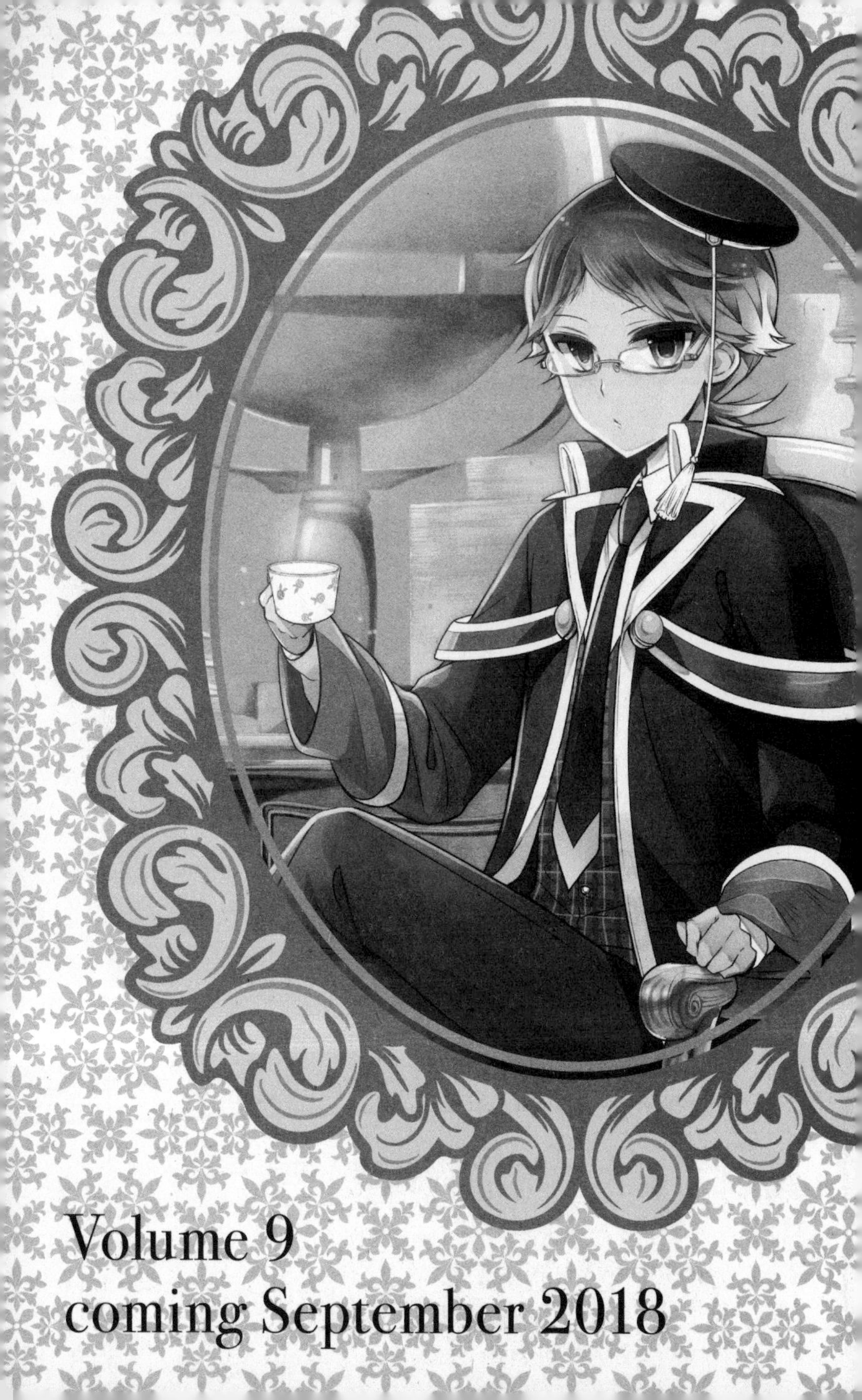

Volume 9
coming September 2018

The Royal Tutor ❽

Higasa Akai

Translation: Amanda Haley • Lettering: Abigail Blackman

THE ROYAL TUTOR Vol. 8 © 2017 Higasa Akai / SQUARE ENIX CO., LTD. First published in Japan in 2017 by SQUARE ENIX CO., LTD. English translation rights arranged with SQUARE ENIX CO., LTD. and Yen Press, LLC through Tuttle-Mori Agency, Inc., Tokyo.

English translation © 2018 by SQUARE ENIX CO., LTD.

Yen Press
1290 Avenue of the Americas
New York, NY 10104

Visit us at yenpress.com
facebook.com/yenpress
twitter.com/yenpress
yenpress.tumblr.com
instagram.com/yenpress

First Yen Press Print Edition: July 2018
The chapters in this volume were originally published as eBooks by Yen Press.

Yen Press is an imprint of Yen Press, LLC.
The Yen Press name and logo are trademarks of Yen Press, LLC.

The publisher is not responsible for websites (or their content) that are not owned by the publisher.

Library of Congress Control Number: 2017938422

ISBNs: 978-1-9753-5333-9 (paperback)
        978-1-9753-5437-4 (ebook)

10 9 8 7 6 5 4 3 2 1

WOR

Printed in the United States of America